P9-CSE-839

GOD ENCOUNTERED

OTHER WORKS BY FRANS JOZEF VAN BEECK:

Christ Proclaimed: Christology as Rhetoric
Grounded in Love: Sacramental Theology in an Ecumenical Perspective
Catholic Identity After Vatican II: Three Types of Faith in the One Church

GOD ENCOUNTERED

A Contemporary
Catholic Systematic Theology

Volume One:
Understanding the Christian Faith

FRANS JOZEF VAN BEECK, S.J.

1817

Harper & Row, Publishers, San Francisco

New York, Cambridge, Philadelphia, St. Louis
London, Singapore, Sydney, Tokyo

Grateful acknowledgment is made for use of the following material. Part of §27 and all of §32, appeared, slightly modified to suit the format of an article, in the fall issue of *Studia Liturgica*. The illustration on the dustjacket, Fol. 112r of Codex Sanhippolytensis N° 1 (15th cent.), is used by kind permission of the *Bischöfliche Alumnatsbibliothek*, Sankt Pölten, Austria.

Imprimi potest:
Very Rev. Robert A. Wild, S.J., Provincial, Chicago Province
April 27, 1988

Nihil Obstat:
Rev. Charles R. Meyer, S.T.D., *Censor Deputatus*

Imprimatur:
Rev. James P. Roache, Vicar General, Archdiocese of Chicago
May 26, 1988

The *Nihil Obstat* and *Imprimatur* are official declarations that a book or pamphlet is free of doctrinal or moral error. No implication is contained that those who have granted the *Nihil Obstat* and *Imprimatur* agree with the content, opinions, or statements expressed.

GOD ENCOUNTERED: *A Contemporary Catholic Systematic Theology, Volume One: Understanding the Christian Faith.* Copyright © 1989 by De Nederlandse Provincie S.J. (F. J. van Beeck, S.J., agent). All rights reserved. Printed in the United States of America. No part of this book may be used or reproduced in any manner whatsoever without written permission except in the case of brief quotations embodied in critical articles and reviews. For information address Harper & Row, Publishers, Inc., 10 East 53rd Street, New York, NY 10022. Published simultaneously in Canada by Fitzhenry & Whiteside, Limited, Toronto.

FIRST EDITION

Library of Congress Cataloging-in-Publication Data

Beeck, Frans Jozef van.
　　Understanding the Christian faith.

　　(God encountered; v. 1)
　　Bibliography: p.
　　Includes index.
　　1. Theology, Doctrinal.　2. Catholic Church—
Doctrines.　I. Title.　II. Series: Beeck, Frans Jozef van.
God encountered; v. 1.
BX1747.5.B4　vol. 1　230'.2 s [230'.2]　88–45694
ISBN 0–06–068828–9

89　90　90　91　92　RRD　10　9　8　7　6　5　4　3　2　1

To friends living and dead
especially
Edward J. Barron, S.J. †
Raymond P. Bertrand, S.J. †
Kathleen A. Bower
James Hennesey, S.J.
Virginia M. Ryan
John W. Lewis III
John L. Urban

"A faithful friend: a tonic of life"

(SIRACH 6,16)

O admirabile commercium!
Creator generis humani,
animatum corpus sumens,
de Virgine nasci dignatus est:
et procedens homo sine semine,
largitus est nobis suam deitatem.

What admirable exchange!
Humankind's Creator,
taking on body and soul,
in his kindness, has been born from the Virgin:
and, coming forth as man, yet not from man's seed,
he has lavished on us his divinity.

(Antiphon at vespers, January 1,
Feast of the Holy Mother of God)

Contents

Preface

This book started as a dim (and quite frankly, implausible) idea when I first taught the required course in systematic theology during the 1982-83 academic year at Boston College. Joan Nuth and Kathleen Sands were students in that course; at the end, they enthusiastically made photocopies of the extensive notes they so capably took, when I had to admit that I had said far more in class than I had been able to prepare in my lecture notes. The puzzlements, the excitement, the questions, and the suggestions of other students—too many to mention—in subsequent years contributed to the development of the project. Loyola University of Chicago offered me the freedom to work on it by inviting me to accept the John Cardinal Cody Chair of Sacred Theology in the fall of 1985. Among my friendly critics, advisors, and supporters, Jan-Maarten Bremer, Charles Hallisey, Charles Hefling, James Hennesey, S.J., Mark Henninger, S.J., Gerard Magill, George Peck, Thomas Tobin, S.J., James J. Walter, James Michael Weiss, and John L. White deserve to be especially mentioned; among other services rendered, they saved me from many an embarrassing error of detail, that bane of the systematician. A fine lecture on postconciliar mariology by my colleague Eamon R. Carroll, O. Carm., served to uncover more than one serious gap in a manuscript already well on its way to completion and, thus, became the happy occasion for substantial improvements. William L. Newell was a very good, affirming, and reliable editor to work with; in due course John V. Loudon and especially Kathryn Sweet and Philip Harnden competently directed my involvement in the circumstantial process of the book's production. José Pedrozo, my graduate assistant, took upon himself the thankless task of putting the indexes together; even more remarkably, Walter Krolikowski, S.J., in a gesture that must surely rank as a close thing to an argument for the existence of God, volunteered to read all the page proofs. Most of all, however, I am indebted to three accomplished theologians: George Schner, S.J., of Regis College, Toronto, and Jon Nilson and John J. McCarthy, my colleagues at Loyola University of Chicago. With the generous abandon that is the mark of passionate scholars, these three friends read almost everything I wrote and gave me the benefit of their frank and able advice; it is not their fault that this book falls short of doing justice to the holy encounter it bears witness to.

Frans Jozef van Beeck, S.J.

Abbreviations

AAS	*Acta Apostolicæ Sedis* (Rome, 1909ff.).
ACW	*Ancient Christian Writers: The Works of the Fathers in Translation.* Edited by J. Quasten and Joseph C. Plumpe. Westminster, MD: Newman Press; London: Longmans, Green, 1946ff.
AF	*The Apostolic Fathers.* Edited and translated by Kirsopp Lake. *Loeb Classical Library.* 2 vols. London: William Heinemann; New York: G. P. Putnam's Sons, 1930.
AG	*Ad Gentes*: The Decree on the Church's Missionary Activity (Vatican II).
ANF	*The Ante-Nicene Fathers.* 10 vols. Reprint. Grand Rapids, MI: Eerdmans, 1980–1981.
Barry	*Readings in Church History.* Edited by Colman J. Barry. Rev. ed. (3 vols. in 1). Westminster, MD: Christian Classics, 1985.
Bettenson	*Documents of the Christian Church.* 2d ed. Edited by Henry Bettenson. London, Oxford, and New York: Oxford University Press, 1967.
CC	*Corpus Christianorum* (Turnhout, 1953ff.).
CD	*Christus Dominus*: The Decree on the Bishops' Pastoral Office in the Church (Vatican II).
CF	*The Christian Faith in the Doctrinal Documents of the Catholic Church.* Edited by J. Neuner, S.J. and J. Dupuis, S.J. New York: Alba House, 1982.
CrC	*Creeds of the Churches: A Reader in Christian Doctrine from the Bible to the Present.* 3d ed. Edited by John H. Leith. Atlanta, GA: John Knox Press, 1982.
Cross	*The Oxford Dictionary of the Christian Church.* 2d ed. Edited by F. L. Cross and E. A. Livingstone. Oxford: Oxford University Press, 1974; Reprint 1977.
CSEL	*Corpus Scriptorum Ecclesiasticorum Latinorum* (Vienna, 1866ff.).

DH	*Dignitatis Humanæ*: The Declaration on Religious Freedom (Vatican II).
DictSpir	*Dictionnaire de Spiritualité*. Paris: Beauchesne, 1937–.
DS	*Enchiridion Symbolorum Definitionum Declarationum de Rebus Fidei et Morum*. 32d ed. Edited by H. Denzinger, revised by A. Schönmetzer. Freiburg: Herder, 1963.
DV	*Dei Verbum*: The Dogmatic Constitution on Divine Revelation (Vatican II).
DocVatI	*Documents of Vatican II, The Conciliar and Postconciliar Documents*. Edited by Austin P. Flannery. Vatican Collection, vol. 1.
DocVatII	*Vatican Council II, More Postconciliar Documents*. Edited by Austin P. Flannery. Vatican Collection, vol. 2.
DocVatAb	*The Documents of Vatican II*. Edited by Walter M. Abbott.
Easton	*The Apostolic Tradition of Hippolytus*. Translated by Burton Scott Easton. Reprint. Ann Arbor, MI: Archon Books, 1962.
GCS	*Die griechischen christlichen Schriftsteller der ersten drei Jahrhunderte*. Leipzig, 1897–1941; Berlin and Leipzig, 1953; Berlin, 1954ff.
GE	*Gravissimum Educationis*: The Declaration on Christian Education (Vatican II).
Goodspeed	*Die ältesten Apologeten*. Edited by E. J. Goodspeed. Reprint. Göttingen, 1984.
GS	*Gaudium et Spes*: The Pastoral Constitution on the Church in the Modern World (Vatican II).
Jaeger	*Gregorii Nysseni Opera*. Edited by W. Jaeger. Leiden: E. J. Brill, 1921–.
LG	*Lumen Gentium:* The Dogmatic Constitution on the Church (Vatican II).
LThK	*Lexicon für Theologie und Kirche*. Edited by Josef Höfer and Karl Rahner. Freiburg: Herder, 1957–65, suppl. vols. 1967–68.
NA	*Nostra Ætate*: The Declaration of the Relationship of the Church to Non-Christian Religions (Vatican II).
OE	*Orientalium Ecclesiarum*: The Decree on Eastern Catholic Churches (Vatican II).
OT	*Optatam totius*: The Decree on Priestly Formation (Vatican II).
PG	*Patrologia Græca*. Edited by J. P. Migne. 162 vols. Paris, 1857–66.
PGL	*A Patristic Greek Lexicon*. Edited by G. W. H. Lampe. Oxford: Clarendon Press, 1962–68.

PL   *Patrologia Latina.* Edited by J. P. Migne. 221 vols. Paris, 1844–64.

PLS   J. P. Migne. *Patrologia Latina, Supplementum.*

R   *Enchiridion patristicum.* Edited by M. J. Rouët de Journel, S.J. Freiburg: Herder (many editions).

SC   *Sacrosanctum Concilium*: The Constitution on the Sacred Liturgy (Vatican II).

SC   *Sources chrétiennes.* Paris: Cerf, 1940ff.

TDNT   *Theological Dictionary of the New Testament.* Edited by Gerhard Kittel and Gerhard Friedrich, translated by Geoffrey W. Bromiley. 10 vols. Grand Rapids, MI: Wm. B. Eerdmans, 1964–76.

TDOT   *Theological Dictionary of the Old Testament.* Rev. ed. Edited by G. Johannes Botterweck and Helmer Ringgren, translated by David E. Green. Grand Rapids, MI: Wm. B. Eerdmans, 1977–.

UR   *Unitatis Redintegratio*: The Decree on Ecumenism (Vatican II).

Vat II   *Sacrosanctum Oecumenicum Concilium Vaticanum II, Constitutiones Decreta Declarationes, Cura et studio Secretariæ generalis Concilii oecumenici Vaticani II.* Reprint. Rome: Typis Polyglottis Vaticanis, 1974.

Introduction

The present volume, while a coherent whole in itself, constitutes the finished first part, under the subtitle *Understanding the Christian Faith*, of a theological system *in statu nascendi* in three parts, under the collective title *God Encountered: A Contemporary Catholic Systematic Theology*. The present introduction is meant to acquaint the reader, mainly by description but also somewhat by sample, with some of the basic characteristics and expository methods of the entire work.

Above all, the present attempt at systematic theology is marked by a deep, pervasive concern for *catholicity* [a]. This, it is hoped, will place the book firmly in the framework of the Church universal. But this stated concern for catholicity does something else as well: it implies a statement about the specifically *Roman* Catholic commitments and loyalties in this book.

The Second Vatican Council declares that the unique Church of Christ, which we profess in the creed as one, holy, catholic and apostolic, "subsists" in the Roman Catholic Church. This implies, among other things, that "many elements . . . of truth are found outside its visible confines" (LG 8), in other "Churches or ecclesiastical communities" (LG 15). To the extent, therefore, that this systematic theology will succeed in being catholic, it will accomplish two things. First and foremost, it will represent Roman Catholic Christianity, though it will also set standards for it. Second, it will represent Christianity as it has taken shape outside the boundaries of Roman Catholicism and set standards for it, too. The reason for this is that catholicity, while being a major formal, determinative element in Roman Catholicism, is a force that must cut deeper and reach wider than catholicism as it actually exists, even in the Church of Rome. For catholicity is *normative*, not only for the Roman Catholic Church, but for other Churches and ec-

---

[a] For the range of meanings of "catholic," cf. Avery Dulles, *The Catholicity of the Church*, p. 185. To prevent misunderstandings, "Catholic," in this volume, is synonymous with "Roman Catholic"; "catholic" means "characterized by catholicity."

clesial communities as well. This normativeness involves two features: *integrity* and *openness*.

Catholicity involves the *integrity* of the faith. It cherishes the fullness of the Christian faith without the kind of selectiveness that arises whenever there is too much interest in seeking to accommodate the Christian faith to the transient and scattered demands of times and places. It is sensible to recall that the root meaning of the word *heresy* (Gk. *hairesis*) is "choice."

Catholicity is equally a matter of *openness*. From the outset, the Christian Church has resisted the urge to reduce itself to a sect; it has always professed to be, by divine grace, the fulfillment of all that can be recognized as naturally true and valuable in the world. Thus, the splendid variety of times and places is taken seriously and accorded the respect it deserves. The Church, therefore, must appeal to the sound judgment of all people of good will, in a gesture of broad, if searching, welcome extended to the deepest concerns of every time and place. For catholicity is deeply antisectarian. It is sensible to remember the root meaning of another Greek word: *katholikos* means "universal."

Wherever integrity and openness are harmoniously combined, the results bear the hallmark of catholicity. Avery Dulles has well characterized catholicity as "reconciled diversity," "not homogeneous but heterogeneous unity," and "identity in diversity."[1]

All of this implies something else as well, of course. In the author's understanding, this theological system will succeed in being ecumenical to the extent that it will succeed in being catholic, and succeed in being catholic to the extent that it will succeed in being ecumenical.

[§2] THE UNITY OF THEOLOGY

[1] To the extent that this book is successful in its search for catholicity, it will also turn out to be a successful attempt at demonstrating the *organic unity of Christian theology*. That unity is fundamentally grounded in the unity of *God* but also, derivatively, in the fundamental as well as ultimate unity of the *world*—a unity that in every place and time remains to be explored and actualized by human understanding, ingenuity, and cooperation. Not surprisingly, therefore, the unity of theology is also required by the unity of *the human mind* as it endlessly thirsts for understanding and love. After all, if theology must mediate between the One God and the one world, it can only do so because the theologizing human spirit is natively attuned to both. In the words of Thomas Aquinas:

The human soul becomes, in a way, all things, in virtue of sense and intellect, by which all beings that have knowledge approximate, in a way, the likeness of God, in whom all things pre-exist.[2]

In this sense it can be said that in doing theology, the human mind actualizes, by the practice of disciplined thought, the depth of its native power of mediation between God and the world.

[2] But there is another, rather more contemporary reason for the search of the unity of Christian theology. Given the present fragmentation of scholarly disciplines, including the theological disciplines, and given the philosophic, social, political, and cultural pluralism that surrounds us today, attempts at recovering the unity of theology are a matter of special urgency. The catholic theological tradition has always maintained that there is much theological insight to be gained from the demonstration of *connections*; the current trend towards specialization jeopardizes the availability of that insight.

Attempts at recovering the unity of theology, however, must be undertaken in such a way as to demonstrate two things. First of all, no matter how distressing the fragmentation, theology must show that a unified understanding of the Christian faith is an exercise in intellectual *freedom*: unified understanding need not, and indeed must not, be enforced or imposed by dogmatic, totalitarian control. Secondly, however, theology must also show that a unified understanding of the Christian faith is not something merely *ad hoc*, something produced by knocking together an occasional, contemporary, "relevant" version of Christianity. Neither impatient integralism nor impatient modernism is catholic; critical appreciation of tradition and long-suffering openness to the ever-evolving world is.

[a] In opting for catholicity in recovering both the integral essence and the open structures of the Christian faith, and in equally seeking to avoid the pitfalls of integralism and modernism, the present attempt at systematic theology declares its indebtedness, both to the inspiration generated by the Second Vatican Council and to the painful polarizations that have arisen in connection with it [b]. Another area of indebtedness is more personal. The author, while a European by birth, upbringing, and education, has—much to his advantage— lived and learned and taught in North America for roughly the past two decades; he hopes that this, too, will have left its mark on his pursuit of catholicity in theology.

A reasonably effective demonstration of integrity and openness in catholic theology may, perhaps, be of incidental relevance to the authentic, magisterial teaching office in the Church. Unity in believing and thinking is not a function of magisterial control, except, perhaps, for a while and by way of discipline, to deal with a *status crisis* of the Church. Nor is that unity a function of tolerant, adaptive accommodation, except, perhaps, for a while and by way of necessary ad-

---

[b] The author's reflections on this subject are contained in his *Catholic Identity After Vatican II*.

justment, after a period when normal *aggiornamento* and always needed, continuous reform of the Church (UR 6) have stagnated.

[§3] UNDERSTANDING, NOT CORRECTION OR JUDGMENT

[1] These allusions to the problems of disunity in the Church as well as in the theological academy bring up another feature of catholicity. Catholicity in theology, as a matter of principle, implies that theology is not homiletic, let alone remedial; it may incidentally heal rifts, but that is not its primary goal. Catholic theology has traditionally been attuned to the glory of God and the ever-increasing attractiveness of the truth rather than to special concerns—such recurring problems as human sinfulness in all its varieties, the prevalence of error, and the consequent need for admonition. It has been its central vocation to understand the mystery and its structures, not to correct misunderstanding and abuse. It has insisted on making available to all, without exception or partiality, "the entire counsel of God" (Acts 20, 27). This has two sides to it.

On the one hand, while respectful of the teaching authority of those charged with the guardianship of the great Tradition, theology in the tradition of catholicity has consistently insisted on the right—and indeed the duty—to engage in responsible searching and questioning; it has refused to recognize any claims, on anybody's part, to "lord it over [anyone's] faith" (cf. 2 Cor 1, 24). Catholic theology does realistically recognize that the integrity of the faith is always in danger of being contaminated by narrow or superficial ideologies; yet it resists the temptation to reduce the faith, even for practical ("pastoral") purposes, to a form of narrow or anxious ecclesiastical obedience. The enormous claims which the faith involves invite, justify, and indeed demand, the utmost efforts of the honestly inquiring mind.

On the other hand, while respectful of the special temper of times and places (for new ideas and manners—good, bad, and mixed—will occur no matter what, and neither pope nor Council can do anything about it!), the catholic tradition in theology has always denied that everybody's Christian faith-experience is as valid and authentic as anybody else's and that it is cultural or personal relevance that really counts.

Consequently, neither "monarchy" nor "democracy" are to be invoked as ultimate authorities here. The faithful need not, and indeed must not be shielded from the full breadth and length and height and depth of the mystery of God; they have the baptismal right to be introduced to the great Tradition of the Christian faith and to seek to ponder and understand it in its entirety according to the capacity of both their faith and their understanding. The Tradition pre-exists all believers, and, hence, it is owned by none; and its authority is so great and so inalienable that affirming the Christians' right to seek to understand it is normally not a gesture of defiance. On the contrary, it is usually a gesture of respect for the Tradition, which has faced (and survived!) critical challenges before and is now the better, both for the challenges and for the survival.

[a] If all of this sounds a bit polemical, let it be understood what the polemic is mainly about. The present book wishes to avoid the authoritarian, pervasively polemical style that for so long used to characterize the various theological methods of expounding and commending the great Christian Tradition and that never quite seems to die out. This book has not been written *against* anyone inside or outside the Church—at least not consciously. It is true, positions are adopted in this book and options made; this means that other positions are implicitly or explicitly criticized and other options are passed up or even expressly rejected. And, since positions and options can never be wholly separated from the persons that hold them, this book contains criticisms (and, it is hoped, reasoned, measured criticisms) of other theological authors. This is not done in order to cast them in permanently adversarial roles, let alone to cast aspersions on them; rather, it is done to express real disagreement.

Such disagreements derive their importance, not from the intelligence, the authority, or the reputation of the parties involved, but from the weight of the issues on which the parties disagree. And the parties are very much in agreement about the weight of the issues— so much so, in fact, that they find them worth disagreeing on, in a spirit of respectful, if sometimes passionate, inquiry ultimately born out of worship. After all, I may have profound differences about God and matters godly with other persons, but I have to remain aware of the perspective. Not every theological conception is equally true, so there is room for debate and disagreement; yet all theological differences are as nothing in comparison with the infinite difference that obtains between all our different conceptions of God and matters godly (even the truest), and God and God's matters in themselves.

If, therefore, there should be critics who wish to turn their approval of positions taken in this book into a rallying cry against others, they should realize the following. While the author is not in a position to turn down whatever compliments may come his way, he will accept those that call for crusades as insults. Offers of friendship are offensive if the price of friendship is enmity with others; politico-theological alliances have no place in the Church of Christ; theologians should know better than anyone that the Lord our God is the God of all at the expense of none.

If real errors should indeed be going around inside (and outside) the Church today, they must, like all evils, first of all be noticed, then absorbed and suffered through, and thus understood, before they can be finally corrected and turned into sources of truth. Impatient dismissal or refutation of error may well be the practical thing to do, but it can never claim the example of Jesus Christ to justify itself, nor, for that matter, the example of the great saints and doctors. And if some should wish to point out that there is a pressing need for the enforcement of orthodoxy today, let them be assured that, for the theologian, such enforcement is a matter of hard work, intellectual integrity, and (perhaps, on occasion) patient ecclesiastical obedience, not of the arrogation of ecclesial authority. The theologian's proper charisma is not magisterium but understanding, and such teaching as understanding may give rise to.

The kind of orthodoxy that becomes a theologian, therefore, is first and foremost the intellectual kind. Consequently, the first authority theologians must recognize is the great Tradition; the first demands they must experience are the demands which that Tradition makes on their present ability to understand. For theologians, therefore, orthodoxy is not a matter of protestations of ecclesiastical loyalty; rather, it consists in deeply respecting, understanding, trusting, and thus attempting to further, the great Tradition of the undivided Church. In virtue of this vocation, theologians may occasionally or even ceaselessly have to remind the Church of its faith, lest the Church become simply part of the world; yet as theologians they do not have the right to declare the *status crisis*, to tag heretics or tar them, or to call for excommunications. They should, in fact, be the last to arrogate to themselves what is the privilege as well as the dread (and often enough precarious) duty of bishops: to be the judges of the faith of their fellow Christians.

[2] In short, this systematic theology will attempt to follow the advice of St. Ignatius Loyola:

It is to be premised that every good Christian will be more inclined to put a good construction on another's statement than to condemn it. If he is unable to put a good construction on it, let him enquire how the other understands it. If the latter understands it wrongly, let him set him right, in a spirit of love. If this is not enough, let him look for all the means proper to get the other to understand it rightly, and thus to attain salvation.[3]

[§4] THE GREAT TRADITION

[1] In taking its cue from catholicity, the present treatment also commits itself to a high regard for what this book will very frequently refer to as "the great Tradition." That great Tradition comprises, first of all, Scripture: Scripture read, by way of *lectio divina*, as the living Word of God, within the community of faith, and understood in the context of that community's present experience of the Holy Spirit; Scripture

read, too, in its organic entirety, and reverenced as the first and original fruit of the community's Tradition of worship, conduct, and teaching, as well as the abiding canon by which the authority of all subsequent Tradition must be measured; Scripture read in accordance with its diversity as well as in accordance with the unity which encompasses the diversity; and hence, finally, Scripture read, not as one single, undifferentiated book full of timeless doctrinal and ethical propositions, but as the authoritative collection of documents reflecting the great variety of historic Judaeo-Christian faith-traditions, to be interpreted in accordance with the demands implicit in their literary forms (cf. DS 3826–30; cf. CF 234–36).

But furthermore, the great Tradition is the Tradition of worship, life, and teaching of the undivided Church. This implies that this book regards the record of the Christian Tradition before the Schism that divided West from East in the eleventh century as especially authoritative. But even after the Schism, East and West continued to cultivate what was in fact the great Tradition—even though unfortunately marred by very particular, neuralgic, overspecialized debates, and especially by increasingly divergent traditions of spirituality. The elements of the great Tradition, therefore, remain fairly accessible even during that painful period, when the hope for unity restored never quite died out; this book will attempt to recognize and respect them.

The retrieval of the great Tradition from a Christendom thoroughly torn apart since the sixteenth century is a great deal more difficult. The Roman Catholic Church has always continued to cultivate and proclaim its fidelity to the Tradition, but both the theological scholarship and the faith-experience of the mid-twentieth century have demonstrated that Roman Catholicism has, in fact, needed both *aggiornamento* and *ressourcement* to revive the great Tradition and to retrieve it from the clutter of particularist and often polemical accretions. Classical Protestantism accomplished its share of particularisms and polemics, and, hence, it came to suffer in its own way from the loss of living contact with the great Tradition. Still, in its search for the purity of the faith, it has often cherished and recovered precious elements of it. Finally, the ecumenical movement has, in fact, been a movement to recover the great Tradition of the undivided Church, and it has done so for the only sound theological reason there is: that the great Tradition must be furthered against the Day of Christ's coming, by mutual love as the sign of Christian discipleship and by unified witness to a divided world. Far from being an exercise in historical atavism, therefore, seeking out the constitutive elements of the great Tradition is an essential effort in the total process of gathering up of treasures of the historic Church of Christ, in order to bring them home to the God who entrusted them to it.

[2] The present treatment, therefore, is as committed—of course, within the limits of its scope and even more within the limits of the author's knowledge and experience—to the *discovery* and the *recovery* of the great Tradition, as to having a high regard for it. This also means that this book will make no proposals to *define* very precisely just what constitutes the great Tradition. What will result, it is hoped, is the emergence, from the treatment itself, of a broad, *organic* picture of the great Tradition. A single treatment cannot encompass, let alone exhaust, the great Tradition any more than a single fish can encompass the stream that carries it and in which it lives and moves. A truly catholic treatment of the great Tradition, therefore, will bring out and put in bold relief its central themes, but also create, *from inside*, an impression of the breadth of its purview. Again, the catholic combination of integrity and openness.

[a] To make tangible both the core of the great Tradition and the breadth of its perspective, this book uses a method which is in part *anthological*: to make its points, it often has recourse to representative vignettes. Historical incidents related to the great Tradition will be told—sometimes in surprising detail. Great texts from the Tradition as well as great commentaries on the Tradition will be quoted and discussed—sometimes at surprising length. The principal reason for this is that the Christian Tradition is innately historic; systematic theology cannot claim to do justice to the Christian faith if it gives no tangible evidence of its attempts at interpreting the great Tradition. And as in the case of all anthologies, the selection of the incidents and texts in *God Encountered* is the result of a combination of the author's respect for tradition and his personal tastes and preferences.

There is a second reason for the occasional detailed treatment of representative events, texts, and themes: *education*. It seems useful, in a book partly written to teach, to include some detailed demonstrations of the various methods of enquiry, analysis, and interpretation that can be used in systematic theology; representative vignettes afford an opportunity to do so. Systematic theology may, of its nature, have to be generalist; it need not be sloppy. Cooks as a rule enjoy serving up their creations in such a way as to hide, rather than display, the careful work that went into them; occasionally, however, they will take their guests into the kitchen for a detailed demonstration.

[§5] OBJECTIVE REFERENCE

[1] Systematic theology in the catholic tradition, it has been explained, is a reflection on the Christian faith as it comes to us in the form of the great Tradition. This position has occasioned the clarifications offered in this introduction thus far. It is time to turn to another theme:

systematic theology is also *a scholarly, reflective discipline*. It is useful, therefore, to show, by means of a first, preliminary statement, how the commitment to the great Tradition is connected with a fundamental, pervasive *intellectual commitment* implicit in this book.

The language philosopher John Verhaar has sounded an important warning. He points out that conceptualized thinking, and the technical terminology associated with it, are characterized by a tendency towards *internal reference of thought* and *hypostatization of language*. Scholars rightly get interested in the *immanent consistency* of their reflections and thoughts, and in due course they develop a tendency *to treat their concepts as if they were the reality* that is the object of their study. In the long run, this typically takes the form of their attributing "hypostatic existence" to concepts. In Verhaar's words:

> The law operating here is that the more we are concerned with what is meant by what we say, the more we seem to be separated from what we are speaking, and thinking, *about*. From transparent, our words become opaque. The clearer the meanings, the more arbitrary. In this shifting spectrum of increasing reflexivization we finally arrive at the level where words have become terms, and meanings concepts; natural language has been left behind. . . .
> A . . . variety of the "hypostatization" of language is the replacement of meanings by concepts, which is what happens if we replace words by terms. . . . Though it is not in all cases necessarily confusing to speak of "the concept of grace" when we mean "grace," or of the "idea of God," when we mean "God," the tendency seems a doubtful one. . . .[4]

The present book wishes to heed these warnings. In making the great Tradition its focus, it attempts to counteract a tendency that is endemic to the academy: the inclination to make academic disciplines, including theology, entirely self-supporting, self-referent, and (ultimately) self-contained. To put it bluntly, this sets out to be a book *of* theology, not a book *about* theology (or theologies). Throughout this system, therefore, *the reference will be mostly objective*; for example, very few words with the ominous prefix *meta-* will be used. *What* is being *primarily* discussed and reflected upon, in other words, is not the religious self-consciousness, the nature and methods and presuppositions of theology, or the positions taken by theologians, let alone their self-consciousness, but the historic Christian community's faith as well as its commitments: God, Jesus Christ, the Holy Spirit, the Church, Christian worship, conduct, and doctrine. As a result, there will be much emphasis on *sources* and their *interpretation*. The conviction behind this position is partly that there is intellectual danger in the fact that in our day the language of self-conscious, quasi-professional expertise is often mistaken for the language of realism—everywhere. The phrase "I have psychological problems" often stands in for "I am feeling horribly confused and impotent; could it be that a psychologist, who has studied this kind of thing, can help me?" In the same way, the cool, unbiased expression "I have theological problems" is a frequent surrogate for "I am totally at sea about my faith in God." In such cases, the *relatively* sterile language of expertise is inappropriately used to shield the speaker from a full awareness of reality. In the long run, this is the death of all real thought. No wonder some theology is sterile: purely academic discussion, book learning, or intellectual fencing in the interest of senior common room victories, of the kind that engages in intellectual experiments for the sake of display or in order to relieve its inherent *ennui* by "trying something new."

[2] The picture just painted is, of course, a caricature—but one painted in the service of a caution [c]. Needless to say, the refusal to reduce theology to discussion, among theologians, of other theologies does not exclude dialogue with other theologians; as a matter of fact, rather the opposite will prove to be the case. Nor does the recognition of the intellectual risks involved in self-conscious reflection justify the exclusion of serious reflection on human intellectual integrity or awareness of the implications of scholarly method. But in all discussions, focused clarification and interpretation of the "objective" faith-issues will be the intended task—a task which, it can be expected, will *indirectly* demand that the scholarly self-consciousness and the discussion in the academy stay focused, too.

[a] The decision in favor of direct reference has helped shape the decision with regard to the *authority* of the *references to other authors*— a decision any author has to face. While reading has to be the main activity that supports substantive writing, the former also tends to inhibit the latter; ultimately, the thoughts of those who feel they must read everything tend to remain unpublished. Each author, therefore, must find a suitable balance. In this book, the references stated are meant to be just that—stated references. Hence, too, the bibliography has no claims to make besides that of offering a listing of the works quoted or referred to. Many important books and articles that have gone into the writing of the present work have remained unlisted because unquoted; a great many more have remained unread. Consequently, if the reader should wonder, *à propos* of any particular passage, if the author has read such-and-such, the safer assumption is that he has not. Meanwhile, the author consoles himself (with varying degrees of success) with the thought that there exist sources of insight and knowledge besides the exponentially increasing realm of the printed word.

---

[c] As is the joke told about a highly respected university in the midwestern United States. If Hegel and an expert on Hegel, so the story goes, were to apply for the same teaching position, this university would hire the expert.

[§6] EXPOSITORY METHOD

[1] In keeping with the catholicity of its intent, this book attempts to base its expository method on the twin foundation of integrity and openness. That is to say, while striving for a coherent theological presentation of the Christian faith in its entirety, the system offered here does not propose everything either as equally important or with equal emphasis. This is concretized in the typographical arrangement of the exposition as a whole—an arrangement also designed to provide *an internal reference system independent of pagination*.

[2] The *chapters* constitute the largest organizing elements of the book's total argument; their function is aesthetic and broadly thematic. In this first page, the chapters can be grouped in three main blocks.

[a] The first four chapters form a block under the rubric "Raising the Issue." In the interest of establishing a common understanding with the reader, this unit opens with a broad, rather general exploration of the nature of systematic understanding (1) and its application in systematic theology (2). Sound systematic theological understanding is then more precisely characterized by being marked off against integralism and modernism (3). Finally, systematic theological understanding is placed in the context of the theological community. This is also where the present volume offers a first, preliminary characterization of the particular theological system attempted in *God Encountered* (4).

The second block consists of the next two chapters, taken together under the rubric "Clearing the Ground." Christian theology cannot be naively confessional ("positive") today; in the "global village," it must face the universalist claims of common human religiosity ("natural religion"). This issue, compellingly raised by Friedrich Schleiermacher at the end of the eighteenth century, is explored, both in its classical dimensions (5) and in its modern shape (6).

The last five chapters constitute the most thematically theological block of the present volume. It is aimed, under the general title "Understanding the Christian Faith," at the presentation of the Christian faith as a positive, "confessional" religion. By interpreting Jesus Christ's Resurrection, respectively, as the revelation of his divine identity as well as the divine vindication of his human life, these chapters explore, first of all, the "doxological essence" of the Christian faith (7) and its "soteriological structure" (8). This leads to a conception of the Christian religion as an organic, dynamic system subsisting in three integral components, among which worship ("cult") holds pride of place (9). A study of the remaining two components, life ("conduct") and teaching ("creed") rounds off this presentation of the Christian faith as a positive religion (10). A final chapter on the dynamics of faith which the three components give rise to, and on the authority of Christian theology, concludes our introduction to systematic theology (11).

[3] Within the chapters, but running on through them, *numbered, titled sections* of very unequal length and marked by the § sign (a feature borrowed from Friedrich Schleiermacher's *Der christliche Glaube*) serve to unfold the *principal argument*. This argument is articulated in the *main text* of the book. With very few exceptions, the paragraphs (or more often, groups of paragraphs) of this main text are *numbered*, by means of arabic numerals in square brackets; the numbering is *continuous within each titled section*. Theoretically, it is possible to read this book by reading only the main text.

[4] Many numbered paragraphs comprise *indented subparagraphs* (or, again, groups of indented subparagraphs), marked by lowercase letters in square brackets and arranged in alphabetical order within each paragraph. These subparagraphs accommodate, first of all, many of the *important quotations*. More frequently, however, they contain materials *subordinate* to the main text yet immediately related to it: *supporting arguments, discussions, clarifications, elaborations*, and *illustrations*—sometimes fairly detailed.

[5] *Footnotes* are marked by *italicized* lowercase letters in square brackets and arranged in alphabetical order within each *chapter*. They contain materials *incidental* to the passages to which they refer. Typically, they accommodate *corollaries* and *anecdotes*—again, sometimes fairly detailed—as well as occasional *asides*.

[6] Finally, *references*, in the form of endnotes in the back of the book, are marked by italicized numbers in superscript and arranged in numerical order within each *chapter*. With few exceptions, they contain simplified *bibliographical references*. (Full bibliographical data about the literature quoted are given in the bibliography at the end of the volume.) Sometimes, however, they contain other materials: comments too technical or marginal to deserve a place in the footnotes or, more frequently, the (Latin, German, French, etc.) *originals* of texts quoted in translation in the main exposition and the subparagraphs; this tends to be especially the case where the author has prepared translations of his own.

[a] A final word about the references within the text. Throughout, the following references have been placed in the main text itself and in the indented subparagraphs: (1) references to Scripture; (2) references to two authoritative collections of magisterial documents: the one edited by Denzinger-Schönmetzer (DS) and the (rearranged) English version of this by J. Neuner and J. Dupuis, entitled *The Christian Faith* (CF); (3) references to the documents of the Second Vatican

Council (see the complete list of abbreviations in the front section of this volume).

The references just listed, it could be argued, put enough of a burden on the printed text to rule out any further encumbrances. Still, at the risk of pushing the capacity of the text (not to mention the reader!) beyond its limits, one more kind of reference has been incorporated into the text: *cross-references* that make use of the above mentioned "internal reference system independent of pagination" (§6, 1). The reason for this is the nature of the present work itself. Insight into the *coherence* of the system, as will be explained later, is one of the principal sources of understanding in systematic theology. Intratextual cross-references, therefore, while a burden, are far from incidental to the task at hand: they provide a guide to the skeletal structures of the system. While the author expects that his readers will establish their own connections and notice patterns of coherence on their own, he wishes to point out the correlations he himself put in place as an integral part of what he wants to offer in this book. At the same time he wishes to encourage readers to claim their freedom, by availing themselves of the cross-references only insofar as they will prove to be helpful.

Part I

RAISING THE ISSUE

CHAPTER 1

Theology and Understanding

PRELIMINARY: SYSTEM AND SUBSTANCE

[§7] SYSTEMATIZATION, EXPOSITION, AND UNDERSTANDING

[1] In January 1857, the Russian novelist Ivan Turgenev wrote a letter to Count Leo Tolstoy. Tolstoy was neither a stranger to theology nor to the search for truth; yet he did believe, in the words of a modern commentator, "that truth could be rationalized and systematized to suit his purposes." Turgenev wrote:

You are growing calmer, improving and—what is most important—you are becoming free, free from your own views and prejudices. . . . God grant that your mental horizon may grow wider every day! Systems are only dear to those who cannot take the whole truth into their hands, who want to catch it by the tail; a system is just like the tail of truth, but truth is like a lizard; it will leave its tail in your hands and then escape you; it knows that within a short time it will grow another.[1]

There are good reasons to start a systematic theology on this note of mild skepticism. It brings home that there is an inherent risk to the whole enterprise of systematic theology: systematization does not necessarily lead either to the truth or to understanding. That is why the first four chapters of this introductory volume must give an account of systematic theology: its nature, its tasks, its hazards. We must discuss, in a preliminary fashion, what kind of systematization is likely to lead to true understanding and what kind is not. The first part of this book, therefore, will set out to give a fairly systematic account of the main tasks, methods, procedures, and basic assumptions involved in the systematic theology that is to follow.

In spite of this, however, it can provide no more than a *provisional* statement. Why is this so?

The reason lies in the nature of the relationships between the *subject matter* of knowledge and the *procedures* of knowledge, between "truth" and "method," between "content" and "form"—relationships that are far from simple or innocent. This is going to be a "systematic theology," but what does that mean? The term *system*, and its traditional companions *method* and *encyclopedia*, have indeed come to enjoy much respect in the more recent history of Western theology; still, it must be remembered that they are at least partly of dubious pedigree. They are associated with the tendency, especially strong since the mid-sixteenth century, to make, whether overtly or covertly, a claim that looks promising but that is, in fact, very dangerous. That claim is this: that there is one single reliable, objective, universally applicable "way to pursue" (Gk. *methodos*) and to "put together" in a system (Gk. *systēma*) the "teaching" of the whole "round" of truths available in any given subject (which is what the late medieval neologism *encyclopædia* means).

[a] The study of Christian doctrine began to feel the impact of this approach in the sixteenth century, which witnessed the rise of the type of *théologie savante* that has remained the ancestor of modern systematic theology. The intellectual style characteristic of the New Learning involved the development of bodies of objective truths systematically and methodically exposed and argued. The movement had strong links with two interconnected sixteenth-century cultural developments: an enormous emphasis on *definition* and the rise of *print literacy*. It is arguable, of course, that the tendency to control knowledge by objectifying it and putting it together in an orderly fashion can be traced back long before the invention of the printing press; in the medieval period, names like those of Andrew of St. Victor[2] and Robert Bacon come to mind. But then, every age has its antiquaries, collectors, encyclopedists, and polymaths, who tend to glorify the systematic accumulation of truths as the ideal method to pursue the truth.

It was the rise of the printed book that caused a quantum leap in the development of literacy's influence on the habits of the human mind: it created a new norm for learning. Among other things, it gave rise to an unprecedented capacity to store and disseminate information in a uniform fashion, and it did so by creating *texts* for the purposes of concentrated *study*. Now since the medium tends to influence the message and form tends to determine content, the implicit conviction could arise that spatial, visual, objective, and, indeed, mechanical containment of truth *more geometrico* represents the ideal shape of knowledge. An aggressive tendency to lay down *definitions* arose. In the schools, this objectivist conviction caused profound changes in the process of education, which affected teachers and students alike. "System" and "method" took their cues, not so much from the processes of *inquiry* into the truth, as from the need for authoritative *instruction*; they came to serve the purposes, not so much of understanding, as of the classroom drill. Once this kind of method had become the norm for learning, the tools of understanding were no longer derived from the matter under study, but from the need for clarity of presentation and efficiency of exposition. System, in other words, increasingly won out over understanding. Eventually, the eighteenth-century encyclopedists—those ardent advocates of rationality—came to systematize knowledge by means of that most extrinsic, "unprejudiced," and "objective" of all ordering devices, the alphabet.

Encyclopedias doubtlessly provide clarity, accessibility, and fullness of information, but all of these may serve to cloak some very real prejudices. Most insidiously, they tend to give the impression that true understanding is tantamount to objective description and classification, and that understanding is substantially dependent on the availability of mechanical storage-and-retrieval devices to supplement that original storage-and-retrieval device: the human mind.[3]

[b] In the theological sphere, examples of this objectivist cultivation of accumulated, authoritative truths are Melchior Cano's *De locis theologicis* and Philipp Melanchthon's *Loci communes*, as well as the various *catechisms*. Despite the great difference in level between them, both kinds of writing aim at presenting authoritative, and especially *complete* and *detailed*, renditions of orthodox faith.

There is indeed a world of difference between Cano's far-flung, learned elegance and Melanchthon's baldness. Still, their intentions are identical: to present a systematic, learned account of the faith by methodical recourse to authoritative sources, put together in print.

The popular catechisms are even more typical products of sixteenth-century concern with objectivity. (It is hard to tell if objectivity was perceived to be needed to order and control a situation of political, intellectual, and theological disarray, or if the search for objectivity helped cause it; odds are it was a matter of two-way traffic.) Despite their cultivation of oral rehearsal, catechisms are steeped in the world of print culture, which also permitted their large-scale dissemination. The word *catechism*, in fact, dates from the sixteenth century, even though its etymology (second-century Gk. *katēchizō*—"give oral religious instruction") harks back to the ancient catechetical practice of handing down the faith by means of live speech. What betrays the modern catechisms' profound indebtedness to print is the practice of *literal, rote memorization* to insure orthodoxy [a], a practice en-

---

[a] Cf. Cross, *s.v.* "Catechism" (p. 249). For an example, both of the enormous authority catechisms came to enjoy and of the contempt in which they were to be held by eighteenth-century rationalists as well as pietists, cf. the following story told by Gotthold Ephraim Lessing (*Axiomata*, pp. 124ff.). A German army chaplain and some crew members of an English vessel discovered, in the Bermudas, a group of naked Christians, "as orthodox as any army chaplain," who spoke the language of Luther's *Catechismus*. All they had left of their catechism, though, was the two wooden book covers that had once

tirely foreign to oral and primary literate cultures, where tradition is ensured by flexible variations on familiar, formulary themes (cf. §43, 4, a).

One conclusion to be drawn from all of this is that systematic theology should draw upon a broader array of sources than catechetical systematizations; this is of some relevance to our discussion of integralism later on in this volume (§19).

[2] There exists, in other words, a history of *inadequate systematization*. It is, therefore, imperative from the outset of this systematic theology to make an important distinction; there is a difference between the task of *systematic exposition* and the task of *systematic understanding*. This implies that not every exposition equally favors understanding; in fact, there are expositions that, far from favoring understanding, are in the service of rather different aims—for instance, the creation of conformity.

The present work is committed to the fundamental decision to have *exposition firmly subordinate to understanding*—just as firmly as method is to be subordinated to truth and the pursuit of scholarship to the quest for content. At times, perhaps, the need for effective exposition may demand methods and systematizations relatively independent of the subject matter, just as the need for a complete *tour d'horizon* of Catholic theology may occasionally require the treatment of relatively unimportant subjects. But neither the needs of the classroom, nor a mistaken demand for total objectivity, nor the need for conformity, nor the merits of encyclopedic knowledge must in the final analysis be allowed to dominate the properly theological treatment of the Christian and Catholic faith. The present work, therefore, will make an attempt to resist the temptation to achieve theological understanding by means of methods ultimately inadequate to the full content of the Christian faith.

This is also the reason why the present introduction must remain provisional: any advance presentation of the tasks, methods, procedures, and assumptions of this system remains, of its nature, firmly within the sphere of *exposition*. It will take the whole *finished* system to settle the question to what extent the treatment offered and the methods used are adequate to the tasks of leading to *theological understanding*. Still, even at this preliminary stage, the theme of theological understanding requires some further explanation, to be elaborated in the next three sections.

---

contained the now worn-away pages. " 'Between these little boards,' they said, 'is everything we know.' '*Was* everything, my friends,' said the chaplain. 'Still is, still is,' they said; 'true, we cannot read, we hardly know what reading is, but our fathers heard their fathers read from them. And they knew the man who cut these little boards. That man was called Luther, and he lived shortly after Christ.' " To the question whether these people were Christians, Lessing characteristically suggests that, of course, they were. Of what interest to a Christian are the opinions of theologians, as long he feels blessed in his faith?

[§8] UNDERSTANDING IN ENCOUNTER: DIMENSIONS

[1] Understanding, Turgenev reminded Tolstoy, is a matter of taking the whole truth into one's hands, not of catching it by the tail. This means that it is a matter of *receptiveness* rather than grasp, of *openness* rather than control, and, hence, a matter of *delight* rather than mastery. Grasp, control, and mastery are faster and seem surer, but in the long run they yield a *reduced* version of the truth—you end up holding the wriggling tail of the lizard, which you soon discover you do not want. The other three, receptiveness, openness, and delight, are slower in the acquiring but much more durable in the enjoyment. They need to be explained a bit further.

[2] Understanding is, first of all, a matter of *openness*. Understanding requires that we attempt to do justice to what we are studying. This means that we should accommodate ourselves to what we seek to understand by allowing the *object* of our knowledge to inform—that is to say, to *actualize* and *structure*—our understanding. When that happens, two interrelated things take place in us, in one and the same act: we *receptively* submit ourselves to the structuring, which is a matter of discipline, and we experience the actualization, which is a matter of freedom.

[a] The position just taken may strike the reader as naively romantic since it does not appear to acknowledge Immanuel Kant's *Critique of Pure Reason*, which sets such sharp limits to the possible relationship between the knower and the object of knowledge. This is an important issue indeed, and it must be taken up later, in the context of natural theology.

[3] Openness leads to the experience of *receptiveness*. The object of our study shapes and determines and chastens our understanding. This not only involves the actualization of our innate potential for understanding beyond its previous limits; it also reveals to us, for our liberation and correction, those limits themselves, and especially our "own views and prejudices." In this way, understanding viewed as openness leads to understanding as an experience of *receptiveness*: if we are to understand, the other must dawn on us.

Receptiveness in turn leads to the experience of *delightful freedom*. Far from being passive, true receptiveness is deeply active: it involves the actualization of our own innate ability to understand and the *delight* that comes from such a self-actualization [b].

---

[b] Readers of Aristotle will have recognized the treatment of the mind as passive and active, in *De Anima*, III, 4–5, 429ª10–430ª25. (All quotations from Aristotle are from *The Basic Works of Aristotle*, edited by Richard McKeon.) For the conception of self-actualization as delight, cf. Abraham Maslow, *Religions, Values, and Peak Experiences*, and *Towards a Psychology of Being*.

[4] Something analogous can be said on behalf of the *object* of under-standing, even though, strictly speaking, our act of understanding it in and of itself does not cause any actualization on its part: nothing "hap-pens to it" in virtue of understanding it [*c*]. Still, in being understood, the object of understanding is, first, drawn out of (abstracted from") and liberated from the limited conditions of its particularity; it is placed in the broad light of reason and attains the freedom of the idea [*d*]. Thus, secondly, in being newly understood, it comes to inhabit a wider world of ideas: it gains in intelligibility. Things and ideas are objectively better off for being understood, or for being understood more widely.

[5] Summing up: in being understood, the *object* of understanding at-tains a new, spiritual identity; in understanding, we *ourselves* come to experience the delight which is: the self-actualization of the human spirit. Understanding, in other words, involves a *mutually actualizing encounter*. There are two sides to this mutuality. Two very important conclusions, therefore, follow.

[6] First, if there is mutuality between the person in the act of under-standing and the matter to be understood, there is an element of *ad-aptation* in every act of understanding. This means that *the method of understanding must be determined by the matter to be understood*. Objectivity, in other words, is the result neither of a subject matter simply imposing itself on the human mind, nor of the human mind imposing an ob-jectively valid treatment on a subject matter. Rather, objectivity results when human understanding receptively focuses on a subject matter that presents itself, and *accommodates itself* to it to the point of *participating in it*, so as to seek to understand it.

[a] In adopting this position, the present book aligns itself with the great ontological-epistemological tradition of the West. Aristotle pro-vides the basic attitude. The quest for understanding, he explains, takes the same shape in the whole gamut of possible intellectual pur-suits, namely, the question "What is it?" Now the fundamental same-ness of the question might lead one to suppose "that there was some single method of inquiry applicable to all objects whose essential na-ture we are endeavouring to ascertain." But that would be too simple a view of the matter; the task of understanding turns out to be "more difficult." We come to the realization that "in the case of each dif-

---

[*c*] Again, readers of Aristotle will have recognized a transposition into the language of intellect of what Aristotle says about sense perception: in the act of perception, there is one single actuation, namely, both of the perceiving sense and of the perceived object (even though the two remain separate in being); still, this actuation occurs only in the perceiving sense (*De Anima*, III, 2, 425^{b}26; 426^{a}10).

[*d*] This applies, not only to our knowledge of particular sensible beings, of which Aristotle says that they are to be "disengaged from matter" in order that their "forms" be understood, but also to ideas, which are immediately ready for understanding, since "what thinks and what is thought are identical" (*De Anima*, III, 4, 430^{a}3–9).

ferent subject we shall have to determine the appropriate process of investigation" [e].

Hegel, who had to deal with the limits of reason uncovered by Kant, with method, and with the claims of objectivism in a way the classic and medieval philosophers never had to, is nonetheless equally emphatic in his insistence that understanding must accommodate itself to the subject matter, not impose itself upon it: "A discipline may organize itself only by means of the idea's own inherent life. A schematic approach will stick determinateness on to things in a merely extrinsic fashion; in a discipline, the determinateness is the living, self-moving soul of the content come to full fruition" [f].[4]

True systematic understanding, therefore, occurs in the *mutually actualizing encounter between human understanding and reality*. This encounter begins by the mind's accommodation to its subject matter, along the lines of the latter's *organic structures*, but it also lays bare and develops the mind's own inherent structures, by which it can understand.

This type of understanding leads to the development of an encyclopedia that is *adequate* to the subject matter. "We can recall here the Tübingen theologian Franz Anton Staudenmaier. According to his 'encyclopedia' of 1834 this discipline offers the 'systematic outline of the whole of theology,' the 'compact sketch of its concrete idea according to all its essential determinations.' He writes: 'For just as the human spirit is organic and is a system of living powers, so also in scientific knowledge it wants to see an organism, a system, and it does not rest until it has produced by its organizing activity a systematic interrelationship among the different parts which form the content. This systematic interrelationship among the different parts of a science in accordance with its essential and basic concepts is presented in the encyclopedia.' According to him, the encyclopedia develops the necessary and organic interrelationship of all the parts of theology, and thus it presents the parts as a real science by grasping them in the unity and the totality of their interrelationships. It is a real organism and bears its life principle within itself" (cf. also §44, 1–2).[5]

---

[e] *De Anima*, I, 1, 402ª10–19. Cf. *Eth. Nic.*, I, 3, 1094ᵇ12–28: "Our discussion will be adequate if it has as much clearness as the subject-matter admits of, for precision is not to be sought for alike in all discussions. . . . It is the mark of an educated man to look for precision in each class of things just so far as the nature of the subject admits. . . ."

[f] Maurice Wiles has proposed, in *The Remaking of Christian Doctrine*, pp. 17–19, to use the criteria of "coherence and economy" to develop a version of Christian doctrine at once coherent and required (as against merely allowed) by the evidence. We may not care to go as far as Hans Urs von Balthasar and simply say, "Whoever says yes to more will be proved right" ("Wer mehr bejaht behält recht": *In der Fülle des Glaubens*, p. 58, n. 42), but it is doubtful whether such extrinsic criteria as "coherence" and especially "economy," with their implied minimalist, lowest-common-denominator definition of "common tradition," can serve as reliable tools for interpretation.

[7] Thus, second, far from alienating the knowing subject from itself, *focusing on the object of knowledge ensures the knowing subject's authenticity.* The focused effort to understand what is outside ourselves actualizes our capacity for understanding; but this capacity is rooted in our inherent integrity as persons. Understanding what presents itself to us, therefore, indirectly causes to grow a new, ever more responsive intellectual identity [g]. The latter will also reveal itself in a growing moral commitment to intellectual integrity [h]. In this sense it is possible to say that the practice of objectivity is a source of mature personal identity.

[a] Subjectively, this moral-intellectual sense of identity in understanding is experienced as a spontaneous, sustained passion for a broader and deeper knowledge and understanding of the object of one's study. The passion is a spiritual one, rooted as it is in the depths of the natural desire to know. It does not spring, therefore, from a need to prove or relish one's intelligence or one's worth, based on the alleged satisfaction involved in "having a subject down" (for instance, for an examination), let alone from the visceral satisfaction that comes from excelling at a subject above others. Nor does this passion come from a desire to correct error, nor even from a desire to teach. This is so because the standard of intellectual excellence is set simply by the object of study itself, not by one's inner needs for self-assurance in its various guises, nor by external norms, such as the crying need for better education, the demand for higher professional standards, or even public authority, which needs scholarship, yet always fears its independence.

Having to measure up to one's object of study has another spiritual benefit: it tends to keep one relatively modest. Those privy to this experience will also testify that it is not their own discipline or sagacity that guides them but only the depth of their own desire to understand and the subject matter to be understood. Discipline and sagacity, of course, are assets in the life of learning, but in the true scholar they are not so much produced by self-conscious or self-righteous effort as called forth by the charm of the object. No wonder

---

[g] This conception of identity-experience as a "responsive" experience will be a recurring theme in this theological system. It is predicated on the thesis, elaborated by Martin Buber in *I and Thou*, that the identity actuated in any encounter depends on the quality of the relationship. Unlike the "I" actuated by the approach to the other as an "It," the "I" actuated by a "responsive" manner of relating, which consists in fundamentally regarding the other as "Thou," is the authentic self.

[h] The young Aquinas is already aware of this connection between concentration on the object and growth in intellectual integrity. He characterizes the contemplative life as one in which a person takes on, preferentially, the search for understanding. But understanding, he explains, is determined both subjectively and objectively. And while in the former respect it is self-regarding ("and so it used to be in the contemplative life of the philosophers"), in the latter respect "it comes out of regard for the object, for where there is love, there is sight (*ubi amor ibi oculus*)": *In III Sent.*, d. 35, q. 1, a. 2, r. [32].

that the life of study can turn into a life of virtue; concentration on the object has something in common with love; real scholars find everything of great interest, just as they tend to have a natural respect for the intelligence of others, as well as for what others know.

The delights of scholarship being so subtle, it is not surprising that the intellectual life can also degenerate. Generations of students have suffered—often unwittingly—at the hands of impatient masters and mistresses more interested in their own superiority than in the delights of their subject matter. In every age, too, scholars of exceptional vision and power of understanding have been criticized and taken to task, with embarrassing confidence and abandon, by smaller minds, who have mistaken the urge to teach, correct, and criticize for understanding.

These sobering points are made here for a special reason. Why do theologians seem to be more than ordinarily tempted to exceed their competence, which consists in understanding? The attractiveness of the study of theology is in no small part predicated on the fact that theology involves the study of a great and authoritative Tradition. Theologians have a tendency to identify so closely with the authority of the Tradition they study that they develop a false sense of responsibility; when this happens, they begin to sound magisterial in inappropriate and mistaken ways, by aggressive teaching, correcting, and criticizing, and even by seeking secret associations with centers of power, ecclesiastical and otherwise. Under this rubric we should also mention sad instances of theologians being called to high ecclesiastical office and inappropriately proceeding to act as if their theological opinions and judgments had been elevated along with their persons. Yet it should be obvious that the fact that the great Tradition is authoritative gives the theologian no authority at all. The theologian's proper authority rests entirely on the quality and depth of his or her understanding of that Tradition; to recall the Church deeply and broadly to its own nature is the theologian's proper ministry in the Church, and in that sense his or her "teaching authority" (cf. §55)

[8] In this way, the act of true understanding turns out to be an experience of transcendence as well as identity: few things are at once so ecstatic and so natural as understanding. No wonder that Plato—and the great platonizers of all times—noticed the deep, spontaneous affinity of the human mind with what it truly knows: ideas suit us so well, they are so natural to us as to make us realize that there must be something about them that is innate in us. And since ideas are bound to exist in a purer, better world, the mind cannot but be at home, ultimately, in the divine world. No wonder, that Aristotle and some of his medieval Arab commentators could associate the light of the intel-

lect with an intelligence that encompasses the whole world, and even with divinity. No wonder, finally, that the mature Aquinas, in a daring aside, could note the awesome perspective in which every encounter that involves understanding occurs: "All those who know know God implicitly in whatever they know."[6]

Aquinas' observation serves to make a final point. Systematic theology, it is often rightly said, should have a mystical side to it. Rather often, though, the phrase sounds like a caution addressed to theologians, to exhort them not to yield to the beguilements of Reason and humbly to stay in touch with piety. But such piety, it is then implicitly conceded, is an enemy of intellectual rigor—the kind of rigor, it is said, that demands of the scholarly theologian that he exercise control, have grasp, and show mastery. What we have implicitly argued in this section is that a mystical element is *naturally* at home in theology, provided theology is practiced properly—that is to say, in the service of *understanding*. This is so because the mystical element in theology derives, not just from theology's theme, nor just from the theologian's sentiments of reverence, but fundamentally from the very exercise of the intelligence with which the theme is so respectfully pursued. In the final analysis, the pursuit of *pia veritas* amounts to *vera pietas*. At heart, the practice of theology is intellectual worship, not only on account of its divine subject matter, but also on account of the God-given thirst for understanding with which the subject matter is pursued.

The assurances just elaborated will have to work themselves out in the course of this entire systematic theology, as was suggested before (§7, 2). Still, we must now begin with a first, preliminary account of some of the main tasks, methods, procedures, and basic assumptions of this systematic theology. The theme of *faith and structures*, in the present chapter (§§9–11), will introduce the issue of the *tasks* of systematic theology in the next (§§12–16). This will be followed, in the third chapter, by a reflection on the ways in which systematization may obscure understanding (§§17–20). Finally, the fourth chapter will discuss pluralism in systematic theology and then proceed to give an introductory account of the *basic theme* of this work, and of its *assumptions and procedures*, in which the theme of *encounter* will play an important part (§§21–23).

FAITH AND STRUCTURES

[§9] FAITH AS ABSOLUTE

[1] There exists, in the Christian tradition, an account of the encounter with God that is starkly absolute: humanity, along with the world with which it is continuous [i], is suspended between God and nothingness,

[i] A crucial conception is implied in this phrase: humanity is truly continuous with

and nothing short of total abandon, shorn of all creaturely, provisional
assurances, will do justice either to the infinite, creative love of God
or to the creature's utter dependence on God—a dependence that coincides with the creature's identity.

> Woe to him who argues with the one who is modeling him—
>   vessel among earthen vessels!
> Does the clay say to the one who is modeling it:
>   "What are you making? Your work is unhandy!"
> Woe to him who says to a father: "What are you begetting?"
>   and to a woman: "What are you in travail with?"
> Thus says YHWH, Israel's Holy One and its Modeler:
>   "Ask me about what is to come,
>   my children and the work of my hands—
>   entrust it to me!"
>
>   (Is 45, 9-10)[7]

Such absolute accounts of the experience of faith are found, not only
in public professions of faith, including numerous scriptural ones, but
also in the highly individuated experiences of the mystics and even in
some of the profoundest statements made by theologians.

[a] Scriptural examples are not only such great cosmic-agonistic theo-
phanies as Psalm 18 but also other professions of radical faith,
whether of the liturgical (e.g., Is 6, 1–8; Ps 115; Rom 11, 33–36),
the self-defensive (e.g., Ps 25, 26), or the sapiential variety (e.g., Ps
73).
    Theological examples are statements like Aquinas' profound for-
mula: "According to what each creature is, it is naturally God's."[8] An
impressive modern example—and one as limited as it is often misinterpreted—is Schleiermacher's analysis, in the second of his
Speeches on Religion, of the essence of "religion." In authentic self-
consciousness, where "the original relation of intuition and feeling"
comes to immediate awareness, we find our self-experience to be
identical with an experience of piety: we allow ourselves "to be moved
by the Whole that man stands over against."[9]
    The most distinctive feature of Karl Rahner's entire theological
effort lies in his combination of Aquinas' ontological approach with

---

the world, and, conversely, the world "is intimately related to man and achieves its purpose through him" (LG 48). This view is both non-Cartesian (there is distinction, but no
separation, between spirit and matter) and non-Kantian (there is distinction, but no separation, between freedom and nature). Much theology since the sixteenth century has
abandoned this classic conception. By being one-sidedly focused on soteriology, it has
unnecessarily colluded with Cartesian and Kantian tendencies: it has tended towards
unworldliness by mainly viewing the world as merely the stage on which the salvation
of humanity, and especially of human souls, is enacted. It is one of the undying merits
of Pierre Teilhard de Chardin to have dealt the deathblow to this prejudice, which—we
are recognizing today—is out of touch with evolution theory as well as the human responsibility for the environment, to mention only two issues.

Schleiermacher's transcendental point of departure. The "idea" (the *Begriff*, that is to say, the normative essence and, hence, also the definition), both of the Christian faith and of the integrity of humanity and the world, lies in absolute dependence on God; in humanity this dependence comes to free and conscious awareness (especially in modern humanity, which has turned, in a decisive cultural move, to transcendental self-reflection). In this way, "faith seeking understanding" encompasses, in Rahner's theology, the quest for human intellectual integrity (*Wahrheitsgewissen*); conversely, "understanding seeking faith" is understood as the openness that must characterize any existential self-awareness in the presence of absolute mystery.[10]

[2] Theologians must recognize and deeply respect such naked accounts; they mark the outer edge of theology—the point where the search for understanding, first prompted by faith, must recognize its limits and press on into a renewed, awe-inspired recognition of the absolute mystery. If such accounts were to be neglected, theology would cease to deal with faith and, as a result, cease to be *theo*-logy and turn into the mere study of religion as a characteristic human phenomenon. Paradoxically, therefore, what guarantees true thought and speech about God is precisely the recognition that God is the absolute mystery and, in that sense, beyond theology's reach (cf. §36, 3).

By the same token, however, neglect of these ultimate accounts would cause theology to lose touch with *humanity*, too. Being related to God is the constitutive ground of creatureliness, and the free and conscious acknowledgment of being so related is the actualization of human creatureliness *par excellence*. Consequently, what guarantees true thought and speech about humanity is the recognition of God as humanity's essential mystery.

These recognitions, therefore, ultimately place *both* God's mystery and the mystery of humanity, which is dependent on it, beyond theology's grasp.

[§10] FAITH AND CULTURE: AN INTERPLAY OF STRUCTURES

[1] Theology, however, while limited *by* these breathtaking perspectives, is not limited *to* them. This is so because our observations about the limits of theology must be matched by an analogous observation about the life of faith as it is concretely lived. Faith is indeed *essentially defined* by the unconditional acknowledgment of God as absolute, but it is not *exhausted* by it. The very fact that it was possible, in the previous section, to point a *variety of forms* in which even the most naked and total abandon to God is conveyed proves that *faith is experienced and exists in structures*—a thesis that remains to be elaborated in a variety of ways (cf. §11, 1–6; §13, 1; §36, 2).[11]

Human faith in God, therefore, is not only, ultimately, suspended between God and nothingness; it is also, proximately, concretized and practiced between religion [j] and world. These latter two, in turn, are not general abstractions; neither religion nor world comes in chemically pure form. They come in a variety of *structures*, according as, on the one hand, the human response to God and, on the other hand, the human response to its own condition and its world have taken shape, in complexes of religious practice and beliefs [k], in complexes of cultural practice and convictions, and in the interplay between the two.

[a] In the Christian tradition, these structures are positively interpreted and appreciated and not considered irrelevant, let alone opposed, to God, in the name of some form of superior *gnōsis*. This conviction is rooted, ultimately, in christology and its threefold structure: incarnation—life and death—resurrection and eschatology. Consequently, the Christian faith cannot endorse, as a matter of principle, the contention (whether Platonist, Gnostic, Romantic, or existentialist) that structures are inevitably alienating. This thesis, however, must remain to be argued. For the moment we are merely observing that the life of faith, while *essentially defined* in absolute terms, is *practiced* in structures that are not ultimate.

[2] The subject of structures must come up, in a variety of ways, in the course of any systematic theology. For present purposes, however, only those *general* points about structures must be made that are relevant to the issue of the tasks of systematic theology.

[§11] NATURE AND DIMENSIONS OF STRUCTURES

[1] A first point concerns *freedom and encounter*. If modern anthropology and modern linguistics—to mention only two disciplines—have taught us anything, it is that meaningful human life cannot exist apart from relatively stable structures of shared life and communication: language, family, ritual, to mention only some of the most obvious. We live in a structured world that is being continually restructured—mechanically, biologically, economically, sociopolitically, legally, internationally, ethically, religiously. The existentialist movement was fond of

---

[j] A terminological clarification may be useful here. The word *faith*, in this book, is used to refer to the central act of total abandon to God; *the faith*, (or *the Christian faith*, or *the Christian religion*) refers to the entire complex of structures in which Christian faith subsists and is practiced. *Religion* has a wider meaning: it refers to the entire complex of structures in which any form of faith-abandon to God subsists and is practiced.

[k] For the present purposes, it is sufficient simply to make the point that faith is embodied in structures. The *nature* of these structures is to be initially explored in the second half of this volume, where we will also argue that the basic structural components of the Christian faith are "teaching, life, and worship" (DV 8), or "creed, conduct, and cult" (cf. §44, 3). This conception is also the point of departure of Louis-Marie Chauvet's interesting general sacramental theology, *Du symbolique au symbole*. Eventually, we will have to explain how the structures of Christian faith, despite their obvious inadequacy and partiality (or rather, by virtue of their very inadequacy and partiality) are experienced as symbolic and, thus, refer to the essential act of faith which is their soul.

pointing out that involvement with particular things and structures must necessarily estrange us from our freedom and our authenticity [*l*]; the structuralist reaction has pointed out (in fact, somewhat over-emphasized) that we necessarily exist in a whole gamut of structural arrangements, both natural and cultural. It is important to note, there-fore, that the structures in which we exist and communicate are not merely practical, mechanical *tools*—that is to say, purely practical and tactical compromises by which we succeed in negotiating our necessary minimum of freedom and interpersonal communication. Quite the con-trary. Freedom and personalness cannot exist apart from structures, and it is far from true that slavery and mutual estrangement are nec-essarily rooted in structures as such. Thus, structures are an *ontological* given: human life is meant to be organic, not shapeless; structure is not the enemy of freedom and personalness but their matrix. This means that structures are deserving of our commitment; we can entrust ourselves to those that already exist, and we can trust ourselves to forge new ones. Freedom and interpersonalness emerge in the school of structure, where we also learn how to meet new challenges and to shape new structures to complement, and even to replace, existing ones.

[2] There are, of course, elements of contingency and even arbitrari-ness in every structure, which accounts for the fact that no single struc-ture is ever wholly convincing. Hence, while existence-in-structures is an inevitable ontological given, no single particular structure can lay claim to total authority. This means that structures have built-in ca-pacity, and indeed demand, for change, and it is part of human re-sponsibility to test structures and to renew or even replace them. And so, we have arrived at our next point, which concerns *stability and change*. Structures are intrinsically capable of providing *both*, by being relatively stable as well as relatively flexible. Again, this relationship has to be dialectically conceived; stability and change can be understood only in function of each other. Without openness to change, structure becomes rigid; without openness to stability, change becomes shapeless; it takes *both* stability and change to have a sound structure. Make either one absolute and you are courting death, whether by fossilization or by diffusion. Tame the tension between the two elements and you have locked yourself up in a spatial or temporal prison, without possibility to communicate.

[*l*] Existentialism may not be simply identified with Jean-Paul Sartre's "L'enfer, ce sont les autres"; still, the tendency towards individualism, in the name of "authenticity," is unmistakable. For a fascinating, if somewhat perverse, analysis of language as "un per-sonnage gênant," breathing down our shoulders and preventing us from freely saying what we mean and meaning what we say, cf. Brice Parain, *Recherches sur la nature et les fonctions du langage*, capably discussed by J. W. M. Verhaar, *Some Relations Between Per-ception, Speech and Thought*, pp. 149–150, 154.

[3] This leads to another point. Precisely because of their relative stability and mutability, structures are *innately partial*, as well as *essentially multiple*. Structures are finite, and, hence, they connote, by virtue of their very being-so, the existence, or at least the possibility, if not the high probability, of other structures. This must be understood in a twofold way. First, it must be understood in a *spatial* and *temporal* sense: different structures coexist in space, and structures become different as they move in time. Second, it must be understood as applying *internally* as well as *externally*. Structures are not simply and massively locked into themselves; rather, they are *internally differentiated*: each structure is, in itself, a cluster of structures. Accordingly, other structures are not purely unrelated to any one structure; structures *interlock*. Structures are multiple, both in the sense that they interlock with other structures and in the sense that they internally consist of structures; structures are con-structured [*m*].

> [a] Let us leave the cool cellars of abstraction for a moment and apply what has just been said about structures to one particular issue in Christian theology. If, as was argued, faith is experienced and exists in structures (§10), and if structures are what we have argued they are, then such structures as the Church Community and the Church Tradition are bound to be, respectively, a "communion of communions" and a "tradition of traditions" [*n*] with different, though related, forms of worship, life-styles, and doctrinal traditions. This, needless to say, has consequences for theology, to which we shall have to revert (§§21–22); for now, we must take our discussion of structures a few steps further.

[4] Structures—and this is the fourth point—are *the matrix of all encounter and dialogue*. The dimensions of existence-in-structures discussed so far—freedom and encounter, stability and change, and coexistence in space and time—show that human beings exist in structures as in microcosms. Still, it is one of the proofs of humanity's basic openness to the infinite that, while necessarily existing in structures, we are (though often unthematically) aware that the small world

---

[*m*] Readers familiar with scholastic philosophy will have recognized in this discussion the classic thesis—Aquinas' constant teaching—that "everything comes into being [*fit ens*] to the extent that it becomes one, undivided in itself and distinct from other things" (*ScG* II, 50, *Item*). Structures are finite unities, imperfectly undivided in themselves and imperfectly distinct from other structures.

[*n*] In an important Unity Week address to the University of Cambridge in 1970, Cardinal Willebrands revived this ancient synodical conception of the Church, with far-reaching consequences for ecumenism. Referring to LG 23, he explained that there can be a plurality of different ecclesial "types" (*typoi*) within the communion of the one Church of Christ. Text in *Documents on Anglican/Roman Catholic Relations*, 1972, pp. 32–41. Yves Congar has authoritatively written on the relationships between the Tradition and traditions, in a book with that title. Cf. also F. J. van Beeck, *Catholic Identity After Vatican II*, pp. 76–78.

of our structures is limited—even if it is often as hard to tell, *from within our structures*, exactly *how* it is limited as it is for a fish to imagine anything but water. Unlike fish, though, human beings are made for an essentially wider world than they inhabit [*o*], and, hence, the issue of transcendence—of encounter across structural divides—will have to occupy us. This is the same as saying that *we exist in an ongoing interplay of structures* and that the dynamism of our human spirit as well as the partiality of the structures in which we exist urge us *to seek to widen that interplay* by always seeking to *encounter reality as it exists in structures outside our own*, whether spatially or in time. Is this why peoples of old have— proudly *and* precariously—cultivated *both* their identity *and* their openness by means of mythical stories recounting their own sacred memories from time immemorial as well as the travels of some of their daredevil heroes to faraway, dangerous, and inaccessible places?

[5] We must continue our discussion of structures by briefly pointing to the connection between *structure and interpretation*. We not only exist in structures; we also understand and communicate in them. Again, this involves both wealth and poverty. The structures we live in form the matrix of our understanding and communication, but they also set their limits. There is indeed much we have come to understand, though we have not attained it through any simple, intuitive shortcuts, nor are we likely to find such shortcuts in the future or elsewhere. We understand by "taking things apart" and by "putting things together," by "reading"—that is, by discerning, by *interpreting*—whatever offers itself to our understanding,[12] and in this way we also come to deeper self-interpretation and self-understanding.

This can be elaborated under the rubric of "horizon."[13] We all live, not only individually but especially also socially, in a world that is limited and, in that sense, defined. We live in a world bounded by a horizon (Gk. *horizon*: "that which limits, defines"). *That horizon structures our world*. Negatively, it sets limits to our world and, hence, to the understanding available to us. Positively, it allows us to understand our world; we cannot make sense of anything except in function of the horizon, by "putting it in perspective." Yet the curious thing is that the horizon itself is determined by our own stance; when we shift, our horizon shifts, and, as a result, our perception of everything in our world changes. *Self-understanding and understanding of the world are mutually conditioned*. Are we, then, locked into our worlds? The horizon, again, assures us that we are not: it is not only the structuring limit of our world; it also conveys the unknown worlds that are beyond. The horizon, therefore, also appeals to the innate *Wanderlust* of the human heart. It acts as the invitation extended to us to go beyond our world

---

[*o*] Allusion to Rupert Brooke's poem *Heaven*, in ridicule of analogy and of Aquinas' proofs of God's existence, quoted by Maurice Wiles in his *What Is Theology?* (pp. 80–81).

by changing our stance, just as the partiality of the structures we live in determines our understanding and, in doing so, invites us to understand what is beyond. No wonder, then, that understanding has been described, by Hans-Georg Gadamer, as a "fusion of horizons," in which understanding is a process of mutual interpretation in a "hermeneutical circle": we interpret what presents itself to our understanding and place it within our intellectual horizon; and in doing so, we are newly interpreted to ourselves, which, in turn, enhances our ability to open ourselves to new understanding and interpretation.

[6] A final point. Understanding—that is to say, the ongoing interpretation of ourselves and of the structures of existence—is, at a deeper level, a matter of *liberating encounter*. It is so in two ways.

In the first place, interpretative understanding is *remedial*; it plays a reconciling role in what we have called the "interplay of structures." The interplay itself occurs in a bewildering variety of culturally conditioned ways. Among these, commerce[14] and conquest have, perhaps, been the most customary. But the smart winners of the marketplace and the battlefield do not ordinarily have the gift of understanding, and their successes end up breeding resentment and contempt in those whom they have taken advantage of. What has been acquired by mere purchase or mastered by sheer power will mulishly resist integration until it is recognized and understood and thus set free. Interpretative understanding can heal, once we learn, patiently and hospitably, how to become partners and allies, sharing goods instead of merely trading them, and learning how disarming we can be when we stop defeating each other and ourselves. Interpretative understanding, however, must not be content with being merely remedial; it must also be *constructive*. Understanding is in and of itself a positive way of initiating the interplay of structures, and one, on the whole, more humane and peaceful than coin and cannon.

Second, understanding the interplay of structures is, ultimately, a matter of *hope*. For not everything can be brought within the compass of understanding. The very source of all our understanding, namely, our self-awareness in light of our awareness of God, can never be completely gathered in, as in an intellectual harvest [p]; it must remain implicit in all our structured understandings. Still, while remaining implicit, it powers the search for expanded horizons as an inner thirst—a thirst matched by the potent, though equally implicit, appeal of the horizons themselves. Horizons are never reached; they will always recede, and, hence, they ultimately offer to the infinite yearning of the human heart a daunting perspective: the whole world [q].

---

[p] "Gathered in" renders Gm. *einholen*—one of Karl Rahner's favorite metaphors to express the idea conveyed here.

[q] Readers of Kant's *Critique of Pure Reason* will have noticed in this paragraph an

[7] In this way, our discussion has finally come back to its properly theological point of departure, so it is possible to sum up. Faith in God involves identity-experience, from which arises a deep-seated thirst for self-awareness—a thirst that we can never fully "gather in." But the thirst is there: self-awareness demands that we live "examined lives." Examination of life, however, involves ongoing awareness of the world we live in, both of our microcosms and of the structures of the larger world. All of this occurs in the ultimate perspective of an understanding of "the whole world"—an understanding, again, that we cannot ever gather in, as in an intellectual harvest. Bringing the whole world home is, ultimately, to be entrusted to God (cf. Mt 13:39), and as for our own deepest selves, for now I can be content to "know in part," in hopes of "knowing as I am known" (1 Cor 13:12).

It is time to return to the subject of theology as a discipline, by developing, in light of our discussion thus far, a first definition of theology, as well as an understanding of the tasks of systematic theology. This, then, must be the agenda of the next chapter.

---

ontological transposition of the Kantian interpretation of "I," "World," and "God" as purely formal categories.

CHAPTER 2

Systematic Theology and Its Tasks

THEOLOGY

[§12] FAITH AND UNDERSTANDING

On the basis of our discussion of the nature of understanding in the previous chapter, the present chapter will proceed to explore one specific form of understanding: systematic theology. After pointing out the connection between systematic theology and the structures of faith (§13), we will argue that systematic theology is characterized by unity of pursuit and that its various tasks, therefore, are arranged on a continuum. At the same time, however, we will argue that within this continuum it is possible to identify three distinct tasks: constructive theology, dogmatic theology, and fundamental theology (§14). After this, it will be explained that systematic theology must look for coherence, without, however, reducing the Christian faith to its manifest elements, lest the reference to the mystery be lost (§15). This will bring up for discussion a difficult matter, which is related to, but by no means identical with, the issue of faith and understanding: the problem of faith and uncertainty (§16), which will bring the chapter to a close.

Before all of this can be accomplished, however, we have a few preparatory matters concerning faith and understanding to treat. Let us begin, therefore, with a first, preliminary definition of systematic theology and a first, introductory discussion of it.

[1] It should be clear from the previous chapter that *Christian theology* must be minimally defined as a form of *disciplined intellectual understanding related to the Christian faith*. This relatedness, we argued, is substantial, not extrinsic or forced; ultimately, it is rooted in *a deep affinity between understanding and faith*. That affinity is a matter of *mutuality*. On the one hand, all acts of human understanding, including acts of theo-

logical understanding, in and of themselves encompass a fundamental aspiration to worship (§8, 8). On the other hand, acts of faith give rise to thought: because faith is experienced and exists in structures (§10), it demands, like all structures, that it be interpreted and understood— ultimately in the light of the absolute dimension it incorporates (§9).

[a] At the core of the great Tradition of Christian theology, there is a fundamental and continuous recognition of this mutuality between faith and understanding, even though it must be granted that the pendulum has markedly swung between the two extremes of naturalism and fideism at certain times and in certain places. These pendulum swings have been most characteristic of the Protestant traditions, although they are far from unknown in the history of Catholic theology; Eastern Orthodox theology has remained relatively unaffected by them. On a total perspective, however, it is fair to say that the fluctuations have served to mark rather than mask the point of balance.

On the one hand, there is the human need—which is individual as well as communal-ecclesial—to make intellectual sense of the Christian faith-commitment and its structures. Faith-commitment thus naturally activates the search for understanding: theology is "faith in search of understanding" (fides quærens intellectum). At the practical level, this means that theology can at times be truly instructive and corrective: it is able, in certain situations, to give insight into the meaning of faith, to settle questions arising from ignorance about matters of faith, to remove misconceptions and prejudices about it, and even to liberate from mental blocks against it. At a deeper level, however, theology must be mystagogical. Animated and guided by faith, theology is meant to lead the mind to a "most fruitful understanding" (DS 3016; CF 132; cf. §15, 2, a) of the mysteries of the faith; in doing so, it must lead the mind into the depth and fullness of its own native potential in the very process of leading it to its limits, as well as beyond them [a].

Thus, on the other hand, theology is also meant to be an education of human intelligence precisely insofar as it is natively in search of the infinite: theology is "understanding in search of faith" (intellectus quærens fidem).

The dialectic of the two movements prompts the conclusion that, as a matter of principle, theology is practiced in the service of faith as well as intellectual integrity. Whole, free, self-aware persons, along with their vital connections with the outside world, must be drawn to do

---

[a] In this light it is understandable how the best of the great tradition could come to positively commend faith as a road to understanding. A classic instance of this is Anselm's credo ut intelligam ("I believe so that I may understand": Proslogion, chap. 1, Fateor; cf. St. Anselm's Proslogion, M. J. Charlesworth, ed., pp. 26ff., 54, 114–15)—the echo of Augustine's crede ut intelligas ("Believe so that you may understand": Sermo 43, PL 38, 237–38).

justice to God by faith. In turn, faith in God must be the exaltation of humanity, otherwise the Christian faith-commitment would be merely superimposed, adventitious, and sectarian, and its only possible defense would be of the fundamentalist kind.

Not surprisingly, therefore, the central tradition has always resisted the temptation to conceive of faith and reason as opposed, or as fundamentally alien, to each other. Tertullian is the classic example of this deviation. It is true that the hyperbole *credo quia absurdum* ("I believe because it is senseless") is wrongly attributed to him [*b*]; still, it is also true that his passionate search for total certitude (a holdover from Stoicism?) resulted in a theology that curiously combines a massive affirmativeness about Christian doctrines with nervous disclaimers of any kind of human reasonableness in believing them. This makes him the prototype of the fundamentalist intellectual: Tertullian came home when he came to Montanism.

None of this, however, has ever been accepted by the great Tradition, no matter how attractive and sincere the various a-rational and irrational interpretations of the act of faith (Søren Kierkegaard!) have been. This applies especially to Roman Catholic fideism and traditionalism, strong movements in nineteenth-century France, and associated with the names of Louis de Bonald, Félicité de Lamennais, Louis Bautain, and Augustin Bonnetty (DS 2765–69, 2811–14; cf. CF 101–05). That the traditionalists and the fideists were disgusted with the individualist rationalism of the eighteenth and early nineteenth centuries is understandable; what is theologically unacceptable was their irrational (and often very authoritarian) acceptance of only one truly reliable source of faith-understanding: an alleged primitive self-revelation of God, handed down by the common consent of the human race, and developed by the revealed Christian faith-tradition authoritatively handed down by the Church's magisterium.

[*b*] It is important to note at this point, without much elaboration, a basic decision implicit in the position adopted in the present book. It is the following. The reality of *sin* weakens, but does not nullify, the fundamentally positive relationship between faith and understanding. In making this decision, the present systematic theology places itself squarely in the Catholic (and Eastern Orthodox) tradition; the construal of an *adversary* relationship between faith and understanding is one of the characteristic features of the many theologies inspired by the Reformation. This Protestant construal of a

---

[*b*] The famous text in *De carne Christi* (5, 3–4; *SC* 216, pp. 228–229; cf. R 353) actually reads: "Why do you wish to tear down the dishonor that is indispensable to the faith? Whatever is beneath God's dignity is to my advantage. I am saved if I am not ashamed of my Lord.... God's Son was crucified? I am not ashamed, for it is shameful. And God's Son died? It is thoroughly believable, for it is senseless. And having been buried, he arose? It is certain, for it is impossible."

fundamentally adversary relationship between faith and understanding rests on a *theological* foundation: a keen awareness of the pervasiveness of sin and of the deep corruption resident in the human predicament—a common awareness, no matter how variously interpreted in the various Protestant traditions. This very basic feature of Protestantism has important consequences for the place of *soteriology* in Christian theology (cf. §20, 1–3).

Needless to say, catholic theology must agree to take sin seriously, and any positive construal of the relationship between faith and understanding must never become a matter of lighthearted naturalism. In due course it will be argued that the construal proposed here ultimately offers a sounder, because more *theological* (rather than merely existential-anthropological), interpretation of sin; hence, we will claim, it does more, not less, justice to the deep depravity involved in sin and to the effects of sin on the human mind's ability to know God [c].

[2] The present chapter intends to approach the relationship between faith and systematic theology in a *descriptive* fashion. Of course the issue can, and must, also be approached *normatively*: just what is the *authority* of theological understanding in relation to the understanding involved in faith, *and vice versa?* The latter approach will be touched on in the next chapter, but its proper treatment must wait till much later in this introductory volume (§55).

However, these two approaches do not exhaust the subject; the theological tradition has had a lot more to say about the relationship between faith and the use of reason in theology; it has explored the inner affinity between faith and understanding in a variety of ways. This will have to engage our attention at greater length later on, when a fundamental treatment of the relationship must be attempted in the context of fundamental theology. For the present moment, it is our task to develop an understanding of the relationship between systematic theology and the Christian faith in a descriptive fashion.

SYSTEMATIC THEOLOGY

[§13] UNDERSTANDING STRUCTURES AND SYSTEMATIC THEOLOGY

[1] Faith is experienced and exists in structures (§10, 1); meaningful human life cannot exist outside relatively stable structures of shared life and communication (§11, 1). As a result, the human response to

---

[c] Readers of Paul Tillich will have noticed, in our treatment, a parallel to Tillich's discussion of autonomy, heteronomy, and theonomy (for example, *Systematic Theology*, I, pp. 84–86). But Tillich, for all his liberalism, remains firmly within the Protestant tradition when he claims that humanity finds itself locked into a sin-produced, sinful situation of existential estrangement from God as well as self (*Systematic Theology*, II, pp. 29–78).

God and the human response to humanity's condition and its world have taken shape, *and are taking shape*, in complexes of religious practice and beliefs, in complexes of cultural practice and convictions, and in the interplay between the two (§10, 1) [*d*]. This process of "taking shape" is a function of the dialectic of stability and change inherent in all structures (§11, 2), as well as of the interplay among structures in place and time (§11, 4; 3), in a dynamic that engages the ongoing human search for freedom and communication (§11, 1), which turns natural process into history proper [*e*].

The *specific task of systematic theology* is the study of these complexes of religious practice and beliefs, of cultural practice and convictions, and of the interplay between the two. In and of themselves, both religion and culture are *structured* as well as *structurally interrelated*; hence, they lend themselves to the kind of *systematic* study that does justice to the "self-moving soul" of religion and culture, as well as to the living movement of their interplay. Systematic theology, therefore, does not have to resort to "stick[ing] determinateness on to things in a merely extrinsic fashion" (cf. §8, 6, a) [*f*].

[a] Needless to say, this definition of systematic theology in terms of *structures* makes it essentially *interpretative* and *generalist* and, hence, always open to the charge—not infrequently justified and never entirely avoidable—of dilettantism. The charge is most often brought by the practitioners of the *theological specialisms*: biblical scholars and

---

[*d*] The entire chapter 2 of part 2 of GS 53–62 is of great relevance to the present discussion of the structures of faith and culture, and of their mutual interplay.

[*e*] Note that there is no suggestion of simple, unqualified *progress* implied in all of this; nor, for that matter, is it denied that progress has, in fact, occurred. What *is* implied, however, is that development of doctrine has involved, not only progress, but also *loss of tradition*. J. P. Jossua has convincingly proposed the thesis that development of doctrine first of all involves, not progress, but "successive structurings" (cf. his "Immutabilité, progrès ou structurations des doctrines chrétiennes?"). This thesis has a wider application, to all the structures of faith and culture. It may be suggested, too, that an analogous thesis could be added to Jossua's thesis: if the living unity in faith *in time* involves successive structurings of doctrine, then the living unity of faith *in space* involves, not standardization by uniformity, but respectful, pluriform mutuality of "co-existent structurings." Cf. §19, 1, b; §51, 4, b, [*s*].

[*f*] George A. Lindbeck's plea, in *The Nature of Doctrine*, for a structural, "cultural-linguistic" understanding of doctrine succeeds in noting some of the weaknesses of the objective "propositionalist" and the transcendental "experiential-expressive" interpretations of doctrine. It succeeds less well in taking seriously the fact that doctrines ultimately make *truth*-claims: their structures are not independent of the faith they mean to express. Hence, while interpretation and comparison of doctrines must take "grammar" seriously, they must eventually go beyond it. This is also possible, because grammars are *open structures*: they admit of translation, comparison, and hence dialogue—they even prompt them (cf. §22, 2, a). Like all structures, therefore, doctrines, whatever their various grammars, demand to be *interpreted*, and interpreted *in light of the integrity of their intent*. This is consistent with Aquinas' observation that "the believer, in believing, aims not at the proposition but the reality; for we formulate propositions only with a view to having knowledge of reality, both in natural-reason knowledge and in faith" (*S. Th.*, II-II, 1, 2, *ad* 2). Cf. also §51, 4, d, [*u*].

church historians, not to mention the liturgists, the pastoral theologians, and the psychologists and sociologists of religion. The charge is as often heard from *non-theological specialists*, who are understandably wary of theologians treating philology, history, literature, law, anthropology, history of religion, and especially philosophy with what they view as cavalier disregard for scholarly research and method. Systematic—and especially dogmatic—theology has indeed a lot to answer for in this regard. Naive dogmatism has been its historic sin, and serious Christian scholars in all disciplines have often been embarrassed by the lack of professional integrity on the part of their colleagues in theology.

Such a lack of integrity is especially undesirable today. The twentieth century has witnessed a spectacular involvement of conscientious Christians in all branches of scientific and scholarly pursuit— a development that especially Pope Pius XII (1939–58) welcomed with unusual, if critical, care (cf. also GE 10–11). In the modern context, systematic theology can no longer plead innocent if it is found to cultivate naiveté, whether of the dogmatist or—on the rebound—of the liberal kind. It must methodically respect and profit from the findings of the theological and non-theological specialisms and let itself be corrected by their astringent criticisms. Fortunately, the authority of critical biblical studies has been increasingly recognized by Catholic theologians ever since the encyclical *Divino afflante Spiritu* of 1943 (cf. DV 12; also DS 3826–31; cf. CF 233–36); this has had an enormous impact on Roman Catholic (faith and) theology. An equally conscientious hermeneutic of church history is still outstanding and must be considered a top priority; it could have a comparable impact on dogmatic theology in the Roman Catholic Church. Analogous points could be made with reference to the possible contributions from other disciplines, especially the social sciences.

[b] It still pays to re-read an encyclical like *Humani generis* of 1950 (DS 3875–99; CF 144–48; 238–39; 419–20; 858–59; 1571) to appreciate the landslide that occurred at the Second Vatican Council in this regard. The document aptly reveals how reluctant the traditional doctrinal establishment was to recognize the relative autonomy of professional scholarship. However, *Humani generis* should not be too easily dismissed; it may still serve as a reminder, by way of counterpoint to the present discussion, that the authority of the disciplines should not be accepted uncritically. Like all modern-day specialisms, all scholarly disciplines suffer from the current fragmentation of specialized academic pursuits; they are far more subject to fashion than they like to admit; they are often unaware of the ideologies implied in their methods and assumptions; they do not always resist the temp-

tation of dodging important theological questions under cover of "professional method" and "objectivity."

Hence, while systematic theology must learn from the disciplines, it must do so in an attitude of *discriminating* openness. Its principal strength must be its *integrity* [g], as it seeks to do justice to the great variety of available data in the midst of a great variety of pressures while also seeking to find the vital coherence among those data that are found to be reliable. Needless to say, finally, that systematic theologians must willingly resign themselves to not being up to date; integration takes time; systematicians tend to bring up the rear.

[§14] THE TRIPLE TASK OF SYSTEMATIC THEOLOGY[1]

[1] The interplay between the structures of the Christian faith and the structures of culture varies enormously from place to place and from time to time. Yet the two are nowhere completely separable, nor have they ever been, if for no other reason than that Christian believers spontaneously bring their cultural patterns, along with their underlying meanings and values, into the Church, to be welcomed, tested and re-formed, and put in perspective.[2]

The great Christian Tradition, however, has never simply contented itself with this natural, spontaneous interplay between religion and culture. It has always also sought to *influence* and even *transform* culture; the Church has always been missionary, even before, in the course of the fourth century, the Christian religion became an active, decisive factor in the normative cultural climate. The Church, by design, has a civilizing bent, and it feels responsible for culture (GS 57–61); hence, even in its properly missionary activity it acknowledges the cultural structures of time and place (AG 6).

In any case, the structures of religion and culture form a *continuum*, both spontaneously and by design, and it is as a continuum that they present themselves for *systematic theological study*, thus guaranteeing its *unity of pursuit*.

[2] The systematic theological study of the structures of religion and culture is not of purely speculative interest. In fact, the cultivation of understanding is, in and of itself, an influential cultural *and* theological activity; understanding, in and of itself, enhances the mutual interplay and integration of religion and culture. Hence, *the central*—or in any

---

[g] The personal side of this requirement is intellectual integrity and habitual purity of intention: systematic theologians must seek to be aware of their motivations and prejudices. The less systematicians depend on "hard data" to keep them honest, the more they must rely on imaginative interpretation; the more daring and imaginative their interpretations, the more they are likely to disguise their personal preferences and prejudices as reliable teaching. No wonder that sound systematic theology is heavily dependent on the systematician's emotional maturity and intellectual integrity.

case most challenging—*task of systematic theology is the search for new forms of unity between religion and culture.*

This requires true spiritual discernment on the part of theologians, for any configuration of the structures of the Christian faith-experience, situated as it is between Church and Culture, worship and worldliness, witness to the world and willingness to learn from it, is a matter of "discretionary fit." A very attractive part of the systematician's vocation is precisely to understand existing configurations *and* to improve on them and carry them further. To achieve this, he or she must be as reliable a *mediator* as possible, interpreting religion and culture to each other. Needless to say, this requires, in the theologian, a special sense of balance between *the appreciation of existing harmony and order and the power of imagination.* Not surprisingly, systematic theology that focuses on this task is often referred to as *constructive theology* [h] and that the history, not only of theology, but in many cases even of *doctrine*, is marked by the names of great constructive thinkers and saints: Irenaeus; Origen; Clement of Alexandria; Athanasius; the Cappadocians—Gregory of Nazianzus, Gregory of Nyssa, and Basil the Great; Augustine; Maximus the Confessor; Anselm of Canterbury; Thomas Aquinas; Gregory Palamas; Martin Luther; Friedrich Schleiermacher; Johann Adam Möhler; John Henry Newman; Karl Barth; Karl Rahner.

[3] The configurative balance between religion and culture, it was just stated, is a matter of "discretionary fit." This is connected with the fact that the interplay between religion and culture is a function of the dynamics of freedom and encounter, and of stability and change, both of the spontaneous and of the intentional kind (cf. §11, 1–2). More fundamentally, however, it is connected with the fact that both the Christian faith and cultures make *demands*: they present themselves as *authorities*. The Christian faith cannot but present itself as a body of time-tested and widely shared conviction that demands attention, ultimately on the basis of a divine authorization; at the same time, it must recognize any culture's rightful demands. Analogously, any culture cannot but demand that justice be done to it in accordance with its deepest intentions and aspirations; at the same time, if it refuses to entertain strangers like the Christian faith, it will do so only at the price of becoming its own prison [i]. Any configurative balance between Chris-

---

[h] Construction is invariably the product of genius steeped in the tradition and at once so deeply original as to create new tradition. T. S. Eliot's essay "Tradition and the Individual Talent" (cf. *Selected Essays 1917–1932*, pp. 3–11) remains one of the profounder statements of this dynamic as it applies to literature. It equally applies to development of Christian doctrine and theology. Cf. §55, 4.

[i] For a historic (if idealized) example of this openness, cf. the account of bishop Paulinus' reception at the court of Eadwin, king of Northumbria, in the Venerable Bede's *Ecclesiastical History*, II, 13, ending with the words of the councillor; "Therefore if this new teaching brings us any more certain knowledge, it seems right that we should follow it." (Also quoted in *A New Catechism*, p. 3.)

tianity and culture must work itself out on the basis of a genuine, discriminating welcome mutually extended and received, and it depends
on the authoritative mutual approval ("reception") of both religion and
culture whether and to what extent such a configurative balance will
be found satisfactory. Systematic theologians are in the service of the
ongoing search for such a configurative balance.

[4] This analysis leads to a conclusion: within the continuous range
stretching from religion to culture *three areas of concentration* can be
distinguished.

The first is the central task that was just discussed; it occupies the
middle ground, where the configurative balance between faith and culture always remains to be forged, in the concrete "teaching, life, and
worship" of the living, historic, universal Church—in "all that [the
Church] itself is, all that it believes" (DV 8). Here also lies, as pointed
out, the theologians' first loyalty, as well as the core of their vocation:
*in the present moment to understand, and perhaps to further, the Church's liv-
ing, historic Tradition as a whole.*

The second and the third areas of concentration concern the two
authorities on either side: the Church and the Culture. This yields two
more theological tasks. The task that matches the former (which is also
the task that places the heaviest demands of *competence* on the theologian) is *dogmatic theology* or *church dogmatics*, whose object of study is the
integrity of historic and universal Christianity. The theological task that
matches the latter is *fundamental theology* in its various forms, whose
object of study is the human condition as it harbors the possibility of
being integrated into God's kingdom as essential to its own integrity.
It is in the force field between these two that *constructive systematic theology* must operate, by mediating between dogmatic theology on the
one hand and fundamental theology on the other.

Again, this involves *discretionary judgments.* Sometimes and in some
places theologians will have to represent the concerns of the world, of
the surrounding culture—the concerns yet to be integrated into the
Christian faith-experience. At other times they will have to represent
the basic experience of the Christian faith, in order to recall the Church
to its original and normative nature.[3]

[a] There is a natural affinity between, on the one hand, dogmatic
theology and *positive theology* and, on the other hand, between fundamental theology and *speculative theology*, the latter often referred
to, especially in the past, as "scholastic" theology. "Positive theology"
refers, roughly, to the theology of the patristic period and to all theologies whose principal focus is the Church's faith as laid down in
Scripture and the great Tradition and in the authoritative traditions
of worship, life, and teaching that comment on Scripture and the
great Tradition. A significant characteristic of positive theology is

that it takes the authority of the Church's faith as axiomatic and that the human ability to understand is used not so much to test the faith as to orchestrate it, in order to arrive at a deeper, richer, more appreciative understanding. "Speculative theology," principally associated with Peter Lombard and the later scholastics, refers to all methods of theology that seek to reveal the credibility of the Christian faith by showing its intelligibility. In doing so, speculative theology invariably also shows a more astringent side; one of its characteristic pursuits is testing the faith by critical questioning, in order to determine the extent of its intelligibility. Speculative theology typically attempts to come to an understanding of the faith that is characterized by intellectual integrity; in this fashion, it often displays a deep, if at times sober, appreciation of human reason and desire as naturally oriented to God [j].

Positive and speculative theology are no strangers to the struggles of modern and contemporary theology. The historical record shows that the two are best kept in a balance, for too rational a fundamental theology tends to drive dogmatics into the pietist or traditionalist corner, and too doctrinaire a dogmatics tends to drive fundamental theology into rationalism. Bishop Joseph Butler's classic *Analogy of Religion* of 1736, while slightly biased in favor of fundamental-theology issues, represents the great, balanced tradition begun by Aquinas' *Summa contra Gentiles*. John Henry Newman, in his own inimitable manner, is in the same tradition of balance; he is as sensitive and respectful an interpreter of the great Tradition (*An Essay on the Development of Christian Doctrine*) as he is a principled seeker for the roots of intellectual integrity in believing (*An Essay in Aid of a Grammar of Assent*). Theologians in the idealist tradition, such as Friedrich Schleiermacher and Paul Tillich, are much more one-sidedly concerned with fundamental-theology issues. On the other hand, the Tractarians and the great Matthias Scheeben are examples of theologians with basically dogmatic commitments. Karl Barth's principal inspiration is dogmatic, too, although speculative issues—no matter how vigorously he denies their importance—are never far from his mind. While Karl Rahner showed a lifelong interest in, and respect for, positive theology, his leading idea hails from fundamental theology [k]; in many ways, his thought can be interpreted as a consistent effort to settle Roman Catholic theology's arrears with the Enlightenment, which had charged that Christian dogma was an insult to hu-

---

[j] Note that Aquinas' famous thesis, "Grace does not abolish nature, but perfects it," occurs right in the first *quæstio* of the Summa Theologica, in the article that deals with the question about the role of argument in theology (I, 1, 8, *ad* 2). The underlying issue is, of course, whether faith recognizes the integrity of human understanding.

[k] In this context, Heinrich Ott correctly observes that Rahner typically reflects on man (foundationally) as the *possible* rather than (dogmatically) as the *actual* recipient of God's self-communication (*Wirklichkeit und Glaube*, 2. Band, *Der persönliche Gott*, p. 346).

man intelligence and freedom. Hans Urs von Balthasar's literary tastes have spontaneously driven him in the direction of positive, dogmatic theology; his appreciation of Barth is far from incidental to his thought [l].

[5] Let us close this brief discussion of the tasks of theology with a piece of sound pastoral advice that is sound theological advice, too. It may help enhance the unity of pursuit so necessary to theology, as well as help ensure that theology make its own proper, theological contribution to the unity of Church and Culture. It is found in the *Spiritual Exercises* of St. Ignatius of Loyola. He writes:

We should speak highly of both positive and scholastic theology; on the one hand, the positive doctors, like St. Jerome, St. Augustine and St. Gregory, have the special gift of moving people's hearts to a generous love and service of God our Lord; the scholastics, on the other hand, like St. Thomas, St. Bonaventure, the Master of the Sentences and the rest, have their own special gift, which is rather to give precision to and clarify, in a way suited to our age, those truths which are necessary for eternal salvation.[4]

SYSTEMATIC INTERPRETATION

[§15] SYSTEMATIC THEOLOGY: UNDERSTANDING THE COHERENCE

[1] We have already touched upon the idea that religion and culture are the outcome of development and that both of them, as well as their interplay, continue to be a matter of ongoing process and even history (§13, 1). This raises several issues. For the Church as such, in its worship, its life, and its teaching, it raises the issues of *pluriformity* (unity existing in simultaneous variety in space) and *tradition* (identity sustained through successive variations in time). Both will be discussed in their proper contexts.

For *systematic theology*, this raises a serious question of *method* [m]. We

---

[l] It must be said, however, that von Balthasar has not shown the kind of appreciation for fundamental theology that Rahner has shown for dogmatics. In *Neue Klarstellungen,* he writes, under the prejudicial title "Menschheitsreligion und Religion Jesu Christi," an essay in which numerous phrases from Rahner's works in fundamental theology are taken out of context and put together in a tendentious manner (pp. 44–51). Then, in a final note that shows at least the edge of a guilty conscience, von Balthasar writes: "We do not maintain by any means that we have rendered (or 'unmasked') K. Rahner's central intention; it is clear that, as a Catholic theologian, he thinks in a more subtle and differentiated manner. But formal foundational structures will have their way, no matter how many devices to retard their influence are built in; and so it seemed a useful idea to put together—after extricating them out of a great deal of cotton-batting—a number of statements, with the object of showing that, out of a dynamism of their own, 'they lead to where you do not want to go.' " Von Balthasar touches on a very serious issue indeed; hence, it should have been treated in less journalistic and insinuating a manner. His thesis about "formal foundational structures" necessarily having their way is belied by a long tradition; the Cappadocians' critical Platonism and Aquinas' adoption and transformation of Aristotelianism come to mind. And as for cotton batting . . .

[m] That there is a connection between the tasks of systematic theology and its methods has already been suggested (§8, 8). We are now ready to discuss this.

have already pointed out that the understanding of structures is a matter of interpretation and that any such understanding is, of necessity, *perspectival* (§ 11, 5). We have also laid down that the reason why systematic theology can be both *realistic* and properly *systematic* lies in the fact that there are religious *structures* to be understood (§13, 1).

Now does anything follow, for the *practice* of systematic theology, from the recognition that the structures of the Christian faith, are, in and of themselves, *amenable to multiple interpretative systematizations*, and that *all these systematizations are perspectival*, that is to say, that none of them are exhaustive or final? The answer to this question must be explored under two headings. The first concerns *the nature of theological interpretation*, which is the subject of this section; the second, to be elaborated later (§22), concerns the fact of *pluralism, both historical and contemporary, in systematic theology*.

[2] Structures, it was argued, are innately partial as well as multiple in time and space (§11, 3). If the method of understanding must suit the structure of reality (§8, 6), and not consist in the imposition of some extrinsic framework of understanding (§8, 6, a), then it is to be expected that any attempt at understanding by systematization will reflect this "open" character of the structure to be understood. This is the reason why the search for systematic understanding must involve, first of all, a search for the *inherent coherence* of the Christian faith—that is to say, for the connections between the structural elements of the great and universal Tradition. However, the coherence of our world is contingent on our horizon as the symbol of a coherence that eludes our grasp (cf. §11, 5); hence, the search for connections must also involve the search for *ultimate coherence*—that is to say, for the connections between the structural elements and God, whose glory and mystery must be the ultimate reference of all the structures of the Christian faith-experience (§10, 1).

[a] The First Vatican Council, in a very important text, seeking to avoid the extremes of rationalism and fideism, combined the thesis that our understanding of the structures of the Christian faith is essentially "interpretative" (§11, 5) with the two points that have just been made, as follows: ". . . if reason, illumined by faith, inquires in an earnest, pious and sober manner [cf. Tit 2:12], it acquires by God's grace a certain—and most fruitful—understanding of the mysteries, both *by analogy of what it naturally knows*, and *from the connectedness among the mysteries themselves* and [from their connectedness] *with humanity's ultimate end*" (DS 3016; cf. CF 132; cf. §12, 1, a; §21, 4, a, [e]).

[3] This applies primarily to *dogmatic theology*, whose task it is to come to a systematic understanding of the authoritative structures of the Christian faith. In seeking for a *greater and deeper and more coherent un-*

derstanding of those structures, however, dogmatic theology must do justice to them *as they are*. The danger is that systematization has a tendency to seek the kind of coherence and economy (cf. §8, 6, a, [b]) that serves the needs of the system rather than of the matter systematized. The antirationalist eighteenth-century theological writer Johann Georg Hamann, acutely conscious both of the truth of human understanding and of its essential incompleteness, put his skepticism vis-à-vis systematization more bluntly: "System is in and of itself an obstacle to truth."[5] On this crucial point, therefore, we need reliable guidance; let our guide be John Henry Newman. In his tract "On the Introduction of Rationalistic Principles into Revealed Religion" of 1835,[6] he writes:

Of course I do not deny that Revelation contains a history of God's mercy to us; who can doubt it? I only say, that while it is this, it is something more also. Again, if by speaking of the Gospel as clear and intelligible, a man means to imply that this is the whole of it, then I answer, No; for it is also deep, and therefore necessarily mysterious. This is too often forgotten. Let me refer to a very characteristic word, familiarly used . . . to designate [a mistaken] view of the Gospel Dispensation. It is said to be a *manifestation*, as if the system presented to us were such as we could trace and connect into one whole, complete and definite. Let me use this word "Manifestation" as a symbol of the philosophy under review; and let me contrast it with the word "Mystery," which on the other hand may be regarded as the badge or emblem of orthodoxy. Revelation, as a Manifestation, is a doctrine variously received by various minds, but nothing more to each than what each mind comprehends it to be. Considered as a Mystery, it is a doctrine enunciated by inspiration, in human language, as the only possible medium of it, and suitably, according to the capacity of language; a doctrine *lying hid* in language, to be received in that language from the first by every mind, whatever be its separate power of understanding it; entered into more or less by this or that mind, as it may be; and admitting of being apprehended more and more perfectly according to the diligence of this mind and that. It is one and the same, independent and real, of depth unfathomable, and illimitable in its extent. . . .

No revelation can be complete and systematic, from the weakness of the human intellect; *so far as* it is not such, it is mysterious. . . . A Revelation is religious doctrine viewed on its illuminated side; a Mystery is the selfsame doctrine viewed on the side unilluminated. Thus Religious Truth is neither light nor darkness, but both together; it is like the dim view of a country seen in the twilight, with forms half extricated from the darkness, with broken lines and isolated masses. Revelation, in this way of considering it, is not a revealed *system*, but consists of a number of detached and incomplete truths belonging to a vast system unrevealed, of doctrines and injunctions mysteriously connected together; that is, connected by unknown media, and bearing upon unknown portions of the system.[7]

Newman is saying that Revelation insofar as it is "manifestation" does not tell the whole truth. The manifestation, that is to say, the ascertainable structures of the Christian faith, must be left to convey their reference to the ungraspable; this involves that they are *essentially open* and that *in this way* they convey Revelation insofar as it is "mystery." In the faith, as in a twilight landscape, there is a balance between the manifest and the hidden, between the prominent elements and the recessive. By themselves, the patterns of prominence can never give an adequate account of the integral act of faith. We may be painfully aware of the inadequacy and provisionality of what we understand of the faith and of the way we understand it, yet there is blessing in that awareness. For it implies that we are operating on a fullness of understanding that remains implicit, and that implicit understanding is the true source of our certainty and assurance in believing. There is, thank God, always more to be expressed; there is always much that is left unexpressed; in fact, positive attempts at non-expressing are part and parcel of faith, to do justice to its mystery. This applies, not only to the *doctrine* of faith, but also to the *life* of faith and to *worship*: the Christian commitment to the good life involves behavioral commitments too deep to be entirely brought to the surface, and while the Church's worshipful response to God's presence does prompt its every word and gesture of prayer, the basic act of worship eludes the grasp of those who pray.[8]

[4] Theological systematization must respect this openness. It must see to it that coherent understanding is attained, but such understanding *must not be achieved by the introduction of massive theological-systematic fixity* where the *faith* exhibits an organic—that is to say, *open*—unity of *structure* (cf. §11, 4–5; also, cf. §17, 1). Attempts to introduce *total* systematic coherence, in other words, involve theological methods that are inadequate to the task of theology. Such inadequate methods of systematic interpretation, we will argue, tend to be initially characterized by *systematic reduction*, but eventually they tend to degenerate into interpretation by *systematic selection* [n].

The adoption of inadequate *methods* is usually connected with misconceptions about *tasks*. For this reason, the present chapter must once again turn to the subject of the tasks of theology and raise the question of the place of *certainty* and *assurance* in believing (§16). Assuming that the quest for certainty and assurance is legitimate, is it also part of the task of systematic theology to deal with these two issues, and if so, in what way?

This order of treatment will enable us later on to discuss some important dimensions of *theological systems*. We will approach this in two steps. The third chapter will argue that, if the task of theology is mis-

---

[n] Such reductions and selections invariably also present themselves as *authoritative* interpretations of the Christian faith. This is a doctrinal problem, and it concerns the relative authority of doctrine, defined doctrine, and theological interpretation; it will be treated in a different context, in the second half of this volume.

understood, overconcern with certainty and assurance will replace the quest for understanding, which in turn will result in systematizations that are inadequate (§§17–20). This realization will prepare the ground for a treatment, in the fourth chapter, of legitimate, and indeed necessary, pluralism in systematic theology (§§21–22). This in turn will enable us to make a first statement about the dimensions of the theological system of which the present book is the opening volume (§23).

FAITH AND UNCERTAINTY

[§16] THE DARK SIDE OF OPENNESS

[1] The ascertainable structures of the Christian faith, it was pointed out, are *essentially open*, and it is precisely in this way that they convey their reference to the ungraspable (§15, 3). We must be careful here, however, lest we run the double danger of too narrow a purview and too optimistic an attitude.

First of all, there is the risk of narrowness. The openness under discussion is not limited to the structures of religion, whether these structures are of the cultic, the behavioral, or the doctrinal variety; it is found much more broadly. In fact, it is a quality that religious structures have in common with *all* structures of finite being. Existence-in-structures, or "structuredness," is the hallmark of finitude as such. Finite beings are only imperfectly self-identical; finite unity is marked by inherent multiplicity (§11, 3 and [m]).

Second, in the human sphere this inherent finitude of self, others, and world is experienced as *ambivalence*. This rules out all easy optimism and opens the possibility for existence, both in its unity and its multiplicity, to be experienced as problematic, erratic, and thus burdensome. What fullness finite human beings enjoy carries in its bosom an element of void; as a result, one's sense of identity may turn sour and become a nasty prison of self-centeredness, just as one's inner variety may turn into inner dividedness, brokenness, and dissipation, a far cry from harmony, roundness, and completion. Hence, to be oneself is *also*: to suffer one's self.

[2] Finitude also affects the finite being's relationships with other realities: elements of alienation as well as confusion are inevitably mixed in. In the human world, this, too, is a matter of explicit and often puzzling experience. While it is true that the structures of existence are the matrix of liberating encounter and dialogue (§11, 4; 6), there is a dark side to them, too. Our self-identity can *also* turn into a capsule that limits our access to the other; and when we do reach the other, whether persons or things, we *also* tend to find out that part of the price of encounter is confusion, as we more or less lose touch with ourselves. To be with others is *also*: to suffer being with others.

[3] Existence in structures is living in ambivalence, is existing precariously; and since there is analogy between the way we exist and the way we understand, our understanding is ambivalent and precarious, too. The openness of structures, on the one hand, makes them alive, transparent, and liberating, and prevents them from being inert, opaque, and oppressive; this makes structures suggestive and symbolic, which stimulates the imagination and gives rise to thought. However, that same openness also makes them irresolute, uncertain, and inconclusive; there is a puzzling side to everything, which makes it often hard to decide just what sense to make of them.

It is easy to see how a person, a community, a culture, and even humanity as a whole should have to struggle with this experience of finitude, by existing in what Paul Tillich has aptly called the ontological quality of anxiety: "Finitude in awareness is anxiety" [o]. It is also easy to see how human beings should be profoundly inclined to look for certainty and assurance and that they should be looking for them in either of two directions: either in the direction where the anxiety might be *alleviated* or in the direction where it would be *illuminated* [p]. The former would be a mistake, for it would lead away from reality; the latter an enrichment, for it would deepen one's realism.

[4] All of this has theological consequences. While it may be a matter of philosophic realism to accept and even cherish the structures of finitude, facility in interpreting them in the light of the infinite does not by any means come automatically, no matter how deeply natural this interpretation may be. In fact, for many honorable men and women, and in many serious circles, it is a matter of special disappointment and even scandal that the structures of religion are as finite as all other structures and, hence, as open-ended and as inconclusive.

[5] It remains true that, on the one hand, the openness and inconclusiveness of the structures of all religion, including the Christian faith, *can* help convey their reference to the ungraspable. A sense of incompleteness is what gives rise to mystical excitement in Jesus Sirach, when he concludes his hymnodic meditation on the marvels of creation with the words:

---

[o] *Systematic Theology*, vol. 1, pp. 191–201; quotation p. 201. Cf. also his *The Courage to be*, esp. pp. 41–88. It should be pointed out, however, that Tillich's interpretation of the awareness of finitude is biased in favor of anxiety viewed as a negative experience; he overlooks its potential for excitement, adventure, confidence, trust, surrender, and abandon.

[p] This brief analysis must suffice for the moment; the present discussion has to be limited to the relationship between theological systematization and the Christian faith. It is obvious, though, that the issues raised here are far from exhausted. In due course, they will have to be taken up again, in two fundamental-theological contexts: (a) the exploration of the relationship between the creature and God, and (b) in the search for an ontological foundation for the theological and soteriological understanding of sin. Still, even the present limited discussion may already suggest that there are forms of theology that are either philosophically inadequate, or marked by sinfulness, or both.

However much we say, we fall short,
and the sum of our words is: "He is the all."
Where shall we find the strength to praise him?
For he is greater than all his works.

(Sir 43, 27-28)

Such a sense of incompleteness, which yields a dynamism toward God, is not limited to Scripture. To mention only one contemporary example, the Catholic American novelist Flannery O'Connor, very consciously writing "about people in a world where something is obviously lacking, where there is the general mystery of incompleteness and the particular tragedy of our own times to be demonstrated,"[9] has pointed to her faith as the factor that enables her to acknowledge and embrace incompleteness, tragedy, and even sin and thus to make sense of them.

[6] On the other hand, though, it remains true that there is something deeply disappointing and unsatisfactory about the openness of the structures of religion. If God is meant to be the ultimate foothold of humanity and the world, both in the structures of the individual religious consciousness and in those of the shared religious life, why are these structures, in which our faith exists and is experienced (§10, 1), so full of dark, empty spaces? Why do they leave so much to be desired, so much room for interpretation, uncertainty, and irresolution? The demand for naked, unconditional abandon to God in faith is liable to make us stumble; faith's foothold is slippery; it is even like walking on water (Ps 73, 2; Mt 14, 28–31). Why would it be unreasonable to expect that we should find in the structures of the faith in which we live—the various forms of cult, conduct, and creed—a coherent, and especially a *complete* and *compelling*, set of pointers for our minds' and hearts' ascent to God?

In this way, religious faith, including the Christian faith, raises, in its own way, the urgent question of *certainty* and *assurance*. The question deserves critical reflection, for it is not only a matter of intellectual and doctrinal interest—faith's *certainty*; it also affects people in a variety of practical and emotional ways, thus raising the problem of religious *assurance*. Newman's appeal to the moonlit landscape (§15, 3) may satisfy the romantic and the contemplative; but can ordinary everyday faith be blamed for wanting the clear light of day to travel by, in a landscape with definite contours, along safe roads with assured destinations?

For the purposes of this book, we will limit our discussion to Christian faith and theology and leave out of consideration other, less intellectual ways of securing certainty and assurance in believing. Given the fact that certainty and assurance are an issue, theology must meet the challenge. It can do so *adequately*, if it succeeds in *interpreting*, and thus *illuminating*, the Christian religion's lack of compelling coherence; this is the option in favor of *catholicity*, which, in Hans Urs von Balthasar's words, "does not cancel anxiety, but transforms it."[10] It can also offer an *inadequate* analysis, by giving in to the temptation to come to the rescue by *removing* the lack of compelling coherence; this is the option in favor of a *closed system*.

The next chapter will start by discussing the dimensions of this serious temptation, which threatens the catholicity of theology (§17), and then proceed to give an account of the two principal ways in which the theological traditions of the West have succumbed to it (§§18–20).

CHAPTER 3

The Loss of Catholicity

CERTAINTY AND ASSURANCE?

[§17] UNDERSTANDING REPLACED BY CERTAIN KNOWLEDGE

[1] The second chapter concluded on a note of concern: theology is tempted. Solicitous to meet and alleviate an understandable need for certainty and assurance, it is tempted to misconstrue the Christian faith. Where the temptation is not recognized and resisted, what results is theology in the service of *certainty and assurance* rather than *understanding*. What then also results is that, rather than *interpreting* the given, spacious structures of the great Tradition of the Christian faith in the interest of contemporary Christian life [a], theology will attempt to *replace* these structures, or at least part of them, by offering an allegedly surer or more relevant rendition of the Christian faith, which, however, is in reality a *reduced version* of it. Such reductions are sometimes merely muddle-headed; more often they are quite consistent. In fact, the main characteristic of such reduced versions of the faith is a curious sort of heady, invincible, comforting, but ultimately confining coherence, achieved by "the introduction of massive theological-systematic fixity where the faith exhibits an organic—that is to say, open—unity of structure" (§15, 4). With the loss of that organic, open unity of structure, however, the *catholicity* of theology is lost, too.

[a] In the West, this tendency to introduce massive fixity by means of theology has strong cultural connections with the development, roughly since the sixteenth century, of scientific and technological Reason, whose influence on *all* forms of knowledge has not gone unnoticed in theology and whose cultural connections with the spread of print culture are now well known (§7, 1, a–b). *True* knowledge came to be identified with *certain* knowledge; the latter, in turn,

---

[a] Note that it is precisely by virtue of *contemporary interpretation* that theology must respect, and leave intact, the great Tradition (cf. DS 3020; CF 136). Cf. §21, 3, a; c.

was widely identified with definitions—explicit, objective statements of ascertainable or arguable fact, of the kind that the New Learning began to call, characteristically, "literally true" [b]. In this way, certain understanding got identified with the kind of knowledge that can be adequately conveyed in *manifest elements*. Any reference to hidden dimensions or elements in knowledge came to represent *lack*, not *depth*, of knowledge.

However, this newly enquiring and inquisitive human mind, so excited by all its new discoveries, was eventually forced, by its own logic, to turn in upon itself. It began—methodically, of course!—to doubt itself, in order to assure itself of the reliability of its knowledge. This was bound to have consequences for theological understanding. Given the transcendent nature of the subject matter, certain knowledge of God and of matters divine, it began to be thought, could only be anchored in the mind's own assurance about itself. Descartes' account of his search for an unshaken foundation of certain knowledge is paradigmatic. It is interesting to watch him, in his *Meditations*, ground certain knowledge of God in the mind's being aware, to its own satisfaction, of its ability to know what is certain and consequently true. The givenness of the clear and distinct concept of God must be taken as proof postive of God's existence, for the possibility of God leading the mind astray—that is to say, of God being a deceitful God, a *deus deceptor*—must be excluded.[1]

Eberhard Jüngel, in his important book *God as the Mystery of the World*, has traced—successfully, it would seem—the characteristically *modern loss of certainty about God* to this revolution in Western thought. The traditional certainty and assurance about God (*Gottesgewißheit*) had been based on a metaphysical and ultimately religious insight, namely, that *God accounts for the human mind's intrinsic desire and ability to know*, and to know, not only finite realities, but also, by analogy, God and matters divine. The new certainty, which ended up setting itself in opposition to the traditional one, was based on *the mind's own self-assurance*: it *made* God a matter of assured conviction (*Sicherstellung Gottes*) on the basis of *its own self-awareness*. Traditionally, God's ultimate unknowability and the mysteriousness of matters divine had lent depth and even religious assurance to the human knowledge of God; in the new framework, God's mysteriousness became an irritant, a source of alienation to the self-assured mind. Jüngel does not hes-

---

[b] This also marked the end of the *lectio divina* tradition, in which the word of Scripture was interpreted in the light of the *present experience of the Holy Spirit* in the Church and its members. Accordingly, the practice of interpretation recognized a variety of meanings in Scripture; over and above the historical sense (often called "literal"), there were the anagogical, allegorical, and spiritual senses (cf. §54, 1). The new literalism changed all this. Karen Jo Torjesen (*Hermeneutical Procedure and Theological Method in Origen's Exegesis*, p. 1, n. 2) rightly observes: "According to Melanchthon allegory no longer mediates the 'Spirit.' The naked text alone can do that."

itate to give a telling account of the history of that irritation, through Fichte, Feurerbach, and Nietzsche, down to the modern theme of the "death of God."[2]

Both the Reformation and the Counter-Reformation, together with the theological traditions they generated, were deeply affected by these developments. Clarity and authority began to play disproportionately important roles. Religious *knowledge* became so propositional that it was bound to lose some of its credibility. The traditional conception of religious knowledge—both of the natural and the revealed variety, with appropriate qualifications—had been based on *analogy*, in which the mixed perfection of finite knowledge had been the wings on which the mind's ascent to God took place— an ascent ultimately warranted by God as the transcendent guarantor of truth, "who can neither err nor deceive" (DS 3008; CF 118). Once that confidence was replaced by the mind's ultimately restless lack of assurance about itself [c], it should not come as a surprise that an enormous need for *external authorities* arose, among Protestants and Catholics alike, to furnish the theological mind with the certain premisses it needed. Scripture, to which Roman Catholicism added Tradition and what has since come to be called the "magisterium,"[3] came to be viewed, not principally as living, authentic witnesses to a living truth, but above all, as *authoritative sources* (*loci*) of objectively true teachings.

[2] In such an intellectual and ecclesiastical context, dominated by a culturally determined thirst for certainty and assurance, theology has quite often succumbed to the temptation to develop interpretations of the Christian faith that sacrifice the fullness of the truth and its spaciousness to the coherence of the system—a system that, it is implicitly claimed, can be made fully *manifest* and hence compelling (cf. §15, 3; §16, 6). Such interpretations of the Christian faith not only cease to be catholic; they also end up providing only apparent solutions to the problem of certainty and assurance. The next three sections (§§18–20) will explore the two principal—and extreme—forms that such apparent solutions have taken.

INADEQUATE SYSTEMATIZATIONS

[§18] REDUCTION AND SELECTION

[1] Systematic theology has, in fact, succumbed to the temptation to create certainty by introducing the kind of massive fixity that fails to

---

[c] George Herbert's *The Pulley*, with its Augustinian overtones, is a typical product of the religious sensibilities of the age: not faith and trust, but "repining restlesnesse" will toss the person—perfectly characterized as "rich and wearie" by God's own creative design—to God's breast (*The Works of George Herbert*, p. 159). Paul Tillich's anxiety has deep roots in history!

respect the organic openness of the structures of the Christian faith, and it has done so chiefly by moving in two opposite directions. In the Christian West, these movements have taken on very definite historic shapes, which originated in the cultural and religious crisis that began in the sixteenth century. In the course of the last four centuries, however, the serious differences that marked the first clash between Reformation and Catholicism have slowly come to manifest their *fundamental* tendencies. As a result, the differences between the Catholic church and the mainline Protestant churches, while far from resolved, have been considerably rearranged. Fundamentally at issue are no longer the classic topics of sixteenth- and seventeenth-century controversial theology but the nature of the Christian faith itself and its relationship to world and culture. And since doctrine is one of the principal ways in which Christianity embodies and enforces its distinctiveness, the status of doctrine itself—its status as a credible mediating expedient between faith and culture—is at stake.⁴ Theological navigators must now define their position and chart their course, if only in the interest of avoidance, in relation to two commanding landmarks, which, like Scylla and Charybdis, dominate the straits theology has to negotiate: *integralism* (or "integrism") and *modernism*.

Integralism and modernism are extremes and equally undesirable. Integralism wholly severs the structures of the Christian faith from the influence of cultural structures; modernism confuses them. Both, therefore, refuse to involve themselves in the central task of theology, which is the *search for new forms* of unity between faith and culture (§14, 2).

To avoid inadequate theological systematizations, therefore, it is important to understand and recognize the tendencies towards integralism and modernism. These tendencies are twofold: theology can fail by reduction and by selection. *Reductive* systematizations take the *depth* out of the structures of the Christian faith; they create forced coherence by *reducing the faith to the totality of its manifest, objective elements*. *Selective* systematizations take the *breadth* out of the structures of the Christian faith; they create forced coherence by *selecting one of the faith's manifold themes and forcing all other themes into subordination around it*. The former introduce totalitarian principles into the Christian faith, which tends to turn it into an ideology; the latter introduce rationalist principles, which tends to lead to heresy; both set themselves up as authorities over the living Tradition. In Western Christianity, integralism has been the characteristically Roman Catholic problem, although, since the Enlightenment, there have been orthodox Protestant parallels; modernism has typically threatened neo-Protestantism (*Neuprotestantismus*), especially of the pietistic, Evangelical variety.

[2] With this last observation, it has been implicitly recognized that inadequate systematizations have, as a matter of historical fact, occurred

outside the area of learned theology; they have affected *church doctrine, discipline, and worship*. One of the tragedies of the Reformation and Counter-Reformation lies precisely in the fact that, not just theologies, but entire *churches* gave in, to a greater or lesser extent, to the temptation to create massive fixity where the great Tradition had exhibited open, organic unity of structure.

The sixteenth-century Church witnessed, not only tension and disagreement, but division. The spacious house of Christianity was first split up into cramped apartments. Then some moved into separate houses, and all closed the shutters. All, too, in varying degrees, lost the patient realism that comes from living together in quarters just spacious enough for all. More and more houses arose, cluttering the neighborhood. Eventually, many began to find the atmosphere stifling and went to live elsewhere, in new, airy houses, easy to remodel, with no shutters, and with windows and doors that opened with ease; some even went to camp outside, to find God in nature, in no particular house.

This is, in many ways, the ecclesial world we have inherited: churches caught between tendencies, on the one hand, to close the shutters and, on the other, to live out in the open. If, therefore, we now turn to the two principal forms of inadequate interpretation of the Christian faith, we are engaging in an exercise that is of more than merely theoretical interest. Theology must explore the roots of division also in the interest of *ecumenism*, that is to say, in the interest of recovering the possibilities and the limits of Christian *unity and pluralism*, not only in theology, but also in *doctrine* and, indeed, beyond doctrine, in the life and worship of the Church and the churches.

[§19] INTEGRALISM: SYSTEMATIZATION BY REDUCTION

[1] All typically Roman Catholic theological systematizations spring from a profound concern with the wholeness, catholicity, and integrity of the faith and with the Church's unity around the successor of Peter as the permanent principle and the visible basis of the unity of the Church universal (cf. DS 3051; LG 8, 14; UR 2–3). But where concern turns into preoccupation and even compulsion, what results is reductive interpretation. The reduction occurs when the faith is pared down to its manifest, prominent elements and then tightened up into a *closed system*. Usually, this happens in the interest of *control*; reductions make the faith—and hence, indirectly, the faithful—manageable, both intellectually and practically.

The *Roman Catholic* variant of this degeneracy is known as *integralism*. "Integral Catholics"—as the militant antimodernists of the early decades of the twentieth century called themselves—identify the faith completely with its *manifest elements*, usually presented, in the interest of uniformity, as *authoritatively defined elements*. These elements are then treated as—in Newman's words—"a revealed *system*." Integralists overlook that these elements are, in fact, no more than "detached and incomplete truths belonging to a vast system unrevealed, of doctrines and injunctions mysteriously connected together; that is, connected by unknown media, and bearing upon unknown portions of the system" (§15, 3). The mood of integralism is authoritarian and objectivist—even totalitarian. Integralists have a tendency to make the area of doctrine their special concern, but experience shows that they treat matters of life and worship in exactly the same manner.

It is worth noting that the essence of integralism does *not* lie in its alleged regard for the authoritative tradition, no matter how fervently integralists will project that as their central concern. In reality, integralism is simply a body of *theological opinion* [d], parading as the Christian faith, but in fact replacing it with a *reductive interpretation*, or rather *systematization*, of it. This systematization is harsh: it makes of *manifest* doctrines, precepts, and liturgical forms something that they are not, namely, the be-all and the end-all of the Christian faith. In this way, the undifferentiated acceptance of all doctrines, norms, and liturgical forms comes to be presented as both the essence and the sum of the act of faith.

As a result, the *structure* of the faith is lost sight of; the price of complete certainty is loss of organic coherence and depth. The elements of the faith turn into almost purely catechetical counters and lose their vital connections with one another, and, most importantly, they lose their reference to the mystery [e]. Rather than inhabiting the spacious structures of the Christian faith, the integralist turns into its landlord. Rather than being content to be held and contained by the faith, the integralist wishes to hold and contain it. Doctrine ceases to be "a gateway to contemplation" and "an instrument of freedom," which "preserves mystery for the human mind";[5] instead, its every detail turns into an inert article of belief ("il n'y a pas de petits dogmes"), allegedly proposed with equal emphasis by the Tradition; the latter is interpreted in almost exclusively magisterial, and even authoritarian terms.

[a] A telling implication of integralist thought is its redefinition of the *hierarchy of truths* as a hierarchy of doctrinal *certainties* (cf. §21, 4, a–c). The manifest structures of the Christian faith, as Newman reminds us, are coherent because of their association with the hidden mysteries. Hence, while it is "essential that doctrine be clearly pre-

---

[d] To all those who propose reduced versions of the Christian faith, Newman's firm phrase about the Rationalist applies: "He professes to *believe* what he *opines*" (*Essays Critical and Historical*, vol. 1, p. 35). A fuller discussion of the relationship between faith and theological opinion must wait till the next chapter; on this subject, cf. also §55, 3, a.

[e] And since theological understanding results from establishing connections among the mysteries and between the mysteries and God (DS 3016; CF 132; cf. §12, 1, a; §15, 2, a), it is easy to understand how integralism should be profoundly anti-intellectual and anti-theological.

sented in its entirety," it should be remembered that "in catholic teaching there exists an order or 'hierarchy' of truths, since they vary in their relationship to the foundation of the Christian faith" (UR 11). Johannes Feiner draws the correct conclusion from this important passage from Vatican II (and from the commission reports behind it) when he writes: "Thus the importance of a doctrine is not determined by the degree to which it is theologically binding, as though a defined doctrine belonged to the first rank of truths solely on the basis of the fact that it had been defined, while a non-defined truth of revelation was *eo ipso* of a lower rank."[6]

Integralism ignores this distinction between integral truth and defined truth; it fails as a theological system precisely because it does not respect, paradoxically, the integrity of the Christian faith *as an organic whole* [f]. Analogous biases in interpretation are found in theological systems, which, while not technically integralist, *de facto* tend to treat magisterial definitions as the core of the Christian faith. Unfortunately, influential representatives of this tendency have a firm foothold in several Vatican offices and in some schools of theology, in Rome and elsewhere.

[b] Theologies with an integralist perspective tend to idealize *past developments of doctrine* as well as *past forms of unity* in the Church. These idealizations, typical of the sensibility of the modern age, show how doctrinal overdefinition has a very close affinity with the failure to distinguish between truth and certainty (cf. §7, 1, a–b). Accordingly, integralists ignore certain inconvenient features of the *history of catholic doctrine*, like the fact that the reception-process of such an important council as Chalcedon was not only tortuous but also dubious in some respects, and that one patriarch could at least insinuate that Chalcedon enacted not only "right decrees" but also, presumably, wrong ones.[7] In the teeth of this kind of evidence, integralists will naively insist on reducing the history of catholic doctrine to a history of authoritative, manifestly defined "*dogma*."[8] They will interpret that history of dogma as a process of sustained, coherent, cumulative progress and, hence, as a simple matter of linear devel-

---

[f] Pope Benedict XV, therefore, was being thoroughly traditional when, in his encyclical *Ad beatissimi Apostolorum* (ET AAS 6(1914) 647–60) he alluded to the much-heard expression "integral Catholics," and wrote: "We desire that that practice, lately come into use, of using distinctive names by which Catholics are marked off from Catholics, should cease; such names must be avoided, not only as 'profane novelties of words' [1 Tim 6, 20] that are neither true nor just, but also because they lead to grave disturbance and confusion in the Catholic body. It is of the nature of the Catholic faith that nothing can be added to it, nothing taken away; it is either accepted in full or rejected in full: 'This is the Catholic faith, which unless a man believe faithfully and steadfastly, he cannot be saved' [Symb. Athanas.]. There is no need to qualify by fresh epithets the profession of faith; let it be enough for a man to say: 'Christian is my name, Catholic my surname'; only let him take heed to be in truth what he calls himself" (pp. 656–57).

opment in certainty and clarity. Theologies more realistic and less anxious about certainty tend to view doctrine and its developments in organic terms, as the record of the Church's historic interaction with culture, deeply guided by the Spirit. What presents itself to view then is a fine, varied history of assimilation supported by a living tradition,[9] but also a history marred by both rigidity and dissipation, *both* caused by forgetfulness of that same tradition (cf. §13, 1, [*e*]).

[c] In placing magisterial definitions at the center of the faith, integralism and allied movements often cannot avoid lapsing, first, into the creation of division and schism and, eventually, into *selective*, and even heretical (from Gk. *hairesis*: "choice"), interpretations of the faith. Integralists *need* to look for, and indeed create, opponents—heretics and schismatics—in the interest of shoring up their own intransigent convictions. Eventually, faith is totally replaced by ecclesiastical obedience (or alleged ecclesiastical obedience). Debates about doctrines concerning the visible Church and the magisterium move into the center of the experience of faith; they are less and less presented as the *outgrowth* of the catholic faith and more and more as the indispensable *preconditions* for its integrity. This tends to yield versions of the catholic faith with strongly totalitarian features, crowding out the central elements of traditional orthodoxy. Typical examples are the rigorist interpretation given to *Extra ecclesiam nulla salus* ("Outside the Church there is no salvation") by Leonard Feeney (cf. DS 3866–73; CF 854–57) and the traditionalist rejection, by archbishop Marcel Lefebvre and his separatist movement, of the "modernist"—but, in fact, thoroughly traditional—teachings of Vatican II.

[d] Integralism is deeply *secular*, despite its protestations to the contrary; it attempts to secure faith in God by anchoring it in temporal assurances. Fyodor Dostoyevsky's ominous account, in the legend of *The Grand Inquisitor*,[10] of the Catholic Church as a totalitarian theocracy may be a caricature; it is also a serious warning against tendencies to favor the kind of popular Catholicism in which the faithful are denied access to the living Christ and instead must live on assurances furnished by an authoritarian, secular, hierarchical system.

In actual fact, integralists do tend to cherish surprisingly close alliances with secular ideologies and political causes with a penchant for *simpliste* interpretations of culture. Feeney's anti-Semitism and anticommunism drove him in the direction of a fascistoid Americanism. Archbishop Lefebvre had early associations with the notorious Abbé Le Floch, who was one of the associates, in the Action Française, of the freethinker Charles Maurras, who saw in an authoritarian Church one of the best guarantees for the restoration of the French monarchy.[11] Present-day traditionalist, authoritarian currents in North American Roman Catholicism often have surprisingly strong

ties with, and fairly easy and independent access to, great individual
and corporate wealth to support their causes.

[e] Roman Catholicism must be on its guard against what may very
well be its greatest weakness: a systemic affinity with sectarian, monolithic conceptions such as those favored by integralism. The mainstream catholic tradition agrees with Newman and views the Christian
faith as a fundamentally *open* system. In fact, this is part of what
"catholic" means: one of the Church's principal qualifications to meet
and welcome the whole world consists precisely in the capaciousness
of its manifest structures. These manifest structures are associated
with hidden mysteries; in this way they convey their *reference to the*
mystery of God in the very act of *opening themselves to the surrounding*
culture. Tightening them up into a massive system robs them of their
religious significance but no less of their "power of assimilation" in
regard to the culture.[12]

This conception understandably affects the catholic interpretation
of culture. The great Tradition understands that humane cultural
developments will prosper, not in a setting of total control, but in a
basically free, dynamic openness that favors the human potential; not
in the securing of things, but in the cultivation of constructive relationships. Culture, therefore, deserves a discriminating welcome; it
must not be fought and tamed. A post-Christian believer like Antoine
de Saint-Exupéry reflects this deeply catholic conception of culture—
one that perfectly dovetails into Newman's conception of the Christian faith—when he writes, in 1943: "I don't care if I get killed in
action. What I have loved—what will remain of that? As much as
about things that exist, I am talking about customs, irreplaceable intonations, a kind of spiritual light. Lunch on a farm in Provence,
under the olive trees, but also Handel. I couldn't care less about
things—they will endure. *What is important is a certain arrangement of*
things. Civilization is an invisible good because it has to do, not with things,
but with the unseen links which bind them to one another, thus and not
otherwise. We will have perfect musical instruments, custom-made,
widely distributed, but where will the musician be?"[13]

[f] For orthodox Protestant forms of integralism, or at least tendencies in an integralist direction, the picture just drawn should be appropriately modified. The center of authority tends to be the text
of Scripture—often in an authoritative translation going back to the
Reformation, and often in the form of a "canon within the canon,"
with pride of place usually given to Paul's teaching on justification.
The Bible is often joined by other sources of great (though often
unavowed) authority: confessional writings, rhyming psalm translations and hymns, along with their traditional tunes, and even theological writings by classic authors who embody a *de facto* normative

tradition. There is often a curious but characteristic tendency, too, to support the tradition by appealing to key biblical texts, decisively interpreted in a manner strongly reminiscent of neopositivism, as adequate statements of revealed propositions. Unfortunately, the important work of Karl Barth has been misinterpreted here and there, with more zeal than understanding, in a fashion that smacks of integralism.

[2] Finally, a passage from a letter by Flannery O'Connor, an altogether traditional American Catholic, is as remarkable for its theological accuracy as for its insight into the integralist personality:

I know what you mean about being repulsed by the Church when you have only the Jansenist-Mechanical Catholic to judge it by. I think that the reason such Catholics are so repulsive is that they don't really have faith *but a kind of false certainty*. They operate by the slide rule and the Church for them is not the body of Christ but the poor man's insurance system. It's never hard for them to believe because actually they never think about it. Faith has to take in all the other possibilities it can. . . . In any case, discovering the Church is apt to be a slow procedure but it can only take place if you have a free mind and no vested interest in disbelief. . . ."[14]

[§20] MODERNISM: SYSTEMATIZATION BY SELECTION

[1] The characteristically neo-Protestant (or "liberal Protestant") systematization of the Christian faith is the offspring of the fundamental inspiration of the Reformation: the assurance of the God-given, gracious salvation proclaimed by the gospel. This is indeed a central theme of the Christian faith, and the Reformation owes both its seriousness and its inner coherence to its passionate affirmation of it. But just as the Roman Catholic concern with the integrity of the faith harbors a tendency toward integralism, so the Protestant concern with assurance of salvation favors a tendency towards a modernist version of the Christian faith. If integralism is the outgrowth of overconcern with *certainty* and *control*, modernism is rooted in overconcern with *assurance* and *experience*.

This experientialist bias has deep roots in the Protestant tradition, which construes the sinner's experience of salvation by grace, manifested and extended by the gospel message, as the principal element of the faith and the decisive theme around which its coherence is established. The mood of this selective systematization of the faith is anthropological and subjective, and even individualistic: its central focus is the divinely reconstituted integrity of the believer rather than the integrity of the faith or the visible faith-community.

This tendency to identify the Christian faith with its *manifest message of salvation* accounts for the traditional Protestant construal of *soteriology* as the central theme of the faith and its only principle of coherence

[g], so much so that it is often hardly noticed that we are dealing with a selection, and a dangerous one at that, since it has a tendency to sacrifice two themes from the great Tradition to the coherence of the system.

[2] First of all, it implies an interpretation of God's Trinity in terms that are so predominantly *economic* and *soteriological* that God's own glory and mystery comes to be placed outside the experience of faith and moves into an infinite distance in such a way as to cease to function positively, as a central theme. Consequently, faith introduces the believer, not so much to God, as to God's work; it becomes a matter, in Melanchthon's classic phrase, of "knowing his [Christ's] benefits,"[15] rather than of becoming, in Christ, "partakers of the divine nature" (2 Pet 1, 4). This has profound consequences in the area of Christology. It removes from the heart of Christian theology what is perhaps the most central theological theme of the patristic tradition—a theme that gave rise to endless variations: "Out of limitless love God's Word, who is God's Son, became what we are, so as to make us what he is."[16] This broad and capacious theme, known as the "exchange principle" (§23, 2), had warranted, since Irenaeus, the Christian conviction that humanity and the world are called into participation in the divine life. In the new system, *one* of the theme's constitutive elements, namely, that of redemption from sin by divine grace, is selected to stand in for the whole.

Second, once assurance of salvation by the grace of God is taken to be the central, determinative theme of the Christian faith, the experience and awareness of *sin*, mostly thematized under the rubric of "the Law," becomes the adequate correlate of grace and salvation [h]. As a result, the theme of sin, in the whole of the Christian faith, comes to be viewed as second only to the theme of salvation (cf. §12, 1, b). However, once God is principally known as Redeemer, and humanity as corrupted by sin, the fullness of the Christian faith as an account of God's mysterious relationship with humanity and the world has been tightened up into a system of human salvation—a system that fails to

---

[g] Cf. Melanchthon: "But as for one who is ignorant of the other fundamentals, namely, 'The Power of Sin,' 'The Law,' and 'Grace,' I do not see how I can call him a Christian. For from these things Christ is known, since to know Christ means to know his benefits, and not as *they* [i.e., the Scholastics] teach, to reflect upon his natures and the modes of his incarnation. . . . In his letter to the Romans *when he was writing a compendium of Christian doctrine*, did Paul philosophize about the mysteries of the Trinity, the mode of incarnation, or active and passive creation? No! But what does he discuss? He takes up *the law, sin, grace, fundamentals on which the knowledge of Christ exclusively rests*" (Melanchthon, *Loci Communes Theologici* [1521], pp. 21–22; last two sets of italics added).

[h] Cf. Melanchthon's statement: "All the benefits of the Gospel are included in the idea of the forgiveness of sins" (quoted by Hans Engelland in *Melanchthon on Christian Doctrine—Loci Communes 1555*, p. xl).

do justice, not only to the full glory of God, but also to the full vocation of humanity and, indeed, of the whole world (cf. §9, 1, [i]).

[a] Both tendencies are readily visible in the structure of Calvin's *Institutes*. The first book—like so many of Calvin's writings—is still strongly reminiscent of the classic sequence: it opens with the treatment of God as Creator. However, Calvin immediately proceeds to point out that the human recognition of God the Creator is perverted by sin. Quite consistently, then, Book 1 goes on to base its treatment of most of the traditional themes of natural theology, as well as God's Trinity, exclusively on scriptural revelation—the only *locus* that deserves to be recognized as a reliable warrant for divine truth.

The real sweep of the *Institutes*, however, starts in Book 2, which deals with God as Redeemer, and is continued in Book 3, where the trinitarian account of redemption quickly turns into a very full treatment of grace and its application to the believer, under the rubric of God as Sanctifier. Book 4, finally, explains the "external means or helps," by which God invites persons to fellowship with Christ or keeps them in it. Thus the visible, symbolic communication structures of the faith, in which the Church exists in the world on its way to God, are reduced to pure instrumentality.

The selection of soteriology as the focus of the Christian faith is far more explicit and thematic in a much earlier, equally foundational document of the Reformation: Melanchthon's *Loci Communes Theologici* of 1521, "the first systematic theology of the evangelical Church."[17] After a characteristically *anthropological* introduction on the human faculties and on free will, the theological sequence proper sets in: sin—law—gospel—grace—justification and faith, followed by other themes. In this way, creation followed by the Fall, redemption, and sanctification become the central "storyline" of the Christian faith. In fact, that is exactly what Melanchthon explains in the foreword to the 1555 edition of the *Loci*: "God has given us the most fitting order. . . . He puts his doctrine in the form of a story."[18] And that story turns out to be the sequence: creation—sin—grace—law—promise of a Savior. If it is the great merit of the Reformation to have recovered salvation history, it is its great limitation to have made it into the one central theme of the faith.

There is no doubt that the construal, at the heart of the Christian faith, of the message of sin and redemption as mutually proportionate has given Protestantism, and pietistic Evangelical Protestantism in particular, its distinctive, if at times narrow, earnestness, its potential for adaptation and revival, and its broad popular appeal. However, the same feature also tends to make *the human understanding and experience of sin and salvation the norm* of what the Christian faith can possibly involve [i]. This requires elaboration; let us return to John Henry Newman.

[3] Newman, an Evangelical born and bred, not only noted the profound change of perspective caused by Evangelicalism's selective systematization of the Christian faith; he also recognized its deep potential for Rationalist secularism (cf. §28, 1, a, [c]). He wrote:

That theology is as follows: that the Atonement is the chief doctrine of the Gospel; again, that it is chiefly to be regarded, not as a wonder from heaven, and in its relation to the attributes of God and to the unseen world, but in its experienced effects on our minds, in the change it effects when it is believed. To this, as if to the point of sight in a picture, all the portions of the Gospel system are directed and made to converge; as if this doctrine were so fully understood, that it might fearlessly be used to regulate, adjust, correct, complete, everything else. Thus, the doctrine of the Incarnation is viewed as necessary and important to the Gospel, *because* it gives virtue to the Atonement; of the Trinity, *because* it includes the revelation, not only of the Redeemer, but also of the Sanctifier, by whose aid and influence the Gospel message is to be blessed to us. It follows that faith is nearly the whole of religious service, for through it the message of Manifestation is received. . . . Thus the Dispensation, in its length, depth, and height, is practically identified with its Revelation, or rather its necessarily superficial Manifestation. Not that the reality of the Atonement, in itself, is formally denied, but it is cast in the background, except so far as it can be discovered to be influential, viz., to show God's hatred of sin, the love of Christ, and the like. . . . And the Dispensation thus being hewn and chiselled into an intelligible human system, is represented, when thus mutilated, as affording a remarkable evidence of the truth of the Bible, an evidence level to the reason, and superseding the testimony of the Apostles. That is . . . Rationalism, or want of faith, which has in the first place invented a spurious gospel, next looks complacently on its own offspring. . . . [19]

[4] With this trenchant observation we have also come to the point where *selection* turns into *reduction*. This is where neo-Protestantism parts company with the main tradition of the Reformation. The reduction is experientialist, in line with the selection; but more importantly, the reduction has a deep-seated tendency towards secular experientialism, usually referred to as *liberal secularism*. The message of salvation, which the classic Reformers had always recognized as God's word of *power*, predicated on the saving death of the Son of God, has been turned into a word of *reassuring truth*, *taught* and *exemplified* by Jesus and by many passages in the Bible; both the message and the

---

[i] Paul Tillich's interesting "method of correlation" (*Systematic Theology*, I, pp. 30–31, 59–66) is a good example of this tendency. Tillich states that the faith-answers given in revelation can be derived neither from the form nor from the content of the questions implied in human existence. As a matter of fact, however, it can be shown that the shape of Tillich's questions does determine the answer that the Christian faith can give. Cf. §22, 3, d.

example can, as a matter of principle, be called to account by the standard of any known, normative experience of human growth and development. The "true meaning" of the Christian faith has been reduced, in principle, to cultural concerns. This reduction is the central
inspiration behind theological, intellectual modernism, with its tendency to view the Tradition as obscurantist, and intent on replacing
traditional interpretations by "the latest findings," in the interest of
"relevance" and "experience."

[a] This leads to an immediate insight into the modernist interpretation of *development of doctrine*. Precisely because classical Protestantism tightened up the core of the Christian faith to the extent it
did, it could scorn doctrinal developments as merely human accretions. But ironically, the rejection of Tradition as a reliable authority
and the insistence on the *sola Scriptura* and on the centrality of salvation eventually opened *neo*-Protestantism to uncontrollable modernist compromises. The soteriological preserve was jealously
guarded, but the surrounding area became ever more freely accessible. This has led to much doctrinal relativism, often justified under
the rule laid down by Friedrich Schleiermacher: doctrine must be
continuously pruned of elaborations that have become obsolete or
irrelevant with the passage of time (cf. §51, 5, a).[20] Curiously, the
assumption behind this is analogous to the one behind the integralist
interpretation of doctrinal development: a naively optimistic conception of progress.

This is also the modernism that the Catholic church has found
itself faced with ever since the mid-nineteenth century. The rejection
of the movement by the Church's magisterium was for a long time
characterized by total incapacity for dialogue and understanding and
by incessant, categorical appeals to authority. For years, both sides
traded overstatements in a war of mutal misinterpretation that was
symptomatic of the depth of the impasse between faith and culture,
Church and Modern World. The crisis finally peaked in a tide of
integralism, between, roughly, 1900 and 1914. The record makes
miserable reading: *Qui pluribus* of 1846 (DS 2775–86: CF 106–11),
Quanta cura (DS 2890–96; CF 815–16) and the *Syllabus errorum* of
1864 (DS 2901–80; CF 112, 411, 1013, 2010), *Lamentabili* (DS 3401–
66; CF 228, 650, 846, 1326, 1437, 1660, 1729) and *Pascendi* of 1907
(DS 3475–3500; CF 1327), and the Oath against Modernism of 1910
(DS 3537–50; CF 143). *Humani generis* of 1950 (DS 3875–99; CF
144–48, 238–39, 419–20, 858–59, 1571) was in many ways the final
act in this painful drama.

Not until the *Théologie nouvelle* and the Second Vatican Council
did the Catholic Church begin to deal with the real issue: the relationship between faith and culture, and between the Church and the

World. Not surprisingly, a wave of "liberalism" accompanied these developments—doubtlessly a belated abreaction of the harsh repression of the legitimate issues underlying modernism [j]. It is likely that true healing and reconciliation is only to be expected from a patient "re-arrangement of the themes and emphases of the Catholic faith and identity experience," as mandated by Vatican II. What is needed is a sense of Catholic identity less dependent on a panoply of defenses, and a form of Catholic openness that will not sacrifice its distinctiveness.[21]

[5] Modernism in North America has a distinctive atmosphere of its own. It is a prevailing cultural climate at least as much as a theological and ecclesiastical concern. It is a residual, secularized, strongly acculturated type of Christianity of liberal-Protestant extraction, which especially—but by no means exclusively—threatens the faith of Protestant churches. Flannery O'Connor, who made no secret of her Catholic convictions and who was at the same time deeply appreciative of the biblical religiosity of the South, had no illusions about this. "Unfortunately," she wrote, "the word Christian is no longer reliable. It has come to mean anybody with a golden heart."[22]

[a] Understanding this form of modernism is of great theological importance, especially in the United States. There was a natural affinity, from the early seventeenth century on, between the Puritan Evangelicalism that European dissenters and nonconformists of every stripe brought to the New World and the ideal of freedom of religion, the spirit of enterprise and exploration, and, eventually, the constitutional separation of Church and State. This alliance amplified and deepened the traditional affinity between Calvinism and the spirit of capitalism and free enterprise[23] and contributed much to the widespread tendency, in the United States, to interpret salvation in terms of individual and communal happiness, growth, and progress, and vice versa [k].

---

[j] Cf. the testimony of Henry St. John, O. P. (in J. Dalrymple et al., *Authority in a Changing Church*, pp. vii–viii): "I was led during 1916 from anglicanism into the Roman catholic church. I took nearly all that I had learned, up till then, with me. . . . Looking back over the years to those days one seems to see modernism, in its beginnings, as a movement of living truth set up by the impact of new and rapidly growing human knowledge, brought to bear upon revelation, in itself immutable, but needing to be constantly viewed, under the Holy Spirit's leadership, individual and corporate, from new standpoints and with new light, in order to be more fully grasped and lived by the people of God. This new movement was met by an absolute authority, fearfully demanding a submission that was not and could not be freely given. It failed, as such authority will always fail, to serve truth, because it greatly inhibited freedom; and many, humanly speaking, were driven into extremes that might well have been avoided by open consultation and free expression, under an authority of genuine love and service. Today the postponed crisis of authority seems to be calling for a deeper realisation of the lessons of past history. Dominative authority never pays dividends in the long run; in the end it will always strangle and kill, in the effort to secure outward conformity in place of free assent."

[k] The affinity is not exclusively North American. British Evangelicalism, both of the

Popular, if primitive, examples of the reduction of the faith to cultural and personal concerns are stories of great individual success and accounts of intense happiness attributed to faith [*l*] and the naive identification of positive mental attitudes with the saving presence of God.[24] More insidious examples are cases in which biblical faith and science or psychology are made to yield identical certainties, claimed to be universally valid.[25] Unqualified identifications of the Christian faith with very partial political or social causes present an analogous problem.[26]

For sincerely orthodox Evangelicals, all of this is a distressing test of faith. They know that their biblical faith does have universalist and public features, yet they must object to having their universalism and their commitments dictated to them by the culture and its causes; they rightly doubt if biblical faith can be so readily identified with secular certainties.[27] This, however, also shows a basic weakness of Evangelicalism. The ardent proclamation, on the sole authority of the Bible, of salvation by grace as the focal theme of the Christian faith is not deep enough to support a confident sense of Christian identity combined with a critical openness to the world; these two can only come from the integrity of the faith. However, there is widespread reluctance, among conservative and liberal Evangelicals alike, to adopt, say, the creed as a normative, shared symbol of such an integrity; this tends to keep neo-Protestantism painfully torn between fundamentalism and secularism, between ardent reliance on the biblical message of salvation by faith alone and doubts about its application.

[6] Having identified and explored Scylla and Charybdis, it is time to return to our main trajectory. Systematic theology, we have argued, must respect the openness of the structures (§15, 4). It must *interpret* the structures, not *replace* them with something more solid (§17, 1). Reducing the integrity of the faith to an authoritarian system is a sin against catholic openness; reducing the openness of the faith to a scheme of human well-being is a sin against catholic integrity. Both integralism and modernism reduce faith to theological opinion. But in doing so, they also rob theology of its freedom, for freedom can be enjoyed only in the latitude afforded by the structures themselves: in the spaces left open by the interplay between the manifest elements and the hidden, between what is definite and what is undefined, be-

Anglican and the nonconformist variety, with its individualistic doctrine of grace, has produced many hard-working men and women of great wealth that have been examples of deep interest in, and dedication to, the alleviation of the plight of the poor and the improvement of public morals. A man like William Wilberforce comes to mind.

[*l*] Ridiculed as follows by Flannery O'Connor: "... 'pray and your food will taste better' is just another version of 'Grace before meals is an aid to digestion' which is what religion is coming to in some parts" (*The Habit of Being*, p. 89).

tween what is explicit and what is understood—which is where true understanding occurs (§15, 3). Both, too, prevent theology from pursuing its main task: the creation of new forms of unity (§14, 2), which can only occur in the interplay between faith and world. Both, furthermore, are intolerant: integralism is intolerant of any pluriformity, whereas modernism is so intolerant of intolerance that it will commit itself to no definite form. Both, finally, in opposite ways, do a serious disservice to the Church's attempts to *mediate* between God and World. Integralism mistakes the structures of faith, which are meant to mediate the relationship between God and humanity, for faith itself; modernism, in dissolving the faith's mediating structures, insists on immediacy at every turn and thus sets itself adrift in an ever-shifting tide of *ad hoc* mediating structures. Thus, in refusing to interpret and illuminate the faith's mediating structures, both integralism and modernism obstruct the Church's continuous inner reform required by the fidelity it owes to God's call (UR 6), as well as its ongoing missionary renewal required by its commitment to the world—integralism by canonizing fixity, modernism by courting dissolution.

CHAPTER 4

Catholicity and Systems

PLURIFORMITY AND COMMUNICATION

[§21] CATHOLICITY: PLURIFORMITY AND HIERARCHY OF TRUTHS

[1] Under the rubric of the loss of catholicity, the previous chapter treated, and rejected, two styles of "the introduction of massive theological-systematic fixity where the faith exhibits an organic—that is to say, open—unity of structure" (§17, 1; cf. §15, 4). A recent monograph devoted to the Church's catholicity made the same suggestion, only positively: the Church's catholicity is a matter of "reconciled diversity," of "not homogeneous but heterogeneous unity," of "identity in diversity."[1]

Now the manner of understanding must fit the object of understanding (cf. §8, 6); it follows, then, that systematic theology must respect the catholicity of the faith—its integrity-in-openness. It must resist the temptation to *replace* the spacious structures of the great Tradition with a more unyielding rendition of the Christian faith, which, however, is in reality a *reductive or selective version* of it; instead, it must *interpret* these structures, in the interest of carrying forward the great Tradition in contemporary Christian life (cf. §17, 1). Respect for the open structures of the Christian faith, in other words, yields and sustains sound catholic systematic theology, that is to say, systematic theology that fits the faith it sets out to understand, and thus indirectly conveys its openness, both to the mystery of God and to the whole world.

There is a difficulty, though. Sound systematic theology means: *multiple, perspectival* systematic theologies (§15, 1), if for no other reason than that the structures of the Christian faith, like all structures, are poly-interpretable. This multiplicity, or pluriformity, in theology is what we must further explore now, starting from the pluriformity within the great Tradition of the Christian faith itself.

The great Christian Tradition, we have argued, is a tradition of open structures, but the question remains whether the Tradition itself has been *conscious* of this. Contrary to a widespread misconception, which doggedly keeps insisting that the great catholic Tradition has always been monolithic and of one piece, it must be demonstrated that the catholic Tradition has been a consciously open tradition. Such a demonstration will greatly strengthen the case for pluralism in theology. We must begin, therefore, by briefly indicating two telling ways in which the Tradition has given evidence of its conscious awareness of the openness of the structures of the Christian faith.

[2] The first is a piece of tradition that was vigorously recovered at Vatican II. The Church universal, Vatican II declared, is a fellowship of local Churches, whose "variety aspires to unity and thus gives splendid proof of the catholicity of the undivided Church" (LG 23).[2] This clearly implies the conviction that the Church's unity does not demand uniformity [a] and that collegiality is the hierarchical sign and symbol of this unity-in-diversity. There are not a few Roman Catholics who have been disappointed by what they view as so timid an implementation of the Second Vatican Council's emphasis on collegiality as to raise suspicions of Roman reluctance and mistrust vis-a-vis pluriformity.[3]

[a] The Oriental Churches bring this out with special clarity: they have always insisted that their historic traditions be respected. Proponents of high papal privilege often see little more that the specter of conciliarism in this, and many other Western Christians have often mistaken it for mere traditionalism. Still, where the West tends to smell schism, the East smells Roman imperialism. In fact, the Oriental insistence on their privileges and rites has deep ecclesiological roots: it is predicated on the conviction that diversity of customs and traditions is an inherent feature of the Church's communion (Gk. *koinōnia*, Russian *sobornost*) and, hence, something that must be valued, not fought (UR 14–18; OE 2–3).

[3] The cultivation of legitimate variety by means of open communion and dialogue, therefore, must be a feature of the life of the Church universal *ad intra*. However, it is important to see that is must be matched, *ad extra*, by the openness of any truly catholic Church's relationships with other, separated Christian Churches and communions,

---

[a] Note that the Latin text of LG clearly states that *it is the variety itself that tends to unity*—something left unexpressed in the currently published English translations. The theological basis for this doctrine will have to be treated later, in the context of ecclesiology. For the moment, suffice it to point to the teaching that local Churches have their rightful place in the universal Church; this is especially reflected in the doctrine of episcopal collegiality (cf., e.g., LG 13, 26; CD 11). Cf. also the important letter of the German bishops of 1875, confirmed by Pius IX in an apostolic letter of the same year: DS 3112–17; CF 841.

and with the cultural variety in which all Christians live (UR 4, parr. 6–10; GS 92, parr. 1–2) [b].

This openness, again, must prevent the catholic faith from degenerating into an inert, monadic system. The faith must live and move in space and time, influencing and being influenced, in an organic variety of simultaneous and successive arrangements.[4] These particular arrangements, however, may not turn into ghettos; again, they are only as good as they are in active communication with one another. Not surprisingly, therefore, the great Tradition must be characterized by *qualitative catholicity*, which naturally generates and sustains a wealth of traditions.[5] Many of these traditions are doctrinal; they are the record of sound theological reflection and imagination, received, assimilated, and turned into doctrinal developments. Dialogue on doctrine among different traditions, therefore, in the form of an appreciative hermeneutic across space and time, is an essential ingredient of the living catholic Tradition.[6]

[a] Two passages from the decrees of the First Vatican Council seem to preclude any such living, interpretative tradition in the understanding of either Scripture or dogma. In the construction of doctrine, the Council teaches first of all, biblical arguments must adhere to the true sense of Scripture, which the Church has always held and still holds (DS 3007; CF 217). Second, the dogmas themselves are to be interpreted as meaning what the Church has once and for all declared them to mean (DS 3020 coll. 3043; CF 136 coll. 139). However, the problem is only apparent: what the Council means to reject is not the *renewal* of traditional understanding but its *replacement*.

It is not surprising that this was not more clearly expressed. The First Vatican Council was a Council under siege. This prevented it from being very clear about the enormous difference between, on the one hand, *judgments on* the Tradition, handed down by the allegedly superior tribunal of culture or science, and, on the other hand, *interpretations of* the Tradition and new, legitimate questions occasioned by cultural shifts (cf. §17, 1, [a]; §51, 2, [o]).

[b] In the period after Vatican I, these problems continued to plague the dialogue between authority and modernity in the Roman Catholic Church for a long time. In the biblical area, the early responses of

---

[b] Both passages quote the well-known saying *In necessariis unitas, in dubiis libertas, in omnibus caritas* ("unity in what is necessary, freedom in what is debatable, love in everything"). The source of the maxim is unknown. Its import has strong roots in "ecumenical" debates at the time of the Reformation, but it can also be shown to reflect a conviction that was widespread in the undivided Church (cf. Joseph Lecler, "A propos d'une maxime citée par le Pape Jean XXIII," and "Note complémentaire sur la maxime: *In necessariis unitas, in non necessariis libertas, in omnibus caritas*"). Pope John XXIII had already quoted it in his encyclical *Ad Petri Cathedram* (AAS 59[1959]497–579), explaining that the saying, known in various forms and attributed to various authors, "must always be remembered and shown to be true" (513).

the Biblical Commission (DS 3373, 3394–3400, 3503–28, 3561–93, 3628–30) still embody the old, defensive mentality. The encyclical *Divino afflante Spiritu* of 1943 (DS 3825–31; CF 232–36; cf. also DS 3792–96, 3862–64) is the first milestone marking the difficult road toward recognition and encouragement of the present practice of responsible critical exegesis in the Catholic Church.[7]

In the field of doctrine, antimodernism proved far more tenacious, witness the encyclical *Humani generis* of 1950 (DS 3875–99; CF 144–48, 238–39, 419–20, 858–59, 1571). As a result, a real hermeneutic of the doctrinal and magisterial Tradition is still largely outstanding, even though Vatican II has recognized, in principle, the emancipation of ecclesiastical scholarship from doctrinaire neo-scholasticism (cf. GS 44; OT 14–16; AG 16),[8] as well as the legitimacy of historical hermeneutics (cf. DV 8–10; UR 9–10; OT 16), the latter being impressively exemplified by the return to the sources ("*ressourcement*") advocated by the *Nouvelle théologie*, with its monumental series of patristic texts *Sources chrétiennes*. Happily, modern exegesis and modern systematics in the Catholic Church have recovered the traditional realization that the catholic faith was never monolithic and that a generous measure of pluralism is integral to true catholicity [c].

[c] In this context, the so-called Vincentian canon—"*quod semper, quod ubique, quod ab omnibus*"—is often alleged to maintain that the catholic faith does not recognize any real development in the faith. This canon is a maxim drawn from Vincent of Lerins's first *Commonitorium*; it means that "we must hold on to what has been believed everywhere, always, by all."[9] It is important to interpret this quotation in context. First of all, Vincent is specifically referring to the central truths, and especially the teaching of the Councils of Nicaea, Constantinople I, and Ephesus.[10] Second, Vincent explicitly raises the question whether the faith develops and answers it *in the affirmative*. To make his point, he surprisingly uses the very analogies that John Henry Newman was to use and elaborate fourteen centuries later, namely, the growth of the human body and the development of plants, both of which keep their several *identities* while changing their shapes.[11] Finally, Vincent explicitly limits his canon to the central truths, called the "rule of faith" (*regula fidei*; cf. §43, 4–6), and spe-

---

[c] In the meantime, however, the subtlety of the hermeneutical effort required should not be underrated: "Moderns would, it appears, most easily translate the New Testament into their own poetic idiom rather than dialogue with the troublesome idioms of the Bible" (Pheme Perkins, *Resurrection*, p. 34, n. 31). The statement would lose none of its truth if "the New Testament" were replaced by "Catholic doctrine" and "the Bible" by the "the Tradition." There is a world of difference between patient interpretation and self-serving revisionism that cuts corners.

cifically denies that the "consensus of the Fathers" is to be found "in all the little questions of the divine law" (cf. §48, 3, b).[12]

[4] In emphasizing the centrality of the *regula fidei*, we have arrived at a second way in which the Tradition has given evidence of its awareness of the openness of the structures of the Christian faith. The proposition that the faith is structured around a core of central truths is a thoroughly traditional theological theme, recovered by Vatican II in the form of the idea of the "hierarchy of truths" (cf. §19, 1, a).

Not even the post-Tridentine theological tradition, with its inventorial leanings, had ever completely lost sight of this idea. It had always taught that doctrines and teachings enjoy neither the same status nor the same degree of certainty. This was usually treated under the rubric of "theological notes and censures." In this arrangement, "notes" indicate positive degrees of authoritative certainty; "censures" indicate various levels of authoritative rejection. Taken together, they form a series of qualifiers used to determine the value of particular doctrinal and theological statements; they are traditionally set out on a broad range, from "*de fide divina*" ("of divine faith," i.e., a matter of divine revelation) on the positive end of the spectrum to "*hæretica*" ("heretical") on the negative.

[a] If there was a problem with the traditional use of the theological notes and censures, it lay mainly in its uncritical identification of *rank* and *certainty*. This is mainly attributable to the fact that the notes were first developed in the sixteenth century, which tended to depend excessively on the authority of *loci* and magisterial pronouncements to explain and certify doctrines (cf. §17, 1, a). Vatican II restored the traditional distinction between a doctrine's *certainty* and its *rank* in the "hierarchy of truths." For a sound understanding of the faith, the Council teaches, the "manner and order in which catholic belief is expressed" is important. Thus the Council connects, in one and the same paragraph, two issues: the need for a profounder and more precise explanation of the faith for the benefit of *both* Catholics and non-Catholics [d], and the fact that doctrines have varying relationships to the foundation of the faith (UR 11) [e].

This implicitly restores, it would appear, the classical conception that the *understanding* of the faith is best secured by insight into its *structure*. Understanding, therefore, is to be guided, not so much by magisterial authority, but by a doctrine's rank—that is to say, by the

---

[d] Note that the conciliar text implies the ecumenical significance of the hierarchy of truths: the faith is to be explained "in a way and in language which our separate brethren, *too*, can truly understand" ("modo et sermone qui *etiam* a fratribus seiunctis possit vere comprehendi": UR 11; italics added).

[e] It is not difficult to recognize in this an analogue of the teaching of Vatican I that very fruitful understanding may be obtained from the study of the connection between the mysteries (cf. §12, 1, a; §15, 2, a).

position it occupies in the total structure of the faith. Magisterial authority does not in and of itself determine a doctrine's relative importance in the Christian faith as a whole (§19, 1, a) and, hence, its full meaning [f]. What magisterial authority does do, however, is to impose on all the faithful, including the theologians, a serious obligation to receive and treat its teachings in a respectful, open-minded, conscientious, and constructive fashion [g], even in cases where the matter is not definitively—that is, "infallibly"—settled (cf. LG 25).[13]

[b] Only an authoritarian (and ultimately integralist) view of the Christian faith will reject as unorthodox this broad interpretation of the Church's teaching office. "The bishop of Rome and the other Catholic bishops are called upon to exercise a prophetic role in the world today, as spokesmen of a well-informed Christian conscience. If even non-believers listen with respect to their voice, there is all the more reason for Catholics to do so, even without the mistaken belief that every pronouncement that they make must be infallible."[14]

In this context, it should also be pointed out that no note or censure is ever meant to silence serious discussion. Even the most solemnly defined doctrines are capable of being further understood, interpreted, and even developed. In fact, the very authority with which they are proposed requires that they be taken seriously. Hence, authoritative magisterial pronouncements are to be conscientiously and even critically discussed, since the solemnity with which a doctrine is taught creates the presumption that it will hold up under serious scrutiny. Such discussion—along with the kind of earnest disagreements that prove the seriousness of the discussion—must never be caricatured, dismissed, or forbidden as "dissent."

[c] Lastly, there is one final, if marginal, indication that catholic doctrine is not an ideological prison. Mere lack of assent to definitive magisterial teaching has never been taken to be, as such, a sufficient ground to incur a canonical anathema. For the latter, the tradition has held, "contumacy" is needed: public, impenitent persistence in

---

[f] Gerard O'Collins, in *The Case Against Dogma*, has aptly elaborated this theme, by showing that the concept of "dogma" has far less real significance, both in theology and in Christian life, than is suggested by the connotations of authoritativeness it has acquired over the past two centuries and its frequent use.

[g] This is often conveyed by saying that magisterial teaching is the "proximate norm of truth" (cf. Francis A. Sullivan, *Magisterium*, pp. 206 ff.). The relationship between the theologian and the magisterium is, of course, an issue in all this; it will have to be discussed at greater length in due course. For the present, suffice it to say that it is the magisterium's authentic, though not exclusive, responsibility to teach *the faith* in such a manner as to *guard* it, by making sure that it is neither enslaved by definitions nor replaced by a profusion of largely secular concerns. Could it be that in more than a few cases a bishop's teaching office is profitably exercised simply by his occupying his *cathedra*, in such a way as to prevent others from attempting to occupy it with the aim of teaching reductive or selective versions of the faith?

thematically denying defined doctrine or spreading condemned doctrine.

[§22] A PLURALITY OF THEOLOGICAL SYSTEMS

[1] Good systematic theology respects the fact that the faith is not a closed system. It understands that the inconsistency of the faith is only apparent; it thrives on the freedom afforded by the faith's open structures. All construal needs latitude; interpretation prospers only if there is room for variety; there is always more than one way for the Christian imagination to establish patterns of connection among the mysteries. And with regard to the mysteries' connection with God, who is humanity's ultimate end (cf. §15, 2, a), "it is very dangerous to want to drive all people to perfection by the same path; such a one has no idea of the variety and multiplicity of the Holy Spirit's gifts."[15] A healthy variety of theological traditions, schools, and systems, interpreting the great Tradition in various perspectival fashions, is integral to systematic theology's catholicity. "Truth is symphonic."[16]

This variety is also *theologically* meaningful, and hence, worthy of being sought, cherished, and cultivated; it is not just a concession to modern tolerance, an instance of trendy liberalism, or an example of *l'art pour l'art*. First of all, a rich variety of theological systematizations more eloquently conveys the reference to the inner wealth of God's *mystery*—something any single system can intimate only in a limited way; many analogues better convey a prime analogue's transcendence. But second, variety is significant in an *eschatological* perspective: it shows theology's own participation in the process of *recapitulation*, by which "the catholic Church strives energetically and constantly to bring all humanity *with all its riches* back under Christ its Head in the unity of His Spirit" (LG 13).

[2] This can be further developed by means of an analogy. Vatican II points out that the Church community is built through "the common sharing of gifts" and "the common effort to attain fullness in unity." The community of the Church, however, is *organic*: "the People of God is not only assembled from various peoples" [*ex diversis populis congregetur*], but also a community "intrinsically joined together in a variety of *ranks*" [*in seipso ex variis ordinibus confletur*] (LG 13). In this regard, the Church community mirrors the structure of the Christian faith, which is not a mere congeries, but a hierarchy of truths.

Now what holds for the Church and the faith is likely to hold for theology in the Church as well. Theology is to be practiced in community. In a true community setting, variety is constructive (or "edifying") to the extent that traditions, schools, and systems seek active *communion* with one another. Where real dialogue and sharing occur, what is of central importance tends to emerge. Hence, given active

communion among theologians and schools of theology, we are justified in anticipating the emergence of a clearer sense of the *organic
integrity* of the catholic faith. This in turn can be expected to produce
an emergent consensus about the structure and the content of the *hierarchy of truths*. The self-correcting dynamics of open communication
among theologians can, in most circumstances, be safely trusted to
produce respect, not disregard, for the catholic faith.

In this way, finally, what Vatican I says of the mysteries of the faith
may very well apply to different theological systems, too. True, reliable
theology is likely to result from the willing exploration of the "connections" between the systems as well as from the study of the ways in
which each system conveys the reference to "humanity's ultimate end"
(cf. DS 3016; CF 132; cf. also §15, 2, a). The practice of theology in
the Church, therefore, does not need supervision at the hands of any
single "authoritative" theological school which views orthodoxy, or loyalty to the faith, as its singular privilege and which from that alleged
privilege derives the right to criticize other traditions in an especially
authoritative fashion. To the extent that systematic theologians are in
search of understanding, they are involved in an appreciative, interpretative, critical *dialogue* with other systematicians across time and
space. They may differ and disagree; they have no enemies.

[a] In view of this pluriformity, there is much to be said for George
Lindbeck's proposal, in his book *The Nature of Doctrine*, to interpret
doctrinal (and, derivatively, theological) systems, neither as statements expressive of subjective experience nor as propositionalist
statements of objective truths, but as "cultural-linguistic" structures
with distinctive grammars that must be learned before they are correctly used. If the proposal were left here, however, it would stop at
the first step. What Lindbeck correctly views as cultural-linguistic
structures with different grammars are very often not simply juxtaposed, but, in varying degrees, interlocked; and even if many do
seem completely juxtaposed, there is always room for interpretation
by means of patient moves towards a "fusion of horizons" (cf. §13,
1, [f]).

The Nature of Doctrine, however, does succeed in bringing home
two realizations. First, interpretation of doctrine by way of ecumenical dialogue among traditions—and Lindbeck is an experienced
practitioner of both—is a very delicate matter. Second, if the book
suggests that complete doctrinal consensus is a practical impossibility,
this reinforces that positive need for pluriformity as integral to true
ecumenical catholicity in doctrine and, *a fortiori*, in theology.

[3] In the interpretative dialogue with other systems, it is not unimportant to understand particular elements in each system in the context
of the system's broad characteristics, since the latter are frequently in-

dicative of the system's resident genius. This can be illustrated by means of a number of sets of possible dimensions. Our purpose in detailing a number of them at this point is purely descriptive, not normative or systematic; some of the dimensions overlap. Our principal aim, at this point, is to enhance and sharpen the reader's appreciation of legitimate variety in systematic theology.

[a] First, since systematic theology moves on a continuum between religion and culture (§14, 1), and since the search for new forms of unity between the two is every theology's first task (§14, 2), it is to be expected that theological systems show *fundamental biases* either way. In some cases, *the legitimate demands of the culture* constitute the basic inspiration behind the system; in others, it is *the integrity of the faith*. In many ways, Karl Rahner's systematic achievement is an example of the former. Its transcendental starting point implicitly endorses some of the principal concerns of the Enlightenment: the fundamental integrity of the human person and the need for intellectual integrity and freedom in believing. Both turn out, in Rahner's analysis, to be entirely recognized by the Christian faith: far from being a sectarian prejudice, it is the gracious fulfillment of the human subject's deepest aspirations. Karl Barth's system is governed by the opposite concern: it insists on keeping the Christian faith from becoming a mere function of the culture. If Rahner stresses theology's missionary accountability to the culture, Barth stresses its fundamental indebtedness to the Word of God.

[b] The comparison between the systems of Rahner and Barth leads to a second pair of dimensions. Both are instances of strongly *corrective* systematizations. Rahner wishes to free Catholic theology from its overdependence on authority and from the tyranny of vulgar understanding, symbolized by the seminary textbooks; Barth insists on recalling the Church to its normative essence, away from its accommodations, whether to fashionable liberalism or (before and during World War II) to fashionable, Nazi-inspired demands for a truly "German Christianity."

Corrective systematizations differ from *expressive* ones in that the former derive much of their agenda from reform or even polemic, whereas the latter mostly attempt to elaborate a vision. Aquinas' *Summa contra Gentiles*, while ostensibly written to correct the errors of non-Christians, is in reality an expressive exploration of natural reason's capacity for faith, demonstrated when reason is given the freedom to operate, to the full extent of its constructive powers, within the setting of Christian orthodoxy. And while criticism and polemic are by no means absent from Hans Urs von Balthasar's vast systematic effort, his theology is principally characterized by its intention to give theological expression, not only to the vision of Adrienne von Speyr, but also, and especially, to the full catholicity of the Christian faith.

[c] Most of the systems cited so far are instances of *intentional* constructs: they embody their authors' conscious, reasoned attempts to connect the Christian mysteries in a coherent way. The recent rise of historical consciousness has made us far more systematically aware of unintentional, *unstated* features of systems. If even defined doctrines can incorporate elements of historic prejudice, how much more the writings of individual theologians! Not all theologians have equally well developed tastes for historical perspective, and even those who show a good deal of spontaneous or cultivated awareness succeed only to a limited extent in taking their distance from the unthematized tastes and prejudices and ideologies of the culture that surrounds them.

Thus, for instance, we have come to realize that many features of Schleiermacher's theology show him to be a characteristic exponent of the Romantic movement, and this realization should rightly influence our interpretation. Analogously, we have come to recognize the irony of much preconciliar Roman Catholic theology: it demonstrated its transience by dint of insistence on its perennial validity. It was, in fact, a typical product of a particular period of Western *Geistesgeschichte*, namely, the period that was characterized by its unawareness of historical process.[17]

The "hermeneutics of suspicion," meanwhile, do not stop at historical and cultural blind spots; they have also made us extremely sensitive to *symptomatic* elements in theological systems. Interpretation of theological systems must take into account biases that are symptoms of individual authors' unstated personal agendas. Intelligence and learning, we have discovered, are not the same as self-awareness or mental health; capable theologians have this in common with most other men and women, that they enjoy only limited access to their motives and, hence, that their insights may be twisted by psychodynamics that are less than entirely sound or constructive. "God made the angels to show his splendor—as he made animals for innocence and plants for their simplicity. But Man he made to serve him wittily, in the tangle of his mind!"[18] Systematicians, therefore, are well advised to cultivate what the ascetical tradition calls "purity of intention."

[d] Closely connected with the relative bias in favor of either faith or culture already mentioned is another pair of dimensions of theological systems: some systems explicitly move *from universalism to particularity*, others from *particularity to universalism*, with characteristic consequences.

The former tendency has been favored by the great tradition of systematics, which started with Aquinas' *Summa contra Gentiles* and his *Summa theologica*, and which found its last classic, if embattled, representative in Bishop Joseph Butler's *Anatomy of Religion*. In the twentieth century, Karl Rahner and Paul Tillich have developed that tradition, with distinctive results. The risk inherent in this option is the possible loss of the particularity of the Christian faith. This risk is particularly clear in the case of Tillich, where the relationship between universalist claims and Christian particularity is set up by means of the "method of correlation," in which "theological answers" are correlated with "existential questions." In Tillich's systematic arrangement, a stated bias in favor of a universalist existential ontology determines the shape of the questions that demand theological answers. However, contrary to his stated intentions, Tillich's rendition of the Christian tradition's theological answers is determined by that same ontological, existentialist bias; this causes them to lose much of their traditional specificity (cf. §20, 2, a, [i]).[19] Rahner's carefully argued relationship of mutuality between universal ("transcendental") and particular ("categorical") elements[20] is more balanced than Tillich's—more balanced, too, than has been imagined by liberals who have misinterpreted Rahner's concept of "anonymous Christianity" in a one-sidedly universalist fashion[21] and by conservatives who have tried to discredit him on that score (cf. §14, 4, a, [l]). What does remain open to criticism is that Rahner's reflections focus on the human person as the potential rather than the actual recipient of God's self-communication (§14, 4, a, [k]).[22]

Matthias Joseph Scheeben, Karl Barth, and Hans Urs von Balthasar are examples of the reverse tendency: they move from particularity to universalism. Scheeben opens his system with trinitarian theology and treats the issue of faith and reason last of all. Barth and von Balthasar have both insisted that the universalist claims of the Christian faith are best appreciated if they are systematically shown to be warranted by the particularity of the Christian confession itself. Barth argues his case on the basis of an epistemology that is more indebted to his *prophetic* rejection of liberal theology than to the needs of theological argument. In the case of von Balthasar, it would seem, the decision to start with particularity is fundamentally aesthetic: if the Catholic faith's tradition of attractive holiness, theological creativity, and humane civilization is properly understood and appreciated, its inherent capacity for true universalism will be manifest.

[e] An important set of dimensions has been developed by Bernard Lonergan in his *Method in Theology*, by means of a coherent taxonomy of *functional specializations*: research, interpretation, history, dialectic, foundations, doctrines, systematics, and communications. Especially

the latter five provide useful tools to characterize and understand the resident genius of particular theological systems.[23]

[f] In many cases, characteristic dimensions of theological systems are connected with the arrangement of *theological themes*. A few examples. In Schleiermacher's strongly universalist system, the theme of "Christian self-consciousness" dominates theology, a feature consistent with his characteristic emphasis on *anthropology*;[24] Tillich's choice of the ontological-existentialist concept of *the New Being* as the focus of his system is a close twentieth-century relative of Schleiermacher's.[25] In the case of Karl Rahner, who evinces a similar predilection for anthropology, we find a characteristic emphasis on *grace* as the central theme of theology. To mention some systems with a particularist bias, Matthias Joseph Scheeben's theology is based on the concept of *mystery*,[26] Barth's thought centers around the theology of the *Word of God*, Dietrich Bonhoeffer's around *representation*,[27] and Hans Urs von Balthasar's around the theology of the *Blessed Trinity*. Two influential postconciliar Roman Catholic systematizations in the Western hemisphere, by Juan Luis Segundo[28] and Richard P. McBrien[29] respectively, have taken the emphasis which Vatican II has placed on *ecclesiology* as the principle of coherence. Geoffrey Wainwright has given us a very interesting attempt to place *worship* at the center of systematic theology.[30]

[g] In some cases, finally, systems are held together as well as characterized by *unresolved underlying tensions*. Thus, in the interest of treating very different themes, and in very different—and by no means fully satisfactory—ways, Edward Schillebeeckx,[31] Hans Küng,[32] and Gordon Kaufman[33] have all taken the troublesome issue of the *relationship between faith and history* as one of the main operative principles of their respective systematizations. The fact that they have taken on this particular problem places them in the forefront of contemporary theological reflection; the relationship between faith and history is one of the characteristic features of modern theology and one fraught with consequences in the area of systematics. It will have to occupy our attention more than once in the course of this work.

Another unresolved underlying tension that has resulted in significant systematic theologizing is associated with *feminism*. Thus, without offering a full-fledged systematic theology, Anne E. Carr has recently turned her familiarity with an exceedingly varied and growing body of literature into an articulate agenda for the theological reinterpretation of the Christian Tradition in the light of experiences all too often rejected or at lease neglected: those of women. She has done so in a manner not often practiced in the past; broad-minded yet discriminating, her treatment[34] happily avoids the agonistic, combative elements of style so prevalent while theology was still a pre-ecumenical, narrowly ecclesiastical, and largely clerical preserve: dogmatic assertion of truth-claims and blindly adversarial criticism.

[4] To say that these points omit more than they state is an understatement; the choice of authors mentioned conveys the limitations of the present author's studies at least as much as his awareness of the broad variety of systematic theology. However, the enumeration just given has two points to make.

The first is *programmatic*: if systematic theology is to be catholic, it must be an exercise in dialogue, that is to say, in mutual trust. This also enables systematicians to overcome the inhibitions imposed on them by their ignorance. Mutual trust, after all, is not only shown in appreciative interpretation of what others have said and written; it is equally well demonstrated by not insisting on being part of every conversation.

The second point is *expository*: we have now established the context in which it is possible to give a survey of the principal themes and dimensions of the present attempt at systematic theology. It is, therefore, the purpose of the next section to give a preliminary account of the principal features of the systematic theology that is to be elaborated. While this account will contain a few arguments, it will be realized that points will have to be made succinctly as this time; full argumentation and discussion must be kept in abeyance until the issues reviewed present themselves for treatment at the appropriate points in the system as a whole.

"GOD ENCOUNTERED"

[§23] THEMES AND DIMENSIONS

[1] A first significant feature of *God Encountered* is its underlying conviction that *worship is fundamental to doctrine*. This is suggested by the motto of this book, which is taken from the *liturgy*. In the Liturgy of the Hours of the Latin Church, *O admirable commercium!* are the opening words of the first antiphon at evening prayer on January 1, the octave day of Christmas, and the Feast of the Mother of God. This recognition of liturgical worship as a primary source of sound theology is to be understood at two levels. Proximately, theologians must regard liturgical *texts* as a principal source of sound doctrine; more importantly, however, they must regard the *practice of worship* itself as fundamental to doctrine. This claim, to be elaborated later in this volume (§43; §48), is intentional and programmatic, on three counts.

[a] First of all, there is the traditional thesis that universal practices of official, public worship establish the Church's rule of faith. This principle is first made explicit as a decisive theological argument in the *Indiculus*, an anti-Pelagian document of great authority, probably

composed from various sources by Prosper of Aquitaine in Rome between A.D. 435 and 442. The crucial phrase reads: ". . . . we must also take into consideration the high-priestly prayers used in liturgical celebrations, which, handed down from the Apostles, are uniformly observed in the entire world and in every catholic Church, *so that normative prayer may determine normative faith*" (DS 246).

Second, there is a cultural-historical argument that favors renewed attention to liturgy in our day, and it concerns the *act* of worship rather than its texts. This can be argued as follows. Up to the sixteenth century, Christian theology had not been forced, for a long time, to develop any critical awareness of the traditional connection between the Church's authoritative habits of worship on the one hand and doctrinal and theological discourse on the other [h]. From the early seventeenth century onward, however, orthodox Christianity came to be increasingly replaced, as the normative intellectual climate, by various forms of natural rationality. As a result, the authoritative conversation about God and matters divine had to be carried on in a new climate; the latter's pervasive interest was in the common search for objective truth as such, quite apart from the practice of worship, which, sadly, had become the symbol of division rather than concord in the world of learning. Worship thus became a matter of ecclesiastical discipline or individual piety. The aftermath of these developments is still with us. We can no longer assume, in the secularized context of the modern age, that discussions—even serious ones—about God or Christ are always and everywhere backed up by worship or prayer and, hence, a matter of Christian faith. Theology, therefore, must renew—and renew critically—its traditional appreciation of the fundamental significance of worship.[35]

Third, at the apparent suggestion of Pope John XXIII, Vatican II took on the draft decree on the renewal of the liturgy as its first task. Not only did this (arguably providential) move set the tone for the rest of the Council; the reform of the liturgy (however much it still leaves to be desired) has been, to date, the Council's most pervasive achievement, with the deepest impact on the faithful at large. For reasons yet to be explained, the present work consciously intends to interpret the catholic faith in the light of the events and the doc-

---

[h] The eucharistic debates at the time of the Reformation afford a telling instance of this disease. Most Reformers opposed what they saw, with reason, as an illegitimate clericalization of the Eucharist by means of the idea of priestly eucharistic sacrifice. They proceeded to change, with astonishing ease, the immemorial doxological shape of the eucharistic liturgy into a purely commemorative one. Their move, however, is largely accounted for when it is recalled that the principal doctrines developed in the course of the medieval eucharistic debates had failed, almost without exception, to pay any attention to the doxological shape of the Eucharist; this greatly facilitated the Reformers' move. It looks as if all of Western Christendom, once cut off from the great doxological tradition of Orthodoxy, lost sight of the crucial *doctrinal* significance of what Dom Gregory Dix, in a classic treatment, called *The Shape of the Liturgy*.

uments of Vatican II; taking worship seriously as a prime source of theology is consistent with this intention.

[2] A second important feature of *God Encountered* is indicated by the *text* of the antiphon just quoted: our systematic interpretation of the Christian faith is committed to *christology as the central focus of Christian theology*. This christology, however, is interpreted dynamically, in terms of *encounter*, and this encounter, in turn, is interpreted in terms of a *mutuality of sharing*: in the person of Jesus Christ, the living God meets humanity and its world, in an "admirable exchange" of natures.[36] This is the theme of the so-called exchange principle, of which the text of the antiphon represents a liturgical version. This deserves to be clarified somewhat further.

Christianity entered a world where religion was often associated with trade and where trade was largely carried on by barter, often across the forbidding barriers of race, language, religion, and spheres of influence and power. In such a world, the image of exchange of goods (along with related images, such as redemption) could furnish the Christian faith with a telling metaphor: God involved the human race in a paradoxical trade-off. The Church fathers, from Irenaeus on, never tired of repeating, in endless variations, the *divinization* theme: "the Word of God, our Lord Jesus Christ . . . , out of his limitless love, became what we are, so that he might make us what he is."[37]

[a] P. Smulders has pointed out how the exchange principle was capable of characteristic permutations. In Irenaeus, it is displayed in its fullness, in combination with the recapitulation motif: the Son of God, in becoming what we are, has summed up and transformed the entire human predicament, so that humanity and the world are now drawn into participation in the very life of God.

Later versions of the principle, Smulders argues, arise in connection with more focused debates and thus tend to lose some of this original wealth. Thus, in Tertullian, there is a shift of emphasis, away from the mutual exchange between God and humanity taking shape in the life of the Incarnate Son, and in the direction of general ethical instruction: "God entered into converse with man, so that man might be taught how to act like God."[38] This tendency is even more prominent in Hippolytus: "[God] has made you a man. But if you are desirous of also becoming a god, obey Him who has created you."[39] Clement of Alexandria's version is more explicitly christological again, but in a gnosticizing vein: "Now the Word himself speaks to you in visible form, putting your unbelief to shame—yes, I mean the Word of God that has become Man, so that you in turn might learn from a man just in what way man can become God."[40]

Eventually, at the hands of Athanasius and the Cappadocians, the principle is turned into a statement about the fullness of Christ's

human nature, which, however, tends to be rather statically conceived.[41] Still, the very wealth of these variations serves to demonstrate the crucial significance of the principle as well as its fecundity
in informing the theologies of the patristic period.

[b] Simply by way of another illustration, a characteristic variant of
the principle that occurs in one of Augustine's sermons is worth quoting. Augustine's focus is on Christ's humanity as the instrument of
his passion, and he explicitly marvels at this under the rubric of
trade: "Thus he engaged us, by mutual participation, in a remarkable
exchange. What enabled him to die came from us; what (we hope)
will enable us to live will come from him. Still, the flesh, which he
took from us to enable him to die, was the very flesh he gave us in
his capacity as creator; but the life, by which we will live in him and
with him, he did not receive from us."[42]

[c] The antiphon *O admirabile commercium* is a late version of the exchange principle.

> *O admirabile commercium!*
> *Creator generis humani,*
> *animatum corpus sumens,*
> *de Virgine nasci dignatus est:*
> *et procedens homo sine semine,*
> *largitus est nobis suam deitatem.*
>
> What admirable exchange!
> Humankind's Creator,
> taking on body and soul,
> in his kindness, has been born of the Virgin:
> and, coming forth as man, yet not from man's seed,
> he has lavished on us his divinity.

In its present form, the antiphon goes back to the fifth century,
to the liturgy of the Roman basilica of St. Mary Major, traditionally
associated with the Incarnation on account of the altar *ad præsepe*,
where a reputed relic of the manger has been kept from time immemorial. The text has embellishments typical of liturgical anti-
phons, yet it clearly recalls conciliar doctrine. It alludes to the con-
demnation, at the first Council of Constantinople (A.D. 381), of
Apollinarius' denial of Christ's human soul (*animatum corpus*); the
strong emphasis on Mary and her virginity enhances the claim that
the Latin text goes back to a Greek original composed shortly after
the Council of Ephesus (A.D. 430).

[d] It is possible to discern, in the history of Christian theology, the
rise of a certain irresolution with regard to the exchange principle.
The expression "God became what we are, so that we might become
what he is" was increasingly felt to be too bold for comfort. This

happened especially in the West, from the early Middle Ages on. There, the focal theme of faith-experience, and, hence, of theology, increasingly became *grace*, won by the merits of Christ, rather than *deification* in virtue of the exchange of natures.

In the capacious vision of Aquinas, however, there is, as yet, no problem. For him, the fullness of grace is still personalized in Christ, which enables him to state the exchange principle in all its vigor: "And so, because the man Christ received the utmost fullness of grace, being the Only-Begotten of the Father, it follows that it should flow from him to others, in such a way that the Son of God, having been made man, should make men gods and children of God."[43] Or even more resolutely: "For the Only-Begotten Son of God, wishing us to be sharers in his divinity, assumed our nature, so that having been made man he might make men gods" [i].[44]

[3] The exchange principle leads to a third feature of the present system: a commitment, also on *theological* grounds, to *fundamental theology*—that is to say, to an interpretation of the Christian faith in terms of *grace and nature*. In the Tradition, God's gracious encounter with humanity and the world has always been understood to be undergirded by a prior commitment on the part of God, transcendently free, original and originating. This commitment has resulted in creation, culminating in humanity. The great Tradition has consistently maintained that the "admirable exchange" involves the full flower of creation, whose latent potential, therefore, must ultimately be interpreted as capacity for actual sharing in God's nature, by grace. Gracious encounter, so the great Tradition has thought, builds upon the simply given; in the event, however, gracious encounter also turns out to make the most of the simply given, laying bare the depth of its capacity for the encounter.

[a] The theme is found with surprising clarity as early as Justin's *Apologies*. In the first, Justin professes how, in virtue of the insight they have gained from the knowledge of Christ, Christians have the ability to discern signs of the divine *Logos*, "of whom all humankind has received a share." Examples are the wisdom of "Socrates and Heraclitus among the Greeks, and others like them," and among the foreigners "Abraham, Elijah, Ananias, Azarias, Misael, and many others."[45] In the second *Apology*, he makes the same point. After appreciatively mentioning "Plato, . . . stoics, both poets and prose-authors," he concludes on a confessional, explicitly Christian note, by

---

[i] It is interesting to note that the Mandonnet edition of Aquinas' *Opuscula* (Paris, Lethielleux, 1927, vol. 4, p. 465) emends the text to read *Deo* instead of *deos*, which yields the following meaning: "so that, having been made man, he might *destine men for God*" (ut homines *Deo faceret* factus homo). For a similar example, cf. note 40 in this chapter. Maurice Wiles is clearly not alone in thinking that "the Fathers did not intend the parallelism to be taken with full seriousness" (*The Making of Christian Doctrine*, p. 107)!

pointing out that ". . . while the seed and imitation of a reality, which is given according to a person's capacity, is something, the reality itself is something very different, and the sharing in it and the imitation of it is given according to his [the Word's] grace."[46]

Hippolytus' *Refutation* states the issue rather more *sotto voce*. The author first sums up, boldly, the divinization theme: "You will be a companion of God and a co-heir with Christ . . . for you have become god." Then he deftly connects divinization with creation, by means of some classic, and quintessentially Hellenistic, pointers to human nature: "*All that you had to suffer as a man*, God gave you, because you were a man. But all that belongs to God, he has promised to give you, because you have been deified and become immortal. This is the meaning of 'know yourself': to acknowledge the God who made you. *Knowing and being known* sums up your lot, for you have been called by God."[47]

Eventually, the theme becomes a patristic commonplace, under the rubric of human wisdom as a mirror of the *Logos*,[48] and even more importantly, under the heading of the creation of Adam as *Imago Dei*. The commonplace is enthusiastically taken up in the twelfth century, not only by the Victorines, but also by Saint Bernard. Thus it enters the bloodstream of both the scholasticism (for Aquinas' teaching, cf. §26, 2, a) and the mysticism of the Middle Ages.

[b] The relationship between grace and nature is a *crux* of modern systematic theology. In due course, the present system, too, will have to meet this radical challenge. Does, for example, Israel's Covenant refer to a *reality* of partnership, or is it a naive picture? Is God really *encountered* in the world? The issue involves, not only the relationship between faith and history, and between positive revelation and fundamental human experience, but ultimately also the intelligibility of Christianity's trinitarian doctrine of God. As long as the normative world-picture was "pre-modern," it had relatively little doubt about divine intervention (or "inbreaking") in the *natural* order. This made *supernatural* intervention, too, (relatively) easy to accept. But we moderns have come to live, if not in a "closed" natural order, then at least in an autonomous one. As a result, the Christian interpretation of life is now forced to choose—or so it would seem to many—between, on the one hand, an allegedly *naive acceptance* of the order of grace as a genuinely *new reality* and, on the other hand, the *critical re-conception* of the order of grace as a mere *interpretation* of *natural* realities.

To sharpen the contrast, the question can be posed a bit more plainly. Are grace and nature two coordinated, relatively independent *realities* within the setting of one integral, ultimately *supernatural* divine plan, or are they to be reduced to two *interpretations* of what is essentially one single, ultimately *natural* divine plan?[49] Are we indeed forced to choose between a naive "interventionism" and a system that David Brown, in a provocative book on the Trinity, has not hesitated to call "Deism"?[50]

[4] It was argued that the method of understanding must fit the matter that is to be understood (§7, 1; §8, 6). This leads to the fourth characteristic of *God Encountered*: the doctrine of the incarnation and the doctrine of creation must together determine the *shape* of the system. In both creation and incarnation, there is a dynamism of mutuality. In creation, we have God's sovereign, creative self-communication, to which corresponds the creation's actualization in absolute dependence. In the incarnation, God graciously and freely encounters humanity and the world with the offer of the gift of divine self-communication; humanity and the world are thus empowered to respond, in turn, to God, in an act of total abandon, conscious and free.

The main body of this systematic theology is modeled on this dynamic; hence, it will develop its understanding of the Christian faith in two matching moves. In the second volume, it will give an account of the divine *exitus*: God's self-communication in creation and incarnation, culminating in Christ's resurrection and the revelation of God's Trinity as the gracious and ecstatic fulfillment of humanity and the world. This will be followed, in the third volume, by an account of the world's *reditus*: the elevation, by way of worship, sacrament, Church community, mission, and Christian ethics, of humanity and the world to full participation in the divine nature.

[a] At this point, it is important to recall the distinction between the order of *exposition* and the òrder of *understanding* (cf. §7, 1). Teaching calls for expository *procedures*, and those procedures are governed not only by laws of logic and dialectic, but also by aesthetics: truth calls for elegance, if possible. Yet exposition and understanding are not identical; they are to be carefully distinguished. In this systematic theology, this applies in two ways.

First of all, within the context of the *exitus*, creation and incarnation are to be treated sequentially, in two moves; the real relationship between the two, however, is a good deal more complex than the treatment suggests, for the two orders are not juxtaposed but intertwined. The order of creation, far from being replaced by the order of the incarnation, remains its abiding setting and is even enhanced by it (cf. §26, 2, a).

Second, sequential treatment will turn out to be even more inadequate in the case of the relationship between the *exitus* and the *reditus* themselves. In reality, the two occur simultaneously and not sequentially. Even more importantly, the *reditus* of humanity and the world is entirely embraced and empowered and carried and borne by the divine self-extension in the *exitus*. True theological understanding will have to hold together in dialectical tension what exposition is forced to unfold in sequential fashion.

[b] Not only must the relationship between the *exitus* and the *reditus* be understood as dialectical; it must also be construed as *asymmetrical*. In the order of creation, this is clear: the initiative is entirely God's, and the actualization of the creature is identical with its relationship of total dependence on God. But even in the order of the incarnation the relationship is asymmetrical, for it is governed by the dynamics of an encounter that is *divinely initiated* and of a partnership that is entirely of God's making. Thus, while in the discussion about the person of Jesus Christ the human nature and the divine nature must be affirmed with equal emphasis, this does not make of humanity an ontologically equal partner of divinity. In the reciprocal sharing and interpenetration (*perichōrēsis*)[51] of divinity and humanity the initiative lies with the divinity, whose encounter with humanity readies the latter for deification.[52]

[c] A very important feature of this theological system follows immediately from this. The theme of the hierarchy of truths was hailed by the Second Vatican Council (UR 11), but it remains yet to be argued and elaborated in detail (cf. §21, 3, c; 4, a).[53] What must be determined is just what is "the foundation of the Christian faith," in relationship to which the hierarchy of truths must take shape. The present systematic theology will argue that the *hierarchy of truths* results from the structure of the divine-human encounter. It will contend that the doctrines treated in the *exitus* represent the *regula fidei* (cf. §19, 1, a; §43, 4–6): the undivided Church's original, expressive account of its *direct* encounter with the divine condescension (cf. DV 13)—which in and of itself remains a mystery of awe and intimacy (cf. §34, 7) beyond all words. The rule of faith, therefore, must be considered the "foundation of the Christian faith" and consequently the standard against which all other doctrines are to be measured. These other doctrines will be explored in the *exitus*, where it will be argued that they represent, in a variety of degrees, the Church's (and, sometimes gladly, sometimes sadly, the different Church*es'*) traditions of cultivating *their own* ecclesial fidelity in believing.

These "further, particular ways in which the ministry of Christ has been and is embodied among believing Christians throughout history are not themselves part of the gospel but means to living and proclaiming the gospel."[54] These latter traditions, therefore, orchestrate and organize and protect the Church's central act of faith in God only in an *indirect* fashion. Consequently, they depend on the fundamental doctrines for their meaning, and, hence, they have to be interpreted and evaluated accordingly (cf. §48, 3, b).

The distinction proposed would seem to be supported by the fact that one of the ways to make the christological decree enacted at Chalcedon generally acceptable was to attribute only a relative authority to it. In the century following Chalcedon (A.D. 451), the "Synod of the 318 Fathers" of Nicaea (A.D. 325) came more and more to be appreciated as the original, truly normative council; the "150 fathers" of the first Council of Constantinople (A.D. 381) had merely ratified and fully orchestrated the work of Nicaea, by laying down (or so it was thought at Chalcedon) the definitive baptismal creed. That is to say, Nicaea, in combination with Constantinople I, came to be appreciated as *liturgical* and *kerygmatic*: the central core of the worship and witness of *the whole Christian community* had been authoritatively laid down. At Ephesus (A.D. 431), the first decision establishing the concept of a hierarchy of truths was made: it was decreed that no new normative profession of faith should ever be allowed to replace the Nicene Creed (DS 265). As a consequence, it came to be increasingly realized that Chalcedon had to be interpreted as a new kind of council—an *instrumental* council, a "telescope" through which the faith of Nicaea-Constantinople could be accurately discerned by the *bishops* as the authoritative teachers and defenders of the faith: conciliar decrees and definitions were henceforth to be subservient to the central truths—that is, they were to be *magisterial* and *apologetic*, not liturgical and kerygmatic.[55]

[5] A fifth important commitment of *God Encountered* involves its interpretation of *Vatican II* and, in that connection, its attention to *history*. Vatican II, of course, made history one of its main *themes* by recovering a salvation-historical perspective in the understanding of the Christian faith. Yet the linkage, in the present system, between Vatican II and history goes deeper than that. This systematic theology is based on the conviction that Vatican II is itself an historic event in the Church's living Tradition, and that it has inaugurated and mandated the elaboration of a new arrangement of the themes and emphases of the Catholic faith and identity experience.[56]

Consequently, this theological system considers the Second Vatican Council the single most important vantage point from which to give an interpretation of the historic Christian Tradition that is both catholic and contemporary. This commitment to Vatican II, in turn, implies a commitment to a serious "dialogue on doctrine," taking into account "different traditions." This will have to be done "in the form of an *appreciative hermeneutic across space and time* [j]," which is something that

---

[j] One fine instance of such a hermeneutical effort is provided by David N. Power in his book *The Sacrifice We Offer*. It honestly faces the twin Tridentine dogmas that state that the Eucharist ("the Mass") is a propitiatory sacrifice and that the ordained ministry ("the priesthood") finds its primary identification in it, no matter how inconvenient these

must be considered "an essential ingredient of the catholic Tradition" (§21, 3; cf. §2, 2, a; §46, 2, [o]).[57]

[a] "The Second Vatican Council's Constitution on Divine Revelation [DV 8] provided a charter which drew the church historian as never before into the heart of the Catholic theological enterprise. 'Tradition,' it became clear, was no arcane treasure trove of propositional statements of revelation awaiting enunciation, but an understanding arising from and discerned in the life, thought and worship of God's people down the ages and around the world. The council also declared that 'this tradition which comes from the apostles develops in the church with the help of the Holy Spirit.' Teaching, life, worship as they change and develop over time and place, these are the proper object of church historical study. Revelation, in the thought of Vatican II, is not seen as a scholastic concatenation of a series of propositional truths. A sense of history has been recovered. God makes himself known by both deeds and words. It is in contemplation of the life and the worship, as well as the thought, of the christian community down the centuries and in its global extent, that God is known."[58]

[b] Needless to say, this commitment to history will have to be practiced, so to speak, "anthologically" (cf. §4, 2, a), rather than with any claims to universal validity or completeness. This is mainly due to two factors. On the one hand, the present author is not a historian, and his knowledge of the history of Christian life and thought is far from comprehensive. On the other hand, the specific nature of *systematic* theology must be allowed to determine the content of this book; this is not a book of history. Yet the *point* must be made: systematic theology essentially involves the interpretation of the great Tradition and of historic events connected with it. It seems preferable, therefore, to demonstrate one's adherence to this proposition by treating and interpreting what history one knows, rather than to enunciate the thesis and leave it a dead letter altogether. It will surprise no one that the particular anthology offered carries, like all anthologies, strong traces of personal taste and preference.

This may also be the right moment to make an analogous remark concerning the *spatial*, that is to say, transcultural claims of the present work. The author's awareness of the cultural diversity of the Christian Church and of Christian theology is as limited as his awareness of history. Yet while recognizing the limitations of their cultural vantage points, theologians must make the *point* that Christian theology is committed to a conversation across cultural divides as much as historical ones. No one can be part of every conversation (§22, 4),

doctrines are ecumenically. But at the end of the day, the Tradition has been fairly interpreted and opened to a brighter, ecumenical future.

yet all can show respect for, and commitment to, what others have said and written elsewhere. Here, too, it seems preferable to demonstrate this commitment by interpreting the relatively small number of theologians one is familiar with than to enunciate the requirement and leave it a dead letter.

[6] Commitment to Vatican II entails a commitment to its vision of the Catholic Church as "in many ways . . . linked with those who, being baptized, are honored with the name of Christian, though they do not profess the faith in its entirety or do not preserve unity of communion with the successor of Peter" (LG 15). *Ecumenism*, therefore, is a dimension of this theological system (cf. §1).

The word *dimension* is used advisedly. Ecumenism can no longer be practiced as a separate or occasional pursuit; it must be pervasive or not be at all. This is so primarily because "the dynamism of the movement toward unity" is a part of "the renewal of the Church," and the latter can only be a matter of "fidelity to its own calling" (UR 6). This means that any attempt at renewed theological understanding of the Christian faith in the Catholic tradition must henceforth simply include the understanding of the faith of other Christians. Confessional documents and theological writings from other traditions, therefore, will be quoted and interpreted with respect for their inherent authority. This applies, not only to classical Confessions and great theological masters, but also, and with special urgency, to the many documents that have been the blessed outcome of so many inter-Church dialogues in recent decades.

[7] Lastly, *God Encountered* intends to interpret Christian doctrine in the light of the essential, dynamic, structural relatedness between *worship*, *conduct*, and *doctrine* (cf. §44, 3; §§53–54).[59] The claim that Christian doctrine is an intrinsically open structure has by now been repeated often enough in this book. It must now be added that this is based on a more fundamental recognition, namely, that Christian doctrine is, in and of itself, one element in a larger, comprehensive, dynamic structure. This comprehensive structure is none other than the Church, which "*in its teaching, life and worship*, perpetuates and hands on to all generations all that it is itself, all that it believes" (DV 8). It will be further argued that these three, while mutually interactive, are ultimately structured as a *hierarchy*, in which teaching is informed by conduct and worship, and conduct by worship (cf. §51, 1). This commitment to the hierarchical connectedness between worship, life, and teaching (or "*cult, conduct*, and *creed*") also involves a commitment to the pursuit of two different, yet related, goals.

[a] The structural connectedness of Christian doctrine with worship and life must intrinsically determine the treatment of Christian doctrine itself. Concretely, this means that moral and ascetical theology,

and liturgical and mystical theology must be integral parts of dogmatic and systematic theology. Part of the tendency towards immobilism and integralism in Roman Catholic theology has been the result of its neglect of the *developmental* and *mystical* aspects of Christian doctrine; this has tended to lead to a characteristic lack of *theological* interest in personal and communal growth in virtue, and in the cultivation of personal and communal reverence and awe (cf. §54, 7).

The themes of growth and ecstasy in relation to Christian doctrine become even more important when it is realized that the Christian faith and identity experience is not simply of one piece, but structurally shaped in a *developmental perspective*. We will argue that there exist three fundamental, hierarchically structured, and theologically intelligible types of faith-experience, to be termed *pistic, charismatic,* and *mystic*. It will also be argued that there is a structural affinity between these three and teaching, conduct, and worship respectively (cf. §54, 6).[60] In this way, the present interpretation of the Christian faith hopes to do justice, in its systematic interpretation of the Christian faith, to what Vatican II has taught about the universal call to holiness in the Church (LG 39–42).

[8] It is time to conclude the first part of the present volume, which has been devoted to an introductory exploration of *the nature and tasks of systematic theology*. This volume must now make good on the commitment implied in its title, by matching the preceding reflections and discussions with an introductory exploration, in the form of a phenomenological sketch, of its subject matter: *the Christian faith* itself.

Yet there is a serious problem here. The cultural biases of the Western world, and of the United States in particular, place extraordinary intellectual and cultural obstacles in the way of any sort of easy, forthright exploration of the Christian faith. It would be a mistake to overlook these obstacles and a worse mistake to walk around them. The second part of the present volume, therefore, must start with an exploration of the question of the relationship between natural religion and positive religion.

Part II

CLEARING THE GROUND

CHAPTER 5

Natural Religion and Positive Religion

INTERPRETING POSITIVE RELIGION

[§24] FRIEDRICH SCHLEIERMACHER ON POSITIVE RELIGION

[1] In the fifth of his *Speeches on Religion*, written—at the urging of his friends—in 1797–99 and published in Berlin in the year in which they were finished, the young Friedrich Schleiermacher wrote, with the fervor of an evangelist:

Go back then, if you are in earnest about observing religion in its definite patterns, from this enlightened [natural religion] to those despised positive religions. There everything proves to be real, vigorous and definite; there every single intuition has its definite consistency, and a connection, all its own, with the rest; there every feeling has its own sphere and its particular reference. There you will find every modification of religiosity somewhere, as well as every state of feeling to which only religion can transport a person; there you will find every part of religion cultivated somewhere, and each of its effects somewhere achieved; there all common institutions and every individual expression are proof of the high value that is placed on religion, even to the point of forgetting everything else. There the holy zeal with which religion is observed, shared, enjoyed, and the childlike desire with which new revelations of heavenly powers are anticipated, are your warranty that not a single one of religion's elements, which it was possible in any way to perceive from this standpoint, has been overlooked, and that not a single one of its moments has vanished without leaving a monument behind.[1]

This is unexpected advice to flow from the pen of the man who has been held responsible, more than any other modern theologian, for some of the most distinctive *universalist* developments in Western Christianity. Those developments have understandably received mixed reviews—which is reflected in Schleiermacher's mixed reputation, down to our day.

On the one hand, neo-Protestants and other liberal Christians have hailed him as the genius who availed himself of the freedom of the gospel to put an end to the long divorce between faith and human reasonableness. They have even credited him with the recovery of Christianity's catholicity, in the form of a new, enlightened universalism—one that has freed Christians from unnecessary bondage to sectarian doctrine and moral precept [a].

The reaction of the orthodox has gone in the opposite direction. In their eyes, especially in the eyes of those who, in this century, have followed Karl Barth in his conclusions (without, however, always appreciating all his arguments [b]), Schleiermacher is the symbol of an historic mistake. By identifying religion as an integral part of enlightened human self-awareness, Schleiermacher was successful, they will admit, in starting afresh Christianity's dialogue with culture and rationality. By the same token, however, he also contributed decisively to the widespread loss of doctrinal and moral determinateness in modern Christianity, not to mention the abandonment of the *sola gratia*. Many orthodox (in the sense of doctrinally conservative) Christians, therefore, have concluded that Schleiermacher, for all his piety, was but the pioneer of modernism.

These contrary evaluations are both one-sided, and both are narrower than the person who prompted them. To confound, or at least surprise, his orthodox detractors as well as his liberal admirers, there is a striking interpretation of the *Speeches* from Schleiermacher's own pen. In a letter to his close friend Henrietta Herz, written on April 12, 1799, three days before the completion of the manuscript, Schleiermacher referred to his first book as his "polemic against natural religion."[2] Contrary to later reputation, therefore, the young Schleiermacher was not on a crusade to reduce the Christian religion to an unspecified, universally available, and, thus, generally acceptable, "natural" religiosity.

In fact, throughout his life he was to keep a high esteem for the concrete and the particular in religion—the same esteem that he commended when he was thirty years old, as he was finishing the *Speeches*. And if he also continued to insist, all his life, on "piety"—that is, reverential, affective consciousness of absolute dependence—as the uni-

---

[a] Schleiermacher's discussion, in *The Christian Faith*, §§24–25, of what he sees as the distinctive difference between Roman Catholicism and Evangelical Protestantism lends support to this interpretation. That difference lies in contrary appreciations of the role of the Church: Protestantism holds that believers depend, for their relationship to the Church, on their relationship to Christ; Catholicism holds that they depend, for their relationship to Christ, on their relationship to the Church.

[b] It is good to recall Karl Barth's opinion, expressed as early as the winter of 1923–24, that Schleiermacher "does intelligently, instructively and generously what the useless folk of more recent times do stupidly, unskillfully, inconsistently and fearfully" (Eberhard Busch, *Karl Barth*, p. 151).

versal *proprium* of *all* religion, he did so on the basis of his interpretation of the Christian faith as he knew it in its particularity.[3]

[2] It is to be carefully noted that Schleiermacher's text treats particular, "positive" religions as *structures* (cf. §10, 1).

[a] The passage from the *Speeches* quite naturally describes *definiteness* as occurring in a *coherent* way, resulting in *patterns*. The definiteness is due to the particularity of intuitions, feelings, modifications of religiosity, states of feeling, parts, effects, institutions, expressions, elements, and moments. Far from being discredited, this definiteness is evaluated in strikingly positive terms: it is a matter of reality, vigor, consistency, culture, achievement, value, zeal, desire, attentiveness, and remembrance. Furthermore, Schleiermacher emphasizes that the variety and multiplicity of positive religion is not a weakness but a strength; for all the profusion of elements, the organic coherence of the whole is never in doubt. Each "intuition" (*Anschauung*) is firmly connected with other intuitions. All feelings are reliably set in a larger whole and have stable objective correlatives. All modifications of human religiosity and all the feeling states to which religion can give rise are found *somewhere* in that larger whole. In Schleiermacher's opinion, whoever is prepared to examine a positive religion attentively and appreciatively, as a multifarious yet coherent structure, will also notice how all the virtualities of religion as such are actualized in it.

In all of this, Schleiermacher is not being naive. Immediately after the passage quoted above, he admits that not everything is constructive about positive religions. They often appear in the form of the slave; they bear the marks of the poverty of their adherents, as well as the vestiges of their limitations in time and space. Religions, Schleiermacher implies, are not above criticism. Still, in order to criticize them correctly, thoughtful people must make an effort to interpret them as they deserve to be interpreted, namely, in the light of the *proprium* of all religion—the reverential feeling of absolute dependence on the Deity. Once this basis is securely recognized, Schleiermacher has no qualms about particularity in religion—rather the opposite.

[3] According to Schleiermacher, therefore, the only truly interesting religion is religion *as it actually exists*—that is to say, particular, "*positive*" religion. However, positive religion is determinate religion, and determinate religion is made up of elements; these elements, in turn, exist in coherent patterns, that is to say, in structures. Now what ultimately accounts for the *coherence* of any particular religion is *an inner quality that characterizes all religions* as such. This underlying quality, according to Schleiermacher, is accessible, but only by way of *a self-authenticating, interior experience.*

This experience is one that cannot be reduced to any particular acts of knowledge, to any specific moral actions, or to any particular states of feeling. It consists in a person's awareness, at once affective and luminous, of self-identity as well as absolute dependence, in such a way as to make these two inseparable. By reflection, this experience can be brought to explicit awareness, and it can be adequately thematized by saying that the person is originally and absolutely related to God—a relatedness whose actuality is experientially available *in* the person's very experience of self-identity or self-consciousness (cf. §35, 3, a; 4).⁴

[4] Let us sum up our discussion so far. Schleiermacher's point in commending the study of particular, positive religions is that they alone are actual religions. It is a mistake, therefore, to despise them. It is true, they are soulless without the core-experience which alone is capable of authenticating them, but that does not mean that they can simply be *reduced* to that core-experience. They should, therefore, be appreciated and understood as they are, in their concrete actuality as positive religions.

[5] Now what Schleiermacher *suggests* is that this appreciation and understanding of positive religions *precisely as religions* is achieved by appreciating and understanding them, along with all their parts and elements, as *coherent structures*. He seems to be implying that the interpretation of a positive religion must be practiced by focusing on its *elements*. He suggests that interpretation by structural elements, in turn, is tantamount to interpreting a positive religion *precisely as a religion*, that is to say, as an actualization of that fundamental religious experience that accounts for its being a positive *religion* in the first place.

[§25] NATURAL RELIGION AND POSITIVE RELIGION IN CHRISTIANITY

[1] Schleiermacher's commendation of positive religion may serve as a first introduction to the phenomenological sketch of the Christian faith to be elaborated in this second half of the present volume. Such a sketch, however, should not be an exercise in naiveté. It would be just that, if it were to consist merely in a cumulative, descriptive account of those elements of worship, conduct, and teaching that catholic Christianity generally accepts as authentic, supported by the principal arguments from the authoritative, historic Tradition. Such a presentation of Christianity as a positive religion, no matter how authoritative or even attractive, would be inadequate for present purposes, which are properly theological. Theology does well indeed to recognize and appreciate mature docility and acceptance, both of which are proper to faith; precisely *as* theology, however, it is concerned, not with enumeration or acceptance but with understanding. Understanding, however, is a matter, not only of doing justice to the matter to be under-

stood, but also of recognizing the demands of intellectual integrity (cf. §§8 and 11). Hence, before we develop our phenomenological sketch, we must show *how a phenomenology of the Christian faith as a positive religion is compatible with the demands of human understanding and integrity in believing.*

To make this case, let us begin by stating and elaborating as a formal thesis what, we have said, is hardly more than a suggestion in Schleiermacher's *Speeches*. The thesis is the following. There are *two mutually complementary ways* of gaining intellectual access to the universal essence of human religiosity: *transcendental reflection* on fundamental human experience and *phenomenological study* of positive religion.

[2] The first—transcendental reflection—is the way principally *practiced* by Schleiermacher in his *Speeches*. By reflection we come to realize explicitly and thematically what is implicitly and unthematically given in all our particular experiences, as the transcendental precondition for their possibility and meaningfulness. That realization consists in the awareness that our fundamental human integrity is ontologically related to the creative transcendence of God. From the point of view of transcendental reflection, therefore, there is a basic religious dimension to all particular, concrete human experiences.

In the systematic framework of *God Encountered*, it will be the task of fundamental theology to elaborate this, as an important element in the account of the divine *exitus*. Still, it is not too early at this point to make an important observation. The development of a theological anthropology, by means of a careful "transcendental" reflection on the depth of human self-awareness, is not a simple concession to the Enlightenment and, hence, an exercise in liberal, agnostic modernism. On the contrary, it is a fundamental requirement of the need for human integrity in believing—an integrity created and cherished by God. Taking human self-awareness seriously guarantees that the *positive* elements of the Christian faith are appreciated as they should be, namely, as historic instances of true divine self-communication to humanity and the world—a self-communication that prompts true faith-responses.

[a] In our own day, Karl Rahner, whose theology shares some striking family features with Schleiermacher's, has argued this point forcefully and, in fact, made it into the heart of his theology. In Rahner's system, this leads to a whole range of conclusions; at this point one telling example must suffice.

Positive (or, to use Rahner's terms, "categorical" or "a posteriori") revelation simply cannot be heard or accepted as *divine* revelation, unless it finds, in the believer, a "transcendental" ("a priori") aptitude to hear and accept it—an aptitude that coincides with the divine immanence in the human person's subjectivity. "Consequently, there corresponds to the objective supernaturality of a revealed proposition a divine and subjective principle for hearing this proposition in the subject who is able to hear it. Only when God is the subjective principle of the speaking and of man's hearing in faith can God in his own self express himself.... [I]f the objective proposition ... produced by God ... enters into a *merely* human subjectivity without this subjectivity itself being borne by God's self-communication, then the supposed word of God is a human word before we know it. The a posteriori proposition of verbal revelation which comes in history can be heard only within the horizon of a divinizing and divinized a priori subjectivity. Only then can it be heard in the way that it must be heard if what is heard is seriously to be called the 'word of God.' "[5]

[3] The second—attentive phenomenology—is the way *commended* by Schleiermacher in the fifth of his *Speeches*. As, in an attitude of careful attentiveness, we focus on the given elements of a positive religion, we can also gain intellectual access to its true religious meaning. This is not accomplished by a mere *enumeration* of elements; mere inventories, no matter how authoritatively proposed, never convey understanding. Complex realities like religions require *interpretation*; but true interpretation occurs only when, in the process of discovering the coherence of a religion's elements, we gain an increasing appreciation of its *structures*. Most importantly, in doing so, we also attain its intelligibility (cf. §13, 1; §15, 1). Far from being an exercise in theological sectarianism, therefore, *an attentive phenomenological study of Christianity as a positive religion is capable of opening our eyes, in an indirect fashion, to its intelligibility and, hence, also to the depth and universality of its significance as a religion.*

It follows that the phenomenological study of positive religion is liable, indirectly, to lead to appreciation of religion as essential to human integrity in its depth, just as reflection on natural religiosity will, again indirectly, lead to an appreciation of positive religion as vital to human culture in its breadth. It also follows that what Schleiermacher calls "natural religion" must never be brought into play against positive religion, to discredit it, nor must positive religion be summoned as a witness for the prosecution in order to mount a case against natural religion. The former is the modernist's temptation, the latter the integralist's.

[a] Natural religion and positive religion, therefore, may never be separated, let alone placed in an adversarial relationship. They are mutually interdependent. Karl Rahner makes the same point when, in the context of christology, he insists on "the relationship of *mutual* conditioning and mediation in human existence between what is transcendentally necessary and what is concretely and contingently historical. It is a relationship of such a kind that both elements in man's historical existence can only appear together and mutually condition each other: the transcendental element is always an intrinsic condi-

tion of the historical element in the historical itself, and, in spite of its being freely posited, the historical element co-determines existence in an absolute sense. In spite of their unity and their relationship of mutual conditioning, neither of the two elements can be reduced to each other."[6] For all his natural preference for transcendental reflection, Karl Rahner never tires of emphasizing that it is only in virtue of positive, "categorical," *historical* experience that we have access to the "transcendental" dimensions of existence.[7]

[4] If, however, the two are mutually interdependent, this entails that they are legitimately used in the service of *mutual critique*. This must be elaborated.

[a] Cut loose from the fundamental relationship between God and the human person, any religion's positive elements have an unfortunate tendency to become opaque and inert and to degenerate into a multiplicity of beliefs and practices connected with "objects of worship" (the *sebasmata* of Acts 17:23!). When this happens, positive religion begins to equate naiveté with faith and starts to foster, and even glorify, authoritarian fideism and traditionalism. It may end up commending sectarian intolerance and even idolatrous slavery of the spirit. Positive religion, in other words, harbors the risk of idolatry.

To counteract this risk, and to anchor positive religion in the native religiosity of the human person, transcendental reflection is required, based on the conviction that fundamental human freedom and consciousness are natively equipped to tell the difference between true faith and naive forms of belief. Insisting on transcendental reflection in theology, therefore, serves to uphold intellectual integrity and freedom in believing as the birthright of all persons. Upholding that right is not only to the glory of humanity but also to the glory of God, who created humanity in the divine image—that is, as natively oriented to God (cf. DH 3).

Positive religion must respect this basic privilege of humanity. In fact, it is an impressive achievement of the great apologetic tradition of the Christian Church to have recognized the rights of the human spirit. This tradition has found eloquent expression in the order of treatment followed by the classic theological systems. From Aquinas' *Summa contra Gentiles* on, systematic theology has habitually started with a theology of creation, an epistemology of religious language, a philosophical theology, a theological anthropology, or another of the many forms natural theology can take.

[b] On the other hand, advocates of natural religion do not always appreciate the extent to which positive religion contributes to the constructive exercise of human consciousness and freedom, in shaping forms of religious community and even in building a common religious culture (cf. DH 3). They often fail to see that the contri-

bution made to civilization by positive religions far exceeds the damage done by their sectarianisms.

Moreover, they tend to be blind to the principal inherent weakness of natural religion itself. This weakness lies, not in its plea for an enlightened humanism, but in the limitations that flow from the theoretical, abstract nature of its claims [c]. These limitations are best appreciated when measured by the standard of *practice*; natural religion does not normally generate vigorous forms of community or generous commitments to values [d]. This can be briefly illustrated by recalling two historic forms which the advocacy of natural religion, at the expense of positive religion, has taken: anti-ecclesial Deism and heroic Romanticism.

[c] Anticlericalism has always been a feature of Deism [e], especially, in recent times, in circles beholden to a militant anticlericalism of nineteenth-century, and especially French, extraction. Consistent with this, there is in the Deist tradition a tendency to treat positive, ecclesial religion as, at best, a concession to the feeblemindedness of the unenlightened, and at worst, sectarian obscurantism and degeneracy fostered by priests. The tendency is not infrequently accompanied by sentiments of shallow condescension parading as profound Enlightenment; of this, Benjamin Franklin's *Autobiography*[8] is a good example.

Unlike this militant laicism, however, the United States tradition of erecting a wall of separation between Church and State (a tradition that is gaining worldwide recognition) does not necessarily involve any sort of secularist prejudice [f]; in fact, historically speaking, the opposite is true; witness, to mention just one example, Thomas Jefferson's high regard for confessional religion. Still, Franklin's polite

---

[c] Charles M. Schulz, the author of the cartoon *Peanuts*, has put this rather well by having Linus confess: "I love mankind—it's people I can't stand!" Cf. Robert L. Short, *The Gospel According to Peanuts*, p. 122.

[d] Cf. Gerald R. Cragg's thumbnail sketch of one of the forebears of the modern advocacy of natural religion, the Latitudinarians (*The Church and the Age of Reason 1648–1789*, p. 72): "A strong ethical emphasis was characteristic of all the Latitudinarians. They constantly stressed man's moral duty. They not only counselled upright behaviour, they themselves were indefatigable in every good work. Unfortunately their moral zeal lacked dignity and urgency. Everything they did or said was moderate in tone; their religion was genuine but never ardent; they stood for a temper rather than a creed. Their outlook was reasonable and dispassionate, magnanimous and charitable. Their virtues easily degenerated; their good will subsided into mere complacency."

[e] Gerald R. Cragg (*The Church and the Age of Reason 1648–1789*, p. 78) mentions "the hatred of priestcraft which became so consistent an obsession of the Deists."

[f] Vatican II opted, as a matter of principle, for a form of separation of Church and State that includes mutual respect and cooperation (GS 76), and while it did not peremptorily exclude the possibility of an ecclesiastical establishment (DH 6, par. 3), it gently but firmly denied the right of Catholic civil authorities to direct the affairs of the Church (e.g., CD 20). In these conciliar developments, a crucial contribution came from the North American experience, so patiently and ably articulated, in the decades preceding the Council, by John Courtney Murray, S.J. and others.

contempt has found followers, too, and some recent political and social developments in the United States would seem to indicate that the First Amendment is increasingly being construed in an adversarial sense.[9]

From a political and cultural point of view, the principal strength of Deist civil religion is that it allows and creates freedom for all forms of worship. In the United States, this is often demonstrated by the presence of a variety of ministers of religion praying at public functions where the unity of the nation under God is cultivated. Theologically speaking, however, Deism suffers from a fundamental weakness: an almost purely theoretical conception of God. In practice, this tends to take the bite out of the very thing Deist civil religion respects and wishes to make possible: common worship—that most characteristic feature of positive religion (cf. §30, 5).

Given the tenuousness of the worship it inspires, it is not surprising that Deism tends to reduce, both theoretically and in practice, the possible meaning of any religion to ethics and, in particular, to a purely universalist ethic based on rationality and individual autonomy. This, however, frequently leads, again in practice, to misgivings about the kind of motivational morality in virtue of which members of Churches (and other positive religions) typically make very particular moral *choices*. In this way, curiously, a public ethic divorced from worship harbors a tendency towards intolerance. In the name of universality, it ends up recognizing as respectable, or indeed acceptable, only an almost purely legal sort of social-contract ethic. Such an ethic, however, may eventually end up publicly discouraging individuals and particular groups from making (and commending!) vigorous commitments—commitments that they consider both objectively good and beneficial, yet that they also recognize as principally binding on themselves and their co-religionists [g]. Seen in this light, the common worship and the shared community values characteristic of positive religions turn out to be rather less sectarian and prejudiced than this brand of intolerant Deism would hold them to be.

[d] There is another tendency in natural religion, and a deep-seated one: it consists in the simple identification of human self-consciousness with immanent divinity. This often takes the shape of an uncritical canonization of individual conscience; sometimes, however, it takes the shape of a heroic cult of human vitality or of human spirit,

---

[g] In the United States, therefore, it is theoretically (as well as practically!) sound to ask some critical questions about the stances taken by organizations like the American Civil Liberties Union. One can think of such public policy issues as prayer in the public schools and the freedom of confessional institutions such as churches and church-sponsored schools to cultivate their own communal ethical values without immediately being accused of narrow-minded intolerance and discrimination.

in which the very conception of God comes to coincide with inner pride.

There is a distinctively Romantic-heroic version of this, well exemplified by the thought of Johann Gottlieb Fichte. For Fichte, any true concept of God is both impossible and superfluous, because assurance about divinity simply coincides with self-consciousness. Fully self-identified by this radical immanence, the completely self-conscious person simply transcends the contingencies of historical existence. "I am a God in the depth of my thoughts, enthroned, in my innermost soul, over myself and the universe," as a late-Romantic Dutch poet was to convey the Fichtean stance.[10] In this way, human self-identity lays claim to a truly meta-physical sovereignty. In Fichte's own words: "Only the Metaphysical, and in no way the Historical, makes blessed."[11]

Rudolf Otto has rightly pointed out that Schleiermacher was very much aware of this issue. In treating the question as to whom Schleiermacher had in mind when he addressed his *Speeches* to the cultured among religion's despisers, Otto answers: "Those 'imbued by the culture of the times' . . . are those who, touched by literature and philosophy, have been grasped and imbued by the great Idealist movement of the day. The readers he has in mind are not the tired skeptics, those who know too much, those defeated in the battle between 'knowledge' and 'faith,' those for whom world, mind and ideas have become a source of discouragement; rather, he is thinking of the disciples of Herder, Goethe, Kant, and especially Fichte. He wants to overcome, not doubts or petty atheisms, but a *conflict of mood*. While vigorously sharing and endorsing the Idealism of his time, he confronts its high-mindedness and its proud self-awareness, and especially Fichte's grand heroic conception of the 'I' as lord of world and things, as gloriously self-sufficient and free. He wants to safeguard gentle humility and abandon, in opposition to all that captivates and carries away, not only the world and things, but also the 'I' and ourselves. Without that humility, the mood and the culture of the day, for all their vitality, are nothing but 'hybris,' nothing but 'promethean insolence—an insolence that steals, with a coward heart, what it *could* have claimed and awaited in quiet assurance.' "[12]

[e] Theologically speaking, therefore, it is important to identify the *agenda* behind the tendency to present the human religious a priori as unrelated to positive religion. In and of itself, we must emphasize, the human religious a priori is the intrinsic, integral, "natural" element (that is to say, the natural "moment": §44, 1–2) within positive religion as it exists in the concrete. Those who, by a process of rational involution, raise it to the power of independent existence tend

to overlook that the resulting conception of God is almost completely theoretical (§25, 4, c).

What is more significant in this move, however, is that those who thus canonize native human religiosity are interested in the affirmation of the human self, not so much as religious, but as *autonomous*, or in cases even as divine in its own right. This may sound noble, but it really amounts to the end of all religion. The human interiority laid bare by transcendental reflection can be safely understood as inherently religious but only on condition that it is not conceived in terms of sovereignty over everything, including sovereignty over positive (or "organized") religion.

Friedrich Schleiermacher and Karl Rahner have understood this. The former conceived of the fundamental religiosity that characterizes the human person as such in terms of absolute dependence on God (in the second of the *Speeches* and in §§32–35 of *The Christian Faith*); the latter stressed the total openness and receptiveness to God and to all of creation that lies at the root of human integrity (in *Foundations of Christian Faith*[13] and elsewhere).

Dietrich Bonhoeffer saw all of this with uncommon clarity when he argued that the real issue is not natural religion but *the human demand for total autonomy*, which has taken, in the course of history, a variety of forms. There are recurrent demands that the Christian faith justify itself before a superior tribunal, whether it be Reason (in the eighteenth century) or Culture (in the nineteenth) or *Volkstum* (in Nazi Germany). All those demands amount to one and the same irreligious demand: that the Christian faith justify itself before the tribunal of human autonomy.[14]

[5] Again, Flannery O'Connor was acutely aware, as well as savagely critical, of one typically North American shape that this identification of inner, autonomous self-assertion with religion tends to take (cf. §20, 5; 5, a). In one of her letters she wrote:

One of the effects of modern liberal Protestantism has been gradually to turn religion into poetry and therapy, to make truth vaguer and vaguer and more and more relative, to banish intellectual distinctions, to depend on feeling instead of thought, and gradually to come to believe that God has no power, *that he cannot communicate with us, cannot reveal himself to us, indeed has not done so,* and that religion is our own sweet invention.

And in a letter to a close friend she explained, savagely:

This girl . . . who shows up here from time to time, was a seminarian at Union in New York and quite snarled up in the emotions, etc. When the psychiatrist got through with her, her emotions flowed magnificently and she believes nothing and she herself is her God, and everything for her depends on her success in the theatre—which I doubt she'll ever have.[15]

[6] Natural religion and positive religion, therefore, are real only in mutual interdependence. To understand the relationship between human nature's transcendental orientation to God and the Christian faith's historic structures is to understand it in terms of a *mutual critique*. On the one hand, the historic, authoritative structures of Christian cult, conduct, and creed are to be tested by the requirements of human integrity. If this were not done, Christians would be forced into commitments unworthy of human dignity but indirectly also unworthy of the God who creates humanity as inherently attuned to the divine majesty and mystery. On the other hand, natural, universal human religiosity must be tested by the standard of the positive, concrete structures of worship, life, and doctrine. If this were not done, natural human religiosity would arrogate to itself an unbecoming autonomy in relation to God as well as in relation to human community. Such an autonomy will also place humanity in an ultimately irreligious (and inhumane!) position of sovereignty over the world.

CHRISTIANITY AND NATURAL RELIGION

[§26] THE ASYMMETRY BETWEEN NATURAL AND POSITIVE RELIGION

[1] Natural religion and positive religion, we have argued, do not exist except in a relationship of *mutual dependence* (§25, 3, a). Consequently, both are legitimately alleged in the service of *mutual critique*, lest both cease to be religion and lest both end up distorting true humanity. These conclusions, it would appear, could conveniently end our argument at this point. There is, however, one important question left— one that will take us far afield. Do natural religion and positive religion have equal standing in the relationship? In other words, is the relationship between the two symmetrical? Or are they related asymmetrically—that is to say, by way of a hierarchical relationship?

At the present stage of our argument, we will answer this question only in a very incomplete manner, on two counts. First of all, we must, for the present, limit ourselves to the Christian faith, without concerning ourselves with claims that can be made in behalf of other positive religions. Second, we must, in the interest of orderly exposition, save the fully orchestrated speculative treatment of this crucial question for later. In the second volume of this system the development of a fundamental theology will require that the relationship between natural religion and Christianity as a positive religion be fully developed. In a different way, though, it will take the entire system of *God Encountered* to argue the thesis about to be proposed.

The decision not to argue the thesis at this point, however, does not mean that we must content ourselves with simply stating it. We will, therefore, state the thesis and then immediately proceed to explore, at some length, some of its principal dimensions and consequences, both historical and systematic. The main reason for this procedure at this time is that the discussion of the relationship between natural human religiosity and the Christian faith has left profound marks on the Christian faith and on Christian theology as they have come down to us.

[2] Our thesis, then, is that, *at least in the case of the Christian faith* [h], the relationship between natural religion and positive religion is asymmetrical, *since the Christian faith as a positive religion must be recognized as the concrete shape of grace and, hence, accorded theological superiority over natural religion* (cf. §23, 3, b; §35, 1, b).

> [a] This is a restatement of two fundamental insights of Thomas Aquinas. The first is that grace, far from "cancelling" nature, both "pre-supposes" and "perfects" it.[16] The second is that "the gift of grace exceeds every power of created nature."[17]

[3] In the following exploration, it is of the utmost importance to keep in mind our previous argument that natural religion and positive religion *do not actually exist except in a relationship of mutual dependence* (§25, 3, a; 7; §26, 1). Hence, any hierarchy occurs, not between two *separable elements*, but *between two distinguishable "moments"* (cf. §44, 1–2) that are related to each other by way of *mutual interpenetration* (cf. §23, 4, b, for an analogous case of *perichōrēsis*). The attribution of hierarchical superiority to one, therefore, does not entail the attribution of a separate existence to it.

The catholic tradition has always understood this rather well. It has always insisted that regard for humanity's transcendental orientation to God is an integral part of the theological task of understanding the Christian faith as a positive religion (§25, 3, a; 4). The advocates of natural religion have not always demonstrated the same understanding; they have often treated natural religiosity as if it were capable of an independent existence. Against this, it is our contention that natural religion cannot but take the shape of a positive religion and, hence, that advocacy of natural religion can never simply claim to be universalist, noncommittal, unprejudiced, or even tolerant. The explorations of the next section are to be understood in light of this basic understanding.

[§27] THE CLASSIC CASE FOR THE SUPERIORITY OF NATURAL RELIGION

[1] The position just adopted is likely to be unattractive to those who do accept an asymmetry between natural religion and positive religion but construe it, whether by design or in practice, in the direction of a *hierarchical superiority of natural religion* over positive religion. The tendency to do so has an influential tradition, which has manifested itself

---

[h] But by no means exclusively in the case of the Christian faith: cf. §35, 1, b.

in several shapes. While it has been especially prominent since the Enlightenment, it was far from unknown to the ancient Church.

Contemporary Christian theology, especially in North America, must obviously concern itself with the contemporary version of the problem. However, it will come to this task better equipped if it lets itself be instructed by the great Tradition. Against that classic background, modern theology will also be able to gain a clearer, and very necessary, understanding of the special features that characterize the modern version of the problem. The present chapter, therefore, will briefly discuss the issue as the ancient Church knew it. This will lay the groundwork for the treatment, in the next chapter, of the modern, post-Enlightenment shape of the problem.

In any case, we are dealing here with a crucial theological issue, to be treated with great care. The thesis that Christianity as a positive religion is hierarchically superior to natural religion must not be lightly asserted. Here if anywhere in theology today, "zeal for God" must not be "unenlightened" (cf. Rom 10, 2). Precisely because it is an essential thesis, it must be very responsibly proposed. It can be so proposed only on condition that it is clearly recognized that the thesis has faced, is facing, and will continue to have to face, serious challenges.

[a] These challenges are more obvious in some periods than in others. One telling way to characterize the period between, roughly, the mid-fifth century and the late seventeenth century is to note that there were no serious *systematic* challenges to the thesis that Christianity as a positive religion is superior to natural religion. This is tantamount to stating that orthodox Christianity provided the culture with its normative intellectual climate. This became especially true in the medieval Christian West. There the pursuit of secular learning, logic, philosophical reflection, and, eventually, natural theology came to be too solidly set in the context of Christian orthodoxy and ecclesiastical sponsorship to be able to direct themselves roundly against the faith. Moreover, the penalties meted out to heretics by the secular arm were too harsh to make a public critique of Christianity an attractive option. Heresies did occur, of course. But the many popular, charismatic uprisings were not so much directed against the Christian faith as against the ecclesiastical establishment.[18] Faith did coexist with heresy and residual paganism in places,[19] but this never amounted to a naturalist critique of Christianity as a positive religion, except in the eyes of those modern observers who see manifestations of such a critique everywhere.

While the instances where the authority of the Christian faith was really contested, therefore, were few and far between, they were nonetheless real. In the case of the extravagant, brilliant thirteenth-century emperor Frederick II, the claim to have transcended Christianity (which earned him a reputation for atheism, among many other things) may have been mainly a matter of swagger. But there are good reasons to think that the medieval Church had to deal with undercurrents of sophisticated critique, in a variety of quarters. The philosophical daring at the universities, the creative independence found in literary circles, and the increasing claims to secular authority voiced among the merchant class stimulated free thought not always compatible with Christian orthodoxy. In philosophy, there were tendencies towards Averroism and rationalism, sometimes feebly defended by means of the theory—frequently attributed to Siger of Brabant, Aquinas' colleague and adversary in Paris—that there exist two independent realms of truth, reason and faith. Much medieval literature, including some religious literature, owed more to pagan philosophy than to faith. It is also hard to imagine that there was nothing serious behind the aesthetic charm—often merely elegant, sometimes delightfully naughty—with which many medieval and early Renaissance authors proposed not a few pagan ideas that, if seriously entertained, would be quite offensive; what comes to mind is the courtly love tradition,[20] and names like Petrarch, Chaucer, and Boccaccio; even Dante has not escaped suspicion.[21] The advice of the humanist Clelio Calcagnini, "speak with the many, think with the few," was widely taken long before it was formulated (cf. §30, 2, a). At least for the record, therefore, it must be noted that real dissent, all the more careful for having to be cautious, was far from unknown in the otherwise very Catholic Middle Ages.

[2] First of all, we will probably do well to go on the assumption that there is something *universal* about the tendency to criticize positive religion and to reduce it, at least to some extent, to its anthropological dimensions. There are aspects to positive religion that simply ask for, and even provoke, criticism—especially of outsiders.

To mention one example, in positive religion the response to the divine is very often ingenuous and unstudied. Yet the artlessness of innocence can turn into naiveté, especially when innocence turns stubborn and resists the demands of rationality and sophistication; and hard though it may be to draw the line, there *is* a decisive difference between ingenuousness and credulity. Hence, when the critique of religion arises, it is often hard to tell which of the two attract the critique: positive religion in and of itself or the immaturity of its forms and the irrationality of its adherents. On the other hand it is also true that outside critics of positive religion frequently make their task rather too easy for themselves by declaring that positive religion is, in and of itself, a form of immaturity or prejudice or, worst of all, insincerity.

[3] Yet not all critique comes from outside. As persons and communities mature and get broader realities to face, their very religions tend

to give rise to thought, and reflection comes to inhibit the spontaneity of the old-time religion. In this way, like an unstable chemical compound, positive religion gives evidence, it would seem, of a native tendency to find a lower energy-state; it appears spontaneously to want to trade itself in for something a little more "realistic."

[a] Martin Buber has laid bare some of the twentieth-century cultural dynamics of this process of reduction, manifested in the development of the modern "darkening of God," in a book with the same title (cf. §35, 2).[22] But the tendency towards this kind of reduction is probably ubiquitous; witness, for example, the ease with which the early eighteenth-century naturalists' religious wonder at the marvels of nature soon drifted off into mere ethical exhortation[23] and, much further back, the naturalness with which Euripides came to psychologize what had been truly cultic and religious-ethical postures and attitudes in Aeschylus and Sophocles.

[4] However, positive religion frequently has to face a rather more *intentional critique*, which at times can turn downright aggressive. Positive religion can indeed be crude and "unspiritual." Not only do its deities and its heroes (not to mention the accounts of their exploits) often look dubious; the blind, partisan devotion often shown by its adherents is disconcerting, if not downright repulsive, even if the object of their cult could, perhaps, be considered acceptable or even attractive.

[a] The Christian Church had to face this issue from the outset. In the ancient world, the crassness and narrow-mindedness of much positive religion caused as much polite embarrassment as they do nowadays, especially among the motivated intelligentsia. Then as now, the need for sophistication and integrity in believing took a number of forms. The yearning for mystery uncluttered by vulgar detail and shared only with the serious and the select was as apparent in the various forms of ancient religious gnosticism as it was ever to be among eighteenth-century Freemasons. Philosophic reflection on humanity's natural religiosity produced allegorized, rationalized, liberal, and, above all, tolerant versions of traditional religions. Stoicism, with its tasteful cultivation of disciplined virtue, proved especially attractive. This was partly due to its ability to interpret traditional polytheism in an urbane, reasonable, profound, and ultimately monotheistic (if pantheistic) perspective. Other religious movements, mostly of Neoplatonic extraction, considered positive religion crude beyond recovery, as Plato himself had tended to do. They tended to opt either for an intellectual philosophic monotheism with ecstatic perspectives, or, in the case of the Isis religion, for a mystical-cultic monotheism with clearly universalist perspectives.[24] All these movements in some fashion appealed to an eternal order of reality, accessible either by Reason or by way of special revelations. Most of

them also agreed in criticizing and rejecting particularity in religion as gross and sectarian.

The ancient Church shared many of these criticisms. It, too, had a universalist outlook. It was developing an increasing respect for Reason, for it saw in Christ the final revelation of the divine *Logos*, which had given evidence of itself at other times and in other places. Finally, it rejected the grossness and the busyness of idolatry as an insult to humanity as much as to God. At the same time, it insisted on being particular as well. This was a demanding combination of claims to defend, but the challenge was met, and it produced a series of capable apologists. Eventually, it produced the brilliant mind who was equal to the ancient Church's task of intellectually confronting the claims of natural religion: Origen. It took the shape of a lengthy diatribe known as *Contra Celsum*—Origen's elaborate rejoinder to a pointed attack on the Christian Church by the late second-century pagan philosopher Celsus, entitled *Alēthēs Logos* ("True Reason").[25]

[b] A substantial part of Celsus' critique of the Christian religion derived from the Stoic elements in his philosophical background. Celsus, therefore, found much to admire in the Church, especially the universalism of its *Logos*-doctrine. As a result, he was all the more baffled as well as offended by the impenitent insistence, on the part of Christianity (and of the Judaism it arose from: cf. Esther 3, 8!), on its particularity.

In Celsus' eyes, absolute claims on the part of positive religions had to be steadfastly denied, and it was a mark of true philosophical intelligence to be able to do so, in a civilized manner. It was best done by interpreting the myths of all religions allegorically (cf. §30, 5). Putting the positive religions in perspective in this way enabled one to view them all together, ultimately, in the light of Reason. Seen in that light, all religions had basically the same import: they were versions of "an ancient doctrine which has existed from the beginning, which has always been maintained by the wisest nations and cities and wise men."[26] No positive religion, therefore, presented a serious intellectual problem as long as it did not insist on professing its particularity as divine. From a philosophical point of view, all particular religious forms and observances fitted into a broad picture of humane civilization ultimately governed by Reason. In practice, this meant that they all must agree to being appropriately fitted into the order comprehensively held together by the divinely imperial State.[27]

Yet it was a matter of long, wearisome experience that particular religions, despite their obvious grossness and particularity, tended to insist on absolute claims. Since this could only lead to barbarism, it was in the interest of humane civilization to keep the positive religions literally in their places. There, in their own contexts, their particularity was to be appreciated.[28] There, too, they could be encouraged to do what they did best, namely, to give concrete shape to the worship of "the greatest God," who benevolently let himself be worshiped by means of the worship extended to his lieutenants, the regional deities and daemons appointed by him.[29]

In the case of (Judaism and) Christianity, therefore, Celsus saw a major problem. What offended him was Christianity's arrogant refusal to let itself be fitted in, to become like the other religions, which were happy to be as particular and as partial as the deities and daemons that were the objects of their observances.[30] Any particular religion that failed to recognize these essential limitations was vulgar; Christianity, then, was the limit of corruption and obstinacy and deserved nothing but contempt. This explains the violence of Celsus' invective: the details of Judaism and Christianity were so crude, he wrote, and so inferior to the mythologies of other nations,[31] that most of them were not even capable of refinement by means of allegory.[32] They could, therefore, only be counted on to mislead illiterate yokels and bumpkins.[33]

Given this background, it is clear why Celsus should have greeted Christianity's claims to *newness* with special scorn. This claim, especially when coupled with the claim to universal significance, involved the rejection of the authoritative religious and philosophic tradition as an acceptable yardstick to judge Christianity by. In the ancient world, however, immemorial tradition symbolized the perennial order and harmony of things; the ancients were inclined to consider antiquity the single most important and incontrovertible sign of truth. "I have nothing new to say, but only ancient doctrines," Celsus boasts.[34]

For Christians to come up with the novelty that "some God or son of God has come down to the earth . . . is most shameful," for if God wanted "to correct men," God did not have to come to earth to "learn what was going on among men"; God could have corrected them "merely by divine power, without sending some one specially endowed for the purpose."[35] The true God does not intervene: "if you changed any one quite insignificant thing on earth, you would upset and destroy everything"; and if we supposed that God wanted to come to earth to throw his weight around, we would be attributing "a very mortal ambition" to God.[36] What is also in bad taste is that Christians sully the goodness and holiness of the universal *Logos*, by bringing forward "a man who was arrested most disgracefully and crucified."[37] But what is fundamentally objectionable in all of this is the particularism attributed to God by Christians. Why was it only "after such a long age" that it occurred to God to redirect the human race? "Did he not care before?" Also, why should God, after such a "long slumber," have sent some one "into one corner"?[38] "He ought to have breathed [his spirit] into many bodies in the same way and sent them all over the world. The comic poet wrote that Zeus woke up and sent Hermes to the Athenians and Spartans because he wanted to raise a laugh in the theatre. Yet do you not think it is more ludicrous to make the Son of God to be sent to the Jews?"[39]

[c] Origen appreciates the import of what Celsus means. In a slightly different context, he agrees with him on an important point. He grants that God does indeed intend that "this world as God's work [should] be made complete and perfect in all its parts. . . . we should agree that in this point [Celsus] was right." But then comes the decisive difference: ". . . God does not take care, as Celsus imagines, only of *the universe as a whole*, but in addition to that He takes particular care of every rational being."[40]

In Origen's view, therefore, the world is not a world as the Stoics (whom Celsus is here following) conceive of it. It is not a quiescent place where differences (such as those between the animal world and humanity) do not really count and where an impersonal divinity permeates all things indiscriminately, like a benign, intelligent gas [i]. Rather, Origen maintains, the world is differentiated and dynamic, and it culminates in humanity; and humanity, in turn, is oriented to God. If, then, God wants to correct the *whole* world, it is not unreasonable that God should visit humanity *in particular* and *in a particular time and place*. Origen's analysis implies that Christianity as a positive, particular religion is the perfection of natural religion, not its deformation.

[5] Remarkably, Celsus' critique of Christianity has some characteristic features in common with contemporary theological positions of the "liberal" kind. While a bit condescending, his appreciation of all positive religions has a familiar ring to it, as does his polite insistence that none of them must make absolute claims. His recommendation that myths and scriptures be interpreted in a sophisticated, allegorical fashion, which will show them to be mutually compatible and harmonious, is reminiscent of modern appeals to demythologize. Even his Stoic refusal to place humanity in a position of eminence over the animal world sounds curiously like some contemporary expressions of ecological concern. Most strikingly modern, however, is his rejection of an "inter-

---

[i] The metaphor is suggested by A. A. Long, *Hellenistic Philosophy*, p. 156; cf. also Pheme Perkins, *Reading the New Testament*, p. 121. In identifying Christ as the *Logos*-Spirit Incarnate, Tertullian (*Apologeticus* 21, edited by Mayor-Souter, pp. 68–69) quotes the Stoic Cleanthes as maintaining that the Spirit (in which are combined the creative *Logos*, fate, the mind of Jupiter, and the inevitableness of all things) is "what permeates the universe" ("Hæc Cleanthes in spiritum congerit, quem permeatorem universitatis adfirmat").

ventionist" God and his pointed insistence that the Christian faith, in maintaining the particularity of the Incarnation, poses a huge theological problem, since it raises the suspicion that the Christian Church is innately intolerant.

Yet there are characteristic differences, too, and these differences should caution us not to equate Celsus' critique too readily with the modern, post-Enlightenment critique of Christianity as a positive religion. In all likelihood, we would be making an error in historical judgment if we were to notice the similarities and immediately jump to the conclusion that Celsus' critique is but an historic instance of a timeless, metahistorical issue in fundamental theology: the affirmation of the universal character of humanity's innate religiosity. Such a conclusion might also blind us to the distinctiveness of this fundamental theological issue as it presents itself today. We must, therefore, somewhat more carefully review the characteristic features of the critique of positive religion, and of the Christian faith in particular, as it has become current in contemporary Western Christianity and widespread in North America. Then we will be in a position to draw conclusions for the further conduct of our argument. The next chapter will be devoted to this task.

CHAPTER 6

Natural Religion Superior?

THE MODERN CASE AGAINST CHRISTIANITY AS A POSITIVE RELIGION

[§28] FROM LATITUDINARIAN CRITIQUE TO DEIST REJECTION

[1] There is something deeply disturbing about the historical ante-cedents of the modern critique of the Christian faith as a positive re-ligion: it is the product, not of outsiders like Celsus, but of *self-destructive tendencies within Christendom itself.*

It arose as a radical reaction, on the part of sincere Christians, to the painful aftermath of the Reformation: the interminable, unprof-itable, and often murderous confessional debates of the sixteenth and seventeenth centuries, carried out amidst the devastation and confusion of the religious wars.[1] It had been difficult to profess a faith broken by the broad divisions of the first phase of the Reformation; it became almost self-defeating to profess a faith progressively shattered into un-numbered factional confessions. There is a world of painful discord behind George Herbert's harmonious lines:

> Come, my Way, my Truth, my Life:
> . . . .,
> Such a Truth, *as ends all strife.*[2]

In the case of the Roman Catholic Church, the real achievements of the Counter-Reformation were painfully offset by a rash of progres-sively abstruse theological controversies, as well as by widespread dis-affection among the learned. But the problem was not limited to Ca-tholicism. Like malignant growths, overspecialized doctrines were everywhere disfiguring the great body of Christian doctrine and drain-ing it of its energy. What made things worse was that all of them were in various degrees being enforced (or, as the case might be, repressed) by authority, sacred as well as secular [a]. This created, among other things, a steady movement of exiles for conscience' sake, which exacerbated the churches' sickness and metastasized many growths even further. This is the period, it must be recalled, that also witnessed a spectacular spread of Christianity outside Europe; but it was religious exiles as well as missionaries that were joining the conquerors and the traders; Europe was bequeathing to the world a Christendom hardened by division. All denominations and churches, from Popery to Puritanism, came to look more and more like intolerant, sectarian theological systems.

Hence, wearied and worn down, and at a loss for constructive alternatives, many middle and late seventeenth-century Arminians, Latitudinarians, Quakers, and quiet agnostics opted out of the Churches. In a platonizing vein, they turned to a simple, direct, pietistic biblicism combined with an ardent trust in the authority of Reason as the only way to recover serenity, peace, and sometimes, as in the case of Rembrandt's biblical etchings, extraordinary spiritual and artistic harmony and depth. Eventually, many came to the conviction that it was in the interest of unity to hold that the Christian faith could, and should, be freely judged by Reason.[3]

[a] John Toland's tract *Christianity not Mysterious*, published at Oxford in 1696, comes to mind as a representative early statement of this position. Toland, an Irish Catholic born in Derry, was not a very capable theologian, but he had his finger on the pulse, and he wrote from experience. Having been brought up "from my Cradle, in the grossest Superstition and Idolatry,"[4] he had traveled, via the Scottish Protestantism of Glasgow and Edinburgh, to the Arminianism of Leyden, from where he moved to Oxford. The little book he wrote there was far from profound, but it startlingly expressed what many people were half thinking, which accounts for its *succès de scandale*.

The preface is the more telling part of the book, for that is where the author shows his hand. Early on, he disarms his reader, "the well-meaning Christian," with the assurance that he is writing "with all the Sincerity and Simplicity imaginable."[5] He implies that those two virtues have long been lost, given the "foreseen Wranglings of certain Men, who study more to protract and perplex than to terminate a Controversy."[6] However, what has really gotten lost is Reason, for the contestants inevitably end up having "Recourse to Railing when Reason fails them." Along with Reason, what has gotten lost is Religion, and Religion "is always the same, like God its Author, *with whom there is no Variableness, nor Shadow of changing.*"[7]

The implication is, of course, that Reason and Religion have a

---

[a] The savage irony of Daniel Defoe's *The Shortest-Way with the Dissenters: or Proposals for the Establishment of the Church* is one among many denunciations of this tendency.

common cause, based on the fact that they are both simple and unchangeable and that both can be had apart from doctrinal and theological systems. "A wise and good Man will judg the Merits of a Cause consider'd only in itself, without any regard to Times, Places or Persons."⁸ John Toland, therefore, will appeal to reason as the tribunal of last resort in matters of Religion. This has the added advantage of also providing a reasonable defense against the "declar'd Antagonists of Religion." What he wants to correct, in sum, is "the narrow bigotted Tenets" of the Churches, denominations, and sects, as well as "the most impious Maxims" of the atheists.⁹

What does Toland mean by this reasonable Religion between impious atheism and sectarian prejudice? Interestingly, it is simply the gospel: "They are not the Articles of the East or West, Orthodox or Arian, Protestant or Papist, consider'd as such, that I trouble my self about, but those of Jesus Christ and his Apostles."¹⁰

It is in passages like this that Toland shows his *mood*. His plea for Reason and Religion arises from an understandable frustration with the divisions, from an impatience that has driven him altogether out of that wearying world of controversy. Once he has gained his distance, he can freely denounce; in this way his initial profession of religious sincerity and simplicity begins to degenerate into a scarcely veiled, spiteful petulance. It comes as no surprise when, with more grandiloquence than realism, he announces his intention to publish an "Epistolary Dissertation . . . entitul'd *Systems of Divinity exploded*."¹¹ This is Toland's real agenda. In comparison with this, his other concern—the denunciation of atheism—is no more than a feeble corollary; could it be that he was taking precautionary measures against accusations of atheism directed at himself?

Toland's advocacy of Reason and Religion, therefore, is governed by a *double negative agenda*. First, but relatively unimportantly, he does not want to pass for a non-Christian or a heathen. The prevailing cultural climate is still distrustful of Socinianism; Deism is on the horizon, but it is not acceptable yet. Secondly, and most important, he has lost faith in the viability of any concrete, historical form of Christianity.

Seventy years before Toland, another former Roman Catholic, John Donne, had still *prayed*, amidst the disorientation of controversy, for a vision of Christ's *spouse*, and he had looked *among*, not *above*, the churches for an answer to his prayer:

> Show me deare Christ, thy spouse, so bright and cleare.
> What, is it she, which on the other shore
> Goes richly painted? or which rob'd and tore
> Laments and mournes in Germany and here?
> Sleeps she a thousand, then peepes up one yeare?
> Is she selfe truth and errs? now new, now'outwore?

> Doth she,'and did she, and shall she evermore
> On one, on seaven, or on no hill appeare?
> Dwells she with us, or like adventuring knights
> First travaile we to seeke and then make love?[12]

Toland no longer prays for a vision of any *Church*; he simply *claims* he has the *true Religion*, "of Jesus Christ and his Apostles," "of the lord Jesus Christ, who alone is *the Author and Finisher of my* [!] *Faith.*"[13] The truth he wants to establish is a *deinstitutionalized, essentially private truth*—the one reasonable, true Christian religion, harmonious above all divisions, serene above all vicissitudes of place and time.

On this airy foundation, then, Toland outlines his project in writing *Christianity not Mysterious*. In the present volume, he writes, he will "prove [his] Subject in general," which is "that the true Religion must necessarily be reasonable and intelligible." Strikingly but not unexpectedly, he will offer this proof while taking "the Divinity of the New Testament . . . for granted" [b].

The second volume will then be devoted to "a particular and rational Explanation of the reputed *Mysteries* of the Gospel"; this will show that the "requisite Conditions" for the true Religion, namely rationality and intelligibility, "are found in Christianity." The third volume will argue that the "clear and coherent System" of Christianity was not framed by human "good Parts and Knowledge," but "was divinely reveal'd from Heaven."[14] Technically, therefore, Toland is not a Deist, for he calls the Christian faith revealed, but his case is flimsy. His demonstration, in the projected third volume, of "the Verity of Divine Revelation" has a *negative* intention: it is to be directed "against *Atheists* and all Enemies of reveal'd Religion."[15]

But in such a framework, the divine authority of Scripture is no more than a voluntarist postulate; there are no cogent reasons, whether communal or intrinsic, why Scripture should still be respected as of divine origin. In this context, it can be anticipated that in due course the free, unfettered flight of Reason will become far more attractive than any forced homage paid to Scripture. It did in Toland's case, as his fantastical *Pantheisticon* of 1720 showed with a vengeance.[16] Still, Toland's almost total surrender to Reason had been noted earlier, when he had repeated, with approval, a remark made by Benjamin Whichcote, the Cambridge Platonist, to the effect that "natural religion was eleven parts in twelve of all religion."[17] Thus, *il n'y a qu'un pas* from Toland to the full Deism of the En-

---

[b] This late seventeenth-century type of pietistic Christian rationalism is still very much alive in North America. A good example of a linear descendant is the influential Baptist theologian D. C. MacIntosh, a fervent pietist as well as a dyed-in-the-wool liberal. Cf. S. Mark Heim, *True Relations: D. C. MacIntosh and the Evangelical Roots of Liberal Theology.*

lightenment, whose theologians "did not reject the Bible; they found in it only natural religion" [c].

[2] A quick glance at the world of the New Learning, which was developing largely apart from the churches, can only confirm this development. Was methodical Reason not proving its ability to provide far more insight and harmony than theological controversy ever had provided, especially in its discovery of the secure laws governing the heavens and the earth—laws that never will be broken, divinely established for the guidance of the universe? Laws of such geometrical purity and harmony that they could not but provide the patterns for the pursuit of all truth and all goodness? Laws that could be discovered by means of one universally applicable method (cf. §7, 1)?

[a] "The force with which the universal-method mentality could move . . . can perhaps be better appreciated when one observes its inroads into . . . theology in such a treatise as *Theologiæ Christianæ principia mathematica*, published in 1699 by Newton's friend, the Rev. John Craig. The Rev. Mr. Craig . . . is under a pious enough compulsion, . . . for he feels that, since nature is governed by geometry (note the unqualified Newtonian assumption here), geometry must lead to God. Most persons would doubtless agree that geometry, like everything else, must somehow lead to God. The question, of course, is how. By geometrical means, says Craig's booklet."[18]

[3] The theological rationality advocated by Christians like Toland was still residually dependent on confessional Christianity; in fact, that was what entitled them to advertise their critique of divided Christianity. That critique was, at least in the beginning, and quite overtly, their principal agenda.

In a more scholarly vein, the reasonable interpretation of Scripture advocated by the German "Neologians" showed a similar combination of basic rationalism with residual biblical Christianity. However, it did not take long for this unstable alliance between rationalism and faith in biblical revelation to be broken up by the progress of rationalistic Deism, which clearly had the force of logic on its side.

[a] Gotthold Ephraim Lessing, a declared enemy of Christian orthodoxy, yet one who greatly respected its intellectual tradition, had only contempt for the feeble compromises of this residually Christian Socinianism and related forms of "enlightened" Christianity. "[U]nder the pretext of making us reasonable Christians," he wrote to his

[c] Thus Henry Chadwick, in a splendid introductory essay, in *Lessing's Theological Writings*, p. 45. Cf. also §20, 3. Cf. also Chadwick's quotation from Matthew Tindal's *Christianity as Old as Creation* of 1730: "The Christian Deists . . . believe not the Doctrines because contain'd in Scripture, but the Scripture on account of the Doctrines" (p. 18, n. 1).

brother Karl, "we are turned into extremely unreasonable philosophers. . . . We are one in our conviction that our old religious system is false. But I cannot say with you that it is a patchwork of bunglers and half-philosophers. I know of nothing in the world upon the study of which human intelligence has been more acutely shown and exercised. What really is a patchwork of bunglers and half-philosophers is the religious system which they now want to put in place of the old; and with far more influence upon reason and philosophy than the old arrogated to itself."[19]

[4] The forced severance of Reason and the Bible led to a real, though relatively minor, change at the level of *content*: by the time Reason *pur et simple* began to advocate and admire a purely natural Religion, there was not much orthodoxy left to lose among the liberal Christians. Some fifty years after Toland, the inevitable conclusions of this development were firmly drawn by Lessing, who—so the story goes—wanted a notary at his deathbed (not a priest, like Voltaire, after all!) to certify that he had died "in none of the positive religions."[20] In Lessing's view, positive religions are nothing but *conventional constructs*, made "out of the religion of nature, which was not capable of being universally practiced by all men alike." In the concrete order, positive religion is indispensable, but this indispensability lies not in its "modifications" but in "its inner truth, and this inner truth is as great in one as in another. . . . Consequently all positive and revealed religions are equally true and equally false. . . . The best . . . positive religion is that which contains the fewest conventional additions to natural religion, and least hinders the good effects of natural religion."[21]

[a] The Deist mood was able to find this natural religion not only in Nature, but everywhere: in the Bible, in Islam, and in the religions of China and other foreign parts, which were just beginning to fascinate eighteenth-century Europe. It found it even in Sephardic Judaism, which was experiencing a revival, not in the last place because of the trailblazing writings of Spinoza in the previous century.

Deism also showed a fairly fertile literary imagination. Lessing found natural religion, with Nathan the Wise, in a philosophy of universal tolerance that vaguely sounded like Jewish wisdom [d]. Dan-

---

[d] Cf. Henry Chadwick's observation in *Lessing's Theological Writings*, p. 27: "The theology of *Nathan* is the familiar eighteenth-century thesis that all the 'positive' religions are equally true to those who believe them, equally false to the philosophers, and equally useful to the magistrates: that the only absolute is the 'universal religion' of humanity as a whole. What is required of man is not adherence to dogma but sincerity, tolerance, and brotherly love." He also quotes Lessing's note: "Nathan's attitude to all positive religions has long been mine" (p. 44, n. 2). It has been suggested that Lessing's Nathan has more than a few touches in common with Moses Mendelssohn, whose *Jerusalem oder über religiöse Macht und Judentum* argued that the power to enforce belongs to the state, not the church, and that the truths contained in Judaism are none other than those God has taught "by fact and idea" to all rational beings, so that what observances Jews adhere

iel Defoe found it, with Robinson Crusoe, on an offshore island near the mouth of the Orinoco River, in the company of noble savages whose opinions sounded surprisingly similar to those of lower-class urban English dissenters.

[5] It is in Jean Jacques Rousseau perhaps more than in any other writer that Deism shows its true face. Several factors contribute to Rousseau's rare clarity and suasiveness. An important one is the fact that he does not set Deism in the accommodating context of British liberal Protestantism but harshly offsets it against a French Roman Catholicism with Jansenist overtones and cast by Rousseau himself as cold, deliberate, and uncompromising, as well as obscurantist and theologically thin. Yet the principal source of the suasiveness of Rousseau's Deism is the sheer fascination that the author's own immoderate personality and his extraordinary talent inspire.

Unlike John Toland, Rousseau is a dazzling stylist. Like Toland, he is not profound. But far more than Toland, he has his finger on the pulse of the intelligentsia of the period, whose sensibility he knows from inside like others in the century. Like Lessing, he is marvelously versatile—an arguer and sophist rather than a thinker; unlike Lessing, who is ultimately interested in solid positions and ideas, he is the past master of charm, beguiling to the point of being seductive, yet in the most innocent of ways. One of the great prose passages of the century, the "Profession of Faith of the Savoyard Vicar," in the fourth book of *Emile; or, Education*,[22] is Rousseau's classic statement on Deism.

[a] The fictitious speaker is a suspended priest professing his faith (or making his confession?) to a young man. In the first half of this profession, the priest gives an autobiographical account of the unreliability of all systems of religion and metaphysics. Duped and driven into perplexity by all the established authorities, but sustained by an inner love of truth as his sole resource, he recounts how he had at long last entered into his own soul, with Descartes and Locke as his principal guides. In this way he has succeeded in constructing the truth he was always looking for. That truth is Deism pure and simple, of the kind that resolutely refuses to make any definitive affirmations about God or, for that matter, anything else [e].

At the end of his monologue, the vicar—presented by Rousseau

---

to on the basis of the written Torah are a matter, not of truth, but (like all matters of organized religion) of chosen obedience to particular traditions.

[e] Cf. Lessing: "If God held all truth in his right hand and in his left the everlasting striving after truth, so that I should always and everlastingly be mistaken, and said to me, 'Choose,' with humility I would pick on the left hand and say, 'Father, grant me that. Absolute truth is for thee alone.' " (Quoted by Henry Chadwick in *Lessing's Theological Writings*, p. 43.) It would be a mistake to take these noble sentiments at face value; in the context of the eighteenth century, such statements always have a rather more immediate agenda, too: the rejection of Christian doctrine.

as the very embodiment of the twin Deist virtues of simplicity and sincerity—abandons himself to the reader's judgment. In doing so, he characteristically appeals only to the sincerity of his unaided effort and deviously suggests that God is to blame for any errors he may have committed: "I rightly mistrust myself, and so I ask [God] for only one thing, or rather, I expect it from his justice: that he correct my error if I am wrong and if this error puts me in jeopardy. Much as I am in good faith, I do not believe I am infallible. Those of my opinions which I consider the most true may be so many lies, for which person does not hold fast to his [opinions], and how many people agree on everything? Much as the illusion by which I am deceived may have its roots in me, only he can cure me of it. I have done all I could to attain to the truth, but its source is too lofty; when the strength to go any further fails me, what can my guilt be? it is up to it [= the truth] to draw near to me. [In the mean time I am happy, because I set little store by all of life's wrongs, and because the price that redeems them is within my power.]"[23]

This last move introduces the theme of the second half of the vicar's profession of faith. It is a typical example of Rousseau's insidious irony. The vicar himself has raised the issue of the need for Incarnation, if God's truth is to be fully known. Yet in reality he has brought up the subject only in order to deny it. Under cover of apparent innocence our priest explains that there are no reasonable grounds to accept the claims of any of the positive religions: "I consider all the religions as so many salutary institutions, which prescribe, in every country, a uniform way of honoring God by means of a public cult. . . . I think all of them are good when people serve God conveniently in them: the essential cult is that of the heart."[24]

Consequently, Rousseau implies, those who say that the Source of Truth has, in fact, drawn near to humanity are expressing no more than a local opinion. The supernatural reality of the Christian faith is but an empty claim; all we have is Nature. There is more than straightforward unbelief here; this is the rhetoric of polite scorn, knowingly aimed at a weakened ecclesiastical establishment only too ready to be infuriated.

[6] If, therefore, the Savoyard vicar's profession of faith is a fine statement of the *content* of Deism, it is vastly more effective in conveying its *agenda*, both the overt and the hidden. The overt agenda of Rousseau's plea in favor of Nature and Reason is a refutation of Christian orthodoxy. That refutation incorporates elements of what used to be the *critique* of Christianity offered by residually Christian rationalists. But that critique has now been absorbed into Deism to add up to a complete *rejection*: the reader is to understand that Reason positively favors the abandonment of the religion of one's immaturity.

But there is something else going on as well: Reason's plea has the hidden support of Sentiment. The *speaker* in the book merely professes to have been awakened from the illusions of his upbringing and education, to set out on an open-minded search for truth, in simplicity and sincerity; the *reader* is meant to *feel* something else. For Rousseau's agenda encompasses, not just repudiation, but *hostility* and, what is more, *unacknowledged hostility*. This feature of the text must be briefly discussed, for it is precisely in this regard that Rousseau is an especially clear and characteristic representative of classical Deism.

[a] The hostility is conveyed indirectly, by means of savage irony. The entire profession of faith is a brilliant pastiche. The speaker is a priest who has abandoned the faith. What he has not abandoned, however, is his priestly style. His confession is a perverse profession of faith, and he still employs, by turns, the language of faith, of the manuals of spiritual direction, of the Sunday sermon, of the confessional, of pious hagiography, and, of course, of Augustine's *Confessions*.[25] He does so while maintaining a pose of harmless, even pious, innocence.

The vicar confesses that his former life was lacking in full humanity, yet not the vicar but "they" are to blame for that. "I learned what they wanted me to learn, I said what they wanted me to say, I made the commitment they wanted, and I became a Priest; but I did not take long to find out that in promising not to be a man, I had promised more than I could keep."[26] Those "they" are, of course, the Church: "This is what complicated my perplexity. Having been born into a Church which decides everything, which permits no doubt whatever, the rejection of one point caused me to reject everything else, and the impossibility of accepting so many absurd decisions also deprived me of those that were not. By telling me, Believe everything, they prevented me from believing anything, and I did not know where to stop."[27]

These quotations call for a moment of realism. There are some choice rationalizations in this second passage. Even if we grant that totalitarian integralism is the systemic temptation of Roman Catholicism (cf. §20, 1) and that the aftermath of the Reformation had shown excessive reliance on enforced orthodoxy (cf. §28, 1), innocence and blame cannot be apportioned that easily.

What we have here is the presentation of an *emotional contradiction*. Rousseau's vicar denounces an unacceptably totalitarian, ecclesiastical logic to justify his abandonment of the Christian faith, but by attributing that logic to the Church, he covers up the fact that it is also his own. This is nothing but a self-justifying move, which enables him to pose as the advocate of a very different logic—that of truth, simplicity, and sincerity.

This contradiction operates entirely at the emotional level. In one move, Rousseau communicates to his reader a double message: hostility towards Christianity and sympathy for himself, all under cover of the advocacy of Reason. In fact, this emotional contradiction accounts to a large extent for the persuasive power of Rousseau's piece: the author expects that his irritation will become contagious and contaminate the reader. On the surface, the vicar's profession appeals to the impartiality of Reason to undergird certain arguments for the rejection of the Christian faith; below the surface, he treats us to a profession of innocence that serves as a cloak for hostility. And precisely because *the hostility is denied*, or at least not acknowledged, it is all the more virulent. Ingenuous readers feel the impact of that hostility without quite knowing where it comes from; the author, whose prejudice is meant to escape them, conceals his animus behind a front of ingenuous reasonableness.

[b] In this regard, Rousseau is, again, very much a child of his time. It is impossible here to give a full account of the conflicted mood that increasingly came to prevail among the sophisticated in the eighteenth century; a few suggestions, however, are not out of place [f].

The eighteenth century gave us the first medical treatises on a new class of diseases. William Stuckely's lecture *On the Spleen* of 1722 and George Cheyne's book *The English Malady* of 1733 contain the first descriptions of the "lowness of spirits" and other "nervous distempers" which a later age would recognize as neuroses. Cheyne explicitly mentions the fact that it is among "people of the better Sort"—the sophisticated—that "this Evil mostly rages."[28]

The causes are not far to seek; they are related to a new, unsettling way of thinking. The early eighteenth century witnessed the beginning of what is easily the most characteristic feature of modernity: the *experimental approach to humanity and the world*. But this curiously detached, empirical way of life had consequences. It gave rise to the "divided self," specifically in the circles whose initiates were on the cutting edge of "progress." The eighteenth century saw the first symptoms of that process of *dissociation*, and even *disintegration*, of *sensibility* that has continued to characterize the social and individual sensibilities of the West down to our own day.[29]

This process of *dissociation* is curiously paralleled, in the objective order, by the ceaseless cultivation of *division of elements* as a most characteristic feature of eighteenth-century rationality. In 1740, Abraham Trembley discovered that it was possible overnight to produce two freshwater polyps by cutting one polyp in half.[30]

---

[f] J. H. van den Berg has successfully placed Rousseau in the context of the general "deregulation" that characterizes the eighteenth century, in a fascinating study with a wealth of telling detail, *Leven in meervoud* ("Living in the plural").

Around the same time, Carl Linnaeus was working on his division and classification of the vegetable and animal realms.[31] The most intricate mechanical devices were being developed on the basis of a division of operational tasks. Last but not least, there were the first moves in the direction of division of labor—the process that for the first time in history was to turn human beings into parts of an industrial machinery [g].

[c] The unconditional cultivation of rationality had a curious side effect. The world of rational objectivity became so mechanical that the worlds of ethical conduct and feeling got cut loose from their anchorage in rationality and objectivity and began to lead unconnected lives of their own. Christian pietism became the emotional refuge against rationalism. Predictably, ethics flourished. The Deists thought of religion in almost exclusively ethical terms; Christianity, in their eyes, amounted to a "perfectly simple ethical teaching, merely loving one's neighbor."[32] This Deist conception is curiously matched, in the eighteenth-century Roman Catholic church, by a distressing impoverishment of dogmatic theology and an extraordinary interest in moral theology of a very undoctrinal kind.

All these dissociative tendencies were not without effect. Modernity came at a price: the cultivation of individuality and freedom, and the displacement of traditional authority by free, and allegedly purely rational, enquiry and discovery, led to maladjustments in many spheres. Both Deism and Christian orthodoxy suffered from these maladjustments; it is not surprising that many of their encounters have remained downright neuralgic, down to our day.

[d] It would be a mistake to overlook the liberating aspects of these neuralgic developments: they marvelously stretched the range of available human experience and thus also demonstrated the depth and the breadth of humanity's capacity for fulfillment. To mention

---

[g] J. H. van den Berg, in *Leven in meervoud* (opposite p. 160), reproduces a plate entitled *Épinglier* ("pinmaker"), found in the fifth volume of Diderot and d'Alembert's *Encyclopédie* of 1755. The text (*Leven in meervoud*, pp. 170ff.) explains that eighteen distinct operations are needed to make a pin. (Cf. also his *'s Morgens jagen, 's middags vissen*, pp. [60–61].) Adam Smith, in the very first chapter of Book 1 of *The Wealth of Nations*, relates that he visited a pin factory in which ten workers produced in excess of forty-eight thousand pins per day, whereas one single pin maker might produce no more than twenty pins per day. I remember seeing, in a museum in Europe, which I no longer recall, an enormously elaborate eighteenth-century machine, powered by a treadmill, on which at one time, it was claimed, a string quartet could be played. The four instruments had mechanical fingers mounted on them, and there were four circular bows that could whir around. One wonders how the music must have sounded. One wonders even more about the sensibility that conceived such contraptions and proceeded to make them. In any case, it is difficult to imagine a more eloquent symbol of the eighteenth century's mechanical mind. Walter J. Ong has pointed out how Dean Swift's metaphors for thought abound with mechanical images; cf. his "Swift on the Mind: Satire in a Closed Field," in *Rhetoric, Romance, and Technology*, pp. 190–212.

only one example, a more sophisticated technology and better playing techniques produced an unprecedented burst of musical invention. It started with the *empfindsamer Stil* ("sensitive style") of the Mannheim school, spread like wildfire, with a rich variety of talent, and attained its full flower in the splendor of the work of Haydn, Gluck, and especially Mozart.

Yet not all is balance even here. To appreciate the ambiguities of the eighteenth-century soul, one should try, by an exercise of the imagination, listening to Sarastro's aria in Mozart's *The Magic Flute* with the ears of an orthodox Catholic Christian:

In diesen heilgen Hallen	In these holy halls
kennt man die Rache nicht,	vengeance is unknown,
und ist ein Mensch gefallen	and if a man has stumbled,
führt Liebe ihn zur Pflicht.	love guides him to duty.
Dann wandelt er an Freundes Hand	Then he walks, at a friend's hand,
vergnügt und froh ins beßre Land.	content and glad into the better land.
In diesen heilgen Mauern,	Within these holy walls,
wo Mensch den Menschen liebt,	where man is loved by man,
kann kein Verräter lauern,	no traitor lies in ambush,
weil man dem Feind vergibt.	since enemies are forgiven.
Wen solche Lehren nicht erfreun,	Whoever is not gladdened by such [precepts
Verdienet nicht ein Mensch zu sein.[33]	does not deserve to be man.[33]

The figure of Sarastro, high priest of Isis and Osiris, is Mozart's monument to a man he much admired. He was the versatile Ignaz von Born, who had once, in 1787, apostrophized Mozart—then at the height of his maturity—as "graced by Apollo" and who had died shortly before Mozart and his friends Schikaneder and Gieseke started work on *The Magic Flute*. Von Born was a representative embodiment of the protean temper of his age. After a brief period as a Jesuit, he had become a widely traveled jurist and mineralogist and the author of many scientific works. But he had also cultivated more idealistic pursuits: he had founded the Masonic Grand Lodge "*Zur wahren Eintracht*" ("To True Concord")—though only to resign from it again, five years before he died.

Mozart's music is heavenly; Sarastro's words are an indictment of the Catholic Church (and the *ancien régime* it was allied with) as inhumane and punitive—an indictment all the more embarrassing for being kept implicit. Even here, in the midst of beauty, the overtones of the conflict between Faith and Reason can be heard.[34]

[7] It is time to sum up. The principal difference between Deism and the Christian rationalism from which it had sprung was that Deism completed the severance between Reason and the Bible. This involved a small but real difference at the level of *content*. Deism did acknowl-

edge the existence of God and commended natural religion, but the intent behind these two affirmations was never far to seek: both served to relativize positive religion in all its forms [h]. However, since all other known religions had already been interpreted as forms of natural religion, the only real target of the Deist critique was orthodox Christianity, as it had been for Celsus.

What was far more significant, however, was the change of *agenda* produced by the shift to pure Deism: critique turned into hostile repudiation. Repudiation had been Celsus' agenda, too. Yet there was a feature that made the Deist rejection of Christianity decisively different from Celsus': it attempted, forced by its own logic, to keep its anti-Christian agenda *unacknowledged*—is Reason not, by definition, impartial, above the fray? In this way, *critique and repudiation turned into prejudice.* The new tolerance became intolerant of Christianity's alleged intolerance; the modern rejection of all prejudice turned into a prejudice against all alleged prejudice. The advocacy of pure Reason had to resort to *repression* to keep its claim to total impartiality alive. *Tacit contempt of orthodox Christianity began to be cherished as the cultural prejudice of the cultivated.* By the end of the century, Schleiermacher would know whom to address.

[§29] CHRISTIANITY AND MODERN CULTURE: EMOTIONALITIES

[1] All of this leads to an important conclusion. The cardinal issue of the relationship between Christianity and natural religion *as it has come down to us* is not a purely intellectual one; it is charged with *deep-seated emotionality* [i]. We have close to three centuries of nervous conflict to teach us that the intellectual, thematic aspects of the problem can only be constructively broached if its emotional elements are squarely faced. It is the main object of the present section to recognize the *neuralgic, conflicted mood* that has been characteristic both of the Enlightenment

---

[h] Pascal had, as usual, been keen enough to notice this while it was happening. He wrote: "I cannot forgive Descartes; in his entire philosophy he would have liked to do without God; but he was forced to have him flick his finger (*il n'a pu s'empêcher de lui faire donner une chiquenaude*) in order to set the world in motion; after that he had no use for God any more" (*Pensées*, edited by Brunschvicg, n° 77). Two centuries later, Lessing was to complete the argument: "Lessing saw that in the scheme of nature that had come to dominate the mind of the age, this transcendent God, who made no special revelations and was only known to all men alike through the book of nature, was no longer necessary. He may have been the first cause of the world, but he had not intervened since the beginning. He might as well be dead" (Henry Chadwick in *Lessing's Theological Writings*, pp. 45–46).

[i] W. H. van de Pol, therefore, was on target when, after a lifetime devoted to ecumenism, he turned to the fundamental question of theology and modern culture and opened his classic book *The End of Conventional Christianity* with a treatment of an *emotional* issue, namely, *prejudice* (pp. 15–59). Incidentally, the English translation of this book missed the hopeful epigraph that opens the Dutch original and beautifully sums up the author's intentions: "At evening time there shall be light" (Zech 14, 7).

and its aftermath and of Christian orthodoxy in the modern era. Both deserve some reflection.

[2] The new authoritative cultural and intellectual climate brought about by the *Enlightenment* was hostile to Christian orthodoxy. That hostility, however, had a tendency to pose as reasoned impartiality, and many Rationalists acted as if this profession of impartiality sufficed to absolve them from serious intellectual effort. The classical rationalists were dexterous and versatile encyclopedists rather than profound thinkers, and their newfound inventiveness often blinded them to the shallowness of their arguments. But the sad truth is that in dealing with the Church, contempt, not argument, had become the accepted, and infuriating, procedure among the sophisticated—something which very much suited the mood of a century that had adopted lighthearted (and sometimes surprisingly vulgar) mockery as one of its favorite genres.[35] Bishop Joseph Butler was being prophetic rather than peevish, when he wrote, in the preface of his *Analogy of Religion* of 1736:

It is come, I know not how, to be taken for granted, by many persons, that Christianity is not so much as a subject of inquiry; but that it is, now at length, discovered to be fictitious. And accordingly they treat it, as if, in the present age, this were an agreed point among all people of discernment; and nothing remained, but to set it up as a principal subject of mirth and ridicule, as it were by way of reprisals, for its having so long interrupted the pleasures of the world.[36]

The Enlightenment, therefore had internal weaknesses and instabilities of its own, often masked and even repressed by a superficial faith in progress. Its apparent advocacy of religion, in the shape of natural religion, masked a lot of emotional ambiguity.

From a theoretical point of view, this should not come as a surprise. Natural religion does not actually exist except in a relationship of mutual dependence on, and *perichōrēsis* with, some form of positive religion (§25, 3, a; 7; §26, 1; 3). Only at the price of inner conflict, therefore, can natural religion regard itself as entirely autonomous and unprejudiced and view positive religion as naive and uncritical. When natural religion locks the front door against positive religion and its "prejudice," they will enter by the back door, in the form of other, rather less easily detectable and less tractable, biases. Such biases will arrive and insinuate themselves strangely disguised, sometimes even as substitute religions. History has witnessed plenty of self-deception in this area, and there are numerous instances of surprisingly naive creeds religiously held by the enlightened, with a devotion worthy of an infinitely better cause and with an intolerance that is all the more stubborn for parading as objectivity and openness.

[3] Not being taken seriously is neuroticizing, especially when one's weaknesses are exposed. The *Christian faith* was not taken seriously, and

its principal weakness was a serious as well as an immemorial one: Christian theology had forgotten how to deal with educated unbelief.[37]

Theodosius' decrees *Cunctos populos* of A.D. 380 and *Nullus hæreticus* of A.D. 381 had banned, not only paganism, but even heresy; Nicaea and Constantinople I had become the law of the land. Over a period of some thirteen centuries, the Church had gotten accustomed to relying on Christian orthodoxy as the normative cultural and intellectual climate. It had come out of the late Middle Ages and the Reformation and its aftermath deeply divided. Accordingly, the Church's (and the churches') sense of theological priorities had gotten seriously weakened by dint of controversy about doctrines most of which were at least once removed from "the foundation of the Christian faith" (UR 11) [j]. Preoccupation with heresy and specialized doctrine had robbed Christians of the habit of giving a focused, confident account of the really fundamental dimensions of their faith to unbelievers.

Thus, when the Enlightenment became the prevailing intellectual climate, the Church's own resolve was wanting, and its perception of its new, elusive adversary lacked theological precision. At times it fought back so fiercely that it did not look carefully just where to land its blows, and it ended up striking out not at enemies but at hidden allies and friends. At other times it sinned by overstatement, discrediting the very truth it meant to uphold. Sometimes, too, it sought refuge in piety and passivity and bitterly complained when it was being attacked. Much of the time, it drew not only contempt but supercilious ridicule.

[4] In this way, cultural developments with deep roots in the sixteenth and seventeenth centuries saddled *the relationships between the Church and the modern world* with deep conflict. Church and culture, faith and Reason came to be habitually antagonistic, leaving a trail of mutual caricatures throughout recent history.

As usual in such circumstances, voices of authority[38] on every side attempted to settle complex issues by enforcing order and hardening boundaries rather than by promoting patient understanding. The conflict became no less painful where it was interiorized: numerous Christians, especially among the well educated, got torn between orthodoxy and modernity. In the process, a great deal of suffering was caused by a shortsighted anti-intellectualism on the part of far too many leaders in the churches.

The mood of nervous conflict persisted and even deepened when, in the aftermath of the Enlightenment, there was a welcome revival of substantial philosophical and theological reflection. The Romantic era saw the rise of the great humanistic theisms and atheisms as well as

---

[j] This had noticeable effects on theology. It is interesting as well as distressing to see, for example, in Yves Congar's *A History of Theology* (pp. 163–82), how meager the theological harvest of the seventeenth and eighteenth centuries really is.

the first great renewals of Christian orthodoxy. Liberal compromises were numerous, but only few of them, like F. D. Maurice's conciliatory latitudinarianism, were deep and broad enough to last; most were short-lived. The nineteenth century continued to bristle with the conflicts bequeathed to it by the intellectual and sociopolitical developments initiated by the eighteenth. These conflicts ran too deep to be quickly settled, and, in addition, new conflicts kept arising; integration was only very partial and in any case painfully slow. Mutual suspicions and accusations continued to bedevil the theological discussion of the relationship between natural religion and positive religion, between the legitimate demands of human integrity and autonomy on the one hand and the integrity of the Christian faith on the other.

All of this has consequences for theology today. Forgetfulness of history condemns the forgetful to repeating history's mistakes. The eighteenth century witnessed the first moves of what was to be known, in the twentieth century, as *secularization*: the definitive displacement of Christian orthodoxy, as the sole normative cultural climate, by autonomous human Reason. The Church cannot be said to have taken its cultural disestablishment graciously, nor can it be said that it was free enough to extend to the new scientific and sociopolitical humanism the critical welcome it deserved. Yet on the other hand the new culture of human Reason was not as open and impartial as it often professed to be. Orthodox Chritians in the West have long felt that frequently an unfairly heavy burden of proof has been on them. They have felt how their intelligence and their integrity have come under the scrutiny of prejudice, in what is now a thematically non-Christian world. In such a situation, Christians may be tempted to evade the tension by a quick retreat into isolationist integralism, of the militant or the defensive variety, or by looking for cheap modernist compromises.

[5] Both temptations must be resisted. Contemporary Christian orthodoxy and theology must achieve a true, contemporary integration of the best of the tradition that has come out of the Enlightenment and the best of the Christian faith. They will do so to the extent that they will learn freely to respect the concerns behind the modern advocacy of natural religion and equally freely to profess the positive elements of the Christian faith.

Neither natural religion nor Christianity as a positive religion occur in the abstract (cf. §10, 1); both occur in time and space, in cultures and in the historic Christian Tradition. We know the guises the problem has taken on: nature–grace, Reason–revelation, Athens–Jerusalem, culture–religion, State–Church.

This leads to a conclusion. If the first task of theology is the search for new forms of unity—or integration—between faith and culture

(§14, 2), theology must be as patient and diligent in seeking *to under-stand the contemporary cultural shape that the native human religiosity has taken* as in giving *an intelligible account of the positive Christian profession of faith* (cf. §14, 4). The sadness of past conflict can become the wisdom of present understanding. Disintegration does not necessarily lead to permanent degeneration; it may lead up to, and provide the stuff for, broader as well as deeper integration. There are good reasons to think that in the long run convergence is dominant over divergence.[39]

[a] These considerations also serve to put in bold relief the historic significance of the Second Vatican Council. In it, the Roman Catholic Church—even though acting later than many other responsible or-thodox Christian bodies—succeeded in putting an end to the "siege mentality" that had long characterized, not only the Church's rela-tionships with the world, but also the practice of theology in the Church. The Council enabled the Church to recognize the two great attainments of the modern age—attainments that will always remain tasks and never turn into achievements.

The first is the recognition of the potential, the integrity, and the fundamental rights of the individual human person; the second is the recognition and appropriation of humanity's power to affect the structures of nature and human society by means of the responsible deployment of scientific and technological knowledge and know-how. Both are precious as well as precarious, as Vatican II recog-nized, especially in the Declaration on Religious Freedom, *Dignitatis Humanæ*, and in the Pastoral Constitution on the Church in the Mod-ern World, *Gaudium et Spes*. That they are precarious implies that their actualization will be beset with hardship and conflict; that they are precious implies that they are worth suffering hardship and con-flict for.

[b] Dietrich Bonhoeffer's welcome extended to secularization, com-bined with his insistence on the primacy of the act of faith, remains an important example of this integration between Christian faith and modern culture.[40]

[c] The search for a new integration may also take heart from one of the fundamental insights of Pierre Teilhard de Chardin, whose genius embodies the best of the Enlightenment as well as the best of Christian orthodoxy. Teilhard came to view the evolutionary history of the universe in the light of what he called the law of "complexi-fication": developing life is capable, by its ever increasing complexity, of opening up to and embracing and assimilating ever more foreign matter, while at the same time developing higher forms of inner, organic unity.[41] Real openness and a true sense of identity, far from excluding each other, are mutually enhancing.[42]

[§30] CHRISTIANITY AND MODERN CULTURE: THEMES

[1] The observations just made have brought us back to the *thematic aspects of the relationship between Christian faith and modern culture*. It was suggested, in a previous section, that there might be characteristic differences between the two shapes which the critique of Christianity as a positive religion has taken: Celsus' version and the modern, post-Enlightenment one. Neglect of those differences, it was added, might blind us to some distinctive theological issues today (§27, 5). The section just concluded has cleared the way for a survey of these distinctive issues.

Four themes suggest themselves as crucial to the understanding of the religious dimensions of modern culture. Understandably, they are also the themes around which much modern emotionality has crystallized. The first is the *basic quality of the relationship between natural religion and positive religion*. The second is the *integrity of the individual human person*. The third is the *authority of the scientific world picture*. The fourth is *worship as the original act of religion*. Interestingly but not unexpectedly, they are also the four points on which the Deist repudiation of Christianity as a positive religion most strikingly differs from Celsus'.

[2] The first is that Celsus saw Reason and positive religion as *positively related*. This position did involve a reservation about the religions; none were to be considered absolute. Yet in Celsus' view, all religions had positive affinities with a supreme absolute, since all of them were forms of an ultimately reasonable, universal cult of the greatest God. Celsus saw universal Reason as encompassing and permeating the whole world; this enabled those who pursued a life of Reason to accommodate and support and even commend all positive religions.

This shows an important aspect of the classic critique of positive religion. Celsus construed the relationship between natural religion and positive religion *asymmetrically*, in favor of natural religion (cf. §27, 1; 4, b); but this asymmetry did not commit him to a rejection of positive religion. Celsus' objection to Christianity was not that it was a positive religion but that it did not accept his reservation.

The Deist critique of positive religion, on the other hand, was, as a matter of principle, *negative*. In reality, Deism reduced religion to ethics (cf. §28, 6, c) and was unaware of the self-defeating tendencies inherent in its claim to purely natural religiosity (cf. §25, 4, b–e; §26, 3; §29, 2). Lessing's professed contempt for positive religion (cf. §28, 4) is more consistent and honest in this regard than the religious claims of many Deists. In any case—and this is our first suggestion—contemporary Christian theology should be realistically aware of the antireligious tendencies that modern humanism has inherited from Deism, and attempt to show that they are unnecessary. This must be done partly by insisting that natural religion does not have an independent existence (§25, 3).

It should also be done by developing an appreciative approach to the non-Christian positive religions, as Vatican II has shown in the Declaration about the Relationship of the Church to Non-Christian Religions, *Nostra Ætate*.

[a] The real contempt of positive religion implicit in Deism is strikingly conveyed by Henry Chadwick. He writes: "The enlightened thought it morally justifiable to conceal their true opinions behind the mask of orthodoxy. John Toland had made a special study of the practices of ancient philosophers of teaching one thing to the crowd and another to the inner circle of chosen disciples" (cf. §27, 1, a).[43] The tradition of Christian orthodoxy has always rejected such gnosticizing mental reservations. It has consistently placed the positive elements of the Christian faith in a position of superiority over the claims of natural, reasonable religion (cf. §26, 2) and denied that intellectual independence requires a certain amount of pardonable duplicity.

[b] One characteristic way in which the Tradition has put the positive elements of the Christian faith in a position of superiority lies in its taking worship seriously. Geoffrey Wainwright is on the mark when he writes: "In comparison with the language of theological reflection, liturgical language is typically and appropriately more poetic, more affective. But this is hardly licence for holding that one may be a trinitarian within the charmed circle of the liturgy and a unitarian in the academic study."[44]

[3] Celsus' universalist conception of Reason had a second important consequence. Reason was indeed found in individuals but only by way of a *logos spermatikos*—a dissemination of the universal *Logos*. Reason, therefore, *connected* the individual, not only with the divine world of encompassing Reason, but also with the whole universe.

The modern critique of religion is based on a very different experience, namely, the modern experience that Reason *individuates* and even *isolates*. Its characteristic feature, therefore, is the tendency to view *individual freedom and self-consciousness* as the prime locus of authentic Reason. For many modern persons, the recognition of the full intellectual and conscientious integrity of the individual is the decisive credibility test of any positive religion. This typically modern "turn to the subject" (*Wende zum Subjekt*) merits recognition as well as a searching, critical welcome in any contemporary catholic theology. It must be added, however, that it urgently raises the issues of community and personal communication and their relationships with personal integrity—which is our second suggestion.

[a] On this point, contemporary catholic theology is most profoundly indebted to Karl Rahner. His insistence that the Christian faith is to

be interpreted as the gracious fulfillment of the human subject's deepest integrity has settled a long-standing debt owed by Christian orthodoxy to the Enlightenment. This may very well turn out to be Rahner's most decisive contribution to Christian theology, especially since he has not tired of showing also how the fundamental integrity of the human subject, not only individuates, but also opens up to the mystery of God and to the whole world (cf. §14, 4, a; §21, 4, a; §25, 4, e).

[4] In *Contra Celsum*, Origen repeatedly reminds his readers that Celsus' philosophical interpretation of all positive religions fails to respect an essential claim of Christianity. The Christian faith is vindicated, not by means of suasive philosophical argument, but by "demonstration of spirit and power" (1 Cor 2, 4).[45] This demonstration, Origen explains, is especially cogent in the fulfillment of prophecy and in signs and wonders.

Now on these issues, Celsus and Origen had their differences: Celsus thinks Jesus' miracles were performed by means of the magic Jesus learned in Egypt, whereas Origen thinks they were morally superior to magic; Celsus thinks that the Old Testament prophecies are so obscure that they might have referred to any number of people, whereas Origen thinks they predicted the events of Jesus' life. These differences, however, are undergirded by a basic agreement. Both believe that *we live in a world in which God can be encountered*: a world in which wonders and miracles occur, and in which divinity manifests itself in oracles, sibyls, and seers.[46]

This is where the modern issue is joined. Can the Christian faith fully respect human integrity and the relative autonomy of the world, and at the same time claim that God has been, is being, and will be (*and therefore can be*), truly encountered in the world—as both Celsus and Origen agreed? Or does human intellectual and conscientious integrity require of us today that we construe the world in a purely scientific fashion? Is Deism right in construing the world as a closed, autonomous system, which implies that God is ultimately marginal and even superfluous? Even if, with Dietrich Bonhoeffer, we agree to the death of " 'God' as a working hypothesis, as a stop-gap for our embarrassments,"[47] does that also kill the possibility of encountering the living God? This crucial third theme (cf. §23, 3, b) will also have to come up again, as the foundational issue of a contemporary fundamental theology.

[a] Lessing is completely aware of this problem and formulates the difference with characteristic resolve. He deals with the issue in a short commentary whose title he derived from Origen's claim against Celsus: "On the Proof of the Spirit and of Power."[48] He writes: "I am no longer in Origen's position; I live in the eighteenth century,

in which miracles no longer happen. If I even now hesitate to believe something on the basis of the proof of the spirit and of the power— something that I can believe on the strength of other arguments more appropriate to my age: what is the problem? . . . The problem is that reports of miracles are not miracles. These, the prophecies fulfilled before my eyes, the miracles that occur before my eyes, are immediate in their effect. But those—the reports of fulfilled prophecies and miracles, have to work through a medium which takes away all their force."[49]

[5] There is a fourth and final difference between Celsus and the Deists. Celsus respected *cult as the most typical expression of religion* and encouraged the cult of the inferior daemons as a vehicle of the worship of the greatest God. Celsus also respected the mythologies of the positive religions, which he wanted to see allegorically understood (§27, 4, b). His eclectic combination of Stoicism and Platonism understandably gave much prominence to ethics, but it had not completely lost touch with worship and creed. His interpretation of cult and mythology was appreciative, not dismissive.

The Deists, on the other hand, tended to pay lip service to cult but were forever reluctant to engage in its practice (cf. §25, 4, c). Understandably so, for worship is the most nakedly positive element in positive ("organized") religion. To justify their rejection of worship, the Deists (starting a tradition that was to become especially widespread in North America) tended to appeal to two mutually related tribunals.

The first was ethics, to which Deist religion typically reduced itself. What really mattered, so the Latitudinarians had already taught, was simple and sincere virtue, which unites—not worship and doctrine, which divide [k].

The second tribunal was individual conscience. The Deists liked to appeal to it in the interest of the assertion of moral rectitude. So did the Romantics, whose idea of conscience, however, was considerably more profound: they appealed to conscience as the *locus* of a person's fundamental awareness of self-identity. Yet both the Enlightenment and Romanticism agreed that it was in the "inner shrine," whether of moral conscience or of original, unspoiled awareness of self-identity, that true religion—that is, religion independent of doctrine and com-

---

[k] Cf. Henry Chadwick (*Lessing's Theological Writings*, p. 44): " 'Truth' for [Lessing] does not consist in dogma, except for the dogma that there is no dogma. 'Truth' is brotherly love, sincerity, and tolerance rather than a metaphysical interpretation of nature, man, and God. His certainties are moral certainties." In our own day, one of the many distant North American relatives of Lessing is Jacob Needleman, whose numerous works define religion simply in terms of consciousness and love, or—in its highest form—in terms of a "direct human relationship to cosmic nature"; this, obviously, implies a purely *instrumental* conception of positive religion. Cf., for example, his *Lost Christianity* and *The New Religions* (quotation, p. 228).

mon worship—was to be practiced, or rather, experienced: "God being with thee while we know it not."[50]

[6] Our analysis so far would seem to suggest that worship is in some way the element that accounts for the coherence of the three traditional elements of all religion: cult, conduct, and creed (cf. §23, 7; §46, 5). The neglect of worship in Deism produced an autonomous, individualist ethic of an ultimately nondoctrinal kind (cf., again, §25, 4, c–e). It is to be expected, then, that concentration on worship will prove to be a productive opening move to explore Christianity as a positive religion. The next chapter will make this move. Still, one final question remains to be discussed.

RESPECT FOR THE POSITIVE ELEMENTS OF THE CHRISTIAN FAITH

[§31] THEOLOGY AND THE SUPERIORITY OF THE POSITIVE ELEMENTS

[1] *God Encountered* is committed, with the great Tradition, to the thesis that Christianity as a positive religion is hierarchically superior to humanity's transcendental orientation to the mystery of God (which is the basis of natural religion) while yet essentially related to it and respectful of it (§26, 2, a). This leads to conclusions for systematic theology. The method of understanding must be determined by the matter to be understood (§8, 6); it follows that *systematic theology must show its respect for the Christian faith as a positive religion before setting out to give a theological account of humanity's native, transcendental aptitude to receive the Christian faith.* This means at the very least that theology should acknowledge that the former is epistemologically prior to the latter.

[a] Thomas Aquinas explicitly makes this acknowledgment at the outset of the *Summa contra Gentiles*. Even though the first three books will be devoted to discussions based on *natural* reason, it is *the catholic faith* that is to be explained.[51] In the same way, the very first article of the opening *quæstio* of the *Summa Theologica* expressly acknowledges the need for, and the actual existence of, revelation.[52]

[b] The epistemological priority of Christianity as a positive ("historic") religion is also what Karl Rahner implies when, dealing with the relationship between humanity's native desire for God's self-revelation in Christ and the actuality of the Christian revelation, he writes: "The radical human hope in the very self of God, who is the absolute future, looks for an absolute bringer of salvation in history. A transcendental christology as such cannot arrogate to itself either the task or the ability to state that this absolute bringer of salvation can be readily found in history and that he has actually been found in Jesus of Nazareth. Both of these are part of the irreducible ex-

perience of history itself. *In our day*, however, we would become blind to this factual history, if we failed to approach it with the kind of reflective and articulate hope for salvation that is featured in a transcendental christology. The latter allows one to seek, and in seeking to understand, what one had already found in Jesus of Nazareth in the first place."[53]

[2] Consequently, even though theology, as instanced by Aquinas and Rahner, has traditionally opened the systematic exposition of the Christian faith by an analysis of natural religious knowledge, this has never served to deny that the Christian faith is epistemologically prior. Those who fail to realize this fact run the risk of misconstruing the catholic natural theology tradition in Deistic terms. Again, this issue will be fully developed later, in the context of fundamental theology (cf. §26, 1).

[3] Yet there are good reasons at this point to raise the question if the *traditional order of treatment* must simply be accepted as normative. We should also question Karl Rahner's thesis that transcendental reflection is the most appropriate starting point for systematic theology *today*.

It is obvious that the integrity of the human person must be fully recognized today and that the Church's mission includes a mission to take the world seriously. Yet it is equally obvious that orthodox Christianity owes, both to itself and the world, an account of the Christian faith that is both true and matured by reflection and that there are good reasons to assume that such an account is not as readily available as it could and should be [*l*]. The principal reason for this is that much Christian theology has lost touch with worship (§23, 1, a), which, as the next chapter will argue, is the core-experience of the Christian faith, which alone will be able to recall the Church to its original and normative nature (cf. §14, 4). Both the liturgical movement and the emphasis placed on the liturgy by Vatican II point in the same direction (cf. §23, 1, a).[54] There exists, in other words, a *present-day* need for a *positive starting point of systematic theology*. This will have to consist in a renewed concentration on the positive elements of the Christian faith— a concentration that careful attention paid to the worship of the Church can be expected to generate and sustain.

Yet it is also clear that the pressure of modernity works against such a positive starting point. In a curious way, this chapter and the previous one are a demonstration of that very fact. At the end of the fourth chapter (§23, 8), we promised that the second part of this volume would be a positive presentation of the Christian faith itself. We proceeded to make the case that a phenomenology of the Christian faith as a positive religion was as essential a theological pursuit as the exploration of natural religion (§25, 1). Finally, we stated that the Christian faith

---

[*l*] Here lies the ground for Heinrich Ott's critique of Karl Rahner; cf. §14, 4, a, [*k*]; §22, 3, d.

as a positive religion must be recognized as the concrete shape of grace and, hence, accorded theological superiority over natural religion (§26, 2).

However, the problem of the relationship between natural religion and positive religion, in its modern shape, turned out to be more pressing than all the good intentions. The claims made on behalf of the superiority of natural religion, especially over the past two or three centuries, had to be recognized (§23, 8). They proved to be so forceful and pervasive that an investigation of their origins, their content, and their agenda was needed to clear the way for the promised phenomenological sketch of Christianity as a positive religion.

[a] The history of modern theology shows the effects of the pressure exercised by modernity in a variety of ways. Working in very different ways but sharing a deep concern, both Karl Barth and Hans Urs von Balthasar have protested that the integrity of the Christian faith is at bottom a matter of God's holiness and, hence, not up for negotiation. They have often expressed their skepticism about tendencies in Christian theology and practice that, in their view, accommodate the world rather than understand it and look for compromise rather than encounter (cf. §14, 4, a, and [b]). They may have overstated their conviction at times, but their very overstatements at least give us an indication of the pressure to accommodate brought to bear on Christian orthodoxy by modern culture. In a very different yet analogous manner, the aggressive, heavy-handed, sectarian intolerance of much contemporary Evangelical fundamentalism is, minimally, an indication to the same pressure.

[4] Much of contemporary Western culture likes to flaunt itself as post-Christian, yet curiously does not succeed in dismissing the Christian faith altogether. Rather, it puts pressure on Christianity to conform. Could this be a sign of a real, if apprehensive, thirst for the Christian faith? If it is, the Church would betray the world as well as its own mission if it were, in the passionate words of Dietrich Bonhoeffer,

so to trim down and lop off the message as to make it fit the fixed framework; until the eagle can no longer raise itself and soar up to his true element, but becomes, his pinions clipped, one more peculiar showpiece among the other tame, domesticated animals. Just as the farmer who needs a horse for his land leaves the fiery stallion in the marketplace and buys himself a spunkless, tame horse, so domestication has produced a serviceable Christianity. When this happens, it is only a matter of time and common sense to lose interest in this whole construct and turn away from it. This type of updating leads straight into paganism.[55]

[5] These are serious words, spoken, in the critical thirties, by one who had studied the history of liberal Protestantism and found it wanting. Words like these deserve to be taken seriously everywhere.

In the West, especially in Western Europe, this could very well take the shape of a reminder that the prevalent, residually Christian culture has not heard for a long time: not only should the Church listen very carefully to the world, but the world should also very carefully listen to the Church.[56] Such a reminder could, perhaps, also move the Church of the Old World closer to the emergent Church everywhere. The present-day mass conversions, especially to Roman Catholicism, in Africa and in some Asian countries, are reminiscent of the spectacular wave of conversions in the late fourth and early fifth centuries, which created the culture of the Christian West. In such circumstances, the Church owes it to the world to speak and act with authority. That authority is not primarily magisterial, although those in ecclesiastical office must exercise magisterial authority in its service. It is the authority that comes from the "demonstration of the Spirit and of the Power"—of the gospel itself, spoken with boldness and lived out with perseverance.

[6] Speaking with boldness, or *parrhēsia*, as the New Testament calls it, is *mediating*: it is done before God (Eph 3, 12; 1 Tim 3, 13) as well as before people (2 Cor 3, 12; Eph 6, 19). It involves openness to God and openness to the world. But it comes from God. *Parrhēsia* comes to the Church from the resurrection of Christ, which is the source of Christian worship and, hence, of the Christian faith. The next chapter must begin to study it.

Our study of the Christian faith as a positive religion, however, must not lose touch with natural religion. We must remember, therefore, that Schleiermacher suggested that the interpretation of a positive religion must be practiced by focusing on its *structures*; our study of Christianity, in other words, must be a study of the *coherence* of its positive elements (§24, 3–5). Only to the extent that we will succeed in doing this will the Christian faith, viewed as a positive religion, reveal the inner quality that characterizes it as a true religion. Our study of Christian worship, therefore, must be the first, and decisive, step in a larger project: to show the coherence of all the structural elements that make up the Christian faith. In fact, it will be argued that Christian worship is the originating source of all those elements. It will be the task of the next four chapters to explain and argue this.

Part III

UNDERSTANDING THE CHRISTIAN FAITH

CHAPTER 7

Doxology: The Mystery of Intimacy and Awe

THE CENTRALITY OF CHRISTIAN WORSHIP

[§32] CHRISTIANS IDENTIFIED BY WORSHIP: PLINY'S LETTER

[1] Between approximately A.D. 110 and 113, Gaius Plinius Cæcilius Secundus, better known as Pliny the Younger, wrote a series of letters to Rome, to the emperor Trajan. He wrote them in his capacity as imperial legate to Bithynia-and-Pontus, the sizable Roman province comprising the northwest section of Asia Minor, which had recently been in a state of unrest due to inconsistent administration. In one of these letters,[1] he requested, in the measured, curial style of the professional administrator, more precise instructions about policies to adopt with regard to the Christians in his jurisdiction [a].

Christians, he explained, were a problem he had never encountered in his judicial and administrative career thus far, so he felt both ignorant and hesitant. Was he to discriminate between the old and the young? Was he to punish Christians simply on account of membership in the group or only on account of scandalous crimes (*flagitia*) connected with it? One thing he clearly saw was that the very fact of the Christians' existence, quite apart from whatever it was they believed, constituted an urgent problem: resistance and obstinacy of any kind were dangerous and must be met with rigor. He had already ordered a few of them executed, after formally threatening them, by means of the customary, twice-repeated judicial warning, with the death-penalty, so as to give them every opportunity to recant. There even were some

---

[a] Robert L. Wilken, *The Christians as the Romans Saw Them*, pp. 1–30, and Wilhelm Weber, ". . . *nec nostri sæculi est.*" offer instructive discussions of the letter.

Roman citizens who were part of this madness (*amentia*); he had sent them, under escort, to Rome for trial [*b*].

The problem was, however, that since the introduction of the new measures, more and more cases had been coming to his attention. If anything, this religion was contagious. Christians came in all sorts: young and old, men and women; also, they were to be found everywhere, among all classes, in towns and in villages, even in rural areas. This was undesirable for it could undo the recent modest revival of the state religion: happily, temples were being frequented again, and the trade in sacrificial meat (a commodity hardly any buyer had cared to touch until only very recently) was picking up.

To get to the truth, he had recently ordered two maid-servants, "deaconesses" (*ministræ*) in the Christian community, interrogated under torture; not surprisingly, their religion had turned out to be nothing but a corrupt and extravagant superstition (*superstitionem pravam immodicam*). What remained worrisome, however, was the Christians' number; proceedings thus far had already been based on a long list of names, circulated anonymously. This warranted the expectation of a heavy load of denunciations; was it wise to prosecute so many? For these reasons, further imperial directives seemed called for. The provisional measures had already resulted in a few apostasies. Some of those accused had denied they had ever been Christians and had confirmed their testimony by invoking the gods, by burning incense and offering wine libations to the official *simulacra* and to the image of the emperor, and by cursing Christ—things, it was said, nobody would be able to get a true Christian to do. Others brought into his court had admitted they were Christians, but had immediately proceeded to deny it again; they had at one time been members but had left sometime in the past—some three years ago, some more than that, one or the other even as many as twenty years ago.

In the course of the interrogations, it had become very clear to Pliny what the central issue was:

They declared [the governor wrote to the emperor] that their crime (or mistake, if you will) had amounted to this [*hanc fuisse summam vel culpæ suæ vel erroris*]: on a fixed day [*stato die*] they would gather before dawn [*ante lucem*] and together recite a hymn to Christ as to a god, alternating back and forth [*carmenque Christo quasi deo dicere secum invicem*], and commit themselves by a solemn rite [*sacramento*], not to anything criminal, but to avoiding theft, robbery, and adultery, to not breaking their word, and to not refusing to deliver up a deposit when summoned to do so. After that (they said) they would disband, and come together again to have a meal, but with ordinary and harmless food [*ad capiendum cibum, promiscuum tamen et innoxium*]. The latter they had discontinued after I had forbidden all secret associations, as per your order.[2]

[*b*] Cf. Festus' irritated remark about madness addressed to another Roman citizen, Paul, who was also due to go to Rome for trial, in Acts 26, 24.

[2] The letter gives a vivid picture, seen through the eyes of an outsider, of the way in which one particular group of early second-century Christians were trying to lead unobtrusive lives, as some of the Testament communities had long done before them (cf. 1 Thess 4, 9–12; Rom 13, 1–7; 1 Tim 2, 1–2; Tit 3, 1–2; 1 Pet 2, 12–19). If they attracted others (as clearly they did), they did so by virtuous community living rather than by notoriety [c]. When a gubernatorial edict had made closed associations and clubs unlawful,[3] they had even given up what appears to have been regular *agapē* meals. Yet they had insisted on continuing their regular early morning *community worship*.

[a] It is very important, in interpreting Pliny's letter, to notice with some precision just which features of Christianity its author is taking exception to. Pliny recognizes that the Christians' religion involves more than community worship. He mentions a number of moral commitments that Christians undertake; nothing in the letter indicates that he finds them objectionable. He also mentions one community practice: the meals.

This latter feature of the letter is of special interest. It was one of Pliny's main tasks as imperial legate to deal with all kinds of associations in the cities in Bithynia-and-Pontus. Most of these were originally based on common interests and concerns, often of a professional nature; all of them helped city people to secure what is so hard to come by in any urban setting: a sense of belonging.[4] But associations had a tendency to develop into clubs (*hetæriæ*) with a political agenda, and thus they became a potential threat to peace and imperial authority; fraternities tend to be stubborn and to develop a penchant for sedition, not to mention debauchery. It is significant, therefore, that Pliny explicitly recognizes, whether in response to actual rumors about atrocities [d] or not, that what goes on at the Christians' meals is harmless—a fact confirmed by the Christians' own willingness to discontinue the meals after Pliny's ban on *hetæriæ*.

---

[c] In the course of the second and early third centuries, as rumors about hideous crime and debauchery at Christian assemblies increased and multiplied, this was to become an increasingly important theme in the early apologists' defense of Christianity. For a typical early example, cf. the *Letter to Diognetus*, 5; *AF* II, pp. 358–61 (Barry, pp. 39–40).

[d] For a New Testament example, cf. 1 Pet 2, 12. Albert Henrichs has capably argued that "as early as the first decade of the second century the Christians were accused of human sacrifice for ritual purposes, and perhaps more specifically of infanticide, with subsequent drinking of the victim's blood or (less likely) eating from his flesh." He adds that "it is tempting to see a connection between the rumors of Christian *flagitia* and an increased anti-Christian propaganda of the Roman Jews" ("Pagan Ritual and the Alleged Crimes of the Early Christians: A Reconsideration," quotations pp. 20, 24). The list of the Christians' alleged crimes was to be considerably expanded in the course of the second century, as the writings of apologists like Justin, Tatian, Minucius Felix, and Athenagoras show. For some later accounts of such alleged Christian wantonness, cf. Robert L. Wilken, *The Christians as the Romans Saw Them*, pp. 18–21.

Pliny's objection, therefore, decisively focuses on the *common worship* of the Christians. In that connection (and only in that connection), Pliny also takes aim at the *account* the Christians give of the faith implied in their worship. That account, he states, proves that this religion is to be dismissed as being nothing but "a corrupt and extravagant superstition." Is this an unintentional pagan witness to the rule, to be formulated at a much later time: *legem credendi statuat lex supplicandi*—normative faith is to be determined by normative prayer (§23, 1, a; §48, 1, a)?

[3] What does this concentration on Christian worship imply? Pliny makes it clear that he fully realizes that here, and, by the Christians' own admission, he has his finger on two things at once: the *summa*—the center of coherence—of the Christian religion and the very thing that places the Christians outside the law. Whatever Pliny's personal conceptions about Christian worship and about Christ as a god may have been, his account must be read as an unexpected pagan confirmation of a conviction implicit in Christian liturgical practice from the beginning. This conviction is that *Christian worship is the identifying mark of the Christians, and Jesus Christ worshiped as divine is its central theme* [e]. A most characteristic feature of this worship is that it is *incompatible with the cult of any other deity*, including the worship of the divine state, embodied in the image of the emperor.

This raises two intriguing questions. First, is it possible to determine the nature of the worship mentioned in Pliny's letter? Second, is it possible to determine just why Pliny—and the emperor behind him—objected so strongly to Christian worship? Let us take up the first question first.

[4] Older commentators held that the worship referred to by Pliny was a morning Eucharist followed by an evening *agapē* meal. In the early twentieth century, H. Lietzmann argued, with great authority, that it was a baptismal service involving solemn vows, followed later by a eucharistic meal.[5] While there are good arguments for this position, it would seem doubtful that the Christians in Bithynia simply abandoned the Eucharist when the governor banned closed meetings. Even though it is unlikely that the matter can ever be conclusively settled, the problem is interesting enough to warrant another attempt at careful analysis of the evidence.

[a] A close reading of the letter, in pursuit of telling detail, is legitimate only if the text is interpreted with caution. This becomes especially urgent if it is realized that Pliny is using the idiom of Roman state religion to describe the observances of the Christians. This specifically applies to the statement that the hymn is recited *Christo quasi*

---

[e] This is in accordance with a conclusion Vatican II was to draw; cf. §34, 7, a.

deo ("to Christ as to a god"). Grammatically and syntactically speaking, the expression is ambivalent: it can be construed to mean both "to Christ as to God" and "to Christ as if he were God." Yet it means neither; in context, the phrase cannot be interpreted as a pagan commentary—whether positive or negative—on the early Church's belief in the divinity of Christ. Like a good Roman, Pliny is simply observing that the Christians have a god of their own; his name is Christ, and they worship him.

For the same reason, suggestions about the exact nature of the worship must be made and argued with caution. *Carmen* ("hymn") can mean any kind of set liturgical text recited or chanted by persons qualified to do so. *Sacramentum* ("solemn rite") certainly does not have a Christian meaning, let alone the modern meaning of "sacrament."[6] It most probably means a solemn oath ceremony, like those practiced in the Roman army, committing those involved to unconditional loyalty to the state religion.

Still, it is far from inconceivable that the worship at issue was, in fact, the Eucharist. The main argument in favor of this is the complete compatibility of Pliny's account with the far more circumstantial description of the Sunday liturgy in Justin's first *Apology*, written in Rome just over forty years after Pliny's letter, which mentions the Sunday, the cities and the outlying districts, the admonition to a virtuous life, and the prayer with the response "Amen" at the end.[7]

Yet it is possible to note further details. The vague reference, in the singular, to the "fixed day," while conveying Pliny's unfamiliarity with the Christians' calendar, suggests regularity, such as that of the first day of the week. The word *carmen* ("hymn") implies the formulary stability typical of public oral performance in a preliterate culture; this would fit the eucharistic prayer [*f*]. The express mention of the alternation in the reciting of the hymn, besides being consistent with oral performance, recalls not only the responsory shape of the eucharistic prayers preserved in the *Didache*[8] and the people's final "Amen" noted by Justin, but also the much later instruction on the introductory dialogue found in Hippolytus' *Apostolic Tradition* [*g*].

[*f*] We must not assume, at this early stage of the eucharistic tradition, that a presider's liberty to pray "to the best of his ability" (Justin, *Apology* I, 67 [Barry, p. 36; Bettenson, p. 67, mistranslates "with all his might"]) yielded extempore eucharistic prayers. The opposite is rather more likely. In a preliterate culture, public community celebrations such as the Eucharist favor formulary language *at once stable and flexible* (cf. Walter Ong, *The Presence of the Word*, pp. 17–53, 111–75; *Orality and Literacy*, pp. 31–77). Presidential freedom in praying is expressly mentioned, though with a characteristic caveat, by Hippolytus (*Trad. Apost.* 10, 3–5); Tertullian compares it favorably with the scrupulously monitored, fixed forms of pagan prayer (*Apol.* XXX, 4; *CC* 1, p. 141). Thus it is likely that the dynamics of oral performance long sufficed to guarantee that freedom stayed "within the bounds of an accepted shape or structure of prayer" (G. Wainwright, *Doxology*, p. 254 and n. 609).

[*g*] The prescriptive tone of Hippolytus' account (*Traditio apostolica*, 4; *SC* 11bis, pp.

Christian worship inherited all of these features from the synagogue; the latter—the introductory dialogue culminating in the solemn invitation to "give thanks to the Lord" and its reply—originally implied that the meeting was public and official.[9]

There are some other less decisive, yet nonetheless telling features. The communal commitment to a virtuous life implied in the ritual recalls the traditional emphasis on the obligations connected with the Eucharist (cf. 1 Cor 10, 21; 11, 27–29).[10] The mention of the separate common meal afterwards recalls the separation (already observable in New Testament Corinth: cf. 1 Cor 11, 21–22, 33–34) between the Eucharist and the *agapē* meal.

Finally, one phrase in Pliny's letter—that the food shared at the common meal was ordinary and harmless—is intriguing enough to warrant that we go back to it once more. In all likelihood, the phrase simply means that Pliny was persuaded that the common meals involved nothing criminal or outrageous, contrary to what recent rumors had suggested. Still, could it be that this reassuring bit of information came from the very Christians Pliny had interrogated? Had they succeeded in reassuring him on this point in order to divert his attention from the fact that at the worship before the common meal, too, food was shared—food of which it would be very hard to explain to a pagan that it was "ordinary and harmless"?

A minimal, negative conclusion must be drawn from all this, namely, that none of the features of Pliny's account run counter to the suggestion that the worship referred to was, in fact, the Eucharist [h].

[5] The second question concerns the reasons why Pliny—and the emperor behind him—objected so strongly to Christian worship. Pliny's own Roman religiosity was unreflective, superficial, and completely traditional—the combined result of the peasant conservatism of his north Italian origins and the dependable habits of a career devoted to patriotic duty. He "practiced" his religion, but in a sober-minded manner, without any zeal or abandon, and with a sober-minded skepticism vis-

---

48–49 [ET Easton, pp. 35–36; Bettenson, p. 75; Barry, p. 48]), however, is an indication of a cultural shift. By the end of the second century, oral habits alone are no longer sufficient to maintain the authoritative tradition; they now need the support of canonical ("normative") writings. Accordingly, G. Wainwright's account of the rise of *textually* fixed eucharistic prayers correctly identifies *heresy*, not lapse of tradition or memory, as the culprit (*Doxology*, pp. 253–55 and nn. 607–18). The same trend is discernible in the canonization of the Scriptures—a process that started quite some time before the principal formularies of the central prayers of the liturgy (such as the "canon" of the Eucharist) were being laid down. There, too, the occasion was heresy: Marcion's reduction of the Scriptures to ten of the Pauline letters and an edited version of Luke, to remove every trace of the Law from the Gospel (cf. §40, 3, d).

[h] Pliny's statement that the *carmen* is addressed to Christ (and not to the Father, to whom official eucharistic prayers are normally addressed) does not count against this conclusion. In his eyes what counts is that the Christians, like other groups, are identified by their own god—Christ, whom he naturally assumes they address their worship to.

à-vis the practice of divination and dream interpretation.[11] Why, then, should somebody so sensible about his own religion be so intolerant of the worship of the Christians?

Pliny's letters make it clear that he shared, in an unthematic manner, the atmospheric Stoicism that was very much part of the ethos of the Roman establishment during the first and second centuries. Seneca and especially Tacitus come to mind as characteristic literary representatives of this mind set. The latter had some correspondence with Pliny and shared Pliny's rejection of the religion of the Christians, calling it a "pernicious superstition" (*exitiabilis superstitio*)[12]—a view shared by his contemporary Suetonius, who approved of Nero's persecution of the Christians, "a kind of people characterized by a novel and maleficent superstition" (*genus hominum superstitionis novæ et maleficæ*).[13] In sum, while it is hardly conceivable that Pliny thought *what* Celsus was to think a good half-century later (§27, 4, b), it is quite likely that, broadly speaking, he thought *as* Celsus was to think.

Not surprisingly, therefore, he came to call the Christian faith what Celsus was to argue it was. First of all, it was a *superstitio*: an unbecoming show of "unreasonable enthusiasm characteristic of the lower orders."[14] But more importantly, it was a *superstitio prava immodica*: corrupt because it soiled the purity of divine Reason and immoderate because, instead of recognizing the inherent limitations of all ritual observances, it insisted on being incompatible with any other worship and thus refused to respect the common piety of the empire.[15] His (and the emperor's) way of making this point was to attach the death penalty to the obstinate practice of so exclusive and intolerant a worship.

[a] Trajan's rescript to Pliny was as severe as it was moderate.[16] Pliny's general course of action, the emperor wrote, had been correct, yet henceforth the following general policy was to be in force. Christians were not to be rounded up but prosecuted only upon denunciation. Those denounced and found guilty should be punished but not till after being given an opportunity to recant. Those who did so must sacrifice to the gods, by way of confirmation; this would suffice to earn them their acquittal. Anonymous denunciations were to be rejected as unacceptable; not only would they set bad precedent, they were also out of keeping with *nostrum sæculum*—the present, enlightened age.

[§33] WORSHIP IN THE NAME OF JESUS CHRIST RISEN

[1] If any positive conclusion is to be drawn from Pliny's letter, it must be the following. Pliny offers striking, unprejudiced evidence for the thesis that *the Christian Church is decisively*—through far from exclusively—*identified by its worship* and *Jesus Christ is the one telling Name always and everywhere invoked in the worship Christians offer to God.* Here we have the most telling feature of the Christian faith as a positive religion.

There are two coequal aspects to this central feature. The first is properly *theological*. Christian worship is concerned with *God*; the Christian religion's essential theme is God, and it is in worship that God is most emphatically encountered in actuality, *as* the living God.

The second aspect is *christological*. Christian worship is essentially specified by the profession of an *inextricable and mutual bond between Jesus Christ and the living God*. "The throne of God and of the Lamb" (Rev 22, 1) is the center of the heavenly liturgy in the Apocalypse— the model as well as the eschatological fullness of the Church's worship—and to God and the Lamb together is the acclamation addressed: "Worthy!" (Rev 5, 9, 12). Elsewhere in the New Testament, God is worshipfully praised and addressed ("blessed") under invocation of ("in the Name of") Jesus: God is "the God and Father of our Lord Jesus Christ" (2 Cor 1, 3). Conversely, Jesus, whom "God has made both Lord and Christ" (Acts 2, 36), is "the only begotten Son of God" (Jn 3, 18), invoked and professed as Lord "to the glory of God the Father" (Phil 2, 11).

This bond is worshipfully proclaimed as a *present* reality, in the confession of *Christ risen*. The various New Testament traditions convey this complete mutuality between the risen Christ and God his Father in a profusion of themes and clusters of themes: *spirit, word, wisdom, power, life, light, image, reflection, holiness*, and *glory*, to mention only the principal ones. Together, as in a mosaic, these and many other images convey the full compass of the Christian confession in this regard.

[2] This second aspect—the acknowledgment of Christ risen—in turn involves two inseparable, though distinguishable, elements: *identification* and *vindication*.

The first element, identification, is characterized by *transcendence*. The central focus of Christian worship is the *person* of Christ: in the resurrection, *Jesus' transcendent, divine identity* is definitively established. God, *and God alone*, has effectively recognized Jesus, "established as Son of God in power, according to the Holy Spirit, by resurrection of the dead" (Rom 1, 4).

The second element, vindication, is characterized by *historicity*. The Christian Church's worship appeals to *Jesus' historical life*. The living Jesus, revealed in the Spirit as God's only Son, is identical with the Jesus who was crucified: "God has made him both Lord and Christ, that Jesus whom you crucified" (Acts 2, 36; implicit in Lk 24, 39 coll. Jn 20, 20). Consequently, Jesus' identification as God's Son also involves, retrospectively, the revelation, by God, *and by God alone*, of the divine depth of Jesus' life and death.

Christian worship, therefore, has its focus, not only in the *person of Christ alive*, but also in the crucial *event of Christ's resurrection* [i]. The

---

[i] The use of the word "event" raises, of course, the question in what sense, and to

former, the living Christ, is the actual *presence* that has established the Church from the beginning, establishes it now, and will continue to establish it; it has always taken, and it will always take, the risen, present Christ to establish the Church as "the Church of God" (1 Cor 10, 32; 11, 22; 15, 9; 1 Tim 3, 5. 15; cf. Eph 2, 21; 1 Pet 4, 17). The latter, Christ's resurrection, is the decisive, originating *moment* in the Church's worship: in praising God and in giving an account of itself, the Church proclaims that Christ, once dead, is now alive (cf. Rev 1, 18b).

Both elements are abundantly clear in the New Testament. The Jesus that is *invoked* is the living Lord *now*; yet in the invocation, it is *recalled* that God raised him from the dead—this very Jesus (*touton ton Iēsoun*: Acts 2, 36), whose death, ministry, and origins are then also recalled [j].

Both elements demand further reflection. The remaining part of this chapter will elaborate, in two sections, the former element. This, it will be claimed, constitutes the original and originating core-experience of the Christian faith. It is the "idea" (cf. §8, 6, a; §9, 1, a), the determinative and, hence, normative, "naked" essence, the "inner form" of the Christian religion. It is the reality that, while itself remaining inexhaustible, is the soul and the source of all the structures of Christianity precisely *as* structures of *faith*; it is the reality that, while itself being perfectly simple, must integrate and bring to coherence and perfection the entire variety of Christianity's structural elements (cf. §44, 2). Hence, it is the reality that all the structures derive from and point to and without which they ultimately disintegrate.

Only on this foundation, therefore, will the next three chapters be in a position to broach the second element, by offering an account of the fundamental *structures* of the Christian faith (cf. §10).

[3] Before we undertake our task, a word of caution is very much in order. The last five chapters of this volume, it was promised, would involve a "phenomenological sketch" (§23, 8; §25, 1; 3) of the Christian religion. Now while the term *phenomenological* was used broadly, it was not used unadvisedly. It does not mean that the picture to be drawn will simply be a "realistic" one, for the term *phenomenological* is not synonymous with *descriptive*. An integral part of the phenomenological attitude is *epochē*—suspension of judgment with regard to reality as it presents itself in the raw, at first blush. Phenomenology is always searching for the *eidos*—the inner form—of the reality considered as it intrinsically shapes that reality.

---

what extent, Christ's Resurrection can be understood as truly historical. This issue is to be discussed later in this systematic theology, in the context of Christology. But cf. F. J. van Beeck, *Christ Proclaimed*, pp. 192–98, 309–22.

[j] When this insight is applied to the Gospels, the result is the now well-known thesis that the memories about Jesus were recounted and recorded by hindsight, in the light of the resurrection.

Phenomenology is not alone in doing so; it must be recalled that even much of the language of the New Testament conveys the Christian faith's *normative essence* rather than simply offering a *descriptive* account. The real Church we live in and the real Christians we live with—including ourselves—are a great deal less ideal than the language we will use may suggest, especially the language inspired by the New Testament. Yet cold description was never theology's purpose. What is to follow, therefore, is an idealized sketch but not, it is hoped, an unreal one. That is to say, it is hoped that it is a sketch that gives insight, sets standards, encourages thanksgiving, and inspires perseverance, not one that endorses or inspires uncritical thankfulness, let alone righteous self-congratulation.

THE CENTRAL MYSTERY IN CHRISTIAN WORSHIP

[§34] WORSHIP: IMMEDIACY TO GOD THROUGH AND IN JESUS CHRIST

[1] First of all, the Church's worship, which is its *present access* to the actuality of God ("the living God"), centers on Jesus Christ, present [k] as the One whom God has raised to Life, revealed as the Holy and Just One, and exalted in Glory. Christ renders, and indeed *is*, in his very person, the perfect worship to God, his dear Father: the worship that does full justice to the Living God, to the divine Holiness, to the divine Glory.

In this total worship-abandon to the Father, Christ in turn receives, and indeed *is*, in his very person, the plenitude of God. His being alive for God is, identically, his own being alive (Rom 6, 10), with the immediacy and actuality of the life of God. His being in the eternal Holy of Holies, with his entire self to offer (cf. Heb 9, 12–14), is, identically, his holiness: he is holy as the Father is holy. The One who does not seek his own glory (Jn 8, 50) is the One who gives glory to the ever-gracious God alone; thus, he is wide open to the Father's glory, which makes him "the Lord of glory" (1 Cor 2, 8) and fills him with the gracious fidelity that is of God (Jn 1, 14). In analogous ways, Jesus Christ, alive and present, is invoked as "the power of God and the wisdom of God" (1 Cor 1, 24), as the light that dispels the darkness of death (Eph 5, 14), as "the Spirit" (2 Cor 3, 18).

[2] The Church worships God by *appealing to Christ's perfect worship*. Its access to God is *mediated*: the Church worships "*through* Christ" (Rom

---

[k] Among modern Christologies, two stand out for making Christ's presence the starting point of the discussion: Dietrich Bonhoeffer's *Christologie* (ET *Christ the Center*) and Hans Frei's *The Identity of Jesus Christ*. Neither, however, opens his treatment with a discussion of worship. In *Christ Proclaimed*, I have attempted to do so. The present discussion retrieves some of the explanations offered there (esp. pp. 232–51; 325–57) and expands them to press them into service as foundational elements in Christian theology.

1, 8; 5, 1; 16, 27; 2 Cor 1, 20; 1 Pet 2, 5; 4, 11; Eph 2, 18; Heb 7, 25; 10, 19–22; 13, 15).

But if Christ mediates, he does so, not as the Church's (or indeed, humanity's) *substitute*, but as their *representative*. Now whereas *substitution excludes participation, representation invites it.*[17] Christ, therefore, mediates, not in such a way as to keep the Church at one remove from God, but precisely so as to unite it with himself *in* the very act of self-abandon that unites him with God. Christ's mediation, therefore, involves *an integral element of immediacy:*[18] in Christ, Christians truly know the God they worship—a God who becomes more, not less, adorable and un-graspable (*akatalēptos*, the Greek Fathers say) for being so intimately known.

Awareness of this immediacy shows in a variety of New Testament assurances and images: Jesus' assurance, to the disciples, of God's own immediate love for them, for his sake (Jn 16, 27); Paul's confidence (*parrhēsia*) before God because of Christ (2 Cor 3, 1ff.); insistence on the community's access to the throne of grace, again in confidence (*parrhēsia*), because of Christ's presence in the eternal sanctuary (Heb 4, 16; 10, 19); the conviction that communal love out of faith in Jesus is evidence of God's immediacy (1 Cor 8, 3 [*l*]; 1 Jn 3, 23–24; 4, 7–12); the unimpeded vision of the throne of God and of the Lamb as the guarantee of Christian hope (Rev 3, 21; 5, 13; 6, 16; 7, 9–10. 15–17; 14, 3–4; 22, 1. 3).

[3] Thus the Church radically worships the Father by *participating in the very being of Christ*, that is to say, *in his perfect worship*. In virtue of the one Spirit, who unites us in the one Body, constituted by the profes-sion of Jesus as the one Lord, we worship the one Father (cf. 1 Cor 12, 3ff.). The essential unity of the Body in all its manifestations, there-fore, is ultimately rooted in the unity of God the Father, worshiped as the One who effectively means to be "all in all" (1 Cor 15, 28) and who is above all and through all and in all (Eph 4, 4–6). In this way, the Church worships the Father "*in* Christ" (cf. Eph 2, 13–18; cf. Rom 12, 1–12).

Jesus Christ, then, is the present One who mediates to the Church the presence of the living God and who prompts and guides and bears the Church's access to the living God, in worship. In Christ, too, the Church is divinely assured that it is worshiping the Father "worthily" or "perfectly" (cf. §38, 3, b)—that is to say, as God deserves to be worshiped, and with a worship whose generous abandon matches the divine graciousness that prompts it. At heart, the Church's worship does complete justice to God: it is offered "in Spirit and truth" (Jn 4, 24).[19]

[*l*] According to the *lectio difficilior* of codex *p*⁴⁶: "But if someone loves, that person is known [i.e., by God]."

No wonder that the Church experiences herself, like Israel just led out of Egypt, as God's own holy, and hence priestly, people (Ex 19, 6; 1 Pet 2, 9; Rev 1, 6; 5, 10; cf. LG 10). In the Apocalypse, this takes the form of the realization that ultimately "God and the Lamb" are not merely the *center* of the Church's worship but also its *encompassing reality*: "I saw no temple in the city, for the Lord God the Almighty is its temple, and the Lamb" (Rev 21, 22).

This worship in Christ is the worship of the Church as well as of its members. The worship of individual Christians, therefore, is analogous to the Church's worship. All Christians are holy and called to holiness. They are temples of the Spirit, united with Jesus Christ and shaped by him, and thus dedicated to the glory of God in their very persons. If, then, the Church worships *in* Christ, so do the individual members, in whom the Spirit is active, in whose hearts Christ dwells by faith, who grow into the fullness of God, and thus personally participate in the praise the Church offers to God (Eph 3, 14–21). The mysticism of the Church is the mysticism of its members. In the worship of the Church, therefore, we strike upon the prototype and the root of what, according to John of the Cross, the soul does in mystical prayer: "In God she gives God to God-self."[20]

[a] The traditional doxological formula "through him, with him, and in him" suggests that *association* "with Christ" should be added to *mediation* ("through") and *participation* ("in"). Curiously, it turns out that the two Greek prepositions *meta* and *syn* (both of them meaning "with") are relative latecomers in the doxological tradition. When the expression "with Christ" begins to occur in the classical doxologies, it serves, not to associate *the Church* with Christ, but to associate *Christ with the Father*. Eventually, its purpose came to be, invariably, to emphasize, against Arianizing tendencies, Christ's coequality with the Father in divinity.[21]

This post-Nicene modification completely determines the theological perspective of the doxology and thus decisively modifies the original meaning of the prepositions *through* and *in*. In the new formula, *all three* prepositions in the doxology serve to express, not the Church's relationship with Christ, but the relationship between Christ and the Father, who is the original focus of the classical doxologies. The meaning thus becomes: the Father receives the Church's glorification through the mediation of Christ, together with Christ, and in Christ; and Christ is the channel, the co-recipient and the summing up of the Church's worship. The idea that *the Church*, in worshiping the Father, is related to Christ by way of *association* turns out to have no support in the doxological tradition, either before or after Nicaea (A.D. 325).

The *doxological* expression "with Christ," therefore, turns out to serve the same doctrinal purpose as the gradual introduction, in the course of the fourth century, of the (coordinating) doxology "Glory be to the Father *and* to the Son *and* to the Holy Spirit" to replace the classic (but seemingly subordinationist) formula "Glory be to the Father *through* the Son *in* the Holy Spirit." This latter, more ancient formula conveys *only mediation and participation*: mediation is conveyed by the phrase "through Christ" and participation by "in the Holy Spirit." The latter phrase encompasses, not only Jesus Christ's unity with the Father and the Church's unity with Jesus Christ, but also the actuality of Christ's resurrection as the effective origin of both (cf. §48, 3, a).

[b] The question remains, however, whether (the doxological traditions aside) there is a sense in which the Church can be said to be truly associated "with Christ" in worshiping the Father. Does the idea of the Church's association with Christ in worship have any support, say, in the New Testament? What, for instance, does the expression "with Christ" (together with its equivalents "with me" and "with him") mean in the New Testament?

Since our theme is the Church's worship now, we should leave aside, for present purposes, the instances where the expression refers, either to the *Father's* association with Christ (as in Jn 8, 29; 16, 32: Acts 10, 38), or to the *disciples'* companionship with the *historical* Jesus (as, for example, in Mk 3, 14). Instead, our discussion must focus on those instances in which "with Christ" conveys *the Church's or Christians' present or future association with the Lord.*

Where the New Testament uses "with Christ" to express this association, it does so by means of two different Greek prepositions. *Meta* is found in the Johannine writings and the Apocalypse. There it signifies the disciples' present communion (Jn 11, 16; 13, 8. 18; 1 Jn 1, 3. 6) and future association with Christ in glory (Jn 17, 24; Rev 3, 4. 20. 21; 14, 1; 17, 14). Nowhere, however, is the reference specifically to *worship*. With one exception, where the reference is eucharistic (Acts 10, 41), *syn* occurs exclusively in the Pauline corpus. There, *syn* is sometimes found as a separate preposition but far more often as the prepositional prefix *syn-*, in compound verbs and (a few) adjectives. In the vast majority of cases, the companionship with Christ is a matter, either of Christians' *present suffering*, or of their *hope of future glory*, or (especially in Colossians) of a combination of these two themes (Rom 6, 4–6. 8; 8, 17. 29; 1 Cor 9, 23; 2 Cor 4, 14; 7, 3; 13, 4; Gal 2, 19–20; Eph 2, 5–6; Phil 1, 23; Col 2, 12–13. 20; 3, 1. 3–4; 1 Thess 4, 14. 17; 5, 10; 2 Tim 2, 11) [m]. Again, nowhere is the reference specifically to *worship*.

---

[m] In Rom. 8:32 the context is, again, Christ's suffering and death, but the theme is God's giving us "all things with him."

It would seem, therefore, that the New Testament places the Church's association with Christ, not so much in the act of worship, as in the *lived Christian life*, viewed, in faith and long-suffering hope, as the *pledge of eschatological association with Christ in glory*. However, Christian worship is not a pursuit entirely separate from life, as will be argued (§41, 2); on the contrary, it involves and engages the entire dynamic of the Christian life (cf. Rom 6, 13; 12, 1ff.; 1 Cor 6, 20; 10, 31; 1 Pet 2, 5). Association with Christ by obedience, in imitation and discipleship, therefore, must be understood as integral to Christian worship. In fact, two powerful New Testament images associated with worship imply this: Body and Temple [*n*]. Praising and giving thanks to the Father in the Body of Christ implies obedience, on the part of the members, to Christ as Head (Eph 1, 15–23; Col 1, 12–20); worship of the Father in the temple of the Spirit implies obedience, on the part of the "living stones" to Christ the cornerstone (Eph 2, 20–22; 1 Pet 2, 4–5).

[4] The New Testament and the doxological tradition, therefore, have their differences; both, however, agree, in their very different ways, on one fundamental idea: in Christian worship, addressing the Father and addressing Christ go hand in hand. This addressing is done by means of invoking, and invoking takes the form of *naming*.[22] It is not surprising, therefore, that the Tradition, from the New Testament onward, has cherished, not only a variety of "divine names" (especially by drawing on Israel's precious heritage of worship), but also a variety of *christological titles*, in which Christ's unity with the Father are conveyed: Lord, Christ ("[God's] Anointed One"), Son of Man, Son of God, the Son, only begotten Son, Son of David, the Savior, to mention only the principal ones [*o*].[23]

[5] How is this inextricable bond between God and Christ, so confidently professed in Christian worship, *established*? Negatively speaking, it is *not* originally established apart from worship—say, by insight and intellectual affirmation, which would then lay the basis for worship. Rather, the reverse is the case: *it is the actuality of the bond, revealed in the risen Christ, that originally establishes the worship*. Insight and affirmation are the *product* of a divinely prompted, original act of worship, and not the other way round.

To express the total originality of the Christian profession, Paul even draws a parallel with the first creation: "For the God who spoke, 'Out

---

[*n*] Eph. 2, 11–22 oscillates between these two images and thus shows their organic connections. It is tempting to connect the interplay between "Body" and "Temple" with the fact that the bodily resurrection of Christ was at an early stage linked up with the Jewish accusation that the Christians, like their Master, were "saying bad things about this holy place" (Acts 6, 13–14; cf. Mk 13, 2 parr.; 14, 58 parr.; Mt 27, 40; Jn 2, 19).

[*o*] Other christological titles principally serve to articulate Christ's relationship with the Church; we will come back to the latter (§42, 2).

of darkness, let light shine,' is the God who has shone in our hearts, bringing the enlightenment which is the knowledge of the glory of God in the face of Christ" (2 Cor 4, 6). This needs an explanation.

In the resurrection, what is revealed is Christ's total worship-abandon to God his dear Father and the Father's total self-commitment to his dear Son, Jesus Christ. These two *are* the actuality of the very life of God. This is the Christian meaning of the confession that *God is Spirit*: the living God has become a matter of actual experience. There are two aspects to this.

On the one hand, the actuality of divine life is *intensity and intimacy*: the Spirit is the inner vitality of the *mutual presence* of the Father and Jesus Christ in an encounter of holiness, glory, power, wisdom, light, and life. On the other hand, it is *majesty and abundance*: the Spirit is the actuality of God's *eradiating presence*, filling and firing (that is, enlivening as well as testing) the whole world (Wisd 1, 7), prompting worship as well as awe (Is 6, 3). The Spirit is at once the *intimacy* between the Father and Christ and the *energy* that emanates from that intimacy; in both senses *the Spirit is the divine actuality that compels and empowers and carries Christian worship.*

> [a] Hans Urs von Balthasar points out that the two are complementary conceptions of the Holy Spirit. The West preferably conceives the Spirit of God in terms of self-contained self-possession, in the mutual reflection of Father and Son; the East favors the conception of God's Spirit in terms of absolute effusion of totality of being—the emanation of life from the Father through the Son.[24] These two complementary pneumatologies are matched, of course, by two complementary conceptions of the reconciliation of humanity with God: the East favors *salvation by divinization*; the West, *salvation by the gift of grace.*

[6] The risen Jesus, present in the Spirit, therefore, evokes, not detached affirmation of, but *participation* in, his divine identity. Professing Jesus' divine Sonship involves *us*;[25] involvement with God's Son makes us children of God. *This participation is gift*, and only God's to give. The New Testament conveys this by having the risen Christ communicate *the Holy Spirit* (Jn 14, 16), "as the one who in himself reveals the divinity of the Lord."[26] It is in virtue of the Spirit, therefore, that we worship God, by professing Jesus as the Risen One,[27] as God's Son, as Christ, as Lord (1 Cor 12, 3; cf. 1 Jn 4, 2–3; Phil 2, 11). By the Spirit, too, we come to fathom the very depths of God (1 Cor 2, 10ff.; cf. Jn 4, 23–24) and receive access to all truth (Jn 16, 13). Drawn by the Spirit into Christ's Sonship, we are God's children (Jn 1, 12; Rom 8, 16), addressing God as Jesus did: "*Abba*—Father dear!" (Mk 14, 36; Gal 4, 6; Rom 8, 15–16). Hence, what Christ is by "birth" or "nature" we are by "adoption" (Gal 4, 5), "rebirth" (Jn 3, 3), or "grace": "sharers of the

divine nature" (2 Pet 1, 4) or, as the Church Fathers liked to say, "gods by grace."

For the Church this means, in its worship, which is truly its own, it is also out of its depth. Having received the Spirit of God, it does indeed "fathom the depths of God" (1 Cor 2, 10); the Spirit testifies, *along with* our own spirit, that we are children of God, addressing God as "Father dear" through and in the Beloved Son (cf. Rom 8, 15–16; cf. 1 Jn 2, 23; 3, 1). Yet at the same time Christian worship runs deeper than our conscious, free participation in the Spirit. The inner witness of our own spirit to God, no matter how divinely eloquent, is ultimately *not* decisive; as a matter of fact, "we do not know how to pray as we should" (Rom 8, 26). Most deeply, therefore, it is the ineffable "groans" of the Spirit that carry the feebleness of Christian worship before God, who fathoms human hearts and understands what the Spirit means (Rom 8, 26–27).

[7] Worship is not the only activity by which the Church is caught up in the very life of God; it is, however, the activity in which this is most manifestly and most irreducibly the case. In its worship, the Church draws closest to the mystery at its center; the direct encounter between God and humanity in the person of Christ (cf. §23, 2)—in a Holy of Holies in which intimacy and awe meet and find one another.

The Church is likely to cherish the infinite intimacy of this mystery only according as it cultivates its sense of awe, and *vice versa*. If, then, the Church is to be faithful to the mystery that is its very life, it must live, both in awe of it and in its intimacy; and live in these two it only can by consistently living in the school of worship—by agreeing to be itself "a temple holy in the Lord," a "dwelling-place of God in the Spirit," (Eph 2, 21–22; cf. 1 Cor 3, 16–17; 2 Cor 6, 16ff.; 1 Pet 2, 5). "Be constant in prayer" (Rom 12, 12; cf. Luke 18, 1; Acts 1, 14; 2, 42; 6, 4; Eph 6, 18; Col 4, 2; 1 Thess 5, 17–18). The great, multiform, truly catholic variety of the Christian Church's living structures—gifts, services, and energies—is ultimately coherent only to the extent that it draws on the inner sanctuary, where the unity of Spirit, Lord, and Father (1 Cor 12, 4–6) is glorified and, in the glorification, experienced as the source of the Christian life. That experience is at the heart of the Church's worship.

[a] "From this it follows that every liturgical celebration, because it is an action of Christ the Priest and of his Body the Church, is a sacred action surpassing all others. No other action of the Church can either claim or equal its efficacy" (SC 7; cf. LG 50).

[b] The fusion of awe and intimacy in worship is the Christian fulfillment of the core of *Israel*'s relationship of awe and intimacy with its God, summed up by Ex 3, 14: "I am who I am"—an expression that acknowledges God's unconditional transcendence as well as

God's unconditional presence. Its meaning (as will be explained later) could be rendered by "I am totally beyond you as much as I am totally with you."

[c] Odo Casel has shown how the fusion of mystery and spirit in the Christian liturgy succeeded in reinterpreting and transforming the yearning for truly spiritual sacrifice in ancient mysticism, both in Hellenism and Judaism.[28] But the experience of worship just described is also the characteristically Christian actualization of the experience of the Holy in *all religions*: the fusion of awe and intimacy. In his masterpiece *The Idea of the Holy*, Rudolf Otto has shown how, while the *form* of the Holy is *mystery*, its substance comprises the qualities of *tremendum* (awe-inspiring) and *fascinans* (attractive).[29]

[d] Finally, since the worship of the living God in and through Christ risen is the activity of the Spirit before it is the Church's activity, the experience of worship most closely approximates the experience of *asymmetry* in the divine-human encounter (cf. §23, 4, b). The next chapter will develop the idea that the concrete shape of Christian worship is an expressive account, uttered by the Church in praise of God, of its encounter with the divine condescension. This account, it will be shown, is a soteriological narrative, which is not only the substance of the Church's worship, but also the warrant for the Christian life and the rule of Christian teaching. The present chapter serves to emphasize that the Church's worship, life, and teaching are indebted, for their very existence, to a divine self-communication that is as inexhaustible as it is ineffable. The self-communication of God permanently encompasses the response it prompts and empowers; the living God remains the transcendent presence, to which the Church is but the response (cf. §23, 4, c). It is principally (though, again, not exclusively) in the act of worship that this asymmetry becomes a matter of actual experience.

[§35] SAFEGUARDING THE INTEGRITY OF CHRISTIAN WORSHIP

[1] The analogy between the traditional Christian understanding of the mystery at the heart of the Christian faith and Rudolf Otto's fundamental analysis of the experience of the Holy is striking enough to invite further reflection. This reflection mainly serves to affirm and emphasize the idea—that is, the normative essence—of worship, as the most direct expression of the encounter between God and humanity and its world. We will argue, therefore, in favor of the originality and authenticity of worship; we will also caution against all attempts, Christian as well as non-Christian, to reduce the central act of the Christian religion, or indeed of any religion, to something else.

The central reality of the Christian faith, we have explained, is *encounter in ecstatic immediacy*, initiated and carried by the Spirit, that is to say, by the very presence of God. God's living presence in Christ both lifts the Church *out of itself* and *identifies* it, and prompts it to *respond to God* by sharing in the living encounter between Christ and the Father. In this way, the Church worships the living God through and especially in Christ, that is to say, it worships God "worthily"—the way the living God deserves to be worshiped.

The Church itself is deeply changed by this; by being united with Christ in the Spirit, it, too, is made essentially holy and glorious. The Church's essential identity, therefore, is not self-established but responsive: it comes about by ecstasy.[30] Only to the extent that the Church responds to God in Christ risen does it *share*, and therefore *mediate*, the divine life, holiness, and glory. Any true attractiveness or effectiveness the Church may have in the world is predicated on this worship-encounter. Yet the inner value of worship lies neither in attractiveness nor in effectiveness, no matter how real they may be. For worship resists reduction. Worship is abandon, not cultivation, of self. Its focus is away from self, on God. Elicited by God's presence, to God's presence it responds, with fruits beyond intending and thus beyond all telling. The only adequate and lasting reason for worship is: that God is God.

[a] David Jenkins, therefore, is right in explaining that there is "an essential element in the knowledge of God which has always been present within the Biblical and Christian understanding of Theism. It is this—that *the authenticating knowledge of God is not derived but direct.*"[31] He might have added that it is the experience of the ecstatic immediacy of worship that principally accounts for this very traditional understanding.

[b] Responsive recognition of divine presence is, phenomenologically speaking, a feature that the Christian faith, *in its own specific way*, has in common with most religions. In fact, it has been argued (though the arguments have not met with universal acceptance) that it is the original characteristic of *all* religions, even of the so-called developed religions, in which the central act of worship is orchestrated, and sometimes even overlaid, by secondary, expressive, *religious-cultural* accretions.

A most important conclusion follows from this. Non-Christian religions must not be exclusively interpreted as *expressive actualizations* of the universal human *religious a priori*, as Deism and allied traditions have tended to do (cf. §28, 4, a). Rather, they must also, and even principally, be interpreted in *positive* terms: as traditions of *responsive encounter* with the *transcendent*. This is most pointedly actualized and concretized in worship, for the heart of all worship is encounter with the divine, in the immediacy of *ecstasis*. In worship, believers of all kinds address themselves, with characteristic, self-less abandon, to a transcendent reality they encounter outside themselves and to which they offer religious homage.

This is also recognized by Vatican II: "From ancient times down to the present, there has existed among diverse peoples a certain perception of that hidden power which hovers over the course of things and over the events of human life; at times, indeed, recognition can be found of a Supreme Divinity and of a Supreme Father too" (NA 2).

From this a basic conclusion must be drawn regarding the theological interpretation of non-Christian religions. Not only should Christian theology interpret the Christian faith as the concrete shape of grace, and, hence, accord to it theological superiority over natural religiosity (§26, 2; cf. §23, 3, b); it should also interpret non-Christian positive religions in the same perspective—as the concrete shape of the actual encounter of human persons with God.

This conclusion is heavy with consequences, the most important being that Judaism first of all, but then also the world religions, can be the vehicles of the acceptance of divine grace as well as its rejection. This applies very concretely to the "sacraments of the Old Testament" and the "sacraments outside Christianity."[32] A full discussion of this, however, will have to wait till later.

[c] Worship gives rise to thought. It is part of human intellectual integrity to wish to understand, interpret, and explain a phenomenon at once so obvious and so mysterious and to attempt a critique of it. Yet a caution is in order: explaining worship is not the same as explaining it away, and offering a critique is not the same as reducing it to something else. It is realistic, therefore, to recognize that the pressures to interpret worship in reductive ways are powerful indeed. These pressures deserve to be clearly recognized as well as firmly resisted, if only in the interest of *safeguarding the integrity of the phenomenon of worship* itself. This observation is especially relevant to non-theological definitions of religion.

A simple example to clarify this. From the point of view of some of the social sciences, it is obviously correct and illuminating to say that a ("primitive") community's religion is the ultimate organizing principle of all its insights, values, and structures. Yet phenomenologically speaking, it is incorrect to ignore the fact that the *obvious intentionality* of what certainly is one of the most characteristic acts of religion, namely *worship*, is towards the *deity*, not the community. To suggest that the "real meaning" of worship lies in its ability to provide the community's structures, insights, and values with their ultimate coherence amounts to giving a reduced account of worship, and hence of religion.

[2] In *Eclipse of God*, Martin Buber has studied the pressures, both the intellectual and the religious-cultural ones, that favor such a reduced account of religion. The fundamental thesis of this important book is worth pondering. Buber writes:

The true character of a period is most reliably known from the relationship between religion and reality that prevails in it. In some [periods], that which people "believe in" as something absolutely independent of themselves and existing in itself is a reality to which they stand in a real relationship, although they can form only a most inadequate representation of it, as they well know. In other [periods], on the other hand, this reality yields to the current representation of it, which people happen to "have" and which accordingly they can handle; in due course [it may] even [yield] to the residue of the representation—the concept, which retains only faint traces of the original image. People who are still "religious" in such times usually fail to notice that the relationship that they conceive of as religious no longer occurs between them and a reality independent of them, but only within their own minds. . . .

Thus what is decisive for the genuineness of religion is . . . that I relate myself to the divine as to a Being which is over against me, though not over against me *alone*. Complete enclosure of the divine in the sphere of the human self abolishes the divinity of the divine. It is not necessary to know something about God in order really to mean God, and many a true believer knows how to speak to God but not about Him. The unknown God is the legitimate object of religion, but only if one dares to lead one's life toward Him, to seek to encounter Him, to invoke Him; those who refuse to limit God to the transcendent have a better conception of His greatness than those who do so limit Him. But those who confine God within the immanent mean something other than Him.[33]

[3] Rudolf Otto has also recognized this, despite the fact that some of his philosophical assumptions made it hard for him to resist the reductionist pressure. Like a good neo-Kantian, Otto is suspicious of the *rational* element in religion: ". . . orthodoxy found in the construction of dogma and doctrine no way to do justice to the non-rational aspect of its subject."[34] However, he hastens to add that it is an equally serious mistake to follow Kant in interpreting religion solely in terms of "the perfectly *moral*." What has to be accounted for is *the Holy*, and if rationality cannot adequately account for it, neither can morality. Instead, it must be viewed as a distinctive, irreducible category, providing us with the proper way to interpret and valuate religion. The Holy is perceived exclusively in "a unique original feeling-response, which can be in itself ethically neutral and claims consideration in its own right."[35]

[a] This insight moves Otto close to Schleiermacher's analysis of religion in terms of the characteristic experience of *absolute dependence* (cf. §24, 1–4; §25, 2; 4, d–e),[36] but with a decisive difference. In Schleiermacher's *Speeches*, not *encounter with God*, but *piety* and *self-consciousness* are the decisive categories: "true religion is sense and

taste for the Infinite,"[37] which implies that "the Infinite . . . we cannot be conscious of immediately and through itself."[38] For Schleiermacher, therefore, the Infinite is attained only *indirectly, in* the depth-experience of the finite self;[39] that experience then provides the basis for inferences about the Infinite, drawn from an analysis of self-consciousness. This is precisely the conception that Martin Buber has criticized. A modern commentator has summed it up by writing, "God is out though godly attitudes may be in."[40]

Otto carefully aims his critique at this crucial thesis of Schleiermacher's. He grants that there is indeed an element of immediacy in our attainment of the Infinite but adds that Schleiermacher's choice of words, "feeling of absolute dependence," curtails the experiential data and thus prejudices their interpretation. A better way, both to describe the experience and to convey what is involved, is to use the term *creature-feeling.* This implies *contrast,* and thus it also implies a reference to *a reality that is experienced as distinct* from the experiencing subject.

Otto explains: " 'creature-feeling' is itself a first subjective concomitant and effect *of another feeling-element,* which casts it like a shadow, but which *in itself indubitably has immediate and primary reference to an object outside the self."*[41] Otto, in other words, recognizes that we deal with the Infinite, not only as it is *mediated by our own subjectivity,* but also (and primarily) *immediately,* in a truly *responsive act* of encounter. Here we again encounter the crucial question in modern theology mentioned before (§23, 3, b; §30, 4): Is God *encountered,* in a true (if, as always, analogous) sense of the word or can we be only (variously) *conscious* of God as the depth dimension of the natural order, as so many modern North American authors suggest (cf., for example §30, 5, [*k.*])?

Interestingly, Otto quotes William James in confirmation of his position. James writes (with, Otto notes, "a certain naiveté"): "It is as if there were in the human consciousness a *sense of reality, a feeling of objective presence, a perception* of what we may call 'something there,' more deep and more general than any of the special and particular 'senses' by which the current psychology supposes existent realities to be originally revealed."[42] Otto correctly notes that James' "empiricist and pragmatist standpoint" forces him "to have recourse to somewhat singular and mysterious hypotheses to explain this fact."[43] Still, he suggests that James' very reluctance to accommodate the realism implied in his "naive" observation is powerful witness to its truthfulness.

Otto might have pointed to a similar feature in Schleiermacher. Arguably, the third edition of the *Speeches* contains a vestigial awareness of encounter. In his account of the religious experience,

Schleiermacher "naively" writes: "[piety] also has a passive side; it also appears *as an abandon*, a letting oneself be moved by *the Whole that man stands over against*."[44]

[4] The great Tradition of the undivided Church recognizes the fundamental concerns represented by thinkers like Schleiermacher. Against Schleiermacher, it is obliged to maintain that worship is not to be reduced to religious self-experience or self-expression. Yet Schleiermacher's underlying concern merits recognition: the act of worship must not be turned into an act of sectarianism or (what amounts to the same) idolatry. On the one hand, therefore, it must respect the absolutely transcendent mystery of God: worship that claims to own God is idolatrous. On the other hand, it demands the full actualization of human integrity: worship incapable of involving the mystery of the entire human person is inherently sectarian, because only what engages the entire *depth* of humanity can be expected to engage the entire *breadth* of humanity. Only the One who is most deeply "my God" can be the God of all.

The great Tradition combines both themes. It holds that the whole world, but especially all of humanity, is most deeply prepared for participation in the divine life—so deeply, in fact, that serious reflection on the depth of humanity and the world is bound to recover the mysterious reflection of God's invisible countenance and thus *indirectly* to see God, as in an image. But the Tradition also recognizes that the act of Christian worship fulfills creation's natural potential for actual, *direct encounter with God*—an encounter in which God graciously and freely both confers on, and awakens in, the creature a new, responsive identity.[45] This new identity does justice to the mystery of the living God, as well as being the full flower of the mystery of humanity, the crown of created nature. The praise of the Father, through Jesus Christ, in the Holy Spirit brings creation home to the God who made it, as well as to its deepest self.

[a] Arno Schilson, therefore, has rightly suggested that there is no contradiction but complementarity, and even the possibility of true reconciliation, between the fundamental concerns of two twentieth-century Catholic theologians who found themselves very much at loggerheads while they were alive, yet shared a fundamental conviction: Odo Casel and Karl Rahner [p]. The two agreed in opposing routine, standardized forms of faith and in giving "a chance of survival only to those Christians who have experienced something of the abiding

---

[p] Rahner was the ghostwriter of a warning issued, in the early 1940s, by the Office of Pastoral Affairs of the Vienna Archdiocese, against some of Casel's positions. He was of the opinion that they were predicated on irrationalism and that they wrongly implied the absolute normativity of patristic theology (Arno Schilson, *Theologie als Sakramententheologie*, pp. 114–15, n. 26).

mystery—the mystery of the living God." Both, therefore, insisted on giving an account of the Christian faith in which doctrine, precept, and feeling had deep roots in mystery. For Casel, mystery was a matter of *sacramental-cultic* experience;[46] he viewed the Christian as "one who experiences, *at the center of the Church* and *in* the living celebration of the sacraments, the *reality of God* as the fulfillment of the human person, as 'mystery.' "[47] For Rahner, on the other hand, the experience of mystery was *transcendental-anthropological* in nature; he consistently viewed the human person precisely as *attuned to the transcendent mystery* and hence as capable of gracious fulfillment.[48]

[b] This has consequences for the practice of theology. Balanced theology involves the coordination of *doxology* and *analogy*. The former is the root of dogmatic theology; the latter, of fundamental theology. Theology, therefore, should combine these two: on the one hand, a deep sense of awe and privilege before the mystery of a God who, in the very act of self-communication, invites human intelligence into an understanding of the divine mysteries present among us; and on the other hand, a deep, courageous trust in the ultimate reliability of human intelligence in its worshipful search for God (§8, 8).[49]

THE CENTRAL MYSTERY IN HISTORY

[§36] FROM DOXOLOGICAL ESSENCE TO SOTERIOLOGICAL STRUCTURE

[1] It is time to review this chapter and to explore some of its implications. This will enable us also to develop a first perspective on the next chapter. Faith, it was stated long ago, is suspended, ultimately, between God and nothingness (§10, 1). This prompts the word "all" as a key word to convey the act of unconditional praise and total abandon that characterizes the naked encounter of faith: "[God] is the all" (Sir 43, 28; cf. §9, 1).

This chapter has explored how this same total praise and abandon lies at the heart of Christian worship, personalized in Jesus Christ. He is, in person, unconditional praise of God and total abandon to God. In his risen life, he is the living warrant for, and the embodiment of, the world's unconditional surrender to the living God, who not only "brings the dead to life" but also "calls into being the things that do not exist" (Rom 4, 17). He is the one whose glory is "the glory of the only begotten one from the Father" (Jn 1, 14), and who is "the only begotten God, the one who is at the Father's bosom" (Jn 1, 18). In him, the Church, and indeed all of humanity and the world, has access to the living God, whose desire it is to draw creation into the divine life and so to make it share in the divine nature.

[a] In technical terms, therefore, this chapter has elaborated the *doxological center* of Christian worship and, with that, the *trinitarian essence* of the Christian faith. Consequently, this chapter also serves as a caution not to *reduce* the Christian religion to a dispensation of redemption (cf. §20, 1–2). The heart of Christianity is not the redemption of humanity, let alone the "Education of the Human Race."[50] The essence of the Christian faith is humanity's worshipful *encounter with the living God*. In this encounter, humanity attains the "vision of God" (that is, participation in the divine nature: 1 Jn 3, 2) and thus comes fully "alive" to "the glory of God" [q]. There are a hundred admirable ways to become better, more just, and more humane, but only one way (Jn 14, 6) to become gods. Christians are very much called to practice goodness, justice, and humanity; they are not sanguine about unaided human effort. Humanity tends to be self-maintaining and self-righteous; even if we practice virtue, we tend to do so with a vengeance, without compassion. Christians expect true justice only from union with God, who, by graciously taking on humanity in Christ, disarms it and unites it with Godself.

In this way, christology, whose origin is in worship and whose focus is the *identity of Jesus Christ*, blocks the reduction of the Christian faith to a system of salvation and, even further down the road, to an autonomous ethic or a philosophical anthropology. Here, therefore, in the christological affirmation of the mystery at the heart of Christian worship, also lies, ultimately, the significance of the crucial decision, made at the first ecumenical Council of Nicaea in A.D. 325, to secure the doxological center of the Christian faith by means of the affirmation of the Son's consubstantiality with the Father in godhead.

[2] Worshipful emphasis on the centrality of the profession of Christ's divine identity is capable of affording yet another insight into the reasons why theology must insist on the irreducibility of the Christian faith's central mystery. The Christian's union with God is and remains pure grace; the experience of this union makes God's sovereign freedom to be a gracious God more, not less, mysterious and ungraspable (cf. §34, 2). It is illegitimate, therefore, to present divinization by grace as some lately revealed "fundamental law" of existence; God's freedom remains above all laws and regularities that human reason can establish. While God may, graciously, in incomprehensible love, *share* the divine glory, *surrender* the divine glory God will not (cf. Is 42, 8).[51]

This realization also serves as the implicitly christological ground rule of what the great Tradition has taught about *mystical prayer*. While the human person is so natively attuned to God that only union with God

---

[q] "For God's glory is Man alive; the life of Man, though, is the vision of God" (Irenaeus, *Adv. Hær.* IV, 20, 7; *SC* 100, pp. 648–49; *ANF* 1, p. 490).

will fully satisfy its fundamental desire, actual union with God is and remains unowed—a totally gracious gift and only God's to give.

The author of the fourteenth-century treatise *The Cloud of Unknowing* formulated this in incomparable fashion:

Beware of pride, for it blasphemes God in his gifts, and emboldens sinners. If you were truly humble you would feel about this activity as I told you, namely, that God gives it freely, apart from any merit. The nature of this activity is such that its presence makes a soul able to possess it and to experience it. And that ability is not available to any soul apart from it [the activity]. The ability to perform this activity is united with the activity itself, inseparably; hence, whoever experiences this activity is able to perform it, and no one else—so much so that apart from this activity a soul is, as it were, dead, and unable to crave it or desire it. For as much as you will it and desire it, so much you have of it—no more and no less; and yet it is neither will nor desire, but something you-know-not-what, that stirs you to will and desire you-know-not-what. Never mind, I beg you, if you know no more; just proceed ever more and more, so as to be ever active.

And if I am to put it more succinctly, let that something do with you and lead you wherever it wants to. Let it be the agent, and you but the recipient; just behold it, and leave it alone, Do not interfere with it as if to help it along, for fear you might dissipate it all. You be but the wood, and let it be the carpenter; you be but the house, and let it be the landlord that lives in it. Be blind while it lasts, and cancel craving for knowledge, for it will hinder you more than help you. It is enough for you to feel enjoyably stirred by something you-know-not-what, as long as in your being stirred you think of nothing specific under God, and as long as your intent is nakedly directed to God.

And if it is thus, then steadfastly trust that it is only God that is stirring your will and your desire, simply by himself, without means either on his part or on yours. And be not afraid of the devil, for he cannot come that close. He can never succeed in stirring a person's will, except on occasion and by remote means, however subtle a devil he is. For adequately and apart from any means no good angel can stir your soul; nor, to put it briefly, can anything, except God alone.

Thus here from these words you can get to understand somewhat—but more clearly from the proof of experience—that in this activity people should employ no means, nor can anyone come to it by way of means. All good means depend on it, and it [depends] on no means, nor yet can any means lead to it.[52]

[3] Human faith in God, thus ultimately suspended between God and nothingness, is *proximately practiced between religion and world*, that is to say, in *structures* (§10, 1). This insight must be combined with another position developed earlier: the Church's worshipful confession of Christ risen involves, besides the *identification* of Jesus as the only begotten Son of God, the historic *vindication*, "in the Spirit" (1 Tim 3, 16), *of his historical life* (§33, 2). It is to this historic vindication and its implications that we must now turn. Having established Christianity's *doxological essence*, we must now proceed to develop *the soteriological struc-*

tures in which it subsists. Christian worship must again be our point of departure here.

Like all worship, Christian worship is set in space and time; like all worship, it reaches out, from space and time, to heaven and to eternity. But there is a difference. Space and time are not just the *setting* of Christian worship; they are part of its substance. *The recounting of the local and temporal origins of Christian worship* (as well as its subsequent fortunes) *is an integral part of Christian worship itself.* The Church's worshipful participation in the life of God is not only a reaching out from space and time into heaven and eternity, "where Christ is, seated at the right hand of God" (Col 3, 1); it is also an ongoing activity whereby space and time are *drawn into worship.* Realities in space and time, in other words, are also the very stuff Christian worship is made of. The "only begotten God, the one who is at the Father's bosom," is at the same time, historically and locally "that very one [who] has been our guide" (*ekeinos exēgēsato*: Jn 1, 18). The one who is "the reflection of [God's] glory and bears the imprint of his very being" (Heb 1, 3) is at the same time the one who is "the original guide as well as the accomplisher of our faith" (Heb 12, 2).

While seeking timelessness, therefore, the Church, from the beginning, makes and remakes salvation history in the very act of its access to the throne of grace; while seeking to reach the heavenly City, the Church travels and retravels a world being made holy by its very act of pilgrimage. And that pilgrimage is itself recalled, too. The Church's praise of God in the Name of Christ, sung *in* the sanctuary, takes the shape of a wayfarers' song sung *on the way to* the sanctuary—a song that recalls the way stations [r].

It was no different in Israel. *Te decet hymnus Deus in Sion*:

> To You our praise is due in Zion, O God.
> To You we offer our vows—You hear our prayer.
> To You all flesh will come, with its burden of sin.
> Too heavy for us, our offenses, but You sweep them away.
> Blessed all those You choose and bring near,
> to dwell in Your courts!
>
> (Ps 65, 1–4)

This transition from doxology to history of salvation, and the mention of the wayfaring daughter of Zion's worship in the Jerusalem sanctuary, call to mind an age-old tradition of the worship and the witness of the undivided Church.

---

[r] A striking instance of this is the liturgical celebration, in the Eastern Church, of the Council of Chalcedon and its christological definition; cf. Alois Grillmeier, *Christ in Christian Tradition*, vol. 2/1, pp. 319–20.

[§37] MARY, MOTHER OF GOD AND MODEL OF THE CHURCH

[1] Very early in the Tradition of the Church, both in its worship and in the catechesis connected with it, a human figure appears in close proximity to the center of the Christian profession of faith. She is the daughter of Zion *par excellence*: the blessed virgin Mary. The focus of this veneration is firmly christological. Ignatius of Antioch is speaking *christologically* when he speaks of the "three mysteries in which God's resounding voice was heard, wrought in all stillness and made known to us: Mary's virginity and her giving birth, as well as the Lord's death."[53]

At the heart of the Church's faith and worship, it is always Jesus Christ risen who is proclaimed, on the strength of the Spirit, as the Son of God, to the glory of the Father. Yet that worshipful access to the Father does prompt in the Church a special veneration for the woman of whom the Father's Son was born: the holy "woman who bore God," the holy *Theotokos*. Not surprisingly, therefore, the oldest invocation addressed to Mary known so far, found on a late third-century Egyptian papyrus, apostrophizes her by that ancient title, which Coptic Christians very probably borrowed from the idioms of the age-old Egyptian Isis cult.[54]

> Under your
> compassion
> we take refuge,
> Bearer of God. Our
> entreaties do not
> disdain in hard time,
> but from danger
> deliver us:
> [you,] alone chaste,
> alone blessed.[55]

[2] The title *Theotokos* [s], dogmatized (with more holy resolve than sensitivity to Church unity)[56] at the Council of Ephesus in A.D. 431 (DS 251–52; CF 605–6/1), best illustrates the dynamics of the relationship between the Church's worshipful profession of Jesus Christ as the Son of God and its veneration of Mary. The *Theotokos* title given to Mary is proclaimed *entirely* in the interest of a *christological* proposition: the identity of the *one person* of "the Lord and Christ and Son," "the same

---

[s] The authoritative title is *Theotokos*, meaning "God-bearer" (Lat. *deipara*). It was this ancient title that Proclus pointedly used in front of Nestorius (who had rejected it), within days after the latter's accession as patriarch of Constantinople (Pieter Smulders, "Dogmengeschichtliche und lehramtliche Entfaltung der Christologie," p. 451). *Theotokos* is much terser than the heavy English phrase "Mother of God"; it conveys only that the Child born of Mary is the Son of God and God. In so far as "Mother of God" carries mythical associations (for example, with Greek mother-goddesses) or suggests psychoanalytic materials (as proposed, for instance, by C. J. Jung) it can lead to serious theological misconceptions.

one clearly God as well as Man," by reason of "the mysterious and ineffable coming together into unity of divinity and humanity" (DS 250, 253; CF 604, 606/2).

Consequently, the recognition extended to Mary in the Church's liturgy and catechesis is fundamentally *indirect*; it is entirely parasitical on, and incidental to, the revelation of the risen Christ as God's Son and the Church's worshipful response to that revelation. But since professing Christ as the Son of God on the part of the Church is a matter of *participation* in his divine identity (§34, 6), Mary is recognized, in the very act of professing Jesus as the Son of God, as pre-eminently participating in the divine nature of her Son herself. That is to say, she is recognized as *holy*—in fact, as holy *par excellence*: *Panagia*. Like knows like: in the very act of being made holy by the praise it offers to God in the profession of Christ as the Son of God, the Church receives the capacity, by affinity and connaturality in grace, to recognize the Holy Mother of God. *Mary is primarily recognized in her fulfillment—at the side of her risen Son.*

[a] It has become a commonplace to say that the figure of Jesus in the gospels is essentially determined by the Church's faith in Jesus Christ alive. *A fortiori*, on account of the fact that the Church's veneration of Mary is parasitical on its christological profession, the image of Jesus' mother in the Gospels is that of "the mother of my Lord" (Lk 1, 43)—that is to say, of the Christ whom the Church proclaims as risen. The attention paid to Mary in the New Testament, therefore, derives not from history but from faith. There is no good reason to doubt that Mary is, historically, the mother of Jesus; but in the case of Mary, it is incomparably harder than in the case of Jesus (if not, in fact, totally impossible) to retrieve, from the text of the synoptics, materials that are historically reliable as well as relevant to faith [*t*]).

The annunciation pericope in Luke's Gospel strongly suggests this affinity with the Church's faith in Christ's Resurrection. The angel's address (Lk 1, 32–33, 35) uses christological titles found elsewhere

---

[*t*] This is said in opposition to the historicist and ethical reduction of the undivided Church's Marian traditions put forward by Hans Küng. From a historical point of view, it would seem, Küng places rather too much hermeneutical pressure on the passages Mk 3, 21. 31–35. He then proposes that only two titles can be reliably predicated of Mary. She is "mother of Jesus" and, as such, "witness" (?) to his true humanity, though also to his anchorage in God. She is also "instance and model of the Christian life"; accordingly, "her faith, according to Luke . . . is typical of all Christian faith." Küng suggests, without saying so in so many words, that whatever *practices of veneration* of Mary have developed in the Church are entirely to be put down to current religious and cultural impulses, often of a dubious nature. Cf. *Christ Sein*, p. 448–52; ET *On Being a Christian*, pp. 458–62. No one doubts that much traditional Marian devotionality has seamy sides; Vatican II expressly recognizes it and cautions against it (LG 67). Still, the postulate that no veneration of Mary may derive from worship and devotion is unwarranted by the Tradition.

in Luke's Gospel: the child to be born will be called "Son of the Most High" (cf. Lk 8, 28) and (by implication) "Son of David" (Lk 18, 38–39; 20, 41) and, especially, "Holy, the Son of God" (Lk 3, 22; 4, 3. 9. 41; 8, 28; 9, 35; 22, 70; Acts 8, 37; 9, 20; 13, 33). And just as the risen one is alive in the Spirit, so the child to be born will owe its conception to the Spirit. To this "anticipated resurrection kerygma," Mary says yes.

[b] In the New Testament context, the fact that Jesus is "born of woman" (Gal 4, 4) [u] adequately accounts for his being a child of Israel and a member of the human race. It is from Mary that Jesus derives what relates him as Savior to all of humanity and the world [v]. Two second-century authors illustrate how quickly this insight— and with it, the figure of Mary herself—became part of the typological arsenal deployed by Christian catechesis; the pull towards mariology was obviously irresistible.

In Justin's *Dialogue with Trypho*, the exploration of Christ's universal significance takes the shape of an exploration of the title "Son of Man." That title is due to Christ on account of his birth from the Virgin, and it can be interpreted in two ways. It either means that Jesus is a member of the race of David, Jacob, Isaac, and Abraham, or it means that he is a member of the race of Adam himself, of whom both the patriarchs and Mary herself are descended. The second interpretation is clearly the preferred one, since Justin goes on to explain that the end of human disobedience corresponds to its beginning: virginal Eve had conceived from the serpent and borne disobedience and death, whereas virginal Mary conceived faith and joy at the message of the Angel and bore the one through whom God destroys the serpent and all those like him and delivers from death those who repent and believe.[57] In this way, remarkably, Mary is drawn from the outset into the christological theme of *recapitulation*.

It was at the hands of Irenaeus of Lyons that the recapitulation theme acquired its fundamental theological significance. Jesus Christ, the second Adam, sums up in his person everything the first Adam represents and thus redeems it; the root of this recapitulation is his birth from the second Eve.[58]

Thus the early Tradition turns out to have found it impossible to

---

[u] Gk. *genomenos ek gynaikos* ("born of woman") in Gal 4, 4 functions as the equivalent of *gennētos gynaikos*, with the same meaning, in the Septuagint. It renders Heb. *yᵉlûd 'iššah* in Job 14, 1; 15, 14; 25, 4. It occurs in the plural *gennētoi gynaikōn* in Mt 11, 11 par. Lk 7, 28. Its meaning is "human individual," with connotations of transience and mortality.

[v] This observation will have to be further explored when the virgin birth will be discussed in its appropriate context. Note the patristic interpretation of the prepositional adjunct "from the Virgin Mary" as involving the reality of Christ's humanity: J. N. D. Kelly, *Early Christian Creeds*, p. 336.

conceive of Jesus as the Savior of humanity without acknowledging the holiness of the mother that bore him. Aquinas, therefore, is simply following tradition when he explains that Mary's motherhood qualifies her for the "special reverence" or *hyperdulia* ("special service") that is appropriately offered to "creatures that have a special affinity with God, like the Blessed Virgin, inasmuch as she is the Mother of God."[59]

[c] There is a further tendency in the Tradition: it consists in conceiving of the Virgin Mary's participation in Christ's holiness as fully accomplished, even down to her sharing in his resurrection. Liturgical feasts pointing in this direction go back to the fourth century. The Roman Catholic Church's papal teaching office defined this in the year 1950, in the form of the dogma of the Assumption of the Blessed Virgin to heaven (DS 3900–3904; CF 713–15).

[3] To sum up: the liturgical veneration of the Blessed Virgin Mary and the recognition of the singular holiness of her person and her life is radically contingent on the Church's profession of the divine identity of Christ her Son. Augustine reflected on this basic connection with uncommon clarity:

After that [Pelagius] recalls those "who are said not only not to have sinned, but also to have lived justly [there follows a long list of names of Old Testament figures]," including the mother of our Lord and Savior herself, of whom he says that "we owe it to piety to acknowledge [*confiteri*] that she was without sin." Granted; let us, then, make an exception for the holy virgin Mary. *In her regard, I am prepared to say, on account of the honor of the Lord, there can be absolutely no question of sin. For can we think of any source from which she could have obtained more grace bestowed on herself to conquer sin in every respect? She was found worthy to conceive and bear the one of whom it is certain that he had no sin!* So, apart from this virgin, if we could assemble all those holy men and women while they were alive, and ask them if they were without sin, what do we think they would reply? . . . "If we say we have no sin, we deceive ourselves and the truth is not in us" [1 Jn 1, 8].[60]

[4] Veneration offered to Mary is radically dependent on the Church's profession of Jesus' divinity; yet from the Lukan and Johannine writings on, this veneration has been undergirded by *a tradition of faith-reflection on the person of Mary herself*. The Church recognizes that Mary's holiness is not just a brute fact materially required by the Incarnation of the Word; it is contingent on Mary's *faith*. This reflection occurs at two levels. The first level of reflection on Mary's faith concerns its *origin*.

[a] Mary's yes to God makes of her the first believer in the Word of God and the Son of God. No wonder, then, that she conceives Jesus in a manner matching the Church's manner of acknowledging Jesus as Lord: through the coming upon her of the Holy Spirit, which is

only God's to give (§34, 6). If her conceiving Jesus is entirely the
work of grace, so is her readiness to say yes to it: she is "the graced
one"; she has "found grace with God" (Lk 1, 28. 30).

The recognition of the Blessed Virgin's fullness of grace lends
depth to the recognition—widespread in the Tradition of the undivided Church—of her sinlessness. In the Roman Catholic tradition,
this sinlessness as well as the Blessed Virgin's readiness to conceive
Christ has been recognized as rooted in her radical redemption by
grace, which includes, by a gift of divine grace in anticipation of the
merits of Christ, her freedom from original sin. This is known as the
dogma of the "Immaculate Conception," promulgated by papal definition in 1854 (DS 2800–2804; CF 709).

[5] Thus Mary comes to be venerated as the first believer, who is
blessed for having heard and observed the word of God rather than
for having borne and suckled Jesus (cf. Lk 11, 27–28). By her free
acceptance of God's prevenient grace, she was enabled to abandon herself to God in a "virginal" faith-abandon.[61] Again, Augustine provides
a classic analysis:

It is written in the gospel that when the mother and the brothers of Christ—
that is, his relatives after the flesh—were announced to him and were waiting
outside because they could not get to him on account of the crowd, he said:
"Who is my mother or who are my brothers? Stretching out his hand over his
disciples he said: These are my brothers; and whoever does the will of my
Father, that person is brother and mother and sister to me" [Mt 12, 47–50].
What else was he teaching us except that we should place our spiritual family
ahead of carnal kinship, and that people become happy, not by being linked
up with just and holy people by the ties of the flesh, but by being closely united
with them by obeying and following what they teach and the way they live? *So
Mary is more blessed by receiving the faith of Christ than by conceiving the flesh of
Christ. For also when someone cried out "blessed the womb that bore you," he replied:
Rather, blessed those who hear the word of God and keep it*" [Lk 11, 27–28]. Finally,
as for his brothers—that is, his blood-relatives—who did not believe in him:
what was the use of their being his relatives? *In the same way, the closeness of
motherhood would not have been of any profit to Mary, had she not more happily carried
Christ in her heart than in her womb.*[62]

[6] There is a second level of reflection on Mary's faith in the Lukan
writings and the fourth Gospel: the *life* of Mary is presented as one of
accomplished *discipleship*, and, hence, Mary herself is cast as the model
of the life of faith in the Church and, indeed, of the Church itself.

[a] In Luke, she becomes the joyful carrier of the Spirit when she
goes to visit Elizabeth and the child in her womb and sings her song
of eschatological praise and thanksgiving to God (Lk 1, 39–56). But
she also becomes the model of patient and even suffering faith. She
hears Simeon prophesy that she, too, will feel the pang of the
sword—the Word of God, penetrating and testing any person down

to the point where the faith-decision for or against Christ is made (Lk 2, 34–35; cf. Heb 4, 12–13; Hos 6, 5; Is 11, 4; 49, 2; Eph 6, 17; Rev 1, 16). She ponders, in faith, the enigmatic events that befall Jesus—the visit of the shepherds and his being found in the things of his Father (Lk 2, 19. 51). Finally, she is found with the Jerusalem Church—the Twelve, the women, and Jesus' relatives—praying in anticipation of the gift of the promised Spirit (Acts 1, 13–14).

In the fourth Gospel, Mary's patient, long-suffering discipleship is cast in even bolder relief. At Cana, she finds her request politely ignored, and at the cross, she is present in complete impotence. Yet this puts her total faith-abandon to Jesus in even sharper relief, as she tells the servants, "Whatever he will tell you, do it," and as she accepts her new relationship with the community of the Beloved Disciple at the hands of the dying Jesus (Jn 2, 5; 19, 26–27).

Finally, in the Apocalypse, there is the apocalyptic symbolization of the persecuted Church as the woman bearing Christ even as she is threatened by the cosmic powers (Rev 12, 1–6. 13–17). Here, the features of the mother of Jesus have completely given way to the features of the Mother Church of the suffering saints; but the liturgical tradition has insisted on recognizing the typology even here and has long used the passage in Marian liturgical context.

[b] The mystical tradition, both in the East and the West, was to discover and cherish a close connection between personal identification with Jesus Christ and deep devotion to the Mother of God. In many instances, this tradition is all the more touching for being devoid of attempts at theological justification. Still, the underlying idea is everywhere clear: personal faith in Jesus Christ is enhanced by contemplation of, and participation in, Mary's faith [w].

[7] Unfortunately, the place of the Mother of Jesus in the worship, the life, and the teaching of the Church has become a matter of deep disagreement among the churches, especially since the Reformation (cf. UR 20). The Reformers took exception, and many still do, to the excessive accretion of popular devotion to the Blessed Virgin. Modern Protestants have long suspected, in the abundant Marian piety of Orthodox and Catholics, not only an attack on the sole mediatorship of Christ, but also—more insidiously—an attempt at symbolic self-canonization of the Church, and even as a concession to popular paganism.

---

[w] By way of illustration, one story out of many. The fourteenth-century monk St. Maximus of Kapsokalyvia, on Mount Athos, is reported to have said: "One day, as with tears and intense love I kissed her most pure icon, suddenly there came a great warmth in my breast and my heart, not burning me up but refreshing me like dew, and filling me with sweetness and deep compunction. From that moment my heart began to say the [Jesus-]Prayer inwardly, and at the same time my reason with my intellect holds fast the remembrance of Jesus and of my *Theotokos*; and this remembrance has never left me" (quoted in *The Study of Spirituality*, p. 248).

Catholics and Orthodox on their part have suspected, in the Protestant neglect of Mary, an attempt to isolate Christ from the communion of the saints, a lack of awareness of the presence of the Holy Spirit in the Church, and, hence, a lack of appreciation of the Church's essential holiness.

[a] Recent ecumenical conversations on mariology have witnessed a guarded but sincere recognition, on the part of many Protestant communities, that fidelity to the New Testament warrants, and even demands, a discontinuation of the total rejection of any recognition of Mary. These conversations have also helped stimulate a renewal of Catholic devotion to Mary in accordance with Scripture and sound doctrine, as mandated by Vatican II (LG 67).

Vatican II made a momentous decision, when, on October 29, 1963, it decided, by a small majority, to integrate a proposed separate document on the Mother of God into the Constitution on the Church as a special section (LG 52–69). This decision succeeded, at least in principle, in countering an unhealthy tendency toward isolation of the veneration of the Blessed Virgin. The passage carefully balances the two elements of the great Tradition's veneration of Mary: the *doxological* element, by which, as *Theotokos*, she is inseparably associated with the Church's profession of Jesus Christ as the Son of God, and the *soteriological* element, by which she is firmly associated with the Church—first unequivocally as a believer, and then also, on account of her rare privilege, as its model.

[8] Vatican II's Constitution on the Liturgy sums up both elements, in words that may also, in the present context, serve to mark the transition to the next chapter, which is to deal with the soteriological shape of the Church's doxological essence.

In celebrating this annual cycle of Christ's mysteries, holy Church venerates with special love the Blessed Mary, Mother of God, who is joined by an inseparable bond to the saving work of her Son. In her the Church admires and exalts the most excellent fruit of the redemption, and joyfully contemplates, as in a faultless model, that which it wholly desires and hopes to be itself (SC 103).

Soteriology: The History of Salvation

THE CENTRAL MYSTERY IN ESCHATOLOGICAL PERSPECTIVE

[§38] CHRISTIAN WORSHIP: FROM DOXOLOGY TO NARRATIVE

[1] The Church's confession of Christ risen, it was explained, occurs in response to two inseparable, though distinguishable, elements: the *identification*, in the Holy Spirit (cf. Rom 1, 4), of Jesus as the only begotten *Son of God*, and the *vindication*, also "in the Spirit" (1 Tim 3, 16), *of his historical life*. The former element, it was stated, constituted the Christian faith's doxological essence; the latter, its soteriological structure (§33, 2; §36, 1–2). We now turn to this latter element and its implications; in the interest of clarity of exposition, let us open the complex discussion that awaits us with a brief survey of its order of treatment.

In the risen Christ, it was explained, the Church acknowledges—and shares in—the fullness of participation in the divine life accorded to an historical human individual, Jesus of Nazareth (cf. §34, 2–3; 6). In the revelation of Jesus' fulfillment, however, the Church also receives the anticipation of *an absolute, universal promise*. The risen Christ is revealed, in person, as the firstfruits of the eschatological harvest—God's own guarantee that all of the world and humanity are to share in the divine nature.

Christ's resurrection, however, was the divine vindication of his historical life. Consequently, we will argue, the assurance of the eschatological fulfillment held out, in his person, to humanity and the world is revealed as the crown upon a *history of salvation* from alienation and sin—a history both revealed and mandated by Christ's life, death, and resurrection. The Christian access to the living God, therefore, must take the shape of a *process*—a process of *divinization*. This process of divinization, we will show, is carried on the wings of a *christological narrative*; this narrative, in turn, inspires and mandates, not only a *tradition of worship*, but also a *tradition of conduct* and a *tradition of teaching*.

To begin the elaboration of this long line of thought, let us return to the theme of the Church's worship.

[2] The focal, determinative theme of the Church's worship-encounter with the living God is the person of Jesus Christ alive and present in the Spirit (§33, 1; §34, 1; 5). This worshipful acknowledgment of Christ's living presence, however, takes the *shape* of a *memorial*. Notwithstanding the immediacy of its access to the eternal God, Christian worship is not immemorial; *it came to be*. The startling freshness and confidence of the rhetoric and the language of the New Testament is a literary witness precisely to the *newness* of the original and originating Christian experience and of the worship it precipitated.[1]

Very importantly, this newness came about entirely unexpectedly, in response to completely unanticipated, startling "visions," "appearances," or (in the case of Paul) "a revelation" (Gal 1, 12). Those privileged to be parties to these elusive, yet compelling, events, also insisted on interpreting them in entirely divine terms: they attributed them to God as to their only acknowledgeable source. The living God, they maintained, had revealed Jesus, divinely brought to life, to themselves as persons divinely chosen. This revelation, they claimed, had completely changed them: it had made of them, not only converts, but also believers and even witnesses. All of this had more than reversed the painful embarrassment, disenchantment, and despair they had suffered in the wake of Jesus' arrest and execution [a]; it had turned those very failures into the stuff of enlightenment, joy, and hope.

[a] God-given *confidence in speech* (*parrhēsia*), we have indicated (cf. §31, 6; §34, 2), characterizes the community's worship as well as its witness. In the person of the risen Christ, and in the act of proclaiming the account of his life, death, and resurrection, the community has confident access to the living God (2 Cor 3, 12; Eph 3, 12; Heb 4, 16; 10, 19); in recognizing God's action in this way, it worships God the way God is worthy of being worshiped.

This frees the community for witness that is equally confident; the kerygmatic proclamation of the Christian narrative (cf. §41, 1) is also

---

[a] "Execution" is used here in view of the fact that many creeds *appear* not to mention Jesus' *death* explicitly but move straight from his "crucifixion" and/or "passion" to the burial. Thus the Nicene-Constantinopolitan creed reads: ". . . who was crucified for us under Pontius Pilate, and suffered, and was buried." The explanation for this is that "crucify" (Gk. *staurō*) implies execution, while "suffer" (Gk. *paschō*) is a technical legal term for "undergoing capital punishment." To solve the problem, the English text of the Nicene-Constantinopolitan creed in present-day liturgical use has inserted the word "died" after "suffered"; it would have been better to translate: "[he was] *put to death* and buried."

characterized by God-given *parrhēsia*. Confidence marks the Christian commitment, both to kerygmatic mission (Acts 4, 13. 29. 31; 28, 31; Eph 6, 19) and to community life (2 Cor 7, 4; Philem 8; Heb 3, 6; 10, 35) [b].²

[3] While alive, Jesus had rendered present among the disciples the actuality of the living God—the God who had been the all-encompassing presence in his own life and ministry. This had made of Jesus the embodiment of the living God's kingship, the actual presence of that kingship in person [c].

He had actualized this divine presence by way of *witness*. What he had said to others ("I say to you") had been but the reflection of his endorsement ("Amen")³ of what he had heard from the Father [d]. The living God had been the mystery behind the original and unprecedented freedom and authority (*exousia*) with which he had encountered people, in word and deed, in a ministry of compassion that had set aside accepted forms of socioreligious discrimination and challenged the sole authority of the Law.

More importantly, therefore, Jesus had represented the divine presence by way of *worship*, in his unique abandon to, and in his incomparable intimacy with, his *Abba*—his "Father dear"—which had marked his life and ministry, and in which he had invited his followers to share (Mt 11, 25–27; 5, 43–48). This familiarity and abandon had especially

---

[b] Paul's entire person is marked by *parrhēsia*, in view of the hope that comes from Christ's Resurrection (Phil 1, 20). In 1 Jn, *parrhēsia* connotes the eschaton: it comes from the forgiveness of sins, encourages access to God in prayer, and enables the faithful to face the coming judgment (2, 28; 3, 21; 5, 14).

[c] "The kingdom in person" (*autobasileia*) is Origen's oft-quoted coinage, an instance of the stylistic device known as personification. In the present context, the title is used to sum up Jesus' *historical* ministry; other modern commentators have done the same. In the original context, however, it is one of a series of analogous, full-fledged *christological titles*: " 'The kingdom of the heavens,' he says, 'is compared [Mt 22, 2],' and so on. If it is compared to such a king, and one who has done such things, who are we to say it is but the Son of God? For he is the king of the heavens; and just as he is the wisdom in person [*autosophia*], and the justice in person [*autodikaiosynē*], and the truth in person [*autoalētheia*], in the same way, surely, he is *the kingdom in person*, too? And this kingdom comprises, not something here below, nor [only] part of what is above, but all that is above—all that is called the heavens. Hence, in seeking to penetrate the text, 'Theirs is the kingdom of the heavens' [Mt 5, 3. 10], you may say, 'Theirs is the Christ,' inasmuch as he is *the kingdom in person*: he reigns in every respect over the person who is no longer under the reign of sin, which reigns in the mortal body [cf. Rom 6, 12] of those who have subjected themselves to it. And in saying that he reigns in every respect over that person, I mean something like this: inasmuch as he is justice, wisdom, truth, and all the other virtues, he reigns over the person who, by bearing the likeness of the heavenly man [1 Cor 15, 49], has become heaven" (*Comm. in Matth.*, 14, 7; *PG* 13, 1197B). Cf. also the title "the Logos in person" (*autologos*), in combination with "the wisdom, the truth, and the justice in person" (*C. Celsum*, VI, 47; *PG* 11, 1372D; ed. Chadwick, p. 365; cf. *C. Celsum*, III, 41; *PG* 11, 973A; ed. Chadwick, p. 156). Cf. also *Hom. in Jer.*, 17, 4 (*PG* 13, 457C), where Origen adds *autohagiasmos* ("sanctification in person") and *autohypomonē* ("patient expectancy in person") to his treasury of personifying christological titles.

[d] Cf. the thematization of this in Jn 8, 26; 15, 15.

expressed themselves in a habit of praise and thanksgiving—the form of prayer characteristic of the new age inaugurated by Jesus (cf. §38, 3, b).[4]

With Jesus' arrest, abandonment, and execution, his life's witness to his Father had been reduced to silence, and eventually discredited, before the tribunal of the powers that judged him. The disciples, scattered, had gone into hiding. Worse still, with Jesus, all hope of salvation and all possibility of access to God in praise and thanksgiving had died. Into this hopelessly dead and empty silence had burst the risen Lord, restoring hope beyond all expectation, and opening, in person, the way to unprecedented worship [e].

[a] Israel's tradition of blessing God (cf., for example, the blessings that separate the five collections in the Book of Psalms: Ps 41, 13; 72, 18; 89, 52; 106, 48; cf. Rom 1, 25; 9, 5; cf. also Mk 14, 61)[5] could now be taken up in a new way, by way of *eschatological thanksgiving*, under invocation of Jesus Christ risen (2 Cor 1, 3; 11, 31; Eph 1, 3; 1 Pet 1, 3).

Similarly, Israel's song of praise and eschatological hope "*Hall^elû Yâh!*" ("Praise the Lord!"), which, in the context of the great "Hallel" (Pss 113–118), had especially characterized the Jewish Passover rituals, could now be sung in celebration of a new Passover and, hence, in a new key—as a cry of eschatological triumph (Rev 19, 1. 3. 4. 6), under invocation of Jesus Christ alive and present. The liturgical tradition of the West was eventually to go even as far as calling the Alleluia the *canticum Domini*—"the song of the Lord" (that is, the Lord Jesus).

In the worship of the Church universal, this triumphant Jewish exclamation was to become one of the most characteristic Christian acclamations, especially prominent during the Easter season. It became so integral a part of the Church's liturgical sensibility that it was never dropped from the liturgy. Not until the sixth century did Pope Gregory the Great order it banned, in the West, during the pre-Lenten and Lenten penitential seasons—a move that was to be held against the West by the Oriental Churches five centuries later, as one of the causes that contributed to the mutual alienation.[6]

[b] In light of all this, it is not surprising to find Hippolytus singling out *thanksgiving* as the distinctive—that is to say, the typically *christological*—feature of the Church's glorification of God (cf. §38, 3). At the same time, however, he clearly indicates that the Church's ability to give thanks and to witness is due only to the *risen Christ's*

---

[e] This imaginative rendition of the disciples' experience of Jesus' death and resurrection is deeply indebted to Sebastian Moore's *The Fire and the Rose Are One*, esp. pp. 80–89.

gift of the *Holy Spirit* (cf. § 34, 5–6; §38, 5). As a result, the complete structure of the Church's *confession* must be *trinitarian*.

He writes: "And we cannot conceive of God as one, except by truly believing in Father and Son and Holy Spirit. For the Jews did indeed glorify God, *but they did not give thanks, for they did not know the Son*. The disciples knew the Son, but not in the Holy Spirit, which is also why they disavowed him. Now the Father's Word knew the plan of salvation and the will of the Father, [namely,] that the Father does not wish to be glorified otherwise than thus; therefore, once risen, he gave the tradition to the disciples, saying: 'Go forth and make disciples of all the nations, by baptizing them in the name of the Father and the Son and the Holy Spirit.' In this way he indicated that whoever leaves one of these out does not give perfect glory to God"[f].[7]

[4] No wonder, then, that the Church, wherever and whenever it worships God in Jesus' name, should consciously and emphatically proclaim that it is relying on, and incorporating into its worship, historic, particular events of divine origin, which first prompted the mystery of its worship and continue to prompt it. *The worship that is the central focus of the Christian community takes the shape of divinely authorized realistic narrative.*

[a] Among the most explicit (and central) examples of worship by memorial narrative is the phrase "*memores. . . offerimus*": "commemorating [Christ's passion and death, resurrection and ascension] we offer," in the classic eucharistic prayers of the West. The expression occurs immediately after the narrative memorial of Jesus' words and actions at the Last Supper. This conveys that the Church's worship in offering the eucharistic sacrifice is predicated, not only on the specific memorial of Jesus' words and actions at the Last Supper, but also on the comprehensive *anamnēsis* of his life, his death, and his resurrection and ascension. The connection of the former with the latter is conveyed, in the original Latin, by "therefore" (Lat. *unde* or *igitur*)—a connection curiously lacking in the English texts of the eucharistic prayers in current use in the Roman Catholic Church.

---

[f] Hippolytus' emphasis on christological thanksgiving in the Spirit is of great theological interest. Still, it must be added at once that he makes his point at the expense of the truth: Israel did, of course, give thanks to God (cf. §45, 2). The passage exemplifies, sadly, the extent to which the early Church had become alienated, both from its Jewish roots and from contemporary Judaism. It is interesting, in this context, to recall Joachim Jeremias' observation (*The Prayers of Jesus*, p. 78) that the *historical* Jesus' "new mode of prayer is dominated by thanksgiving," and his comment: "Thanksgiving is one of the foremost characteristics of the new age. So when Jesus gives thanks he is not just following custom. There is more to it than that; he is actualizing God's reign here and now."

[b] The insight that the worship at the center of the Christian community takes the shape of divinely authorized, realistic narrative is related to one of the more interesting developments in contemporary theology: a *new appreciation of narrative.*

Much traditional theology has been too notional or conceptual and, as a result, insensitive to history—it has given too static and timeless an account of the faith. In our own day, this has been quite openly the case in Paul Tillich's admittedly unhistorical theology; yet even Karl Rahner's theological effort cannot be entirely exonerated in this respect, as J. B. Metz has explained.[8] Such theologies have a tendency to lose sight of the fact that important meanings reside, not only in the words or the "ideas"—the "content"—of the Christian profession of faith, but also in its "form"—its narrative shape. It is a welcome development, therefore, that this has been pointed out.[9] What is even more interesting and welcome is that a few theologians have exemplified the ability of narrative to convey deep meaning by writing theologically relevant narratives themselves.[10]

Nevertheless, a caution is in order. For theologians systematically to pay attention to the meaning of narrative is not the same as to turn *theology itself* into narrative. An indispensable task of theology is *understanding*, which occurs by means of *conceptualization*, not by the avoidance of it.[11] Moreover, if systematic theology embraces narrative too eagerly, it may lose sight of the central mystery of the Christian profession and drift off into a reduced account of the faith—one with modernist leanings (cf. §20)—in which the central mystery is reduced to a narrative account of human salvation.[12]

[5] "Realistic narrative" must be understood, not only in the sense of "true story," but also in the sense of "narrative that affects reality" (cf. § 41, 2). Theologically speaking this means that it must be understood in *pneumatological* terms—whence the phrase "*divinely inspired* realistic narrative." The essential Christian profession of the unity of *Abba*-God and the Son Jesus Christ is established in the divinely prompted act of Christian worship. But true worship is participation in the very life of God; that is to say, it is carried by the Holy Spirit (§34, 5–6). This applies in a twofold way.

First, Christ revealed as risen, vindicated, and present in the Spirit *prompts* the Christian narrative; hence, the narrative is *prophetic*—it is inspired and animated by the effusion of the life-giving presence of God. The worship-narrative itself, as well as the ability to tell it, therefore, are *gifts*; in that sense *the narrative is the living Word of God before it is a human word.*

Second, the Christian narrative is also the Church's *response* to the revelation of Christ risen and vindicated and present in the Spirit. For that reason it does justice, on the strength of the Spirit, to the intimacy between the Father and the Son, *even if those who utter it do not live up to the praise they utter and the narratives they tell, or at least not yet fully* [g].[13] Thus the Spirit both generates the Christian narrative in those who tell and hear it and decisively brings it home to its source, along with those who tell and hear it.

Thus the living Word of God takes shape in the living human word addressed to God, for all to hear. This human word is a *living*, not a purely gnostic, word; it is a *gesture of commitment*, not a mere *idea* [h]. If it does profess and express knowledge of God and Christ, it does so only insofar as it conveys the total faith-abandon to God and Christ in worship: "your self-offering, by way of a living sacrifice, holy and acceptable to God, which is your spiritual worship" (Rom 12, 1). In the act of Christian worship, therefore, those who proclaim and hear the Christian narrative are being drawn, by the Spirit, into a relationship with God in which God graciously does justice to them, and in which, with the freedom only grace can give [i], they do justice to God. Drawn into the life of God, they rise from death and find eternal life; hallowing God's name, they find the forgiveness of God and are made holy.

Still, the gift of the Spirit is in the nature of a down payment (*arrabōn*: 2 Cor 1, 22; 5, 5; Eph 1, 14): the first instalment of the eschatological inheritance that is the final forgiveness of sins and the full participation in Christ's resurrection. The gift of worship in the Spirit always remains to be lived out: those who worship also commit themselves to a history of salvation borne by the Holy Spirit, both in community life and in the community's mission to the world (§42, 1; §43, 2–4; §50, 3).

[a] In offering this account of the inspired nature of the Christian narrative, as it functions *in the Church's worship*, the present treatment makes a suggestion. It proposes that it is legitimate to make very forceful claims on behalf of the living worship-tradition of the Church—claims analogous to the claims the Tradition has made on behalf of Scripture. These claims are based on the recognition of the

---

[g] For the conclusion that follows from this, cf. §34, 7, a. For the implications of this, cf. §42.

[h] This position is predicated, in the last analysis, on a fundamental linguistic thesis, namely, that language is activity before it is cognition, intersubjective before it is objectifying, and rhetorical before it is logical. Dietrich Bonhoeffer used this idea to support one the main contentions of his christology (F. J. van Beeck, *Christ Proclaimed*, esp. pp. 93–101, 235–43). One of the consequences of this, to be explored later, is that the true home of Scripture is not the classroom, nor the study, nor even the chancery, but the Christian community meeting, where the living Word is heard, and where worship and mutual upbuilding take place.

[i] Cf. the Council of Trent's Decree on Justification: ". . . awakened and assisted by divine grace, they conceive faith from hearing and are freely led to God" (CF 1930; DS 1526: "excitati divina gratia et adiuti, fidem 'ex auditu' concipientes, libere moventur in Deum").

Holy Spirit as the carrier and enabler of the Church's worship-response to God.[14]

This would seem to be implicitly recognized by Vatican II when it teaches: "The Sacred Tradition and Holy Scripture constitute the one sacred deposit of the Word of God, entrusted to the Church" (DV 10). What the Council says of Scripture, therefore, can also be analogously said of the Christian narrative, which is the living, normative core of the Sacred Tradition (cf. §43, 1): "In Sacred Scripture. . . , while God's truth and holiness remain what they are, the marvelous *condescension* of the eternal Wisdom becomes manifest, 'so that we might discover God's ineffable loving-kindness, and come to appreciate how far God has gone, out of his provident concern for our nature, in adjusting his Word to our level.' For the words of God, expressed in human tongues, have become like human discourse in every way, just as once the Eternal Father's Word, having taken on the flesh of human weakness, has become human like ourselves" (DV 13).

[6] With the praise of God thus firmly anchored in the life of God, we can now return to our discussion of the Christian narrative. The historic, particular events of divine origin, which first prompted the Church's worship in the name of Jesus Christ alive, are prominently—yet far from exclusively—conveyed by means of the Resurrection *motif* [*j*]. The profession "Jesus is Lord"—which establishes the heart of Christian worship in every present moment—is closely connected with the historic confession that "God has raised him from the dead" (cf. Rom 10, 9).

We have already stated that Christian worship owes its narrative shape to its origins in history (§38, 1). We now add that the *predominance*

[*j*] The words *motif* and *prominent* are used advisedly here. E Schillebeeckx overstates his case when he proposes to view different early thematizations of Jesus' new life as *separate Christologies* (for example, a Q-kerygma with a parousia-christology without resurrection, a purely pre-existence-inspired wisdom-christology, etc.), which in turn point to *different*, and even *separate*, communities (*Jezus*, pp. 327ff; ET 401ff.). This amounts to treating *oral* tradition, which tends to be flexible, dynamic, and open to interchange (and which in its early stages is not replaced but *reinforced* by the production and especially the *exchange* of writings), as if it were *textual* tradition. Written texts exist side by side, whereas word of mouth is continuous; from a linguistic point of view, it is far more plausible to postulate one single broad, loosely coherent response to the living Christ. This would have included distinct motifs like *vindication-justification* (1 Tim 3, 16), *exaltation* (Phil 2, 9; Eph 4, 8; 1 Tim 3, 16; Heb 1, 3–4, 13; 2, 9; 4, 14; 5, 7–10; 12, 2; 1 Pet 1, 11), and *resurrection*, in a variety of interconnected patterns. An example of this is the series of baptismal exhortations in 1 Peter, which is full of resurrection language, yet contains a passage (3, 18–19) in which the antithesis between the death of Jesus and his "vivification" is couched in terms of the flesh-*Spirit* contrast—a scheme that does not fit the death-resurrection sequence. The text indubitably features a Christ who is alive "in the Spirit" preaching to the spirits in the underworld, yet the word "risen" would clearly be out of context here. However, the passage was spontaneously interpreted in a paschal sense, for example, in a fourth-century Easter homily attributed to Epiphanius of Salamis (§48, 2, a, [*p*]; cf. §40, 3, c, [*u*]).

of the resurrection-motif (along with related themes) to convey and orchestrate the revelation of Jesus alive enormously favors the *development
of realistic narrative* as the shape of Christian worship. Let us begin with
an exploration of the meaning of the "resurrection" that prompted the
narrative.

RESURRECTION, NARRATIVE, MYTH

[§39] DIMENSIONS OF THE RESURRECTION THEME

[1] First of all, and very importantly, "resurrection" is a *metaphor*, and
because it is a metaphor, it does not "describe" what the first eye witnesses "saw." Like all metaphors, it does two things at once. It conveys
the power of the *reality* (in this case, the living Christ) that has manifested itself and thus has prompted the metaphor's use. It also expresses the manner in which the metaphor's users (in this case, the
first disciples) have *interpreted* (that is, "cognitively structured") that
reality and its impact on them.[15]

Second, the resurrection metaphor is not of Christian origin. The
theme, along with its train of connotations, had been available in Judaism long before the first disciples grasped at it. When they did grasp
at it, they did so in order to convey what they had so powerfully experienced: first, the actuality of Christ revealed to them as living and,
second, the significance of his being thus revealed to them. In adopting
the resurrection theme in this way, the first disciples obviously also
changed its meaning, so much so that it can be said that "resurrection"
as used by Christians became irreducible to pre-existing Jewish, apocalyptic conceptions.[16] What modified the resurrection theme most decisively was the *central* position it came to occupy in the Christian idiom;
in late Judaism, "resurrection" had only been one of *many* eschatological
themes. In spite of all this, however, the Christian meaning of "resurrection" can only be fully appreciated if its original meaning is properly understood.

[2] "Resurrection" has its roots in Israel's faith in God's absolute mastery over life and death (1 Sam 2, 6; Deut 32, 39), enhanced, by the
prophetic tradition, into a confident hope of life to be restored by a
faithful God (Hos 6, 1ff.; 13, 14; Is 26, 19; 53, 8–12). Israel, in its
recurring faithlessness, may have forgotten the God who "labored to
give birth" (Deut 32, 18b) to it; yet God, who cannot forget Israel any
more than a mother can forget her child (Is 49, 15), will in the end be
known as its Redeemer and Savior, and "all flesh" will witness this (Is
49, 26).

No wonder that this decisively colors Israel's view of the world. In
the very act of joyfully worshiping God as King, Israel recognizes that
the world, though born out of the divine labor (Ps 90, 2), is not ready

for God; it is a world writhing in birth pangs [k] at the prospect of its redeeming and renewing encounter with God. Penitent Israel itself is awaiting, in fear and trembling, the day when God will purify it and restore it to new life (Is 13, 8; 26, 16ff.; Ez 36–37 [l]), to be the center of a world renewed—a world where, by a triumph of steadfast love, God will be king.

Eventually, this theme of renewal and resurrection became part of the Jewish literary tradition that is called "apocalyptic." As such, it eventually became a major theme in Pharisaic spirituality, though it continued to be rejected by the Sadducee establishment (cf. Acts 23, 6ff.; Mt 22, 23). To a faithful remnant aware of Israel's history of waywardness and chastened by centuries of Gentile oppression and injustice, "resurrection" came to convey the *confident hope* that *final justice, for Israel as well as for the world,* was indeed to be expected, though from God alone (cf. Ps 67; Dan 12, 2–3). A final, conclusive paroxysm of natural and human lawlessness, violence, and disintegration would lay bare the fundamental unreliability of all the powers that be. This would be the prelude to the Lord's own Day; on that day, God's true servants, "too good for the world" (Heb 11, 38), would be "raised up," "made alive," "revealed," and "glorified": all those good people who had suffered at the hands of the powers that be for refusing to make common cause with injustice (Wisd 2, 10ff.). Thus, the primary function of the image of "resurrection of the dead" was to help convey *aspirations at once eschatological and universalistic.*[17]

[a] In this way, the general resurrection was expected also to fulfill the prophetic expectation that a renewed Israel would eventually be the focus of the gathering of all the nations for judgment by effusion of the Spirit (cf., for example, Is 2, 2–5; 65, 17–66, 16; Ez 37; Zech 1–8; cf. also the Jewish apocalypse known as the book of the Prophet Joel, and Ps 87).

[3] "Resurrection," therefore, conveys an *integrated vision of God's design for humanity and the world, across space and time.* It is a design whose constitutive themes are *sin, judgment,* and *mercy* [m]. In God's light, the whole world stands convicted; before God's judgment, the whole world must fear and tremble. In the end, however, God is to come; the world is not, in the final analysis, hopelessly mired in its own injustice, for God cherishes it (Wisd 11, 22–26) and will, powerfully as well as mercifully, establish a justice beyond all injustice.

In this way, "resurrection" *comforts* and *encourages* the faithful in a

---

[k] "Trembling" in Ps 97, 4 and 1 Chron 16, 30 is a technical term for labor.

[l] Cf. 1 Thess 5, 3 and Jn 16, 21 for New Testament uses of the same metaphor in eschatological contexts.

[m] Needless to say, these themes will have to be brought up for full treatment in the context of christology and soteriology.

threefold way. First, it anchors their confident praise of God in the assurance of God's ultimate victory and glory [n]. Second, it commits them to a life of patient, long-suffering pursuit of justice, in the firm hope that injustice will be divinely exposed and justice divinely recognized and that all divisions will be divinely overcome. Finally, it reminds them of the ultimate shakiness of all the powers that appear, or pretend, to be lasting and victorious in the world, and of all who trust in them [o].

This, then, was the metaphor, along with the eschatological and universalist aspirations connected with it, that was activated and pressed into service by the revelation of Jesus alive.

[a] The great Jewish prayer, the *T*ᵉ*fillâh* of the Eighteen Blessings, illustrates the prominent place which the hope for the general resurrection came to enjoy in Judaism. The second blessing (*G*ᶜ*burôth*) runs: "You are mighty forever, YHWH, *you bring the dead to life*, you are mighty to save. . . . Who is like you, Lord of mighty acts, and who resembles you, King, you who *kill and bring to life and cause salvation to spring forth?* And faithful are you *to bring the dead to life*. May you be blessed, YHWH, *you who bring the dead to life!*"[18]

[§40] "CHRIST IS RISEN": FROM ESCHATOLOGY TO SALVATION HISTORY

[1] Most importantly, therefore, the revelation of Jesus' vindication by God, and by God alone, decisively put the Christian experience of the present in the perspective of *an imminent eschatological future that would draw the whole world into the presence of God*: "The mystery is this: Christ in you, the hope of glory" (Col 1, 27).[19] In vindicating Jesus, God had at length begun to establish the eschatological kingdom of definitive justice—a justice involving the whole world and all ages—and Jesus had already been divinely identified as *the anticipated agent of God's final judgment*: "God has fixed a day on which he will do justice to the whole world by one he has appointed, and he has guaranteed this to all by raising him from the dead" (Acts 17, 31). Now, in the revelation of Jesus Christ alive, the present world is truly revealed as being in process of all-pervasive renewal (2 Cor 5, 17; Gal 6, 15; Jas 1, 18). It is "groaning in travail," in assured, if still painful, expectation of the full reve-

---

[n] This assurance often expresses itself by means of dubious forms of chauvinism and aggression; cf., for example, Ps 149.

[o] For moderns it is critically important, in interpreting apocalyptic literature, not to be sidetracked by its ostensible interest in *history* (surveys, periodizations, predictions, etc.). Here as everywhere in the apocalyptic genre (and hence, in the apocalyptic literature that arose around the Christian resurrection theme as well) the central point is the same: ". . . the apocalyptic revelation provides a framework in which humans can *decide their commitments* in the full knowledge of the nature of reality present and future" (John J. Collins, "Introduction: Towards the Morphology of a Genre," p. 12; italics added).

lation of all God's children (cf. Rom 8, 19–23); all must be reborn of the Spirit of God, if they are to be part of the kingdom (Jn 3, 3–8).

No wonder, that the Christian cry of worship *"Amen! Alleluia!"* is specified—and tempered—by the prayer that is as much an expression of the disciples' joyful assurance as of their sense of urgency in the face of the fact that the resurrection is still incomplete: *"Marana tha—Our Lord, come"* (1 Cor 16, 22; cf. Rev 22, 20) [*p*]. The joyful praise of God at Christ's personal fulfillment prompts the hopeful petition for the fulfillment of the *totus Christus*—the whole Christ, fulfilled in all those who belong to him (1 Cor 15, 20–28). Thus the praise of God also inspires the resolve to persevere on the road trod by Christ (Heb 12, 1–2): watchfulness and prayer, in mutual concern, sum up the Church's life in expectancy (Mt 26, 41; Lk 21, 36; 1 Pet 4, 7; cf. Eph 6, 18; Lk 21, 34; 12, 45).

[a] The Book of Revelation sounds this theme in full apocalyptic orchestration, with a large cast of angelic powers to carry out and proclaim the divine design. Opening with a vision of the risen Christ (1, 12–18), it anchors present Christian worship in the security of a heavenly liturgy beyond all destruction and persecution; thus it encourages the faithful to accept their present trials in an attitude of "patient endurance" (1, 9), in the certainty of the Lord Jesus' coming (22, 20).

The Letter to the Hebrews plays the same theme out in a different way. The Church knows that Jesus, tempted, tested, and thus made perfect, has entered into the eternal Holy of Holies. In him, the Church has a "sure and reliable anchor of the soul" (6, 19); thus, tempted and tested in its turn, it can travel the road of perseverance to the end.

This urgent yearning for the total fulfillment of God's promise, when it will be given to those who have persevered in faith to be "with the Lord" (1 Thess 4, 17), runs through the entire New Testament, in a variety of other expressions and themes. Not surprisingly, one of the most telling is the ardent expectation of the "resurrection of the dead" (cf., for example, 1 Cor 7, 26. 29–31; 15, 12–28. 51–58). Most impressively, perhaps, the fourth Gospel dramatizes the Christian aspiration conveyed by the prayer *"Marana tha"* by having *Jesus himself* intercede with his Father for his disciples' eschatological sharing in the eternal union of himself and the Father

---

[*p*] Cf. also *Didache* 10, 6 (*SC* 248, pp. 182–83). There is an important parallel here between the synagogue and the Church. Just as *B^erakhôt* ("blessings") provide the setting for the petitionary *T^efillâh* ("intercessions"); cf. L. Bouyer, *Eucharist*, pp. 58–78), so the praise of the Father prompted by Christ's resurrection provides the setting for the petitionary prayer for his coming in glory.

(Jn 17, 6–26; cf. 14, 3), for which they must be prepared by a life of holiness, fidelity ("truth"), and unity.

[2] The new, eschatological perspective brought about by Christ risen, however, also decisively *rearranged the past*. Most immediately, it evoked a new vision of the most *recent* past: Jesus' life and execution. The original witnesses and those who had accepted their testimony began to insist that their new experience of the living Lord was continuous with the past events of Jesus' life and ministry; in fact, they claimed that the unexpected events of Easter gave them access, for the first time, to the full significance of Jesus' life and ministry.

What had been a matter of well-attested (Acts 2, 22; 10, 36ff.), if controversial, *human* history, now proved to have been *God's work*. If Jesus had "gone about doing good and healing all that were oppressed by the devil," this had been because "God was with him" (Acts 10, 38). God had been mysteriously active even in Jesus' death, so much so that it now became warrantable to say that the Christ "had to" suffer to come into his glory (cf. Lk 24, 26). Thus the risen Jesus stands "vindicated in the Spirit" (1 Tim 3, 16): by raising him from the dead, God had revealed the one who had been condemned by the Jewish authorities as a blasphemer and executed by the Romans as a threat to the emperor's sacred authority, as "the Holy and Just One" (Acts 3, 14).

The resurrection of Christ, therefore, causes *retrospect*: Jesus' works and words now fall into a compelling pattern whose coherence is divinely warranted, and even the senseless cross gets filled with meaning.

If [Jesus], crucified, had remained gone and away, I would in all likelihood not have openly acknowledged [the cross], for I would probably have covered it up along with my Master. But with the resurrection succeeding the cross, I am not ashamed to speak about it at length.[20]

All of this means that Jesus' story can now be truly *told*—and told *prophetically*—on the authority of God, not only by way of praise and thanksgiving offered to God (§38, 5), but also by way of witness to the world.

The story of Jesus' life can now also be traced back in such a way as to insure his personal anchorage in God. If he is professed as Son of God, risen in power by virtue of the Holy Spirit (cf. Rom 1, 3), he also comes to be professed as "the Holy One" that will be called "Son of God" (Lk 1, 35) from the beginning of his life, conceived by virtue of the Holy Spirit (Mt 1, 20; Lk 1, 35). If he is professed as the one who, in his risen state, embodies God's offer of eschatological salvation for all (Acts 4, 12), he also comes to be professed protologically, as the key to all of creation (1 Cor 8, 6; Col 1, 16–17; Heb 1, 2–3, Jn 1, 3. 10), as the original Son of God,[21] as the Lamb slain from the foundation of the world (Rev 13, 7–8),[22] and even as the very Word of God, with God before the world was made (Jn 1, 1; 17, 5; 1 Jn 1, 1–2).

In this way, the resurrection motif favors the development of all-encompassing realistic narrative as the shape of Christian worship (§38, 4)—a narrative whose theme is *salvation*.

[a] Edward Schillebeeckx has soundly argued that the *pre-Easter* interpretation of the *historical* Jesus in terms of "the eschatological prophet" amounts to a true, if provisional, christology, which must have mediated between the uninterpreted facts of Jesus' historical ministry and the first post-resurrection christologies.[23]

We may perhaps wonder if Schillebeeckx has not interpreted the Jewish expectation of "the" eschatological prophet a little too rigidly, as if that expectation specifically concerned a single identifiable individual; the classic passage in Deuteronomy (Deut 18, 15–22) in fact suggests the opposite [q]. Popular expectation, especially in oral cultures, is always a function of *aspiration*; it tends to be atmospheric and indeterminate, and all the more potent for being so.

Also, when Schillebeeckx suggests that the resurrection theme obliterated the early interpretation of the historical Jesus as the eschatological prophet, we are justified in wondering if the opposite cannot be argued equally well. Given the fact that "resurrection" is itself an eschatological metaphor, could it be that the resurrection theme, in retrospect, *supported* the interpretation of Jesus as eschatological prophet rather than pushing it into oblivion?

Schillebeeckx' main contention, however, deserves acceptance: it is extremely probable that eschatological expectancy colored the perception that contemporaries had of the historical Jesus. Something important follows from this. The disciples' use of the resurrection theme to convey their faith in Jesus alive is in basic continuity with related eschatological aspirations aroused by Jesus' historic ministry. This means that the Christian confession of the personal identity between the prophetic Jesus of history and the risen Christ of faith (Acts 2, 36) is matched and undergirded by a *continuity in the choice of interpretative thematizations*.

[3] The disciples' new understanding of the past was not limited to a reinterpretation of the recent past—Jesus' person and his ministry. The prevalence of the resurrection motif in the New Testament proves that the new life of Jesus prompted, from the outset, a universalist perspective.

---

[q] This observation, along with the fact that we have no access to Jesus' self-experience, makes it speculative to say, as Schillebeeckx does, that "it is highly probable, historically speaking, that *Jesus understood himself to be the latter-day prophet*" (*Jezus*, p. 251; ET *Jesus*, p. 306; italics added). There *is*, of course, good evidence that "Jesus conceives of [ET envisages] his life in prophetic categories" (*Jezus*, p. 389; ET *Jesus*, p. 477).

This wide perspective generated, first of all, a new, conclusive reinterpretation of the entire *history of Israel* but, beyond that, a conclusive interpretation of the entire *history of the world*. Like the story of Jesus' life, both had fallen into a divinely coherent pattern. Again, this meant that both could now be truly and coherently *told*—that is to say, told *prophetically*—on the authority of God, both by way of praise and thanksgiving to God and by way of witness to the world. Also in this respect does the resurrection motif favor the development of realistic narrative as the shape of Christian worship (§38, 4); again, the narrative involves a *history of salvation*.

[a] In this way, Christian worship and witness continues Israel's tradition of *cultic-prophetic narrative*, which characterizes both its worship (cf., for some obvious examples, Deut 26, 5–10; Pss 105; 106; 136) and its Torah [r]. Of this tradition, 1 and 2 Chronicles are the priestly reinterpretation; Sirach 44–51 offers a sapiential reading.[24]

[b] The eschatological—that is to say, *definitive*—reinterpretation, on the authority of Christ risen, of the cultic-prophetic narrative of Israel's history of faith and faithlessness as it is concretized in the Scriptures, is part of the bedrock of the Christian Tradition [s]. The resurrection-kerygma reflected in Paul's preaching appeals to the Scriptures (Rom 1, 2; 1 Cor 15, 3–4), as do the kerygmatic speeches in the Acts of the Apostles (Acts 2, 17–21. 25–28. 34–35; 3, 12–26; 8, 32–33; 10, 43; 13, 16–22) and Stephen's *apologia* (Acts 7, 1–53). The integration of Israel's Scriptures into the Christian vision of hope, which is the inspiration for present patience, is an explicit theme in Paul (Rom 15, 4; 1 Cor 10, 11; cf. 9, 10). The same is especially notable in the Gospels. Before the resurrection, the Scriptures were not understood (Mk 12, 10. 24; Mt 21, 42; 22, 29; Jn 20, 9); now they are. In the synoptics, the rereading of the Scriptures is an all-pervasive theme. To mention only one example, the formulaic expression *gegraptai* ("it is written") occurs as many as twenty-four times. In Matthew, oft-repeated references to the "fulfillment of the Scriptures" are among the most notable ways in which Israel's tradition is integrated into the Christian gospel (Mt 1, 22; 2, 15. 17. 23; 4, 14; 8, 17; 12, 17; 13, 35; 21, 4; 26, 54. 56; 27, 9). Luke's Gospel

---

[r] The Law (*Tôrâh*) comprises both the Pentateuch and the books of Joshua, Judges, 1 and 2 Samuel, and 1 and 2 Kings. It is not without significance that the Jewish Tradition calls the latter six (which later, non-Jewish interpretation has tended to refer to as *historical* books) the "Former *Prophets*."

[s] Simply from a literary point of view, reinterpretation and fulfillment of the past are integral to the Bible's inner coherence, not only between the New Testament and the Jewish Scriptures, but also within the tradition of the Jewish Scriptures and within the New Testament themselves. Writing as an experienced and sensitive literary critic, Northrop Frye has shown, under the heading "Typology" (*The Great Code*, pp. 78–138), how an adequate interpretation of the Bible is utterly dependent on the reader's ability to appreciate this fact.

very effectively dramatizes the theme by having the risen Christ personally "open" and "interpret" the Scriptures (Lk 24, 27. 32. 44–45; cf. 18, 31; 22, 37) to show that especially the Messiah's many *sufferings* were integral to God's saving design [*t*]. Throughout the fourth Gospel, the Scriptures are being "remembered" (Jn 2, 17; 12, 16), "fulfilled" (15, 25; 19, 24. 28. 36–37), and "accomplished" (19, 28); in fact, Jesus, resolutely identified, in the prologue, as the divine Word in person (1, 1–2, 14), is cast in the role of the definitive interpreter of the Scriptures (5, 46; 6, 45; 7, 38; 8, 17; 10, 34–35; 13, 18; 15, 25 ["in *their* law"!]; 17, 12). A rather different version of the fulfillment tradition, combined with motifs from Jewish angelology, is found in the Letter to the Hebrews. There, Jesus is presented as the most recent prophet, decisive because he is the protological and eschatological ("in these last days": 1, 2), unmediated revelation of God's own being. Accordingly, he is also presented as the fulfillment of Israel's temple worship, now extinct (4, 14–10, 25), and of Israel's long tradition of prophetic, long-suffering faith (11, 1–12, 2).[25]

[c] The Christian reinterpretation of Israel's history of salvation, however, came to be set in an even broader perspective. Christ came to be seen as the key to an understanding of *the whole world* and its history of faith and sinfulness, from the beginning on. These universalist dimensions of the gospel are powerfully suggested by the genealogy in Luke (3, 23–38); it interprets Jesus as "son of Adam, son of God" (unlike Mt 1, 1–17, which confines Jesus' ancestry to Israel). In the *Prima Petri*, universalism is dramatized by having Jesus go, "in the Spirit," into the nether world to evangelize the cosmic spirits imprisoned there (1 Pet 3, 18–20): the gospel reaches back, down to the world's roots, down to where the universe is enchained [*u*]. In the same perspective Paul can boldly speak of God reconciling, in Christ, "the world" to himself, which amounts to a "new creation" (2 Cor 5, 17–19; Gal 6, 15), with Christ as the "new Adam" (Rom 5, 12–21; 1 Cor 15, 47–49)—a vision already adumbrated by the synoptic accounts of Jesus' baptism, under the wings of the Spirit hovering over the waters (cf. Gen 1, 2).

The universalist perspective is very eloquently brought home where the Christian community came to anchor its interpretation of Christ's significance for the salvation of the whole world in the bed-

---

[*t*] Cf. the Lucan use of Gk. *dei* or *edei* ("must") to denote "divine necessity" revealed by the post-resurrection retrospect: Lk 9, 22 par. Mk 8, 31; Lk 17, 25; 24, 26; cf. also 22, 37; 24, 7. 44. If Lk 2, 41–51 is read as a legendary rehearsal of the theme of Jesus' death and resurrection, retrojected into his infancy (cf. F. J. van Beeck, *Christ Proclaimed*, pp. 371–72), then Lk 2, 46–47 can be added to this list. Jesus' word that he "must [*dei*: verse 49] be in the things of his Father" supports this interpretation.

[*u*] The passage inspired an account of the descent into hell in which Christ, alive in the Spirit, preaches to Adam, with the same universalistic implications (§48, 2, a, [*p*]; cf. §38, 6, [*j*]).

rock theme of *Wisdom*. In royal Israel, wisdom traditions had already provided connections with the wider world of the surrounding cultures. However, when postexilic Judaism began to personify Wisdom, the latter soon acquired features that were fully cosmic: Wisdom was now seen as God's own agent in Creation (Prov 3, 19–20; 8, 22–36), the Word by which God had created the world (Sir 24, 3). It is hardly surprising that Wisdom should have acquired divine features (Wisd 7, 25ff.; 8, 3; 9, 4; Sir 24, 3–4) in the process. As such it came to be thought of as present "in every people and nation" (Sir 24, 7). As pre-existent Torah, however, it had found its preferred dwelling place in Zion (Sir 24, 8–12), without, however, losing its original omnipresence.

No wonder that Christ, once risen, came to be definitively interpreted as the divine Wisdom in person, especially in the fourth Gospel (Jn 1, 1–18) and in the Letter to the Hebrews (esp. Heb 1, 1–2),[26] in a bold move that succeeded in conveying at once his saving significance for the Church and his foundational significance for the world. Finally, the christological hymn in the Letter to the Colossians (1, 15–20) shows the same combination of particular and universal elements but in reverse order: cosmology here precedes ecclesiology.

If Christ came to be seen as the key to the salvation history of the world, it is not surprising that the New Testament, which connects Jesus Christ with the Father by means of themes expressing complete mutuality (§34, 2), also identifies him as the agent of the Father's will for universal salvation. The fourth Gospel is especially rich on this score by its use of mutually related themes like *mission* (Jn 4, 34; 5, 23–37; 6, 38–44; 7, 16–33; 8, 16–29; 12, 44–49; 13, 16–20; 14, 24–26; 15, 21–26), *authorization* (Jn 5, 27; 17, 2), *obedience* (Jn 4, 34; 5, 30; 6, 38–40), *indwelling* (Jn 14, 20; 17, 21; cf. Col 1, 19; 2, 9), *manifestation* (Jn 9, 3–4; 17, 6; cf. Rom 16, 25–26; Eph 3, 3–4), *glorification* (Jn 8, 54; 12, 23; 13, 31–32; 14, 13; 15, 8; 16, 14; 17, 1–5), and *predestination* (Jn 17, 24; cf. Eph 1, 3–10). In this way, the history of the world's salvation, brought to a head in Christ, is ultimately anchored in God's own mystery.

[d] In the earliest decades of the second century, Ignatius of Antioch is already thematically insistent on Christianity's "gathering together all nations and tongues" (cf. Is 66, 18) as well as Judaism. Borrowing the language of Hellenistic Jewish universalism with the intention of surpassing it, he writes: "It is senseless to profess Jesus Christ and practice Judaism. For it was not Christianity that came to believe in Judaism, but Judaism [that came to believe] in Christianity, in which every tongue that came to believe in God was gathered together."[27]

Never, perhaps, was the Christian Church's determination to be universalist and catholic, and not sectarian and narrow, demonstrated more forcefully than a few decades later. It took the shape of the rejection of *Marcionism* (cf. § 32, 4, a, [g]), the most widespread and successful of the second-century heresies, as well as the prototype of all subsequent forms of rigorism in the Christian Church.

In his eagerness to proclaim the newness of the Christian revelation, Marcion saw the gospel, not as the mandate for the (ongoing) fulfillment of the history of Israel and the world, but as its definitive *replacement*. In Marcion's view, the God of the Jews was no more than the subordinate Demiurge—the Creator-God who had made the world and who had exacted obedience to the law. The gospel (which Paul had been the only one to understand fully) had at long last proclaimed "the greatest God" (cf. §27, 4, b!)—the God of Love revealed by Jesus Christ.

Faced with this challenge, the Christian tradition opted for a difficult redemptive task, rather than a sectarian and self-righteous one. It resigned itself to asking and answering the many hard questions about the true meaning of the Jewish Scriptures and the religions of the world and refused to turn itself into a completely novel creation with no real responsibilities to the world of time and place.

[e] Many of the classical eucharistic liturgies are striking instances of the way in which Christian worship takes the shape of a christological narrative that encompasses the Jewish tradition of patriarchs and prophets as well as the protohistory of the world. The narrative is extremely concise in the eucharistic canon found in Hippolytus' *Apostolic Tradition* (the model of the second eucharistic prayer in the new Roman missal); it is more elaborate in the Liturgy of St. Basil (many features of which can be found in the fourth eucharistic prayer).[28]

[§41] CHRISTIAN NARRATIVE AND MYTH

[1] There is a reason why the universalist perspective of the Christian narrative urgently invites elaboration in our day. The opening of *Nostra Ætate*, the Declaration on the Relationship of the Church to Non-Christian Religions promulgated by Vatican II, explains this well. "In our times, when every day the human race is being drawn closer together and the ties between various peoples are being multiplied, the Church is giving deeper study to its relationship with non-Christian religions. In its task of fostering unity and love among people, and even among nations, it gives primary consideration in this document to what human beings have in common and to what promotes fellowship among them. For all peoples form a single community. They have a single origin, since God made the whole human race dwell over the entire face of the earth. One, too, is their final goal: God, whose providence, manifestations of goodness, and saving designs extend to all, until the elect

are united in that Holy City ablaze with the splendor of God, where the nations will walk in his light."

This new appreciation of the unity of all humanity, the declaration goes on to state, has also given rise to a new appreciation of the origin of all human religiosity in the ever-questioning human heart and in the universal sense of mystery (NA 1).

[2] The universal human quest for meaning and the human sense of all-encompassing mystery take the shape of narrative: human communities everywhere live by (among other things) *myths*. In solemn acts of rehearsing them (most often in ritual settings), a community finds itself placed in a sacred milieu, in which it enacts and celebrates its origin and destiny in the presence of the divine. Its sense of identity is renewed and once again experienced as rooted in a timeless, transcendent moment, just as the renewal of its sense of purpose opens out once again on the perspective of its share in a total renewal of the world. Both mythic past and mythic future are thus brought to bear on the present moment, enabling the recovery of the community's primal innocence and authenticity, and actualizing and furthering its vital tradition.

What fundamentally constitutes a myth, therefore, is not its content but the manner of its signification. Narratives are myths neither on account of the historical unverifiability of their content nor in virtue of their allegedly timeless significance but on account of *the way they function* in the communal cultivation of awe, renewal, and self-awareness. Myths shape the experience of meaning in the actuality of the present moment, measured as it is by the significant past and the significant future. In casting its narrative account of the saving significance of Christ in ultimately cosmic terms, therefore, the worship of the Christian community joins *both* Israel *and* many other religions in the use of *mythic narrative* [v].[29]

There are some significant differences, too, of course. The single most important is that the Judaeo-Christian myth intentionally avoids giving the impression that it draws only on the ideal past—the *in illo tempore*—of mythic time. It very emphatically claims mythic significance for historic events that took place in real, historical time (§36, 3; §38, 4) [w].

---

[v] Here also lies, at least in principle, the possibility for the further integration of mythological material into Christian worship and witness. Historic examples of this are the integration of Jewish and Hellenistic cosmic angelology (cf. expressions like "choirs of angels," and "powers and authorities") into the praise of God, and the orchestration of the veneration of the Blessed Virgin by means of themes derived from cosmic and anthropological mythology.

[w] Note the exact nature of the difference. Drawing on history for the creation of myth is not a phenomenon limited to Judaism and Christianity. Mircea Eliade suggests other examples of historic personages that have been known to become legendary and eventually completely ahistoric (cf., for example, *The Myth of the Eternal Return*, pp. 34–

Nevertheless, it is wise to be careful here. The shape of the Christian myth is indeed what we have called "realistic narrative" (§38, 4–5). But this narrative is neither a purely objective account of historic events nor a purely figurative, ahistoric "myth." Rather, it is a narrative that, while *relating a true story*, also carries and conveys a commitment, on the part of the narrators as well as the listeners, to the story as *the vehicle of the meaning of their lives*. It is "testimonial autobiography" (cf. §45, 2; §46, 2): while witnessing, in narrative form, to transcendent divine realities as well as to the whole cosmos, myth gives expression to the community's self-identity as it experiences itself in place and time.

The mood of modern historicism, with its exceedingly narrow definition of "truth," has naively tended to relegate this kind of narrative to the realm of fiction and imagination, if not downright projection and even prejudice. In any case, the modern, absolute distinction between historical events (what "really" happened) and myths and legends (what did "not really" happen) is completely foreign to the Bible, including the New Testament [x]. Hans Frei, in his commanding monograph *The Eclipse of Biblical Narrative*, has told the story of how, ever since the eighteenth century, widespread failure to realize this has led to what is still a major exegetical impasse in the present day: the divorce between "fact" and "meaning," or between "history" and "faith."

[a] Some late writings in the New Testament do indeed decry "myths," "fables," and "genealogies," but they do *not* do so because the latter are *not historical*. Rather, those savage denunciations mean to preserve the *community*. What they reject is the esoteric sectarianism inherent in mythic speculations encouraged by deceitful teachers. Such "godless and silly myths" are a far cry from the reliable teaching, which the solid teachers provide (1 Tim 1, 4. 6–7; 6, 4; 2 Tim 2, 23; 4, 3–4; Tit 2, 10–16; 3, 9; 2 Pet 1, 16). The reliable teaching advocated in these passages, therefore, must not be construed (in fundamentalist fashion) as involving only historical events; it also involves what moderns would call myths, fables, and legends.

Hence, what these New Testament passages *are* interested in is the *way* in which any teaching or any narrative, whether it be mythical or historical by modern standards, *functions*. Teaching that leads to speculation, and breeds factions of initiates who claim privileged access to the mystery, will only cause idle discussion and, hence, lack

---

48). Rather, the difference with the Judaeo-Christian myth is that such mythologized figures derive their *significance* from their *mythical* status, not from their being drawn from history.

[x] Speaking far more generally, but with the instinct for accuracy that betrays the experienced reader, Northrop Frye observes that "if anything historically true is in the Bible, it is there not because it is historically true but for different reasons" (*The Great Code*, p. 40).

of mutual concern and division in the community [y]. Consequently, the promotion of such "myths" amounts to an abdication of community life—that is to say, of concrete social responsibility. (Only in this sense could it perhaps be argued that preoccupation with "fables" amounts to a lack of concern with the present, concrete realities of *history*.) Hence also the emphasis, in the Johannine letters, on the coming of Jesus "in the flesh" (1 Jn 4, 1–3; 2 Jn 7)—an emphasis that a century of antignostic Christian writers was to adopt with a passion.

COMMITMENT, COMMUNION, TRADITION, RULE

[§42] THE CHRISTIAN NARRATIVE AS A MANDATE FOR COMMITMENT

[1] The new, eschatological perspective brought about by Christ risen, it was explained, decisively rearranged the past, from the most recent past, Jesus' life and death, to the cosmic past; this made it possible for the past to be *prophetically told* in a divinely coherent fashion (§41, 2)— as a history of salvation. But *prophecy involves a call to commitment*. Just as the risen Christ had mandated the integration of the world of the past into the disciples' thanksgiving to God and into their understanding of that world, so he also made decisive demands on their understanding of, and commitments to, the world of the *immediate future*. We must briefly develop this important function of the Christian narrative.

If Christ was risen, the glory of the true God had dawned, and the whole world must be drawn into true worship as well as readied for the imminent divine judgment, in which Jesus Christ would be the pivotal figure (§40, 1). The resurrection, therefore, was not only a call to worship, in which all of God's past mercies could be thankfully rehearsed in the light of the eschatological assurance of fulfillment extended by Christ's Resurrection. It also came as a summons to *readiness*: it turned the disciples into an *eschatological community*. This sense of eschatological imminence was, in turn, translated into *a commitment to the urgency of the moment*. Having been saved from the power of sin and death and thus summoned into Christ's absolute future, the Christian community must, in its turn, set about *participation in God's activity in making salvation history*: they are to be *servants*, wide awake and sober, and build up the community by good works done in the broad light of day (1 Thess 5, 1–11; cf. the related imagery in Mk 13, 33–37 parr.;

---

[y] The functional modern equivalents of the "fables" denounced in the New Testament, therefore, are not myths, but *ideologies*. What was said of myths can also be said of ideologies: *what fundamentally constitutes an ideology is not its content but the manner of its signification*. Any myth, therefore, can be turned into an ideology, by being misused. Myths serve to enhance a community's sense of identity by actualizing its connections with the transcendent as well as with the world; ideologies fix and isolate. Eventually, this also affects content: myths remain flexible; ideologies turn rigid.

Mt 24, 43–51; Lk 12, 35–46; Jn 13, 3–4 would appear to cast Jesus in the role of the servant).

It was explained before that the worship that lies at the core of the Christian community takes the shape of confident, divinely authorized, realistic narrative (§38, 2, a; 4). We must now add something that has already been intimated: the praise of God inspires the resolve to tread the path trod by Christ (§41, 1). *The Christian narrative of the past turns into the warrant for, and the expressive vehicle of, the Christian commitment to the present in imitation of Christ, who awaits the Church in the future.* Christian worship, which is prompted by the presence of Christ to the Church in each here and now, till the close of the age (cf. Mt 28, 20), inspires and demands the witness of Christian life. No cries of "Lord, Lord!" without doing the will of the Father (Mt 7, 21; cf. Lk 6, 46). No union with God without responsibility in and for the community, and even for the whole human family in the present world.[30]

This commitment to the life of readiness takes shape in the two fundamental forms of Christian *conduct*: *mission* and *common life* (cf. §38, 2, a; 7; § 43, 2–4; §50, 3), both of them marked by their orientation to the eschaton.

[a] Short versions of the christological narrative clearly functioned prominently in the early *missionary practice* of preaching the gospel to Israel and the gentile world, to call them back to their divine destiny. Traces of this can be discovered in the New Testament, especially in Acts, in which short accounts of Jesus' life, death, and resurrection, of Israel's history, and even of universal history, are placed in kerygmatic as well as controversial contexts (Acts 7, 1–53; 10, 34–43; 13, 16–41; 17, 22–31).[31] But accounts of the life of Christ are no less behind the quiet, unobtrusive, yet equally missionary practice of good Christian living, and especially of Christian patience in the face of undeserved hostility (for example, 1 Pet 3, 15–4, 5; cf. §32, 2).

The prominence of soteriological narrative as a means of fostering *the life of the early communities* is equally obvious. As a matter of fact, it was precisely the demanding, many-faceted life in communion (*koinōnia*) that was largely responsible for the production of the entire New Testament as we have it, including, in due course, its canon. The demands of community life (which included, from the beginning, and as an essential element, a gamut of contacts among the various communities) obviously produced many of the examples of teaching (Gk. *didachē*) and exhortation or encouragement (Gk. *parainesis*) based on Christ's example, found in the epistles and the Apocalypse (e.g., Rom 15, 2–3; 2 Cor 8, 9ff.; Heb 12, 1–2,; 1 Tim 6, 11–16; 1 Pet 2, 21–25). But the demands of community life also produced the Gospel narratives: the confident rehearsal of the life, death, and resurrection of Jesus became the mandate for the community's life-style. Communal commitment to the *imitatio Christi*, in other words, is as much the point of the Gospel narratives as the thankful remembrance of God's great deeds.

[2] Commitment to the imitation of Christ is also expressed, in the New Testament, by a striking literary feature, which can be said to involve *implicit narrative*. It was explained that the New Testament traditions convey the complete mutuality between the risen Christ and God his Father by a profusion of themes (§33, 1); these themes give rise to a number of divine titles of Jesus (§34, 4). A matching profusion of themes and images in the New Testament conveys *Christ's saving significance*. Christ's soteriological significance is, therefore, not only conveyed by means of *narrative*, as we have seen (§41, 2); it is also conveyed by means of soteriological *titles*.[32]

Many of these occur in *sets of related images* structured in such a way as to convey a *dynamic relationship* between Christ and those who are called to salvation—that is to say, *a relationship that demands that it be lived out*. In this sense, these clusters of titles *imply a commitment to salvation history*: they shape and thematize the *soteriological dynamic* implied in, and demanded by, the profession of Christ risen. Those who have turned away from sin to profess the risen Christ aspire, with Paul, to being "with the Lord" (1 Thess 4, 17; 2 Cor 5, 8; Phil 1, 23); this aspiration has been a source of inner freedom for them, and in thus freeing them it has shaped, and will continue to shape, their lives.

[a] Like the explicit narratives already treated, these clusters of titles serve a double purpose. They (retrospectively) convey thankfulness for, and appropriation of, salvation already obtained; they also (prospectively) express commitment to the Christian life that remains to be lived. Three principal types may be discerned.[33]

1. *Key and headship sets*. In the fourth Gospel, Jesus' self-designations by means of the titles "vine," "door," and "shepherd" are matched by titles for his followers, expressing organic connection and dependence: "branches," "sheepfold," and "sheep" (Jn 15, 1. 5; 10, 1. 3. 7–9, 11. 14. 27). Analogously, the Pauline corpus refers to Christ as "head," and to the members of the Christian community as "members" (1 Cor 12, 27; cf. Eph 2, 20; 4, 15; 5, 23; Col 1, 18). If Christ is the "keystone," the Christians are the stones that are making up the building (Eph 2, 20–21; 1 Pet 2, 5).

2. *Names of excellence*. There are good reasons to assume that the expression "more than Jonah" and "more than Solomon" (Mt 12, 41–42 par. Lk 11, 31–32), and perhaps "the Son" used absolutely (Mk 13, 32; Mt 11, 27), are historical self-designations of Jesus. In any

case, they *set a standard* for what it means to be an effective prophet, a teacher of wisdom, and a child of God.

The Christian communities came to use this figure of speech with abandon and frequently devised related metaphoric self-designations to convey the *conversion* that their association with Christ had brought about. Thus, Jesus is the true Moses, in whose face Christians have seen the true reflection of God's glory (2 Cor 3, 7–4, 6), and who is faithful *over* God's household, as the Son, just as Moses had been faithful *in* it as the servant (Heb 3, 2–6). He is the new Adam (Rom 5, 14–21; 1 Cor 15, 22. 45), as well as the "image of the invisible God" *par excellence* (Col 1, 15), through whose grace and in whose image all are to be remade. He is the "good" shepherd (Jn 10, 11ff.) and, as such, the model of what it means to love: in giving one's life for those one loves. He is "the Son of God," and, as such, "the heir," raising Christians to the status of adopted children and fellow-heirs (Gal 4, 1–7), the "firstborn" (Rom 8, 29; Col 1, 18; Heb 1, 6; Rev 1, 5) among many younger brothers and sisters.

3. *Radical personifications.* Here, Jesus is identified by means of absolute personifications derived from metaphors expressing soteriological *functions*. Not only is Jesus "the just One," but he *is* "our justice" (Acts 3, 14; 1 Cor 1, 30). Designated as "the author of life," come in order that others may have life in abundance, he is also "your life," and even "the Life" (Acts 3, 15; cf. Jn 10, 10; Col 3, 4; Jn 11, 25; 14, 6). He is the "Amen" (2 Cor 1, 20; Rev 3, 14): the guarantee, in person, of the "Amen" with which Christians worship and witness. Not only is he the prophet who speaks God's word, and a teacher who "teaches the way of God in truth"; he *is*, radically, "the Word," and "the Way, and the Truth" (Mt 13, 57; 22, 16; Jn 1, 1. 14; 14, 6). "The Lord is risen indeed," but most radically he *is* the Resurrection (Lk 24, 34; Jn 11, 25). In the fourth Gospel, these titles occur as radical *self*-identifications of Jesus, as part of a whole series of "I am" sayings, which have overtones of the divine self-designation "I am" in Exodus (3, 14; cf. Jn 8, 58; 13, 19). Hence, not only do these Johannine personifications relate the faithful to Jesus as savior; they also anchor that relationship in God.

[3] The saving history that it is the community's responsibility to make, we have argued, is warranted and mandated by the narrative that informs its worship and witness: the saving story of the life, death, and resurrection of Christ—the key to the salvation history of Israel and, indeed, of the whole world. It must be remembered, however, that the narrative is prompted by Christ's resurrection, that is to say, by *eschatological assurance.* Much as memory and tradition may guide and shape the Christian commitment, its energy comes from confidence in the

promise held out in the person of the risen Christ. The history that the Christian community must forge is prompted by Christ's resurrection; hence, the Church's life occurs in the perspective of *judgment* (cf. § 39, 2; §41, 1).

This eschatological perspective, no matter how sobering, is a source of *realism*—a realism that draws its confidence from the risen Christ. The imitation of Christ, therefore, is not a matter of canonizing precedent and past example but of meeting the challenges of ever-new times and ever-new places in the Spirit of the risen Christ—the Spirit for which the Church must ever pray. In that Spirit, access to "the mind of Christ" (1 Cor 2, 16) is available to Christians, even to the point where they "might venture to predict how he might have acted in this or that situation, indeed even what he might have said.[34]

Finally, the eschatological perspective is a source, not only of realism, but also of responsibility. Judgment on the rightness of history-shaping decisions, the small as well as the great, which the Church must make as it follows Christ, lies with God, whose Christ "will come to do justice to the living and the dead." Freed from the worries of self-righteousness, therefore, the Church is to act responsibly, by doing justice to the world it lives in. In all of this, it must rely on the advocacy of him who pleads on its behalf and on whose mercy it wholly depends.[35] Here lie the eschatological roots of the combination of carefreeness and dedication that must characterize Christian ethics.

[§43] THE CHRISTIAN NARRATIVE AS THE RULE OF FAITH

[1] The Christian narrative, we have shown, was originally prompted by the resurrection of Christ and proclaimed by way of praise and thanksgiving offered to God. It also turned into the inspiration, both of the Christian mission and of the responsible Christian life; in this way, the Christian narrative moved the Church abroad and into the future and thus generated the Christian Tradition. We must end this chapter by pointing to a third function that the Christian narrative came to acquire: guarding this living, authentic, and, hence, authoritative Tradition by serving as the Church's guide as it encountered differences of place and time. The christological narrative, in other words, became not only *the shape of the tradition of worship* and *the mandate for the tradition of conduct* but also *the core of the tradition of teaching*.

[a] This is where faith and theology become most closely allied. Theology, and systematic theology in particular, essentially involves the interpretation of what the great Tradition and the historic events connected with it have understood and taught (cf. §23, 5, a). In a sense, therefore, all of *God Encountered* must be a demonstration of the ways in which the great Tradition is a tradition of *teaching*.

[2] The shared Christian narrative, we have shown, functions as the carrier of commitment, to God and to the world (§38, 5; §42, 1). In virtue of the commitment to God, the community anticipates, in its worship, the fulfillment of the promises held out in the person of Christ risen (cf. §38, 1; 5; §41, 1). In virtue of the commitment to the future and the whole world, the narrative encourages those who live by it to make history, by missionary activity and community-building (§42, 1; §50, 3).

In the process, however, the very experience involved in making history will feed and enrich the narrative that prompted the effort to make history. This is all the more understandable if it is recalled that space and time are the very stuff that Christian worship—the source of Christian teaching—is made of: the Church's praise of God in the Name of Christ has the shape of a wayfarers' song sung on the way to the sanctuary (§36, 3). In this way, as historic experience joins the past, it also enters into the communal account of the past and thus reinterprets and modifies it. *The original Christian narrative begins to augmented by the record of the living Tradition it mandates.* That is to say, as time advances, the narrative turns into *the bearer of the community's ongoing commitment to the authoritative past,* Israel's past, and, indeed, the whole world's (cf. §41, 2).

[a] This process is not exclusively Christian; it can be readily demonstrated in the Jewish Scriptures. The Bible as we have it reflects the entire spiritual history of Israel, its living tradition of common worship and shared witness. It reflects that history, not only in the progressive accumulation of the Law, the Prophets, and the Writings, but also in the Septuagint, which augmented and reinterpreted the Hebrew Bible for the Greek-speaking Jewish Diaspora, in a more universalist perspective. The Bible also reflects all the redactional and editorial activity, which, as the biblical scholars of the past two centuries have taught us, accounts for the shape in which it has been handed down to us. Today, in other words, it is clearer than ever that the Bible is itself the principal piece of evidence for the history of its interpretation and reinterpretation (cf. §41, 2, b, [s]) and, hence, the principal witness to Israel's living tradition.

In the New Testament this tradition continues. In fact, one correct (if unconventional) way to describe the Christian Bible is to call it the most recent edition of the Jewish Scriptures, augmented with a series of documents that offer a definitive reinterpretation of the Jewish tradition—one that finally includes the gentile world.

[3] Just as this ongoing Jewish reinterpretation of the Scriptures was the fruit of Israel's historic experiences, so the New Testament is the fruit of the historic experiences of the first generations of Christians. In the process of praising God in the name of Jesus Christ, the faithful

have brought *the concerns of their own lives* with them.[36] These concerns have so shaped both their worship and their witness, that the Christian narrative and the titles of Christ (which make up the core of the Church's worship and witness) can also be said to be the record of the historic faith-experience of the primitive Church.[37]

[a] The vital concerns of the New Testament communities are visible in the patterns of worship that can be inferred from the many blessings and thanksgiving hymns found in the Epistles and the Apocalypse and especially in the numerous intercessions in the same writings. They clearly follow the established patterns and metaphors of the Tradition yet also incorporate allusions to the community's own situation.

The opening blessing of 1 Corinthians (1, 4–9), for example, shows how Paul is adapting standard blessing formulas to his specific purposes in writing the letter: he praises the Corinthians' speech, knowledge, and gifts, and pointedly does not mention faith, hope, and love. The blessing in 1 Peter (1, 3–12) is strongly marked by the theme of suffering in imitation of Christ—doubtlessly a reflection of actual experience of the letter's recipients, as the remainder of the letter also suggests. Finally, the blessing in 1 Timothy (1, 12–17) is an imaginative characterization of Paul's apostolic life as a testimony to God's merciful patience.

[b] The historic experiences of the first Christian communities have shaped not only the patterns of worship but also the patterns of witness, both in its missionary and in its paraenetic forms.

With regard to the former, it has often been pointed out that the Pauline kerygma shows its indebtedness to the gentile mission by the absence of an account of Jesus' ministry (an account that, understandably, the Palestine communities were to cherish). The author of Acts, too, clearly means to fit the Christian narrative to situations. On the Areopagus, Paul meets the concerns of Gentiles: he uses the theme of universal history, which his audience shares, as a basis for his call to repentance in preparation for the impending Judgment and for his proclamation of Christ's resurrection (Acts 17, 22–31). In Pisidian Antioch, speaking to a Jewish audience, Paul relates both Israel's history and Jesus' ministry and then proceeds to proclaim Christ's resurrection and to call his audience to conversion (Acts 1, 16–41).

In the area of community life, as it appears in the New Testament, the influence of historic experience on the shape of the Christian narrative is, again, hard to miss. The Thessalonians, in accepting the gospel and suffering for it, became imitators of Christ; this, however, took the shape of imitating Paul himself (1 Thess 1, 6; cf. 1 Cor 4, 16; 11, 1), as well as imitating, at a great distance, "the Churches of

God in Christ Jesus which are in Judaea" (1 Thess 2, 14), which had themselves suffered in imitation of Christ. In Ephesians (5, 2), a very brief statement of Christ's way (which, it is implied, was an imitation of God) functions as the key to a long exhortation to virtuous living that even includes household responsibilities.

[4] In this way, it is possible to observe how, from the start, the Christian narrative, while remaining itself, *creates diversity* in accordance with the situations of *time* and *place*. In such a situation, however, the need for *authoritative stability about the true center of the Christian faith* must eventually arise. This need occurred, not only in the context of settling the relations among the Christian communities themselves, but also in the context of mission: a far-flung community of Churches needs the security of a common confession if does not wish simply to be at the mercy of the next questioner.

The need was met, from the second half of the second century on, by the formation of "rules of faith" (*regulæ fidei*; cf. §21, 3, c),[38] which present themselves as the undivided Church's expressive account of its encounter with the divine condescension. They also express, therefore, what must be considered the "foundation of the Christian faith" and, consequently, the standard against which all other doctrines are to be measured (§23, 4, c).

[a] Unlike the later creeds, which are textually fixed and thus can be used as canonical documents, rules of faith are still largely oral and, hence, both stable and flexible. They developed out of short creedal formulas, and became part of the broad tradition of instruction offered to catechumens.[39] Written texts were still entirely in the service of the living, oral tradition; orthodoxy was not yet tied to any letter. The Church largely relied on the formulary stability of liturgical, kerygmatic, and paraenetic oral discourse, which guaranteed the continuity of the Tradition. In that sense, rules of faith are typically catholic. They are examples of *qualitative catholicity* (§21, 3)— of the kind of unity that encourages diversity and the kind of diversity that seeks the common ground (§21, 2, [a]).

The common "rule of faith" thus subsists in a variety of rules of faith. Since these rules of faith present, in a free way, the focal commitments of the great Tradition, they generate and sustain a wealth of traditions. Only on the basis of such rules of faith can there be room for that essential ingredient of the catholic theological tradition: an appreciative hermeneutic of doctrine across space and time (§21, 1).

[b] In the framework of *God Encountered*, the doctrines contained in the rule of faith will be treated under the rubric of the divine *exitus*. The rule of faith involves the account of the divine self-communication in Creation and Incarnation, culminating in Christ's resurrec-

tion and the revelation of God's Trinity as the warrant for the gracious and ecstatic fulfillment of humanity and the world (§23, 4).

[c] Vatican II explains that the Church "has always regarded and still regards [the Scriptures] together with Sacred Tradition as the supreme rule of its faith" (DV 21). In the interpretation here offered, the living Tradition of worship and witness, of which the rules of faith are an apt expression, first produced the Scriptures; the same living Tradition then proceeded to draw on the Scriptures as the most original witness to itself. Accordingly, we have suggested that divine inspiration can be analogously claimed on behalf of both (§38, 5, a).

[d] The formation of three of the Church's fundamental authoritative structures—the rule of faith, the New Testament canon, and the apostolic office—occurred roughly contemporaneously and thus may be viewed as integral parts of the formation of the great Tradition. It is not surprising, therefore, that the Second Vatican Council, following a long tradition, could teach: "It is clear... that, by God's most wise design, the Sacred Tradition, Holy Scripture, and the Church's Teaching Office are so linked together and coordinated, that one cannot exist without the other, and that all of them, each in its own way under the action of the one Holy Spirit, effectively contribute to the salvation of souls." (DV 10)

[5] One of the earliest rules of faith occurs in the first book of Irenaeus of Lyons' *Against All Heresies*, written in the last quarter of the second century. Its orientation is entirely positive. It stresses the worldwide universality of the Church along with its essential unity, across the differences of space and time, in the profession of its central Tradition:

In fact, the Church, though dispersed throughout the world to the ends of the earth, having received, handed down from the apostles and their disciples, the faith in *one God, Father almighty, 'who made the heavens and the earth and the sea and all they contain'* [Ex 20, 11; Ps 145, 6], *and in one Christ Jesus, the Son of God, who was made incarnate for our salvation, and in the Holy Spirit, who through the prophets proclaimed the dispensations* [z], *the coming, the birth from the virgin, the passion, the resurrection from the dead, and the bodily assumption into the heavens of the well-beloved Christ Jesus our Lord, as well as his coming from the heavens in the glory of the Father 'to bring all things under one head'* [Eph 1, 10] *and to raise up all flesh of all humanity, so that before Christ Jesus, our Lord and God and Savior and*

---

[z] This word (Gk. *oikonomias*) sums up, in Irenaeus' idiom, the whole history of salvation, told by way of divinely authorized realistic narrative (§38, 2, a; 4): "the totality of the work accomplished *by the Son* in conformity with the Father's good pleasure, from the beginning, through the Incarnation and the paschal mystery, to the glorious Parousia. It is not surprising that the Holy Spirit should thus have been able to proclaim, through the prophets, the totality of the history of salvation. Recall that for Irenaeus, the Holy Spirit is not just the one who announces the future, but also the one who gives knowledge of the past and uncovers the present" (Adelin Rousseau, in *SC* 263, pp. 223–24).

King, according to the good pleasure of the invisible Father, 'every knee may bend, in the heavens and on the earth and in the underworld, and every tongue may acknowledge' [Phil 2, 10–11] *him, and so that he may render just judgment on all, sending to the everlasting fire the 'spirits of evil'* [Eph 6, 12] *and the angels that have transgressed and become apostate, and well as the impious, the unjust, the lawless and the blasphemous among humankind, but endowing with the life that gives incorruptibility and clothing with everlasting glory the just, the holy, those who will have kept his commandments and abided in his love, some from infancy, others since their conversion,*—having gotten this preaching and this faith handed down, as we said before, the Church, though dispersed throughout the world, carefully guards them, as if it were inhabiting one house, and believes in them, as though it had one single soul and one and the same heart, and unanimously preaches them and teaches them and hands them down as if it had one single mouth. For while the languages across the world are different, the gist [*dynamis*] of the Tradition is one and the same.[40]

[6] The *regula fidei* was apt to be used for polemical uses as well. This becomes apparent in Tertullian's *De præscriptione hæreticorum*,[41] probably written around 200. Tertullian's central thesis is that the Church need not argue with heretics because the Tradition it lives by was in place before the heresies ever cropped up: "After Jesus Christ, we have no need for curiosity, nor do we, after the Gospel, need any further inquiry. Once we believe, we do not want to believe anything besides. For this is what we believe first of all: that there is nothing else we should believe."[42]

This professed refusal to debate does not prevent Tertullian from introducing a few decidedly polemical, antignostic emphases into his version of the rule of faith. Yet on balance, it must be granted, these added touches are relatively inconsequential. What is far more striking, really, is *how little* Tertullian's version of the rule of faith has been affected by the controversial purposes to which he puts it.[43] This helps to demonstrate how reliable an instrument the flexible, adaptable *regula fidei* was for the safeguarding of the Tradition. Tertullian writes:

The rule of faith. . . is that by which we believe [what follows]. *There is one single God, who is none other than the creator of the world, who by his Word, sent out before all else, brought all things into being out of nothing. This Word, called his Son, appeared in the name of God in various ways to the patriarchs, was always to be heard in the prophets, and last of all descended, by the Spirit of God his Father and his Power, into the Virgin Mary, made flesh in her womb and, born from her, lived as Jesus Christ. Thereafter he proclaimed the new law and the new promise of the kingdom of heaven, wrought wonders, was put to death by crucifixion, rose again on the third day, and, taken up to heaven, took his seat at the Father's right hand, and sent in his place the Power of the Holy Spirit to guide those who believe; and he will come with glory in order to take the saints into the enjoyment of the everlasting life and the heavenly promises, and to condemn the impious to the everlasting fire, both parties having been raised from the dead and gotten their flesh restored.* About this rule, which. . . carries the authority of Christ [*a Christo. . . instituta*], there are no questions among us, except those which were introduced by heresies and which produce heretics.[44]

[7] It is time to close. This chapter has demonstrated that the Christian narrative is, not only *the shape of the tradition of worship* and *the mandate for the tradition of conduct*, but also *the core of the tradition of teaching* (§43, 1). In tracing the narrative, we have thus discovered the three integral elements of the Christian faith-experience, namely *worship, conduct*, and *doctrine* (cf. §23, 7). Each of these three, while centered on the Christian narrative, has given rise to broader traditions. Together, these form the threefold Tradition. This Tradition is the comprehensive, dynamic structure of the Church we live in, which *"in its teaching, life, and worship*, perpetuates and hands on to all generations all that it is itself, all that it believes" (DV 8). Three final chapters must study this structure at greater length.

CHAPTER 9

Cult as the Matrix of Conduct and Creed

"CONFESSIO"

[§44] PRELIMINARY: HEGEL ON "SYSTEM" AND "MOMENTS"

[1] Early on in his *Enzyklopädie*, Georg Wilhelm Friedrich Hegel discusses the relationships of the various philosophical disciplines among one another and to philosophy as a whole. In the terse, formal language characteristic of his maturity he sums up his fundamental thesis as follows:

Each of the parts of philosophy is a philosophic whole, a circle that encloses itself in itself. However, the philosophic Idea is present in it in a particular determinacy or element. Each single circle is, in and of itself, totality, which is also the reason why it breaks through the limitation of its element and establishes a wider sphere. Consequently, the whole presents itself as a circle of circles. Each of these is a necessary component [*Moment*], in such a way that the system of its own special, particular elements makes up the integral Idea, while the latter in turn also manifests itself in each single element.[1]

Hegel is here implying that a system is to be distinguished from a mere aggregate. In an *aggregate*, the parts remain foreign to each other, because they are simply contiguous and juxtaposed; the whole, therefore, is no more that the sum of its parts. Ordinary, workaday knowledge by and large obeys the laws that govern aggregates: it works by accumulation. In a *system* of intellectual pursuits, however, the parts are integral: they are organically related to the other parts as well as to the whole. Systematic knowledge, therefore, works by organic, coherent understanding.

Philosophy, Hegel explains, is such an organic, coherent system of intellectual pursuits; it does not operate in a merely cumulative manner. The "idea" of philosophy—that is, its normative essence: what it *is* and therefore what it *should be* (cf. §8, 6, a; §9, 1, a; §33, 2)—is one and the same always and everywhere, no matter in which *particular* area it is exercised. This idea of philosophy involves *totality*: philosophic pursuit is concerned with reality as such, and, hence, it cannot stop at any limit. For this reason, each particular, self-defined philosophical discipline or pursuit will betray philosophy's fundamental allegiance to the totality of being, and this will show in the wider sphere of interests to which each particular philosophical discipline necessarily refers. Thus on the one hand, philosophy as a whole is a "circle of circles": it can exist only in the form of *a system of special disciplines*. On the other hand, each specialized philosophic pursuit bears the imprint of *all of philosophy's concern with totality*.

[2] Hegel's choice of the word *Moment*—one of his favorite terms—to designate the partial pursuits that make up philosophy as a whole serves to make an important point. Hegel borrows "moment" from the science of mechanics, where it is a technical term denoting *power of leverage*.[2]

For Hegel, a part in a whole is a "moment" inasmuch as it is, *not a mere part*, but also, in its own particular way, *the whole*. Precisely because each special philosophic pursuit carries in itself the reference to totality, it establishes a wider sphere of reference: it *dynamically* "raises issues" that are outside its own specialized scope. A moment, therefore, is characterized by its *intrinsic ability to enter into dynamic relationships with other moments*, or, in other words, *to enter into dialectical exchanges with other moments*. Without such relationships, any part of philosophy would cease to be a true moment: it would cease to be integral, lose its allegiance to totality, and thus disintegrate precisely as a part of *philosophy*.

This leads to an important conclusion. The genuineness of each moment is established by reference to the other moments; *moments are verified by their mutualities*. This verification takes a very concrete shape. Because each moment *intrinsically* refers to the other moments of the system, those other moments will "reappear" within the context of each moment; if such reappearances do not occur, we are dealing, not with a moment, but with a nonintegral, isolated—and thus ultimately irrelevant—*part*.

In the sphere of understanding, therefore, *systems create intellectual movement*: each "part" is organically related to the other "parts" and thus gives rise to the dynamic understanding known as dialectic. True philosophic understanding, therefore, is essentially a dynamic process of intellectual growth and development, in which no single component can be understood apart from the others, and in which the understanding of each component affects the understanding of other components and of the whole in function of these components [a].

---

[a] CF. *Webster's Ninth New Collegiate Dictionary*, which includes the following definitions

No wonder that an important twentieth-century Hegel scholar has given a definition of "moment" in which the static aspect is immediately complemented by the dynamic:

A moment is an essential constitutive part of a whole [viewed] as a quiescent system, and a necessary transitional phase in a whole [viewed] as a dialectical movement.[3]

[3] It is the intention of the final three chapters in this volume to bring our phenomenology of the Christian faith (cf. §23, 8; §25; §31, 3) to a close by applying Hegel's insight to it.

We will elaborate an understanding of *the Christian faith as a whole* by means of an understanding of its *three fundamental moments* (or "components")—*worship, life, and teaching*—and of *the dynamic hierarchy that prevails among them* (§23, 7). In doing so, we will be elaborating the broader traditions of worship, life, and teaching to which the central Christian narrative has given rise (§43, 8).

We will also be recovering, in a concrete fashion, the discussion of the relationships between reality-structures and understanding, which was conducted, in a rather more abstract way, at the very outset of the present volume (esp. §11, 3–4).

Very importantly, too, we will be arguing that the relationships among worship, life, and teaching involve *mutual verification*. None make sense apart from essential relationships to the other two; in fact, the other two always "reappear" in each of them, as part of the inner make-up of each. Eventually, this understanding of the Christian faith as a coherent system will enable us to gain an insight into the *dynamics of the Christian faith as a lived reality*. Exploring the patterns of coherence of the Christian faith, therefore, is of decisive significance, not only as an exercise in systematic theology, but also as a way to gain an important understanding, namely, that the Christian *community* is essentially a community of *spiritual growth and development* (§§53–54).

Let us start off this important discussion with a telling, if rather technical, example of the coherence of the Christian faith.

[§45] ONE IDEA IN THREE MOMENTS: *Tôdâh—Homologia—Confessio*

[1] The unity-in-diversity of the Christian faith is strikingly exemplified by a series of developments, both *linguistic* and *semantic*, that have yielded an idea central to the Tradition of the undivided Church. In the language of Western Christianity, this idea is named *confession*. It has its roots in the Hebrew Bible, but its development can be traced through the Greek of the Septuagint to the New Testament [b]. Even-

---

under the entry "moment": "4 *obs*: a cause or motive of action 5: a stage in historical or logical development 6 a: tendency or measure of tendency to produce motion esp. about a point or axis."

[b] For a fine elaboration of this theme, cf. Harvey H. Guthrie, Jr., *Theology as Thanksgiving: From Israel's Psalms to the Church's Eucharist.*

tually, it became the common property of the Greek Fathers. Finally, by a process of consistent translation, it became one of the most typical expressions in the Christian Latin of the Vulgate, which in turn influenced, at least to some extent, the usage of the Latin Fathers and, through them, of large portions of the Christian West.

[a] An important caution. In this section, a series of telling linguistic and semantic developments will be treated. This treatment, however, does *not* claim the *the words discussed, and only they, contain, by themselves, regardless of context, the idea* that is to be developed. Ideas are not "contained" in words; they are communicated in statements and clusters of statements.[1] The conception we are about to develop, therefore, could be very well developed by recourse to many other words, texts, and contexts. What *is* claimed, however, is that the very particular semantic and linguistic developments about to be discussed *illustrate*, *exemplify*, and *sum up*, in a striking fashion, a fundamental feature of the structure of the Christian faith.

[2] At the basis of the tradition lies the Hebrew verb *hôdâfah*, along with its cognate noun *tôdâh* [c]. The verb has two chief meanings that are often distinguishable, though seldom completely separable. The first meaning is "to praise, to sing a hymn of thanksgiving"—an action *directly* addressed to God (cf. §38, 3, b, and [f]).

Frequently, this praise is *narrative*: a jubilant song of *detailed thanksgiving* to the Lord. This narrative feature prepares the ground for the second meaning of the word *hôdâh*: "to confess." Acts of confession are narrative accounts: the speakers praise God *indirectly*, by *witnessing* to God's blessings [d]. They recount, elaborately and repeatedly, in public and for everybody to hear, the distress of the past and the rescue from it, and appeal to others to join in thanking God and in expecting divine rescue from God in their turn.

This witnessing acknowledgment of God, finally, gives rise to another, rather more derivative meaning of *tôdâh*. Since the narrative may also occur in the context of a *penitential* act of conversion, perhaps in the setting of an expiatory sacrifice, offering praise and thanksgiving to God can take the shape of a renewed "acknowledgement of the Name" (1 Kings 8, 33. 35 par. 2 Chron 6, 24. 26). Thus the acknowl-

---

[c] Cf. *TDOT* under *ydh*, V, pp. 427–43. The verb *hôdâh* is the *hiphil* form of the root verb *ydh*; the *hithpael* form of this verb, *hithyadâh*, also occurs in roughly the same meanings, but chiefly in later texts (for example, 2 Chron 30, 22 ["to give thanks"]; Ezra 10, 1; Neh 9, 3; Lev 16, 21; 26, 40 ["to confess sins"]).

[d] It is good to recall, though, that in Hebrew (as in many other languages) the distinction between direct address and indirect address is less sharp than it would seem from a purely grammatical point of view. Syntactically and stylistically speaking, the pronouns and verbal forms of the third person, both singular and plural, are often used by way of second-person address, in a reverential sense. A biblical example is 1 Sam 26, 18, where David says to Saul: "Why does my Lord pursue after his servant?" Cf. also the oscillation between the second and third persons singular to address the Lord in Ps 92.

edgement of past sins begins to approximate a formal *profession of faith* in a God who saves.

The semantic world of *tôdâh*, we conclude, comprises the three elements identified in the previous chapter: worship, witness in the form of a story from real life, and profession of faith—all of them in the form of a "testimonial autobiography" (§41, 2): a narrative of rescue from failure by a God who saves.

[a] In the *cultic* meaning of "to praise," *hôdâh* occurs numerous times in the Hebrew Bible, for example, in the standard hortatory formula: "*Hôdû l'YHWH kî tôv; kî l' 'ôlâm chasdô*" ("Praise the Lord for he is good; for his mercy is forever": Ps 106, 1; 107, 1; 118, 1. 29; cf. Ps 28; 136, 1; 1 Chron 16, 41; 2 Chron 20, 21).

Where *witness* is the principal meaning, the distress of the past is usually stated in standard formulas: the violence or the cunning of personal or common enemies, national catastrophe brought on by enemies, illness, or the threat of death. If the distress is a present one, the praise of God may be incorporated into a lament, in the form of a vow to praise God, often by means of a sacrificial offering—a cultic act to be accompanied by the recital of the God-given rescue. Many of these features can be readily identified, for example, in Ps 30, which quite naturally ends with a vow of perpetual thanksgiving, or in Ps 118, where the *tôdâh* oscillates between direct address and public witness.

In a *penitential* context, the narrative of the "distress of the past" tends to take the form of a confession of *sin*, either of the sins involved in Israel's faithlessness as a nation (cf. Lev 16, 21; 26, 40; Ezra 10, 1; Neh 9, 3, in contexts) or of individual sins (Prov 28, 13; Ps 32, 5, in context).

[3] In the Septuagint, *hôdâh* and *tôdâh* are regularly, though not exclusively, rendered by the compound Greek verb *exhomologein* and its cognate noun *exhomologēsis* [e]. In the secular Greek of the period, these words (as well as the simple forms *homologein* and *homologia*, which are more current) have the basic meaning of "to agree, to admit, to acknowledge," also in the legal and religious senses of "agreeing to a statement," "admitting a charge," "committing oneself to a promise, a vow, or an act of penance." This enables them to render many of the

---

[e] Cf. *TDNT* under *homologeō*, V, pp. 199–220, esp. 200–207. The compound verb *anthomologein*, with the cognate noun *anthomologēsis*, is also found. For the meaning "confession of sin," however, LXX prefers *exagoreuein* (Lev 16, 21; 26, 40; Ps 32, 5b; Neh 9, 3; 2 Esdr 8, 91 [LXX 2 Esdr 10, 1]), although *exhomologein* also occurs in Dan 9, 4 (where it renders *hithyadâh*). *Exhomologein* also occurs in 1 Kings 8, 33. 35 par. 2 Chron 6, 24, where it renders *hôdâh*, which in these places has penitential connotations; *hôdâh* in 2 Chron 6, 26 is rendered correctly, if curiously, by *ainein* ("to praise"). Jerome interpreted *hôdâh* in 1 Kings 8, 35 and 2 Chron 6, 24 in an explicitly penitential sense; witness his use of *pœnitentiam agere* in both places. He rendered *hôdâh* in 1 Kings 8, 32 and 2 Chron 6, 26 simply by *confiteri*.

senses of *hôdâh* and *tôdâh*: "to witness," "to profess," and "to confess sin in view of obtaining mercy and salvation."

Still, there is a most remarkable feature to the translation of *hôdâh* and *tôdâh* into Greek. In the Septuagint, *exhomologein* and *exhomologēsis* also come to mean "to praise and give thanks"—*a meaning they do not have in contemporary secular Greek.* The use of these words in this new sense, therefore, is a linguistic and semantic surprise. A Semitism is being pressed into service to expand the available semantic range of a family of Greek words, thus enabling the Jewish Diaspora to carry forward the *tôdâh*-tradition in Greek. *Exhomologein* and *exhomologēsis* in the Septuagint carry forward the entire semantic cluster comprised by *hôdâh* and *tôdâh*.

> [a] In fact, *exhomologein* and *exhomologēsis*, in the Septuagint, render *hôdâh* and *tôdâh* (and their less frequent cognates) *more often* in the sense of "giving thanks" than in any other sense (for example, Gen 29, 35; 2 Kings [= 2 Sam] 22, 50; 2 Chron 30, 22; Dan 9, 4; Tob 12, 7. 22; Sir 39, 7. 15; 47, 8; 51, 1–2; most consistently and frequently in the Psalms). The simple form of the verb, *homologein*, renders *hôdâh* in the sense of "to give thanks" in Job 40, 9 (14).

[4] The Septuagint is by and large the Bible of the New Testament communities, rather than the Hebrew Bible [*f*]. Not surprisingly, therefore, the New Testament takes up and carries forward the vocabulary of the *tôdâh*-tradition. But unlike the Septuagint, it uses *exhomologein* sparingly. Where it occurs, it means "to give [God] praise and thanks" (Mt 11, 25 par. Lk 10, 21; Rom 15, 9 [rendering *hôdâh* in Ps 18, 49]), "to give public witness in praise of God" (Rom 14, 11 [rendering *šb'*, "to swear, declare," in Is 45, 23]; Phil 2, 11), and "to acknowledge sin" (Mk 1, 5; Mt 3, 6; Acts 19, 18; Jas 5, 16) [*g*].

The simple verb *homologein* and its cognate noun *homologia* are more frequent. In some cases, they have the simple secular meaning of "to assure, to promise" (Mt 14, 7; Acts 7, 17). In the vast majority of cases, however, they refer to *witness* and *profession of faith*—a clear indication to the extent to which the practice of missionary witness and community exhortation have influenced the New Testament writings. Yet in spite of this strong specialization, the full range of the *tôdâh*-tradition is still discernible: *homologein* and *homologia* are used in the context of

---

[*f*] This recognition, it can be responsibly argued, lies at the basis of the undivided Church's position on the Jewish Scriptures. From a Christian perspective, the Septuagint is an indispensable phase in the process of the formation of the Christian Scriptures and in that sense "inspired." It follows that the Hebrew Bible can on the whole be legitimately interpreted by means of the Septuagint and that the Old Testament deutero-canonical writings (or "Apocrypha") are legitimately included in the Christian Bible. Jerome's devotion to the *hebraica veritas* is not supported by the Tradition, from the New Testament on.

[*g*] In Lk 22, 6 it has the secular meaning "to commit, promise."

worship (2 Cor 9, 13; Heb 13, 15), and *homologein* once refers to confession of sins (1 Jn 1, 9).

[a] When the reference is to profession of faith, there are a few cases where the usage is routine (Acts 23, 8; 24, 14; Tit 1, 16). Usually, however, the theme is presented with special emphasis. Thus, in Romans, the open profession of faith is connected with inner justification, in virtue of the Gift of the Spirit (10, 9–10). In the Letter to the Hebrews, the perspective is cultic and, more especially, eschatological. In imitation of Jesus, "the apostle and high priest of our confession" (3, 1), Christians are urged to persevere in the confession and to be unwavering in hope (4, 14; 10, 23), just as they are urged, in imitation of the faith-witnesses of the past, to acknowledge themselves as strangers and exiles and to look, like Jesus himself, to the (eschatological) joy ahead of them (11, 13; 12, 1–2). Christ's example of "fine witness" is also alleged to encourage an apostolic office bearer to the life of virtue called for by his initial profession of faith, again in view of the eschaton (1 Tim 6, 12–13). Throughout the Johannine writings, the eschatological perspective of the confession implies *judgment*: *homologia* is christological profession (Jn 1, 20; 9, 22; 12, 42; 1 Jn 2, 23; 4, 2. 3. 15; 2 Jn 7), frequently (and ominously) mentioned combined with its alternative: denial of Christ (for example, Jn 1, 20; 1 Jn 2, 22–23; 4, 2–3)—a feature also found in the pastorals (1 Tim 5, 8; 2 Tim 2, 12; Tit 1, 16). The most consistently eschatological interpretation of Christian witness, however, is found in Q, which establishes a direct correlation between the Christians' acknowledgment of Christ before others and Christ's eschatological acknowledgment of them (Mt 10, 32 par. Lk 12, 8). The reverse is also true: failure to acknowledge Christ before others amounts to provoking eschatological rejection (Mt 7, 23; 10, 33 par. Lk 12, 9).

[5] In the subapostolic writings, the word-group (*ex*)*homologein* and (*ex*)*exhomologēsis* is found in all the meanings of the *tôdâh*-tradition: "give praise and thanks to God," "bear witness," "profess faith," and "confess sin." The same can be said of patristic literature. Even in the case of *exhomologēsis*, whose meaning gets increasingly specialized in the direction of "confession of sins" (also in the sacramental sense), the liturgical, testimonial, and confessional meanings never completely disappear.[5]

[6] When, around the end of the second century, Latin became the accepted language of the Church in the West, the verb *confiteri* and its cognate noun *confessio* [h] came to be used to translate (*ex*)*homologein*, (*ex*)*homologēsis*, and *homologia*, though only after initial hesitation. The reason for the hesitation is clear: in common usage, the Latin words

---

[h] On the pre-Christian and Christian meanings of *confiteri* and *confessio* and their developments in Augustine, cf. the important article by J. Ratzinger: "Originalität und Überlieferung in Augustins Begriff der *confessio*," pp. 376–79.

had a rather negative connotation. Though their principal meaning was simply "to admit" and "admission," they really connoted "self-accusation," often in the sense of forced admission of guilt in court; honorable, voluntary acknowledgment of mistakes was preferably expressed by *profiteri* and *professio*. The words, therefore, had to be explained in the Christian community. These explanations were needed, not only in the early years of the third century (as passages in Tertullian and Cyprian prove), but even as late as the fourth and early fifth centuries; Augustine still had to remind his hearers that *confessio* meant, not only confession of sins, but also the glorification of God.[6]

Still, it is understandable that the specifically Christian use of *confiteri* and *confessio* should have developed. In the Church of the martyrs, the forced confession of faith before a pagan tribunal was turned into a glorification of Christ. The confession of sin before the community, a practice despised in pagan Rome as something shameful, became a penitential act of humble expiation before God. Once *confessio* had been reinterpreted in this fashion, it could also be understood as a sacrifice of praise and thanksgiving.

When, roughly between A.D. 382 and 410, Jerome translated the Hebrew Scriptures, he rendered *tôdâh* and *hôdâh* by *confessio* and *confiteri* in the vast majority of places. It is not clear how far he went in his revision of the Latin New Testament, but the text he left us renders, with very few exceptions, the word-group associated with *homologein* by *confessio* and *confiteri*. The *tôdâh*-tradition had been firmly incorporated into what was to be the biblical, liturgical, and theological language of the Church of the West for at least the next millennium.[7]

[a] While it is doubtlessly right to point out the difficulties presented by the secular meaning of *confiteri* and *confessio*, there is at least some evidence that the words were used in the Christian sense at an early date. One example is found in Minucius Felix' argument for monotheism drawn from the prayer of ordinary pagans, in his *Octavius*, probably written around the year A.D. 200: "I listen to ordinary people: when they lift up their hands to heaven, all they say is 'God,' and 'God is great,' and 'God is true,' and 'if it please God.' Is this the natural language of ordinary people or the public speech of a Christian acknowledging [God] [*christiani confitentis oratio*]? And those who insist that Jupiter is the principal god use the wrong name, but they agree that there is a single [supreme] power."[8]

[7] The literary, spiritual, and theological potential harbored by the *tôdâh*-tradition is, perhaps, nowhere more evident than in Augustine's *Confessions*. His semantic point of departure was clear: "*Confessio* meant, for Augustine, 'accusation of oneself; praise of God.' "[9]

Written in the form of a prayer of praise and thanksgiving—"the longest prayer in world history"[10]—the *Confessions* are indeed also the account of Augustine's failures and sins, as well as of his probings and his continuing struggles. But the praise of God and the confession of sins and weaknesses are integrated. In the teeth of the mockery of others, who have not yet been brought to their knees, Augustine prays: ". . . let me confess [*confitear*] to you all my shame, to praise you. I beseech you: let me do it, and allow me to walk, in present memory, the tortuous past paths of my error, and offer you a sacrifice of exultation."[11] Augustine's account of his failings thus becomes the very stuff of his song in praise of the divine mercies: "Let me not tire of acknowledging [*confitendo*] your mercies to you, by which you have drawn me away from all my worst ways."[12] Thus his *confessio* is a testimonial to *grace*: it is the account of Augustine's restoration to God as well as to his own inner integrity.[13] In giving thanks, Augustine comes to know God as well as his deepest self.[14]

This *confessio*, however, is far from private. Augustine, that most public and charming of men, very much meant to set himself up as an example: "Behold, you love truth [Ps 51, 6 (50, 8 *Vg*)], for whoever does what is true comes to the light [Jn 3, 21]. I want to do what is true in my heart before you, by way of praise and confession [*in confessione*]; with my pen, before many witnesses."[15]

Much as he is intent on praising God with his entire person brought to self-awareness, Augustine very much wants to *bear witness*, as he most emphatically states in the crucial first chapter of Book 11. In the first nine books, he has confessed what kind of person he used to be; in the deeply introspective tenth book, he has acknowledged who he has become and how far he still has to go [*i*]. Now he is about to share with his readers the wisdom he has discovered in the Scriptures. He resolutely returns to the song of praise with which he opened his *Confessions*: "You are great, Lord, and highly to be praised" [Ps 145 (144), 3].[16] But he does so in a slightly different mode; the witness-function, always intentional, now also becomes very explicit. "Why, then, do I rehearse to you the narratives of so many events? You certainly do not learn them through me, but this is how *I stir up my own heart as well as the hearts of those who read this*, so that *we may all say: 'Great is the Lord and highly to be praised.'*"[17] The praise of God of Augustine the soul-searcher opens out into the call of Augustine the witness, who from his position in the community calls on his fellow Christians (note the "we"—not "they") to praise God. Thus, in the final analysis, both the autobiographical confession and the public, lived witness in Augustine's narrative of sin and salvation are subordinated to the communal praise of God [*j*].

[*i*] "Quis iam sim et quis adhuc sim" ("Who I already am, and who I still am": *Confessiones*, X, 6; *CSEL* XXXIII, p. 230).

[*j*] Ratzinger's opinion that the "*confessio* proper happens in the heart" ("Originalität und Überlieferung in Augustins Begriff der *confessio*," p. 388 and n. 46) is an overstate-

[8] Not surprisingly, the *tôdâh*-tradition is closely allied to the theme of *witness*.[18] This realization is important enough to warrant another, less semantic and more reflective, approach to the issues discussed in the present section. This will take the shape of a meditation on a formula that the previous chapter frequently used but never discussed: worship and witness.

[§46] WORSHIP AND WITNESS

[1] Christian worship is prompted and enabled by a fulfillment that is entirely God's work. The Church has access to the invisible Father; it is united with Christ risen; it worships—even though in groans (Rom 8, 26)—on the strength of the gift of the Spirit, who is the love of God poured out as the guarantee of the resurrection (§34, 1–3; 5–6). At the heart of Christian worship, therefore, there is the doxological encounter, in *ecstatic immediacy*, with God the Father, mediated by Christ risen and embodied in him, and carried by the Spirit (§35, 1).

Still, much as Jesus Christ may be invoked as the "absolute bringer of salvation," *the fulfillment remains only inchoative: the new heaven and the new earth, the general resurrection, the fullness of the love, which comes from God and embraces all, are still outstanding* [k]. At the heart of its worship, therefore, the Church is living off a world yet invisible, off a liberation that is incomplete, off a future that remains to be seen, off a love that for the time being is desire rather than embrace. This is conveyed by the fact that the Church worships with hands lifted up, with eyes closed or raised to heaven, and with hearts groaning in expectancy. Worship, and the life inspired by it, is living, by anticipation, in a spiritual home away from the earthly tent: "If then you have been raised with Christ, seek the things that are above, where Christ is, seated at the right hand of God. Set your minds on things that are above, not on things that are on earth" (Col 3, 1–2).

Here lies a problem, though. Since the Church must mediate between faith and world (§10, 1), worship irrevocably raises the issues of realism and responsibility. Christian worship (and hence, the conduct and the teaching that flow from it) are at heart authorized by God and God alone; but the question is if, and how, a worship so ecstatic and so other-worldly and ostensibly so liberated is related to the world we live

---

ment not covered by the texts he quotes. His conclusion that the Confessions are not a profession of faith (p. 391, n. 66) is correct; still, it should not be overlooked that *professio fidei* is one of the unspoken assumptions behind the whole work.

[k] It remains the merit of Wilhelm Thüsing to have pointed out that Rahner's transcendental christology suffers from a systematic lack of attention paid to the provisional character of the Christ-event in history. Christ may be the "absolute bringer of salvation"; yet this salvation, while absolutely assured, is not fulfilled. Cf. Karl Rahner and Wilhelm Thüsing, *Christologie—systematisch and exegetisch*, esp. pp. 104–7 (ET pp. 63–64). Cf. also J. B. Metz, *Glaube in Geschichte und Gesellschaft* (ET *Faith in History and Society*), where the concern about Christianity's continuing responsibility to *history* is a pervasive theme.

in—that is to say, if, and how, it can be verified as responsible and authentic human behavior. For worship is rightly held suspect—it might just be a matter of self-centeredness and witless tradition. "If the Christian self-expression is uttered *only* to praise God it gets isolated from the world and turns into an act of tribal religiosity—an inauthentic, defensive gesture of self-affirmation directed against outsiders and against all questions, and thus an instance of 'historical atavism' unfortunately popular in certain brands of evangelism ancient and modern."[19]

Hence, if Christian worship is to be believable in the world we live in, it must be proven true—that is to say, *verified* and *tested*. This is done by *witness*, from which worship is inseparable. The ecstatic, worshiping Church must be prepared, this side of the eschaton, both for its own sake and for the sake of the world whose salvation it announces, to be a witness, from Jerusalem to the end of the earth (cf. Acts 1, 8).

[2] What makes a witness? Witnesses are born out of acts of *encounter*, in which persons *address* one another. Addressing someone is more than communicating something to, or getting something communicated from, another person. Underneath *what* is communicated, there is an act (or rather, a dynamic relationship)[20] of *communication-with*: a responsive encounter with an experienced presence. In addressing another person, I personally acknowledge and endorse the reality of the one who prompts me to respond and commit myself to it.

In this way, addressing someone prepares me to be a *witness* to others who were not part of the original encounter, for "it is characteristic of witness for the speaker to present himself personally as the guarantor of the reality he is witnessing to."[21] Only on the basis of that original encounter (or communication-with) can witnesses offer *themselves* for examination, so as to have their personal integrity tested; thus, too, they can claim to tell the truth, by giving a reliable account of *what* was communicated in the encounter.

Ultimately, therefore, witnesses are authorized by an *encounter*. *Proximately*, they are authorized by the fact that they know, and can tell, *the truth*; this knowledge and this ability puts them under an obligation: they are pledged, with the whole integrity of their persons, to reveal and not to manipulate the truth. The original encounter and the proximate claim to truth are *mediated* by the integrity witnesses claim *for themselves*; they press that claim by offering their *testimonial autobiography* (cf. §41, 2; §45, 2) for examination.

Let us apply this brief analysis of the phenomenon of witness to the issue of worship and witness.

[3] *Ultimately*, what authorizes Christian witness is *worship*, for in Christian worship, the Church, prompted and empowered by God's gracious

presence in Christ risen and alive in the Spirit, is encountered by God, and responds by *addressing God*. Addressing God in this way involves a commitment to God; worship is a gesture of acknowledgment of, and total abandon to, the living God, not a purely ideational account of certain truths (cf. §38, 5). This means that the worship of God intrinsically prepares Christians to be witnesses to the actuality of the living, saving God who has encountered them and whom they in turn have encountered as Savior, on the strength of the Spirit, in the resurrection, the death, and the remembered life of Christ.

Thus the Christian worship-response to God involves *commitment* to a style of life; the christological narrative Christians proclaim is also autobiographical, since it is the vehicle of the meaning of their lives (§41, 4). If, then, the Christian faith, especially as it is practiced in worship, is to be perceived as credible, it must be verified by the Christians' moral responsibility, shown in the integrity of the communal and personal style of life. *Proximately*, therefore, Christian witness involves testimony to the truth of the Christian narrative *insofar as it obligates Christians themselves*. It involves fidelity to the rule of faith as the stable center of the tradition of worship and conduct—the center that enables Christians to encounter the innumerable challenges that meet them with consistency, across differences of time and place (§43, 4), without being at the mercy of each occasion.

[4] Witnesses are proved true by being *tested*; this test characteristically takes the shape of *cross-examination*.

The practice of *worship* places the Church closest to the doxological core of the Christian faith—the central mystery of intimacy and awe. This is where it is primarily *God* who examines and tests the Church's faith, and hence, this is where the Church must experience, in total abandon, the test involved in the encounter with God's own divine reliability; that is to say, this is also where it must come face to face with its own unreliability.

The practice of *teaching* places the Church closest to humanity and the world, which are yearning, often unconsciously, for salvation in Christ. This is where the Church must primarily let itself and its integrity in believing and preaching the gospel be examined and tested by *humanity and its world*; it is also the place, however, where the Church must let its loyalty to the teaching tradition be tested.

Finally, the practice of Christian *living* places the Church squarely *between God and humanity and its world*. This is where, in the test of loyalty implicit in the moral demands that each moment makes, the Church must prove its true, responsible freedom, by proving itself true, both to God and to humanity and the world.

[5] It is time to sum up the last two sections. Both the Hebrew, Greek, and Latin vocabulary of the *tôdâh*-tradition and our reflection on the

relationship between worship and witness serve to argue that the central, naked faith-encounter with God (§9, 1; §33, 2; §36, 1) subsists in three moments: worship, conduct, and profession of faith. The core of the Tradition is doxological. In the naked encounter between God and humanity, God is glorified as God, and humanity attains to the glorious summit of its native potential. At this doxological center stands the risen Christ (cf. §34, 2), who is, in person, the "Admirable Exchange" between God and humanity and the world: in him, God encounters humanity and the world (cf. §34, 7) for their salvation and glorification, and humanity and the world come to glorify God. Those who believe in Christ risen share in his worship, which unites them with God, in the Spirit (cf. §34, 6); they also share in his witness, which commits them to the world, in conduct as well as teaching, again in the Spirit (cf. §38, 5). Thus the central encounter with God, played out in the christological narrative of sin and salvation (cf. §41, 2), carries the three constitutive moments of the Christian faith: cult, conduct, and creed.

Each of these moments, if we take Hegel's suggestions (§44, 1–2) seriously, is the whole, although in a particular determination. The Christian faith, therefore, *is* the worship of God, but there is more to the Christian faith than cult. In the same way, the Christian faith *is* "the way of God" (Mk 12, 14; Acts 18, 26), but there is more to the Christian faith than conduct. Finally, the Christian faith *is* "the truth of God" (Rom 1, 25), but there is more to the Christian faith than creeds.

Each of the three moments, therefore, bears within itself the whole of the faith, in the form of *dynamic relationships* to the other moments. *In each of the particular moments in which the Christian faith as a whole subsists the other moments must reappear, as integral to itself.* Without this reappearance, each moment would cease to be a component of the whole and, hence, disintegrate (cf. §23, 7; §33, 2).

The following sections must concretize and elaborate this rather abstract proposition. The first moment to be considered is worship.

CHRISTIAN WORSHIP AND ITS STRUCTURES

[§47] WORSHIP RELATED TO CONDUCT: HOLINESS OF LIFE

[1] Worship intrinsically demands that it be tested and verified by Christian *conduct*. The manner in which this verification must occur is twofold.

First of all, the verification must occur *in the practice of community worship and private prayer themselves*, since in and of themselves they are integral parts of Christian conduct. The verification of Christian worship, in other words, must be partly *internal*: worship must give evidence, in its very structure, of its *moral integrity*. Most importantly, worship must give evidence of its awareness of its own incompleteness. This involves two elements.

First of all, the Church must give evidence of its awareness that it fails, in its conduct, to live up to the praise of God that it utters; hence, *confession of failure and unworthiness* must be an integral part of its praise of God. The Church's awe at God's presence must be borne out by its awareness of the boldness, not to say presumption, involved in addressing God at all. The Church's intimacy with God must be verified by its humble profession of the obstacles that its continuing lack of total abandon to God places in the way of the divine love.

Second, this penitential profession, of the part of the worshiping Church, of its unworthiness and inadequacy, involves an essential commitment to *petition* and *intercession*. The Father's gracious surrender of his only Son for us is indeed the definitive pledge that God will give us "all things" (Rom. 8, 32), but both the Church's growth in the Spirit of Christ and promised gift of "all things" remain the work of grace, to be prayed for, not be taken for granted. No wonder that the Lord's Prayer itself is a petitionary prayer with a consistently eschatological orientation. It prays for the complete actualization of God's kingdom and, in the interim, for the gifts of freedom from worry about sustenance and of readiness to forgive; finally, it prays for faithful endurance of the eschatological tests and trials and, even more pressingly, for the rescue from the evil one that is behind all resistance to God, down to the end.

To sum up, enduring habits of penitence, petition, and intercession (also in behalf of the world) must keep the Church from cultivating, in the very act of its worship, the dreadful illusion that its union with God is complete, and that the rest of the world might as well be abandoned. In this way, the worshiping Church will be able to mediate, in a credible way, its faith in God to a world in whose incompleteness it very much participates.

[2] Christian worship also involves the Church's relationship with the world. Hence, it must allow its worship to be tested and verified *externally* as well. By making Christians witnesses, worship involves them in a commitment to the life of readiness in anticipation of the Judgment, in the imitation of Christ (§42, 1). This verification, in other words, is a matter of observable holiness of conduct.

The profession of Christ risen involves participation, not distance (§34, 2; 6). Far from absolving Christians from a life of holiness, therefore, the worship of God's holiness revealed in Christ risen commits them to holy living. Accordingly, worship *without* a holy life, far from uniting people with God, estranges them from God, not in the last place because it is scandalous: it casts doubts on the credibility of God Most Holy. Exclaiming "Lord, Lord!" without doing the Father's will, therefore, bars access to the kingdom (Mt 7, 21). Confessing Jesus as the Son of God, and thus abiding in God's love and having God's love abide in oneself, is utterly incompatible with hating one's brother (1 Jn 4, 15–21). Living by the Spirit who prompts the faithful to address God in worship as "Father dear" involves the obligation to walk by the Spirit and to produce the fruit of the Spirit in freedom, since the works of the flesh involve slavery and exclude one from the kingdom (Gal 4, 6; 5, 16–23).

It is striking that Paul's call to Christian conduct, in his Letter to the Romans (Rom 12, 2–15, 12), is wedged in between a call to worship in the Spirit, in total sacrificial abandon (Rom 12, 1), and a wish for the joy and the peace of the Resurrection that warrants hope abundant (Rom 15, 13; cf. §49, 1, a). Similarly, the Letter to the Colossians places its exhortation to reject the sins of the past and its commendation of the Christian virtues (Col 3, 5–15a) between a call to the life on high (Col 3, 1–4) and a call to worship (Col 3, 15b–17). The first Letter of Peter consistently oscillates between the themes of worship and holy living (cf. §48, 3, a). The New Testament communities clearly bear out the conviction that it is of the essence of Christian worship that it be verified in right conduct.

[a] Quite consistently, therefore, the Second Vatican Council teaches that the worshipful proclamation of Christ, together with the Father and the Spirit, as "alone Holy" leads to holiness in the Church and that, therefore, all believers are called to holiness of life (LG, esp. 39, 42).

This has consequences for the practice of worship. Mutual encouragement to lead good lives is part of the total function of communal worship; not surprisingly, the order of service of most liturgical celebrations comprises not only prayer but also exhortation. And, to mention a very concrete example, the rite of dismissal in which the worshiping community is entrusted with its mission of peace and service, is an integral part of the Eucharist [*l*].

The obligation to a virtuous life involved in worship is also implied, for example, in the thirteenth-century exhortation first found in William Durandus' *Pontificale*, just before the ordination ritual proper, in the traditional Roman liturgy of the ordination of priests. One of its high points is the pithy phrase *imitamini quod tractatis*: "Live in accordance with [the holy things] you handle."

[*l*] The original name of this rite, in vulgar Latin, was *missa*. In military idiom, the word could mean "dismissal" (also in the sense of "On your mission!"), even though it was also commonly used, for example in the courts, in the more neutral sense of "Meeting adjourned." In the Christian West, *missa* became one of the names of the eucharistic liturgy as early as the mid-fourth century, when Ambrose used the phrase *missam facere* ("to do the mass"). Cf. Cross, pp. 886–87 (bibliogr.).

[3] Worship is verified by conduct, not only in the sense that it demands and generates it, but also in the sense that it *pre-requires* it. Jesus stands in the great prophetic tradition when he calls for forgiveness as a precondition for prayer (Mk 11, 25), and exhorts to reconciliation with a brother who bears a grudge as a precondition for the offering of sacrifice (Mt 5, 23–24). For Paul, living for God is permanently rooted in the Christian commitment, undertaken in Baptism, to the mortification of the sinful passions of the flesh (Rom 6, 3–12; 8, 12–17). In his discussion about the observation of food laws, Paul reminds the Romans that the cultivation of harmony, peace, and concern for each other's weaknesses in the community is a precondition for the glorification of God (Rom 14, 1–15, 6; cf. 1 Cor 8, 4–13; 10, 23–33).

Accordingly, sin makes the sinner unworthy of the communion of the Body and Blood of Christ, and participating in this communion despite habits of sin amounts to drawing divine judgment down upon oneself (1 Cor 11, 27–34). For these reasons, Baptism, which is the original act of worship, by which persons are incorporated into the worshiping community, pre-requires the renunciation of sin. And with regard to the already baptized, the Church's age-old tradition of refusing access to common worship, especially the Eucharist, on the basis of immoral conduct has excellent New Testament credentials in the practice of "binding" (Mt 18, 17–18; cf. Jn 20, 23; 1 Cor 5, 4–5). The *common* worship of the living God would lose all credibility if indiscriminate participation in it were allowed.

[a] Preoccupation with sin and worry about right conduct as a prerequisite for worship, in turn, found their way back *into the structure of the liturgy itself*. The early Gallican Mass-orders and the eleventh-century, so-called *Missa Illyrica*, both of which left their traces in the pre-Vatican II Roman missal, are especially characterized by an awareness of sinfulness, witness the numerous *apologiæ*—prayers for forgiveness—inserted into the eucharistic liturgy, most of them whispered by the priest on his own behalf.[22] All these emphatic penitential gestures, it may be suggested, were not entirely unconnected with the phenomenon of widespread failure to live up to standards of Christian conduct in the popular Church that arose in the West in the wake of the massive tribal conversions after the demise of the Roman Empire. The reforms introduced by the Second Vatican Council have removed most of these—essentially very clerical—prayers from the eucharistic liturgy and correctly replaced them with a firm, communal penance rite at the beginning of the eucharistic liturgy.

[§48] WORSHIP RELATED TO TEACHING: "LEX ORANDI LEX CREDENDI"

[1] To verify Christian worship, witness takes the shape, not only of conduct, but also of *teaching*. Teaching has its roots in the christological

narrative as it came to function both in kerygmatic-missionary and in paraenetic-communal situations (§42, 1). Eventually, it took shape in *rules of faith* generated by the christological narrative (§43, 1; 2–3); remarkably soon after the end of the apostolic era, therefore, Christian worship turns out to have generated authoritative doctrine. It is not difficult to see why.

Within the community, sober-minded, precise, and articulate doctrine helps verify worship by counteracting mindlessness. Teaching, therefore, helps hold together and build the worshiping community, by protecting it against the anarchic sectarianism associated with purely ecstatic, "spiritual" worship (cf. 1 Cor 14) [*m*]. In the community's dealings with its immediate surroundings, articulate teaching prepares Christians "to make a defense to any one who calls you to account for the hope that is in you" (1 Pet 3, 15). Worship, in other words, proves its inherent *intellectual integrity* by *generating teaching*—teaching that is articulate and authoritative and, thus, capable of being *discussed* as well as *shared*, both inside the Church and with outsiders, across differences of place and time.

Here ultimately lies the origin of the theological tradition that views stable patterns of worship as important sources of authoritative doctrine—a tradition usually alleged by quoting the maxim *lex orandi lex credendi*: "the law of praying is (or, corresponds to) the law of believing."

[a] The failure to respect worship as a source of reliable doctrine has been one of the severest limitations of theological method since the sixteenth century. Characteristically, Melchior Cano fails to mention the *lex orandi* in his *De locis theologicis* (cf. §7, 1, b). Sound theological method demands that this failure be rectified (cf. §23, 1, a). The theme, therefore, calls for some careful further discussion.

First of all, the document that first appeals to this rule, the *Indiculus* of around A.D. 440, does *not* show the easy parallelism of the modern expression *lex orandi lex credendi*.[23] It very pointedly presents the *liturgy* as the *source* of doctrine: ". . . the high-priestly prayers used in liturgical celebrations, which, handed down from the Apostles, are uniformly observed in the entire world and in every catholic Church, *so that normative prayer may determine normative faith*" (DS 246; cf. DS 3792; 3828; CF 235; c. §23, 1, a).[24] There is no indication that any reverse relationship is also intended.

Second, the text of the *Indiculus* must be carefully read and restrictively interpreted. The document demands respect for "the high-priestly prayers used in liturgical celebrations, which, handed down from the Apostles, are uniformly observed in the entire world and

---

[*m*] Here lies the root of the Catholic opposition to two related movements: doctrinal liberalism on the one hand and authoritarian, sectarian fundamentalism on the other. For all its biases, Ronald Knox' *Enthusiasm* is still worth reading on the latter subject.

in every catholic Church." While the formula sounds very broad and all-inclusive, its intention is rather limited. The context shows that the author is thinking of the ancient liturgical practice of the *general intercessions* (cf. 1 Tim 2, 1–4), nowadays often called "the prayers of the faithful." This narrow appeal to *intercessory prayers* is clearly connected with the *Indiculus'* main agenda, which is to show, against all forms of Pelagianism, that the Church's constant and universal practice of petitionary and intercessory prayer proves the absolute necessity of grace. For that reason it is probable that the text should really be taken to mean that "normative *entreaty* [*lex supplicandi*] should determine normative faith."

To get to the true meaning of the passage, it must be noted that behind it lies the inspiration of Augustine. Christians, he had argued, pray, as they have always prayed and will continue to pray, for the grace of conversion for those who do not believe and for the grace of perseverance for themselves. The grace to pray in this manner comes from Christ and from the Holy Spirit poured out in the hearts of the faithful, so it is not surprising that the Church has universally prayed in this fashion ever since its apostolic origins. In fact—and here Augustine shows his real conviction—whenever and wherever the Church is assembled around its ordained ministers, its prayer of praise and thanksgiving to the Father comes from that same source.[25] In Augustine's view, therefore, the deeper norms that govern the Church's prayer—and hence its faith—are apostolicity and universality, which in their turn are signs of the deepest and truest law of prayer and faith: Christ at work, in the Holy Spirit, in the Church's worship.

[2] A conclusion follows from this. The maxim *lex orandi lex credendi* is not a general norm that can be indiscriminately invoked to draw doctrine from each and every text used in liturgical settings. It is a general norm only in the sense that it points to Christ, present in the Spirit, as the ultimate authorization of all of the Church's worship.

To determine whether a *particular* liturgical usage qualifies as a source of true doctrine, the *Indiculus*, following St. Augustine, establishes three specific, interconnected norms. The usage must be in the area of *episcopal* (or presidential) prerogative at public liturgical functions; it must have *apostolic tradition* behind it; it must be in *universal* use. These specific norms, it would seem, do not just apply to the *intercessions* mentioned in the *Indiculus* but across the board. With the help of these norms, therefore, it should be possible to identify specific liturgical prayers and suggest that they are authoritative sources of normative doctrine.

[a] The greetings "The Lord be with you" and "Peace be to you" are among the oldest elements in the liturgies of East and West. With

these words bishops and priests embrace the newly baptized (§52, 3),[26] greet the community at the beginning of the liturgy after reverencing the eucharistic table but before anything else is said [n],[27] greet the deacon before he proclaims the Gospel [o], and introduce prayers, especially the eucharistic prayer.[28] The greetings must be understood, not just as wishes ("The Lord *be* with you"), but also, and especially, as authoritative, prophetic declarations ("The Lord *is* with you"). Either way, they are rooted in the Hebrew Scriptures and the New Testament.[29] In the Church's liturgy, they sum up the Christian assurance that the risen Lord [p], according to his promise (Mt 28, 20), is truly present, in the Holy Spirit, to his people, uniting them with himself[30] and thus making them one.[31]

The people return the greeting, traditionally reserved to ordained ministers, by means of the response "And with your Spirit" [q]. In doing so, they acknowledge that the special charism of the Spirit in the presiding minister, ordained to call them together as an organically structured community before God (cf. §22, 2), is pivotal to their own integrity as a worshiping community.

A passage from a Pentecost homily by John Chrysostom may serve to illustrate how this liturgical formula reaches down to the roots of the Christian faith: "If the Holy Spirit were not present, there would be no pastors and teachers in the Church, since they come about through the Spirit, as Paul also says: 'in which the Holy Spirit has made you pastors and overseers' [cf. Acts 20, 28]. Do you see how

---

[n] The post-Vatican II reform of the liturgy has adopted two New Testament wishes as functional equivalents of "Peace be to you" and "The Lord be with you" as alternative opening greetings for the Eucharist: 2 Cor 13, 14 and Rev 1, 4–5 (condensed).

[o] The use of the greeting, addressed by the *deacon* to the *people* before the Gospel reading, is not attested until the tenth century and only in the West (Joseph Pascher, "Der Friedensgruß der Liturgie," p. 34).

[p] The association of *Dominus vobiscum* with the Resurrection is clear from a passage in the fourth-century paschal homily attributed to Epiphanius of Salamis describing Christ's arrival in Hades (cf. §38, 6, [j]; §40, 3, c, [u]): ". . . turning to all those imprisoned with him from of old, [Adam] spoke: 'I hear the footsteps of one coming in towards us; if he should deign to come all the way here, we shall be freed from our chains.' While Adam was saying these and other like things to those condemned along with him, the Lord came in to them holding the implement of victory, the Cross. When Adam, the first-formed man, saw him, he beat his breast in awe, and cried out to all, saying: 'My Lord is with [you] all!' And Christ, replying, said to Adam: 'And with your Spirit!' " (*PG* 43, 439–64; quotation 461AB. For excerpts, cf. the Office of Readings for Holy Saturday in the postconciliar Roman breviary.)

[q] Jungmann's suggestion that this is simply a Hebraism amounting to "And with you too" (*The Mass of the Roman Rite*, I, pp. 19, 236, 363) is not supported by any evidence (W. C. van Unnik, "*Dominus vobiscum*: The Background of a Liturgical formula," p. 273). It is worth noting that the phrase was felt to be a curious one in Greek, too; its meaning had to be explained. The reason why it was retained was obviously that it was felt to be so ancient as to warrant retention. Theodore of Mopsuestia writes: "It is in this sense that the phrase 'And unto thy spirit' is addressed to the priest by the congregation, according to the regulations found in the Church from the beginning" ("Theodore on Eucharist and Liturgy," *Woodbrooke Studies*, vol. 6, pp. 91–92).

this, too, comes about through the Spirit? If the Holy Spirit were not present in our common Father and Teacher [r], you would not, when he came up into this sanctuary a moment ago and gave all of you [the greeting of] peace, have exclaimed to him together: 'And with your Spirit.' That is why you exclaim those words to him, not only when he goes up [into the sanctuary], or when he addresses you, or when he prays on your behalf, but [especially] whenever he has taken his place at this holy table, whenever he is about to offer this dread sacrifice. Those who have been initiated understand what I am saying. He does not touch the gifts until he has first wished you the peace that comes from the Lord, and you have exclaimed to him: 'And with your Spirit.' With that very reply you remind yourselves that he who stands there does nothing and that the gifts that lie [on the table] are not the achievements of human nature. Rather, the grace of the Holy Spirit, which is present and descends upon all, fashions that mystical offering. For while the one who stands there is a human being, God is the one who works through him. Hence, do not attend to the nature of the one you see but regard the grace that is unseen. There is nothing human going on up here in this sanctuary. If the Spirit were not present, the Church would not hold; but if the Church does hold, it is plain that the Spirit is present" [s].[32]

[b] The *basic "binary" shape*—that is to say, the shape that involves the Father and the Son—*of the doxological conclusions of presidential prayers* must be considered another instance of the *lex orandi*. These conclusions are characteristic of "two main types of liturgical prayer": prayer *to* Christ and prayer *through* Christ.[33]

The latter is foundational and, hence, by far the most prominent in the liturgy; in both East and West, the classic liturgical prayers were exclusively addressed *to the Father* "through" Christ living and reigning with the Father—a practice proposed as normative at the

---

[r] Chrysostom is here referring to Flavian, the presiding bishop of Antioch between 384 and 404. This dates the homily between 386, the year of Chrysostom's ordination to the priesthood, and 398, when he became the presiding bishop of Constantinople.

[s] It is in accordance with this that the Council of Hippo (393) should have forbidden lectors to use the words "The Lord be with you," since the people would be unable to reciprocate with "And with your Spirit" (*Liturgisch woordenboek*, coll. 568–69). Even when, in the West, the liturgy (and the Church!) got increasingly clericalized, the greeting *Dominus vobiscum* and its response remained associated, in the self-consciousness of reform-minded clerics, with the unity of the Church at prayer around its appointed, ordained ministers. A good example of this is the advice given to clerics by Peter Damian, in the eleventh century, at the dawn of the Gregorian Reform. Even when reciting the divine office in private, he argued, they should continue to say *Dominus vobiscum*, and themselves reply *Et cum spiritu tuo*, since the Church not only exists as one in many persons (*in pluribus una*), but also as entire in each single person (*in singulis tota*). Cf. *PL* 145, 235AC; also, Adolf Kolping, *Das Büchlein vom Dominus vobiscum*, pp. 29–30).

Council of Hippo in 393: "At the altar, prayer is always addressed to the Father."[34]

Still, the ancient communal practice of addressing supplicatory prayers to Christ did become part of the liturgical practice of *presidential* prayer, early on in the East and not until after the start of the second millennium if the West [t].[35] Not a few of the latter kind took the form of orations, which came to be concluded, in the West, with a doxological address *to Christ* living and reigning "with the Father."[36]

Both types of conclusion—the classic and the more recent—have this in common, however, that they bear consistent liturgical witness to the central Christian profession of the "inextricable and mutual bond between Jesus Christ and the living God" (§33, 1).

[c] The *typical shape* of the classic presidential prayer, too, can lay claim to *lex-orandi* status. This shape is especially clear in the Roman rite, traditionally austere and stylized. While presidential orations are essentially *petitionary* prayers, in their classical form they betray their indebtedness to the fundamental Christian *tôdâh*-tradition.

This tradition demands that prayer should begin with doxology, then move, via a profession of sin and unworthiness, to petition, in order finally to return to doxology.[37] This pattern, discernible in New Testament blessings (cf., e.g., Phil 1, 3–11), is also followed by many of the classic orations. After glorifying God (or sometimes Christ, as the case may be) by means of one or more titles or a blessing couched in a relative clause (or both), they proceed to a humble petition, and again return to doxology [u]. In this respect, the Christian tradition of liturgical prayer remains indebted to the synagogue: it continues the Jewish tradition of consistently placing supplication in the context of praise and thanksgiving; this tradition is especially prominent in the *T^efillâh* of the Eighteen Blessings (cf. §38, 3, a; §41, 1, [p]), of which the first three and the last three are pure blessings, while the intervening ones contain elements of supplication.

[d] This observation leads, finally, to the specific point made in the *Indiculus*, which deserves special attention. The bishops, the *Indiculus* explains, together with their Churches everywhere, pray that faith may be given to unbelievers, that idolaters may be freed from their

---

[t] Both traditions came to be decisively modified, as will be pointed out shortly, by anti-Arian and trinitarian controversy.

[u] By way of example, cf. the collect for the thirty-first Sunday in ordinary time in the postconciliar Roman missal: "Almighty and merciful God, thanks to whose gift it is that your faithful serve you in a manner that is worthy of you and a credit to them: grant us, we beseech you, that we may press forward to what you have promised without stumbling on our way. Through our Lord Jesus Christ. . ." (*Omnipotens et misericors Deus, de cuius munere venit, ut tibi a fidelibus tuis digne et laudabiliter serviatur: tribue, quæsumus, nobis; ut ad promissiones tuas sine offensione curramus. Per Dominum nostrum Jesum Christum. . .*).

unbelief, that the Jews may see the light of truth, that heretics may come to their senses, that schismatics may receive the spirit of charity, that those fallen away may turn to penitence, and that catechumens may receive a share in the divine mercy by Baptism. These prayers are proved effective by the actual enlightenment and conversion of many. This shows that all of this is God's work, to whom consequently all thanksgiving and praise are due (DS 246). The universal apostolic practice of liturgical petition, in other words, bears out the Church's belief that all the blessings of the Christian faith are wholly the work of God's grace.

As a matter of fact, however, the Church's official prayer has a wider purview. Many of the classic orations pray, not only for enlightenment and conversion by divine grace, but also for those natural, temporal blessings that are conducive to faith and support it: peace and tranquillity in our days, health in mind and body, protection against all adversity, freedom from all evil.

In this form of prayer, it would seem, is implicit the relationship that the Church professes between the new creation, marked by Christ's resurrection, and the first creation (cf. Rom 4, 17; 2 Cor 4, 6). The Church, in other words, gives thanks and prays for the latter in the light of the former. The thankfulness for the remembered blessings of divine grace taught by the *lex orandi* teaches the Church to give thanks and pray for the underlying, immemorial blessings of nature (cf. §23, 3). Little wonder that a classic collect in the Roman missal prays that "we, who cannot *be* without you, may be able to *live* in accordance with you."[38]

[e] The presidential sections of the baptismal and eucharistic liturgies are, of course, prime instances of worship-formulas that are authoritative sources of doctrine. We will come back to them, both in this volume (cf. §52, 1–3) and in the context of sacramental theology.

Then there are the age-old communal acclamations and prayers like *Amen* (§52, 4), *Halleluyah* (§38, 3, a), *Maran atha* (§40, 1), *Kyrie eleison*, and the Lord's Prayer (§47, 1); these, too, are obvious examples of normative prayer—universal and traditional-apostolic, even though they fail the test of presidential prerogative, and thus are not covered by the letter of the *Indiculus*.

[3] Finally, just as worship not only generates right conduct but also pre-requires it (§47, 4), it both generates right teaching and re-requires it. It is not surprising, therefore, to find, throughout the New Testament, exhortations addressed to the communities (whose primary focus in assembling, we are to recall, was the communal praise to God) to hold on to the confession (esp. in the Letter to the Hebrews: cf. Heb 3, 1–6; 4, 14; 10, 23; cf. 6, 20) and not to associate with false prophets

and false teachers (Mt 7, 15; Acts 19, 9; Rom 16, 17; Gal 1, 8–9; 2, 4; 2 Thess 3, 6; 1 Tim 1, 3; Tit 3, 10).

The exhortations invariably appeal to such constants as the integrity of the tradition, the force of apostolic authority, and unity in and among the communities. All of these are threatened by heresy (Gk. *hairesis*: "choice")—the habit of "picking and choosing." Heresy involves selective interpretation of the Tradition, replacement of apostolic authority, and factionalism in the community.

The ecclesiastical tradition of excluding from worship those who profess teachings at variance with the Tradition, therefore, has excellent New Testament precedent. It is clearly irrational to claim to address the one true God in acts of worship that are both *common* and *coherent* and at the same time to admit all comers indiscriminately, along with their incompatible convictions. Such worship could hardly be said to involve the whole person in the faith-abandon to the living and true God; it would also be wholly unverifiable as true and thus lose all credibility.

[a] Preoccupation with orthodoxy as a prerequisite for worship, in turn, found its way back *into the structure of the liturgy itself*. There is evidence, in other words, that the *lex credendi* sometimes does determine the *lex orandi*. The classic instance of this occurred in the Church of the East, in the course of the fourth century, when the classical doxological conclusions of presidential prayers came to be rephrased in an anti-Arian direction. Since Arians tended to seize upon the formula "through Christ" to promote their heretical, subordinationist agenda, it became a mark of orthodox worship to associate Christ unequivocally with the Father by means of the preposition "with" (cf. §34, 3, a). To this was added, also in the fourth century, the orthodox insistence of the full divinity of the Holy Spirit.

As a result, in the East, the concluding doxologies of the prayers were turned into full-fledged affirmations of the consubstantial Persons of the Trinity. In the West, some similar developments took place, but much later, and never with quite the determination to promote orthodoxy and root out heresy that characterized the Oriental liturgies. "The Roman liturgy is not concerned to change elements of . . . prayer into formulas of faith, to provide bulwarks against those threatening the faith" [v].[39]

---

[v] This observation affects the interpretation of the phrase "in the unity of the Holy Spirit" in the doxological conclusions of liturgical prayers in the West, whether addressed to the Father or to Christ. In the East, intent on the affirmation of the divinity of the Spirit, the doxology came to include the Holy Spirit by means of the phrase "together with"—a usage not unknown in the West. However, the liturgy of the West was far less nervous about possible subordinationist misinterpretations of the doxology. It also developed the phrase "in the unity of the Holy Spirit." This must be understood, not only of the intratrinitarian unity of the Father and the Son in the Holy Spirit, but also of the

[b] Agreement on doctrine as a prerequisite for common worship is an important contemporary issue in the practice of ecumenism. Joint worship, it must be frankly recognized, may hurt the Church's unity and favor error, scandal, and indifferentism (OE 26). In the context of ecumenism, however, it is at times desirable (UR 8). This applies, in practice, primarily in the relationships between the Catholic Church and the Orthodox Churches (OE 26). But it deserves to be commended everywhere, especially in the form of joint prayer for Christian unity. Still, it is not to be indiscriminately used as a means to restore unity, for the fact that common worship should *signify* unity generally rules it out (UR 8).[40]

In the present context, however, the specific question that must be raised concerns *the extent of doctrinal consensus* that is both requisite and sufficient for joint worship across ecclesial divides. Quite recently, Heinrich Fries and Karl Rahner have responsibly argued that agreement on the "fundamental truths of Christianity, as they are expressed in Holy Scripture, in the Apostles' Creed, and in that of Nicaea and Constantinople are binding on all partner churches of the one Church to be. . . . Beyond that, . . . nothing may be rejected decisively and confessionally in one partner church which is binding dogma in another church."[41]

This position is right in refusing to set up the entire body of doctrine as completely self-sufficient and, hence, as an *absolute* norm of the practice of the faith. It correctly implies that *doctrine is itself subject to verification*: only in relation to worship and conduct is doctrine a reliable expression of faith (§44, 3). If this holds for the central doctrines contained in the *regula fidei*, how much more are the different Churches' derivative teachings dependent on worship and conduct for their verification!

We conclude by proposing that positive agreement on the doctrines professed in the *regula fidei* is, as a rule, both necessary and sufficient *in the area of doctrine* [w]. But making full doctrinal consensus "in all the little questions of the divine law" a prerequisite for common worship would seem to go against the consensus of the catholic Fathers. In this area, it is reasonable as well as in keeping with the Tradition to suggest that it is sufficient for partner Churches to respect, understand, and appreciate each other's special doctrinal tra-

---

Spirit-given unity of *the Church*, which professes, in its worship prompted by the Spirit, the unity of the Father and the Son. Cf. §34, 3; 5–6; also, Joseph A. Jungmann, *The Place of Christ in Liturgical Prayer*, pp. 180–90, 201–6; Cyprian Vagaggini, *Theological Dimensions of the Liturgy*, pp. 217–23.

[w] The decree on ecumenism specifies that there are prerequisites in the area of conduct as well, to be adjudicated by the local bishop, the episcopal conference, or the Holy See (UR 8).

ditions and, on that basis, to refrain from mutually condemning them (cf. §21, 3, c; §23, 4, c).[42]

[4] It is time to terminate this discussion. Christian worship, we have argued, is the most direct response to the transcendent, doxological heart of the Christian faith: the encounter, in the Holy Spirit, between God the Father and humanity along with its world, through and in Jesus Christ. The Church's ongoing practice of worship, however, far from placing humanity and the world at a definitive remove from God, unites them with God. Worship commits the Church to the world, to a history of salvation; union with God in praise and thanksgiving is the warrant of Christian witness, in its twofold shape of conduct and teaching, which are the fruits of worship as well as its verification.

The next chapter must tackle the subject of Christian witness, both in its behavioral and its intellectual shape—conduct and teaching. By way of introduction, however, it may not be entirely inappropriate to match a previous warning about the temptations inherent in worship (§46, 1) with a warning about the temptations inherent in witness. "If [the Christian self-expression] is uttered merely as witness, it turns into proselytizing—no loving surrender to others, but a summons to others to surrender themselves; witness becomes party propaganda. Thus, the Church's witness is not compelling unless she is *over*heard to worship Jesus Christ as she speaks to the world; the Church's worship is vacuous if she drops her witness and loses her confidence before the world."[43]

CHAPTER 10

Christian Witness: Conduct and Creed

CHRISTIAN CONDUCT AND ITS STRUCTURES

[§49] CONDUCT RELATED TO WORSHIP: THE CHRISTIAN LIFE AS CULT

[1] The christological narrative, uttered, in the Spirit, in praise and thanksgiving to God the Father, involves assurance about the establishment of *final, universal justice* (§39, 2), by which God will both reveal the divine holiness and communicate it with the whole world. This perspective warrants Christian conduct and indeed demands it (§42, 1). Definitively anchored (Heb 6, 19) in the eschaton by the resurrection of Jesus Christ, the Christian community is now called to the imitation, on the strength of the Spirit, of him whose past way of worship and witness (§38, 3) is memorialized in the christological narrative. For God's eschatological blessing rests on those who are doers of the Word and not just hearers of it (cf. Jas 1, 22–25).

Out of God's *future*, therefore, comes the assurance of the *glory*—the eschatological fulfillment of the promise, on the Lord's own Day, at a time beyond all time. The Church reaches out to Christ alive in the Spirit, the *Holy One* who is in God's own sanctuary as the embodiment of God's unconditional self-commitment to humanity and the world— as the head of what is to be the *communion of the holy* and as the guarantee of the *new creation*. This new creation is to be actualized in a final, definitive outpouring of the divine Spirit of *all-encompassing and all-sanctifying love*. Out of that promise, the Father is now drawing humanity and the world, in and through Christ, Godward on their way to glory. What commits the Christian to the eschaton, therefore, is *hope* aspiring to universal love, prompted by Christ risen; that hope both inspires *perseverance* and is kept alive by it (cf. Rom 5, 2–4).

In this way the future becomes the modality by which the grace of eschatological assurance impinges on the present as a call, not only to praise and thanksgiving, but also to free and responsible conduct (§42, 3).[1] In the light of the resurrection it becomes clear that what most deeply shapes the Church's moral commitment is not relief at the forgiving clemency once and for all shown by God to sinners, let alone satisfaction with past moral achievement or a noble sense of moral duty in the present. Rather, if the Church acts morally, it does so fundamentally in virtue of the new responsive identity acquired in the act of encountering God (§35, 1; 4).

That identity is "hollow," so to speak, but that hollowness is but the form of its graced capacity for participation in God, for "it is yearning that makes the heart deep."[2] Thus the moral commitment that arises from praise and thanksgiving is imbued with enduring *desire*—readiness to proceed on the road of discipleship not yet traveled to the end, pining for God's promises still outstanding, for virtue not yet acquired, for truth not yet attained, for visions that remain to be seen. "The life of the good Christian is one holy desire."[3]

This eschatological orientation decisively places Christian conduct in the perspective of *holiness* and *glory*. Hence, the characteristically Christian commitment to the moral life cannot be conceived apart from worship, which it serves to verify, nor apart from the anticipation of *divine judgment*, which bars access to all that is defiled and unholy (cf. §44, 3; 6; §46, 1; 4–5; §47, 1–3) [a]. A vital conclusion follows from this: *Christian conduct comprises an intrinsic moment of cult*; in this sense, *there is no such thing as an autonomous Christian ethic*—an ethic without reference to worship. There is ample evidence that the Tradition has been consciously aware of this.

[a] In the New Testament, instances of this realization abound; hence, let a few telling examples suffice to make the point. Exhortation to virtue is grounded in God's call to *holiness*, and failure to practice virtue disregards God (1 Thess 4, 1–8) rather than just ethical values. The long series of moral exhortations in Paul's Letter to the Romans (Rom 12, 2–15, 12) is wedged in between a call to worship (12, 1) and a wish for eschatological abundance of hope, in the Holy Spirit (15, 13; cf. §47, 2).

The first Letter of Peter steadily oscillates between liturgical praise of God for the hope granted to the community by Christ's resurrection and exhortations to the imitation of Christ, especially in patience (cf. §47, 2). That same letter portrays Christian conduct in the explicitly cultic language derived from the levitical holiness code: "Since the one who called you is holy, be holy yourselves in all your conduct"

---

[a] The *Journal of Religious Ethics* (7[1979]139–248) devoted an issue to this subject, under the title "Focus on Liturgy and Ethics," with contributions by Paul Ramsey, D. E. Saliers, Margaret A. Farley, William W. Everett, Martin D. Yaffe, Ronald M. Green, and Philip J. Rossi.

(1, 15; cf. 1, 16; Lev 11, 44–45; 19, 2; 20, 7. 26). To support this precept, the letter appeals to the death of Christ interpreted, again, by means of cultic, sacrificial terms borrowed from the priestly tradition in the Pentateuch: "You were ransomed . . . by the precious blood of Christ, like that of a lamb without blemish or spot" (1 Pet 1, 19; cf. Heb 9, 14) [b].

Little wonder that the New Testament frequently uses the expression "without blemish" along with other cultic-eschatological idioms, so as to convey the ethical demands involved in Christian living [c]. Nor is it surprising that the New Testament uses temple imagery to lend cultic connotations to ethical demands, especially demands for chastity: the metaphors "temple" and "house of God," of which Jesus Christ is the cornerstone or the foundation (1 Cor 3, 9, 16–17; 6, 19; 2 Cor 6, 16; cf. Eph 2, 19–22; 1 Pet 2, 5; cf. 1 Thess 4, 8).

Finally, one of the marks of the Pauline letters is the way in which virtue is oriented to holiness; this is conveyed by the fact that the final wish or prayer for (eschatological) peace routinely concludes the apostolic exhortation (1 Thess 5, 23–24; Gal 6, 15–16; Phil 4, 4–7, 8–9; Rom 15, 33; 16, 17, 19–20; 2 Cor 13, 11);[4] thus, Christian conduct is firmly put in the context of readiness for eschatological worship.

[b] From these Pauline texts it can be reliably inferred that there must be a deeply cultic component in Paul's conception of the life of the Church. If the Christian community is the temple of God, and Christian conduct rooted in spiritual sacrifice (Rom 12, 1), then indeed it does not come as a surprise that Paul characterizes his own *apostolic conduct* as a whole in cultic terms. His preaching—sometimes accepted, sometimes rejected—is a burnt offering, whose fragrance ascends to God as it spreads to more and more places (2 Cor 2, 14–

---

[b] "Without blemish" renders Gk. *amōmos*, a thoroughly cultic word. In the Septuagint version of the Pentateuch it invariably refers to the flawlessness of sacrificial animals, rendering Hb. *tâmîm* ("sound," "whole") in the vast majority of cases (in Ex 12, 5 *tâmîm* is rendered by *teleios*—"perfect"). In Ezekiel, too, *tâmîm/amōmos* consistently refers to animal sacrifices (43, 22–25; 45, 18–23; 46, 4–13), but in one place (28, 15), where it characterizes the king of Tyre, glorious on the "holy mountain of God," its meaning is ethical-cultic. This personalized, ethical-cultic usage of *tâmîm* is very frequent in the Hebrew Scriptures. Significantly, it is found only twice in the Pentateuch: in Gen 6, 9 (Noah) and in Deut 18, 13; in both cases, the Septuagint has *teleios*. In the remaining books of the Hebrew Scriptures, where the Septuagint renders it variously by *amōmos* or *teleios*, the ethical-cultic meaning is the rule. *Teleios* in the ethical-cultic sense occurs in the New Testament in Mt 5, 48; 19, 21; 1 Cor 14, 20; Eph 4, 13; Phil 3, 15; Col 1, 28; 4, 12; Jas 1, 4; 3, 2.

[c] Cf. "God's children *without blemish*" (Phil 2, 15); "*holy and without blemish*" (Eph 1, 4; 5, 27); "[Christ has reconciled you] in order *to present you holy and without blemish and unimpeachable* before [God]" (Col 1, 22); "[God is] able . . . *to present you in the presence of his glory without blemish in exultation*" (Jude 24); "while you anticipate [the new heavens and the new earth], do your best to be found by [God] *spotless and without blemish* (*amōmētoi*) *in peace*" (2 Pet 3, 14). Cf. also Rev 14, 5.

16) [d]. One brief passage in particular is charged with cultic terminology: Paul writes that he has received the grace "to be the cultic minister (*leitourgon*) of Jesus Christ to the Gentiles, serving God's gospel as a priest (*hierourgounta*), so that the offering (*prosphora*) of the Gentiles may be acceptable (*euprosdektos*), sanctified (*hēgiasmenē*) by the Holy Spirit" (Rom 15, 16).

But it is not only the founding of Christian communities by apostolic proclamation that is cultic; their development by incessant apostolic care (2 Cor 11, 28) is, too. Paul labors with discriminating care to build the eschatological temple of God (1 Cor 3, 10–15), and his life is sacrificially spent in the service of the faith of others (Phil 2, 17).

This apostolic labor creates a relationship of mutuality: the community must requite Paul's love (1 Cor 4, 14–15; 2 Cor 12, 14–15). When it does so, this is, again, a cultic act: the support sent to Paul by his favorite community at Philippi is a sacrifice (Phil 4, 18) [e].[5]

[c] Augustine's classic treatment of Christian sacrifice in *The City of God* is informed by this tradition. True sacrifice, he explains in commenting on the opening verses of Romans 12, is "every action that causes us to be united with God in holy partnership, by virtue of its relationship to that ultimate good by which we can be truly happy."[6] Consequently, all who die to the world to live for God are themselves sacrifices. The secret of this union with God is *compassion*; we are to have mercy, both on our own selves and on others, for the love of God. All this sacrificial compassion is encompassed by the perfect sacrifice of Christ. Thus Augustine can conclude that life together in the Christian community is truly cultic: "This is the sacrifice of Christians: many as we are, we are one body in Christ."[7]

[d] The ultimate ground for this fundamental coincidence of Christian worship and Christian life lies in the fact that worship is a matter of *participation*—that is to say, participation in the very being of Christ, who mediates the Holy Spirit, by which those who believe participate in the very nature of God (cf. §34, 2–3; 6–7). Hence, not only does Christian conduct have its *finality* in worship, its *motive* derives from worship, too. The inner transformation by the Spirit

---

[d] "Fragrance" (Gk. *osmē*) and "aroma" (Gk. *euōdia*) occur usually together, in the semitism "odor of sweetness" (Gk. *osmē euōdias*, which, in the Septuagint, consistently renders Hb. *rêªch hannîchoªch* meaning "sweet odor." In the Pentateuch, the expression occurs in the cultic, sacrificial context of the priestly source, in Gen 8, 21 and Ex 29, 18. 25. 41, as well as numerous times in Leviticus and Numbers. In the New Testament, the sacrificial, cultic meaning of the expression is explicit in Phil 4, 18 and Eph 5, 2.

[e] In characterizing his activity, Paul associates the temple-building metaphor with the metaphor of tending the (eschatological) harvest (1 Cor 3, 5–9). He does not seem to associate the temple metaphor with body metaphors to explain the mutuality of service in the community (cf., for instance, 1 Cor 12, 1–30). That association is prominent in Ephesians: cf. §34, 3, b, [n].

prompts those who persevere on the way to fulfillment to act out of *love*: "Hope does not disappoint, for God's love has been poured out in our hearts by way of the Holy Spirit God has given us" (Rom 5, 5).

[e] That the witness involved in the Christian life of virtue is inseparable from worship is very pointedly obvious in *martyrdom* (Gk. *martys* means "witness"). Traditionally regarded as the highest form of Christian conduct, martyrdom cannot be reduced to purely ethical dimensions, let us say, by viewing it in terms of heroic virtue [f].

The essence of martyrdom is *perfect witness*, resembling Jesus' "good witness to the *homologia*" (1 Tim 6, 13). It is the complete living out, in voluntary suffering, of the *homologia*—the sacrifice of praise and thanksgiving in total abandon to the Father, in the Spirit of Jesus Christ, put to death and risen. This accounts for an essential feature of martyrdom: the complete consonance of worship and witness, of the love of God and the love of neighbor. Martyrs do not counter force with force, nor do they simply turn in upon their own conscience—a passive butt for the aggression of others. Like Jesus, martyrs keep themselves related to all those around them,[8] all of them children of God, whether just or unjust (cf. Mt 5, 45; cf. also LG 42). The martyr dies, "not only on behalf of the world's suffering, but also on behalf of the world's oppressors—those violent victims of their own fears of losing their lives. The Christian Tradition has called this loving one's enemy. Loving one's enemy is suffering for him at his own hands."[9]

[f] Loving one's enemy may be the highest form of love, but even in its ordinary, "nonheroic" form, the Christian Tradition resists the reduction of neighborly love to purely ethical dimensions. Both the synoptic tradition and the Fourth Gospel insist on tracing this fundamental command to Jesus' teaching about the love-command—a teaching whose ultimate theme is the way *God* acts (Mk 12, 28–34; Mt 22, 34–40 par. Lk 10, 25–28).

---

[f] Augustine (*De Civ. Dei*, X, 20–21; *CC* 74, pp. 294–95) spontaneously brings up the subject of martyrdom immediately after explaining the one sacrifice of Christ the mediator. By doing battle against godlessness (*impietas*: "refusal to acknowledge God," hence "refusal to worship"), martyrs participate in Christ's sacrifice; on that account, and more properly than the heroes boasted by ancient Rome, they could be called "heroes" in the City of God, except that the Church's idiom does not include this usage. Interpreting martyrdom in *doxological*, not heroic-ethical terms has far-reaching consequences. J. B. Metz has been entirely right in insisting that, since the resurrection of Christ keeps the memory of his *passion* alive, the Christian interpretation of history and the Christian commitment to the future should be radically critical of other, prevailing interpretations and commitments, with their heroic bias. History written by the victorious offends the truth involved in the suffering of the defeated; in the same way, the forces of progress tend to dictate, at the expense of the marginal, what the future of the world shall be. Cf. his *Glaube in Geschichte und Gesellschaft*, esp. pp. 87–103 (ET *Faith in History and Society*, pp. 100–118).

The parable of the good Samaritan (Lk 10, 29–37), which Luke attaches to Jesus' teaching on the love-command, is a classic instance of the Christian conviction that only love fulfills the law and only God accounts for love: "Love is from God" (1 Jn 4, 7). In the telling of the parable, the self-justifying lawyer's invitation to *casuistry* about *ritual-cultic*, legal conditions for love ("Yes, but who is my neighbor?") gets quietly turned into the challenge to show *mercy in actuality*: "Whom am I to be a neighbor to?" (cf. Lk 10, 36). In this way, not ethnically narrow ("tribal"—cf. Mt 5, 43–48) concern about ritual fitness for worship (personified by the priest and the Levite on their way to the Jerusalem temple), but the free, never-ending, all-inclusive, other-regarding, compassionate love of the living God turns out to be the measure of Christian ethics [g].

Thus it is *the Spirit* that produces "fruits" in all manner of virtues (Gal 5, 22–23), tending towards holiness (Rom 6, 22); it is *charity* that brings all moral commandments to fulfillment (Rom 13, 8–10; Gal 5, 14; Col 3, 14; Jas 2, 8). In the fourth Gospel, the love-command is one of the commandments that Christ has received from the Father (Jn 10, 18; 14, 31; the other is to speak the word of life: Jn 12, 49–50). Christ has kept it freely, out of love (Jn 15, 10). Christ now orders his disciples to keep it—again, out of love: they are to love others, as Christ has loved them, that is, by giving up his life out of love (Jn 15, 12–17; cf. 13, 34). The fourth Gospel elaborates this love-command by suggesting a relationship of dependence between Christ's "commandment" (*entolē*) and his "commandments" (*entolai*: Jn 14, 15. 21; 15, 10). This relationship is a major theme in the Johannine Epistles, in which Jesus is presented as the proof as well as the guarantee of the unity of the love of God and the love of neighbor: God's commandment involves the dual command of believing in the name of Jesus Christ as God's Son and of loving the brethren; keeping this dual commandment unites with God, known and loved in the Spirit (1 Jn 3, 23–24; cf. 4, 20–5, 3; 2 Jn 4–6).

[2] The great Tradition, especially in the Christian West, has translated its conviction that the cultic moment is integral to Christian living in two ways.

First of all, it has taken seriously the New Testament teaching that the holiness (Rom 6, 21–22; 1 Jn 3, 3ff.) involved in virtuous living is

---

[g] It is tempting (as well as in harmony with the passage's obvious sense) to read the parable also as a *christological allegory*, in which the Samaritan stands for Christ, professed and celebrated in the Church as the embodiment of God's compassion, taking upon himself, in the person of the robbery victim, the human condition (a commonplace in many Fathers of the Church). In this allegory, the innkeeper stands for the ministry in the Church, commissioned by Christ to show *more than adequate mercy* ("overspend"), in anticipation of the reward "when I return" (*en tōi epanerchesthai me*; cf. "when he returned" [*en tōi epanelthein auton*] in Lk 19, 15). This interpretation of the parable supports the case for a cultic-eschatological conception of the Christian love of neighbor.

the fruit of the *Holy Spirit* (Gal 5, 22–23; cf. 1 John 4, 11–13). Theological reflection has drawn a conclusion from this: *charity*, the divine gift by which we are united with God and made to share in God's love (that is, in God),[10] is the "root," the "mother," and the "formal principle" *(forma)* of all virtues, [11] so much so that no true virtue is possible without it,[12] that whoever has charity has all other virtues,[13] and that charity (and, hence also, patience and wisdom) cannot exist apart from grace.[14]

There is a second way in which the Tradition, especially in the West, has translated its conviction that the cultic moment is integral to Christian living. It has authoritatively taught, against all forms of Pelagianism and moral naturalism, that the virtuous life, along with its growth and development, entirely depends upon participation in the divine life— that is to say, upon *grace* [h]. The Tradition has understood this doctrine to imply, not the removal of human freedom to choose what is morally good, but precisely its flower [i].

[a] The anti-Pelagian document known as *De gratia Dei Indiculus* expresses this with great authority: "Therefore, with the help of the Lord, these rules of the Church and these divinely authorized teachings encourage us to acknowledge God as the author of all good desires and deeds, of all efforts and all virtues by which we move towards God, from the first beginning of faith. And we do not doubt that the merits of everyone are graciously anticipated by him [*ipsius gratia . . . præveniri*] through whom we come to want to undertake any good and accomplish it [cf. Phil 2, 13]. Far from destroying free will, God's help and gift liberates it: from being dark it becomes enlightened, from being corrupt it turns to what is good, from being sick it grows sound, from being reckless it becomes provident. For so great is God's goodness towards humanity that he wishes the gifts he gives us to be our merits, and that he means to grant an eternal reward for the very favors he has so lavishly given. Indeed God moves us both to will what he wills and to do it; he does not allow those gifts to lie idle in us which he has given to us for our use, not

---

[h] According to the most important representatives of the Tradition, this even applies to the *root* of the virtuous life: free will. Writing in his old age, Augustine insists that he always meant to teach that divine grace must preveniently liberate the will's basic freedom, if we are to choose the good *(Retract.* I, 8 [9], 4; *CSEL* 36, pp. 41–43; *CC* 57, pp. 26–27). Karl Rahner's discussion of the "supernatural existential," which is the fruit of an "antecedent self-communication of God which is prior to man's freedom," is a modern instance of the same teaching *(Grundkurs,* p. 135; ET *Foundations of Christian Faith,* p. 129).

[i] Donald M. Baillie's *God Was in Christ* is a classic statement of this thesis and rightly shows the analogy between Christology and the doctrine of grace (cf. esp. pp. 106–32). Christ's full humanity, far from being "taken away," is "salvaged" (cf. DS 302) by the union with the divinity; Christ's human freedom is "divinized, not taken away" (DS 556) by being united with the divine will. In the same way, far from being "taken away," human freedom is "salvaged," and indeed sanctified, by divine grace.

to go to waste. In this way we become cooperators with the grace of God" (DS 248; cf. CF 1914. Cf. also DS 238–45; 246 [cf. §23, 1, a; §48, 1, a]; 1528–31; 1545–49; 1582; CF 1907–12; [1913]; 1932–34; 1946–49; 1982).

[b] Classical Protestantism accepted, and indeed emphasized, the traditional affirmation of the absolute necessity of *actual* grace; it designed its own characteristic doctrine of *sanctifying* grace, by insisting that the person justified is *simul justus et peccator*. It is the great merit of Hans Küng to have demonstrated, in a study of abiding ecumenical interest, entitled *Rechtfertigung* (ET *Justification*), and prefaced by Karl Barth, that there is no substantive difference between the teaching of Catholicism and classical Protestantism on the subject of justification [j].

[c] Yet a caution is in order. It remains possible for the entire doctrine of grace to be misinterpreted. This happens when grace is taken in a largely *anthropocentric* sense, as *the saving gift that graciously heals humanity*, rather than as the *divine life* by which humanity, restored to innocence, is graciously enabled to live in communion with, and for the glory of, God [k]. Where this misinterpretation becomes habitual, union with God fades into the background and an almost purely ethical reduction of the Christian faith is just around the corner [l]. In such a construction, divine grace may still continue to be

---

[j] Calvin characteristically does not lose sight of the connection between the theme of humanity's redemption by grace and the more eminent themes of God's holiness and the communion of the saints; this also enables him to emphasize that there is no autonomous, philosophical Christian ethic. Cf. *Institutes* III, VI, 2–3 (vol. 2, pp. 2–4). The *Confessio Augustana* states that good works should be done for the sake of God (VI; *CrC*, pp. 69–70); the Westminster Confession contains a similar article (XVI, 2; *CrC*, p. 210). Recently, James M. Gustafson has raised the theme again, in his *Ethics from a Theocentric Perspective*.

[k] It is legitimate to wonder if an anthropocentric interpretation of grace does not amount to a psychologically immature interpretation of Christian revelation. Parental love (which is by nature undeserved!) is not meant to encourage the child's tendencies toward narcissistic egocentrism but to equip it for gratitude to parents and altruistic behavior towards others. Analogously, the experience of God's love of humanity (*philanthrōpia*: Tit 3, 4) is not meant to invite Christians to a sustained interest in self-improvement but to equip them for the love of God and the love of all. Such, at least, is the burden, both of the exchange principle and of the teaching on the relationship between nature and grace (cf. §23, 2–3; §34, 7; §35, 1).

[l] In this area lies, in my view, the single most serious problem with Hans Küng's exciting book *Christ sein* (ET *On Being a Christian*). Many features of Küng's book are doubtlessly very well done; its interpretation of Jesus' historic ministry deserves special mention. Yet the structure of the book as a whole suggests a problem. After a lively sketch of the modern world and the spiritual dynamics at work in it (the various humanisms, the God question, the appeal of the world religions), the issue of Christianity's *decisive difference* is raised. The answer is that it is the *historical Jesus*, known from his ministry and death as the totally devoted representative of "God's cause" as well as "humanity's cause." It is in Jesus' resurrection, however, that the ultimate reality professed by the Christian faith is manifested: Jesus crucified lives eternally with God; thus he is the embodiment, *both of our duty and of our hope*. Consequently, the Christian faith de-

affirmed, in lyrical tones, as the central experience of the Church; but the latter is—to borrow from Ernst Troeltsch's typology of churches—more and more reduced to a purely mystical communion. This ultimately involves the implicit reduction of grace to a claim made in behalf of the purely individual consciousness (cf. §20; §25).

To the extent, therefore, that the Church worshipfully lives by God's love shown and offered in the risen Christ, it will come to this crucial understanding: that God's gracious love is an offer of *partnership*, not of mere *indulgence*. Consequently, self-indulgence is alien to Christian conduct. God makes moral demands, although God does give what he demands: "O love, you who always burn and are never extinguished, charity, my God, enkindle me! You command continence; give what you command and command what you want."[15]

Hence, what John Henry Newman says of conscience applies *a fortiori* to the Christian conscience enabled by grace and drawn by Christ: "Conscience implies a relation between the soul and a something exterior, and that, moreover, superior to itself; a relation to an excellence which it does not possess, and to a tribunal over which it has no power. And since the more closely this inward monitor is respected and followed, the clearer, the more exalted, and the more varied its dictates become, and *the standard of excellence is ever outstripping, while it guides, our obedience*, a moral conviction is thus at length obtained of the *unapproachable nature as well as the supreme authority of That, whatever it is*, which is the object of the mind's contemplation."[16]

All of this implies that the cultic component in Christian ethics is the source of a dynamic of generosity. Instead of affirming—with pious self-indulgence—that God loves us as we are, the Church professes that "God loves us *as we will be by his gift* [of grace], not as we are by our own merits" (DS 382).[17]

[d] The conception of an essential cultic component in ethics, which sees to it that Christian conduct remains restless, open, and oriented to God, is not really very much at home in North America, and in the United States in particular. American civil religion rests on an

---

mands that it be verified in the Church's *praxis*, in which Jesus is accepted as the fundamental model of life and action; this leads to an interpretation of "being a Christian" in terms of "being radically human." The problem is that this sequence implies an ethical reduction of christology; *the Christian life is reduced to the living out of Jesus' past example as confirmed by the resurrection*. Whatever christological and trinitarian abridgments (cf. §20, 2) Küng's treatment of Christ's person may contain can be put down to this basic bias. Interestingly, Küng does not mention the historical Jesus' prayer, just as he does not treat the Church's worship in his account of what being a Christian involves. His protest against a self-centered, predominantly ecclesiastical religiosity that stunts humanity is, of course, understandable; but ecstasy, not a new righteousness, worship in Spirit and truth, not furious ethical exhortation, is the answer to that.

almost purely theoretical conception of God, which tends to play down common worship—that essential feature of positive religion (cf. §30, 5). Given the tenuousness of the worship it inspires, civil religion tends to reduce the meaning of religion to a rational, individualist social-contract ethic. Such an ethic tends to excuse people at large from vigorous, generous commitments, except on a voluntary basis. Christian conduct, on the other hand, involves a commitment to neighborly love conceived *as a shared, and hence social, and ultimately religious obligation*. This feature of Christian ethics could well enlighten and stir the public conscience in the United States by bringing home the serious limitations of its otherwise very attractive tradition of voluntarism (cf. §25, 4, c).

It would be a mistake, therefore, to jump to conclusions from the fact that the mass media in the United States characteristically play up and even glorify voluntarism and moral generosity. "By attributing too much importance to admirable actions," Albert Camus cautions us, "one ends up paying indirect but potent homage to evil. For one leads others to assume that such admirable actions are so valuable only because they are rare, and that human activity is far more frequently motivated by nastiness and indifference."[18] The media treatment of generous, and even heroic, moral actions and commitments as if they were spectator sports may thus be symptomatic of a prevalent lack of social responsibility and even of the kind of moral complacency that does not really believe in virtue as a real possibility for all people (cf. §25, 4, b, [d]).

The points just made could, perhaps, act as a caution to the Catholic teaching office in the United States. Local bishops act appropriately in bearing authentic witness to concrete ethical issues, not only to the membership of the Church, but also publicly, to American society at large. Yet there are profound differences between Christian ethics and accepted North American public ethics. It would be a mistake to overlook this, for instance, by habitually treating the membership of the Church and American society at large *as if they constituted one single moral audience*.

[3] Emphasizing the cultic perspective in Christian ethics need not lead to a narrow sectarianism. In fact it can do just the opposite: it can act as an antidote against sectarian intolerance. Christians do understand virtue as a moral obligation, yet they believe that it takes the free gift of divine grace to practice it. This makes for realism and discriminating openness toward the surrounding culture. In many passages the New Testament gives evidence of this. It commends respect for human institutions, and, what is more, it shows clear signs of having incorporated into the community ethic, not only some of the principal Old Testa-

ment ethical traditions, but also common wisdom traditions as well as many naturally virtuous practices readily available in Hellenistic culture.[19]

The great Tradition, in the main, has been faithful to this. Ever since Justin Martyr's *Apologies*, the Christian Church has professed to be, by divine grace, the fulfillment of all that is positive in the world (cf. §23, 3, a). This must enable the Church to recognize and welcome, with discriminating love, Christ in the features of the great souls of all times and to adopt their wisdom. This must also encourage the Church to return the favor by taking economic, social, political, as well as artistic and literary responsibility, and to make its appeal to all men and women of good will, with the intention of sharing its moral wisdom with society at large.

Yet throughout, the Christian sense of fulfillment must incorporate an abiding resolve to be different. The second-century *Letter to Diognetus* combines fundamental openness to the world with the New Testament teaching against conformity with the world (for example, Rom 12, 2; Gal 1, 4; Eph 5, 15–17; 1 Jn 2, 15) with great realism and clarity:

Christians are distinguished from the rest of people neither by country, nor by language, nor by customs. For nowhere do they live in cities of their own, nor do they use some different form of speech, nor do they practice a peculiar way of life. . . . They do not champion, like others, a human philosophy of life. Yet . . . they make no secret of the remarkable and admittedly extraordinary constitution of their citizenship. . . . They marry like everybody and beget children; but they do not expose their newly born. The table they provide is common, but not the bed. *They obey the established laws, and in their own lives they surpass the laws.*[20]

[4] In accordance with this, Aquinas was to develop his teaching on the relationship between nature and grace (cf. §26, 2, a). It is also consonant with this to argue that the Church's witness to the world must *integrate* grace and nature—that is to say, it must *freely combine* its own specific profession of faith with the demonstration, by means of an appropriate apologetic, that its confessional beliefs and practices are also naturally attractive and imbued with reason. The Christian apologists of the second and early third centuries never tired of pointing this out.

[a] Wherever some form of freedom of public religious self-expression is available, the Church can also agree to live with a public moral order that is less than entirely moral, especially (but by no means exclusively) in a pluralistic society. This applies especially (but again, not exclusively) in the United States, where the tradition of religious freedom goes back to the *Catholic* cofounders of the Maryland colony in 1632.[21] Ever since bishop John Carroll in the late eighteenth century, American Catholics have learned to appreciate civil liberties,

even if it means living with some public policies that are imperfect and even sinful from a Catholic point of view. The contribution of John Courtney Murray to this true doctrinal development has been recognized by the Second Vatican Council, in its Declaration on Religious Freedom, which includes a special paragraph on public morality (DH 8).[22]

[§50] CONDUCT RELATED TO TEACHING: THE MORAL LAW

[1] If the *cultic* moment orients Christian conduct to its eschatological *future*, out of the *past* comes another component of the lived Christian life: the *teaching* concerning the Church's way to glory. Jesus Christ is not only the "accomplisher of our faith," but also its "pioneer" (Heb 12, 2); he is both the crown and the prime exemplar of the immemorial tradition of faith in God. The memory of Jesus' historic ministry, death, and resurrection, all of them ultimately anchored in God's original, eternal design for creation, are kept alive in the Church community, on the strength of the gift of the Spirit. The past fulfilled, recalled, kept alive, and pondered, therefore, is the modality by which historic and protological wisdom impinges on the Church in the present, summed up under the rubric of the *imitation of Christ* (cf. §40, 3, a–c).[23]

Thus it becomes clear that *there is a creedal moment* in Christian conduct. *The Church's great Tradition of teaching also encompasses moral teaching*, aimed at insuring a sense of identity by means of insuring *stability of moral commitment* (cf. §43, 1–4).

This moral teaching results from two associated sources. First of all, it encompasses the accumulated normative wisdom of the historic Church community—the *specifically and thematically Judaeo-Christian* moral teaching as it has developed over the centuries. Second, it includes the normative wisdom that human reason has always discerned in the very structures of created reality in all its forms—the moral teaching that is implicit in the created ("protological") *nature* of humanity and the world. Also in respect of moral conduct, the Christian religion means to be the fulfillment of the history of Israel and indeed of "the whole world" (cf. §41, 2; §43, 2).

[a] The former derives from *a history of ongoing revelation* and is, therefore, often referred to as "positive divine law"; an example is the Christian recognition of marriage as unconditionally monogamous and indissoluble (cf. Mk 10, 2–12; Mt 19, 3–9; Rom 7, 2–3; 1 Cor 7, 10–11). The latter derives from *established, immemorial, normative patterns of human behavior*. In the experience of a community, such patterns, whether handed down in the form of oral law or codified, have guaranteed the common good and are therefore to be taken as divinely mandated, even apart from any appeal to special, historic revelation.

[b] Thomas Aquinas has developed the concept of "natural law" to illuminate this latter form of moral law. He explains that the orientation of all created beings to the good is reflected in their *natural inclinations*, which are *normative*.[24] Human persons are no exception to this rule. In them, these inclinations are *naturally* arranged in an ascending order, to which correspond three harmoniously ordered levels of natural law.

The first, most fundamental level, Aquinas explains, is *ontological*: human persons are *beings*. In that capacity they have this in common with all existing beings that they naturally tend to maintain themselves in being. Hence, maintenance of human *life* is the most fundamental precept of the natural law.

The second, still very fundamental level is *biological*: human beings have this in common with animals that they naturally tend to maintain their kind in being. Hence, what nature teaches them concerning heterosexual intercourse and the rearing of offspring and related activities constitutes the second most fundamental precept of the natural law. Because these two levels of natural law are "inherent in human nature," Aquinas considers them "more primary and [hence] more fixed than any additional order [of moral law] whatever."[25] For unlike the natural law obligations that human persons may arrive at by the free use of right reason, natural law precepts that are based on the order of nature come as immediately from God as the order of nature itself;[26] that is also why they can be immediately and absolutely grasped without any recourse to reason.[27]

Lastly, there is a third, specifically *human* level of natural law: moral precepts arrived at by *recta ratio*—human reason appropriately applied. The world is full of natural activity, by which all creatures seek to attain their natural goals; in that sense, everything bears the "imprint" of God's providence. At the human level, this is also the case, though "to a more excellent extent": human reason, provident as it is, can *actively* participate in the eternal providence by which God regulates the world and brings it to fulfillment. This puts human agents under a natural obligation to use their native ability to discern and understand what is conducive and what is harmful to that fulfillment, in order thus to determine what is morally good as well as what is morally evil.[28] Consequently, if human persons act in accordance with the demands of right reason, they act morally, because they act in accordance with what they essentially *are*: *rational* animals. Thus, human rationality is, in and of itself, a fundamental, universal source of natural moral law; the "laws of the Gentiles" are an illuminating instance of this.[29]

In the Thomistic tradition, this third level of natural law has most readily lent itself to further elaborations in the direction of an ethic of *responsibility*, for the morality of all acts is doubly determined. Not only is it determined by the *human agent*'s duty to act according to right reason but also by the just demands of the *object* of the agent's action: reality demands that justice be done to it according to *its* nature—the nature which is interpretable by human reason as an expression of God's will [*m*]. An example of a third-level natural law proposition that covers all the points just made would be the rule that it is everyone's duty to abstain from the practice of slavery, as the natural dignity of all human persons forbids their reduction to chattel.

[c] The term *positive divine law* is often used to denote moral norms that are specifically Christian and not covered by the natural law. The term is somewhat misleading in that it seems to imply the concept of a law directly promulgated by God, apart from any mediation. Such a promulgation, however is an unnecessary hypothesis. Positive divine laws may be as much the fruit of human discernment as is third-level natural law; the difference is that the former are thought of as mediated by *historic experience*, the latter as mediated by *natural experience*.

The two, of course, are only inadequately distinguishable; they are no more separable than positive religion and natural religion (cf. §25, 3–6). What counts as naturally and universally valid (and hence as natural law) is, in fact, always culturally determined, which accounts for the *developments* that have occurred in the Church's understanding, and hence also in the magisterium's teaching, of the natural law [*n*]. As a result, it is hard to distinguish adequately between positive

---

[*m*] By Aquinas' definition, the *entire* area of procreation is excepted from human discernment and the kind of responsibility that flows from it, for *biological* nature is an absolute, timeless expression of God's will, which demands that procreative activity be accomplished in its natural integrity. In making this *rational* argument, Aquinas *de facto* joins a broad, authoritative Judaeo-Christian tradition, which associates naturally procreative sexual conduct directly with *holiness* and *worship*, and unnatural (that is, disordered) sexual conduct with *defilement* and *idolatry* (cf. Lev 18, 1–30; 20, 10–21; Deut 23, 17–18; 1 Thess 4, 5; Rom 1, 22–27; 1 Cor 6, 9–20). This tradition continues to be the foundation of Catholic magisterial teaching in matters sexual. The question is, obviously, whether there have been developments to which Aquinas' definition, arguably, no longer applies. Must the *entire* area of procreation continue to be taken to exclude *all* natural law approaches of the third level and, hence, any form of *responsible parenthood* on discretionary, rational, conscientious grounds? Pius XII and Vatican II seem to suggest the opposite. The former was the first to make periodic abstinence, in certain situations, a morally responsible option (cf. *AAS* 43[1951]844–46; *Periodica* 40[1951]366–71; *AAS* 43[1951]859; *AAS* 50[1958]736–37); the latter recognized responsible parenthood in broad terms (GS 50).

[*n*] Examples are the morality of slavery and of usury and, more recently, the serious questions raised about the continued application of the just war theory to the realities of nuclear armament. Aquinas has neither the historical consciousness nor the global awareness to enable him to recognize that his conception of third-level natural law ethics implies the legitimacy of development as well as cultural diversity in natural law ethics. Hence, he believes that the natural law (at the third level) is in principle ("*in principiis communibus*") one and universally valid. Yet in practice he recognizes diversity of appli-

divine law and natural law. Consequently, it is reasonable for the ecclesiastical magisterium to share Christian moral wisdom with the culture at large and even to invite non-Christians to entertain explicitly Christian moral demands (for instance, the indissolubility of marriage) as "naturally" attractive.

[d] The relationship between positive divine law and natural law raises the difficult, much-debated issue of the magisterium's teaching authority with regard to norms derived from the natural law. There is no doubt that the magisterium is *directly* competent in matters of Christian faith and, hence, in matters of positive divine law. The question is whether the competence of Church's magisterium to teach infallibly can be extended any further.

It would seem that claims to magisterial infallibility in moral matters based *purely* on natural-law arguments of whatever level are hard to sustain. Normally, however, the magisterium uses natural-law arguments only in light of faith-convictions ("positive divine laws") that *are* capable of being infallibly proposed, since "what belongs to the natural law is fully taught [in the gospel]."[30] If, therefore, the Catholic magisterium, in infallibly proposing positively Christian ethical norms, should discern compelling natural-law arguments supporting those same convictions, we might perhaps speak of natural-law norms infallibly taught in an *indirect* fashion.[31]

[2] Thus, Christian conduct is integrally determined by both worship and teaching; the practice of the Christian life is positioned between two assurances to inspire, guide, and authorize it. The assurance of the resurrection—the source of Christian worship—is the motive force; the assurance of the historic tradition—the source of Christian teaching— is the modeling power. The former enables the Church at each moment to face the demands of a future which is ever unfinished and which will find its fulfillment only in God; the latter enables it in each moment to rely on the historic Tradition ultimately rooted in God. The imitation of Christ in the present takes the shape of a never-ending series of responses to God's universal call to new conversion and new holiness, guided by a communal commitment to an ongoing tradition of fidelity and renewal ultimately shaped by the example of Jesus Christ and the models of faith that went before him and came after him.

[3] A final remark to take us back to the theme of *mission* and *community* (cf. §38, 2, a; §42, 1, a; §43, 2–4). The demands of the imitation of Christ, so far mainly expressed in a temporal framework, must also be

---

cation, by making allowances for circumstances; he also recognizes that the natural law exists under the conditions of inadequate understanding, depravity of mind, primitive customs (such as robbery, considered moral by ancient Germanic tribes), and other influences, so that growth and development are possible. Cf. *S. Th.* I–II, 94, 4.

expressed in a spatial one. The *eschatological, future-oriented* challenge to lead a life of virtue is paralleled by the Christian consciousness that the Church, precisely because it is the eschatological community of God, is called together from all the nations. Thus, the imitation of Christ is set, from the outset, in the perspective of a global, universal, all-inclusive love. Christian witness is essentially *missionary*; the horizon of the Church's ethical commitment to abide in mutual love is the commitment to teach all the nations to observe all the commandments it has received from Christ (cf. Jn 13, 35; 15, 4. 8; Mt 28, 19–20). To the demand for fidelity to the *historic and protological tradition* corresponds the community's awareness of "the grace in which we stand" (Rom 5, 2)—the Church is built on the unowed, gracious divine election (Eph 1, 4), and it must be cherished if it is to bear fruit. Seen in this light, the witness of Christian conduct is also directed inward, to the community's self-maintenance. The Church must cultivate and preserve itself, as well as the love that holds it together, to the extent that it has already succeeded in being, empirically, the *global, catholic Church*.[32]

CHRISTIAN TEACHING AND ITS STRUCTURES

[§51] TEACHING RELATED TO CONDUCT: COMMUNITY AND FIDELITY

[1] The christological narrative, uttered in praise of God in anticipation of the fulfillment of humanity and the world in the risen Christ come to perfection (cf. Rom 8, 21–23; 1 Cor 15, 20–28), encourages those who live by it to make history, by missionary activity and community building (§42, 1; §50, 3). In the process, it was explained, the experience involved in the making of that history will enrich the narrative that prompted the effort to make history (§36, 3; §43, 2). In this way, historic experience enters into the original Christian narrative, which, therefore, proceeds to include the record of the living Tradition it originated. That is to say, the narrative turns into the authoritative bearer, not only of the community's central dedication to Christian worship and of its basic commitment to Christian conduct, but also of the community's ongoing fidelity to the Christian past that formed it. Thus worship generates and informs conduct, and worship and conduct together generate and inform authoritative teaching.

In this structure, Christian *worship* is most distinctively characterized by the Christian's orientation to the *future* and to the *whole world*, proleptically embodied in the risen Christ. Christian *conduct*, in its turn, is most distinctively characterized by the Christian's attentiveness to the call of the *present moment* and the *neighbor*—the *locus* where Christ is to be encountered. Finally, the distinctive feature of Christian *teaching* lies in the Christian's attentiveness to the *givenness* of the *past* and to the *established order*. Still, while "the grace of yesterday seems to have become the nature of today,"[33] the past and the established order we have inherited are still redolent of God's free initiative in creation and redemption. Thus the past represents and symbolizes God's initiative, which always grounded, and still grounds, the world as well as the history of salvation and which has continued to harbor, from the beginning, the promise of fulfillment in eschatological worship.

[2] By itself, however, fidelity to the past and to the established order is not *fidelity to the Tradition*. Simple preservation amounts to no more than cultivation of *custom*; as such, it does not guarantee truth. Even a traditionalist like Tertullian recognized this: "Our Lord Christ gave himself the title 'the Truth' not 'Custom.' "[34] The Tradition must be preserved from sclerosis if it is to remain *true* in the *Christian*—that is, historic and eschatological—sense of the world. Mere hoarding and rehearsal would reduce the Tradition to a mere "deposit" of truths. Such an idle deposit may still be ardently hailed as perennial and timeless; in reality it is thoroughly dated and only of antiquarian interest.

To be a reliable guide, therefore, Christian teaching must be *integral*; that is, it must maintain its inner connection with conduct and worship so as to remain the support of the *living* Tradition (cf. again DV 8) [o]. Thus bolstered by the authoritative past, Christian teaching must enable the Church to meet the challenge of the moment with the confidence that only eschatological assurance can inspire; in this fundamental way teaching is intrinsically connected with conduct and worship. *Teaching encompasses ethical and cultic moments.*

Once it is recognized that Christian doctrine is part of the pilgrim community's journeying equipment, to support it on the way to the eschaton, it becomes clear that it serves the community's need for *coherence and fidelity*, both in conduct and in worship. The writings that make up the New Testament do not hang in the air: they reflect traditional practices prevalent in the communities that produced them. These practices include, besides teaching, shared moral practice and shared worship; but in their final, written, canonical form, these latter traditions have clearly relied heavily on teaching, both for their development and their preservation in written form (cf. §43, 2–3).

[a] All the Gospels agree in emphatically casting *Jesus* in the role of *teacher*, not only by word but also by example. This picture of Jesus is very likely to owe a good deal to the prominence of teachers in

---

[o] The teaching of Vatican I on the interpretation of the Tradition is thoroughly consonant with this. It takes careful *interpretation*, not mere verbal *reiteration*, to retain forever "that meaning of the sacred dogmas . . . which Holy Mother Church has once declared" (DS 3020; CF 136; cf. §21, 3, a). It is precisely the Church's *present faith-experience* that calls for a discerning interpretation of the Tradition; thus "an *appreciative hermeneutic across space and time*" (§23, 5) must discern how the authoritative Tradition is to be *understood, appreciated,* and *furthered*, precisely as a *living* Tradition.

the early communities (Acts 13, 1; 1 Cor 12, 28–29; Eph 4, 11; Heb 5, 12; Jas 3, 1), whom Matthew's Gospel reminds of their subordinate position (Mt 23, 8). But the Gospels' picture of Jesus as teacher has been shown to have preserved a number of historical features, too.[35] He acts like a *Rabbi*, accepts being addressed by that traditional title, and has discussions with other teachers in rabbinical fashion. But while acting as a teacher of the Law, the historical Jesus' teaching is thoroughly inspired by *eschatology*. While entering by the door of familiar rabbinical practice, he breaks the school-bound molds of rabbinical custom; he prophetically teaches a new way of life, with the urgency and the radicalism demanded by the closeness of the kingdom. Finally, he teaches with an authority that makes implicit claims of being on a par with God's:[36] the herald of the kingdom calls on his hearers to serve the living God by totally dedicating themselves to the accomplishment of God's design. Thus Jesus' teaching of the tradition is wholly informed by the new conduct required by the kingdom and ultimately warranted by the service of the living God.

In the *apostolic* teaching, some distinctions begin to appear; Paul, for instance, makes a clear distinction between the "foundation" he has laid by the gospel and the teaching that he and others have "built" upon it (1 Cor 3, 10ff.).[37] Still, the dependence of teaching on shared worship and communal conduct in the New Testament is very evident and can be shown in several ways. The apostolic *kērygma* is the core of the Christian *homologia* (cf. §45)—the Church's response, in worship and kerygma, to the risen Christ; but the various formulary shapes in which it has been handed on[38] clearly show that oral rehearsal has readied it for transmission by means of teaching, ultimately in the form of rules of faith (§43). More importantly, apostolic teaching has essential features in common with *Christian worship*: in teaching, the teacher invokes the Name of Jesus (Acts 4, 18; 5, 28; cf. §33, 1; §34, 1–2) and speaks on the strength of the gift of the Holy Spirit (Jn 14, 26; 1 Jn 2, 27; cf. §34, 5–6; §38, 5). In similar fashion, Christian teaching—which constitutes the bulk of the New Testament—is embedded in exhortation to, and instruction in, *Christian conduct*. The Epistles as well as the Gospels as we have them are largely the sediment of the early apostles' and teachers' practice of instructing the faithful in the Christian way of life in the communities they were serving.

[3] In any institution bent on permanence, teaching will press its claims to inherent rights. In some of the later writings of the New Testament, we find a phenomenon that has been called—in a formula whose derogatory connotations were intentional when it was first proposed— "early catholicism" (*Frühkatholizismus*). "Early catholicism" is especially observable in the pastoral Epistles, with their emphasis on authoritative

ecclesiastical office. Still, analogous phenomena can be noticed in the catholic Epistles, too.

In these documents, it is clear that the eschatological mood of the early decades is changing: the communities are getting organized in order to settle in for the long haul, and *patient expectancy and perseverance in good works* [p] are becoming a central paraenetic theme (cf. §32, 2).[39] Teaching—often of the prophetic variety—becomes one of the principal instruments to encourage that basic form of Christian conduct: the cultivation of *community* (cf. §42, 1, a). In this way, fidelity to the Tradition comes to serve the cause of *loyalty*, though this loyalty remains ultimately set in the perspective of God's promise. Thus, to take one example, the Johannine Epistles emphasize, against the false teachers, the truth of Jesus Christ's coming in the flesh, but they do so in the context of communal love, which is of God and unites with God (1 Jn 4, 1–12; 2 Jn 7–11).

[a] The connection of teaching with community conduct is most clearly established by means of the expressions *pistoi logoi* ("reliable things to say") in the pastoral Epistles, and the *logoi [pistoi kai] alēthinoi [tou Theou]* ("[reliable and] true words [of God]") in the Apocalypse. All the *pistoi logoi* have this in common that they illustrate the *practical* element in Christian teaching: teaching serves, not simply to keep the truth intact, but to guide the community on its way, as it travels through the vicissitudes of history to its fulfillment. The connection between "reliable truth" and "way of life toward God" is never lost in the New Testament Churches.

All the New Testament *pistoi logoi* are formulary—a clear indication that they are part of a long-standing oral tradition of prophetic teaching in the communities, pieces of which have now found their way into apostolic writings shared among a number of communities. In the Apocalypse, this *connection with writing* is explicit in every case, which would seem to indicate that writing was becoming an important means to insure that the oral tradition remain true to itself.

The expression *pistoi logoi* occurs three times in the Apocalypse (Rev 19, 9; 21, 5; 22, 6–7). Not surprisingly, its orientation is mainly eschatological. It serves to emphasize and clinch the assurances that are implicit in the heavenly liturgy in celebration of God's eschatological victory. God makes use of the mediating ministry of angels and of the prophetic seer John to turn the anticipation of eternal worship into an *encouragement*, extended to the Churches of Asia, *to persevere in the faith despite present tribulation* (cf. Rev 1, 9).

---

[p] The Greek word *hypomonē*, along with its verbal cognate *hypomenein*, occurs with striking frequency in all the New Testament traditions. In the Pauline corpus, it starts in 1 Thess 1, 3 and runs on, through Romans and 2 Corinthians, into Colossians on the one hand and the pastoral Epistles on the other. It helps convey a major theme in Hebrews, James, 2 Peter, and the Apocalypse.

The context of all but one of the *pistoi logoi* in the pastoral Epistles is *apostolic, authoritative teaching*. This observation is confirmed by the expression "the word [that is] reliable [because it is] according to the teaching" (Tit 1, 9: *tou kata tēn didachēn pistou logou*), which occurs in the context of an enumeration of the virtues required in a bishop (Tit 1, 7–9). Not surprisingly, therefore, one of the reliable sayings explicitly commends, in a similar context (1 Tim 3, 2–7), those who make themselves available for the office of bishop (1 Tim 3, 1). A related saying is a commonplace about the present and future rewards of the life of piety, which a bishop's life tends to be (1 Tim 4, 8–9).

The three remaining *pistoi logoi* are the most interesting, since they are very explicitly christological and manifestly indebted to the *homologia*. The first occurs in the first Letter to Timothy. It is not directly associated with authoritative teaching but set in the context of the letter's opening *confessio* (1 Tim 1, 12–17): an apostolic expression of thanksgiving that contains a confession of sinfulness clinched by the reliable saying "Christ Jesus came into the world to save sinners" (1 Tim 1, 15). The second saying occurs in the Letter to Titus (Tit 3, 8). After a brief confession of past sinfulness (Tit 3, 3), the saying recalls, with trinitarian accents, God's saving work: "When the goodness and humanity of God our Savior appeared, he saved us, not because of deeds done by us in righteousness, but in accordance with his own mercy, by the bath of regeneration and renewal in the Holy Spirit, whom he poured out upon us lavishly through Jesus Christ our Savior, so that we might be justified by his grace and become heirs in hope of eternal life" (Tit 3, 4–7). This is followed by an exhortation to insistent teaching, in the interest of the practice of virtue in the community and the exclusion of dissension from it (Tit 3, 8–10). The third reliable saying, in the second Letter to Timothy, is introduced by a brief allusion to the gospel and the apostolic preacher's hardships (2 Tim 2, 8–10), and then proceeds to place, in a dramatic series of four short sayings, present Christian commitments in the perspective of the eschaton: "If we shall die with him, we shall also live with him; if we endure, we shall also reign with him; if we deny him, he will also deny us; if our faith fails, he remains faithful, for he cannot deny himself" (2 Tim 2, 11–13). This is, again, followed by an exhortation to insistent teaching to counteract tendencies towards factionalism and corruption (2 Tim 2, 14ff.).

There are *pistoi logoi* in the Pastoral Epistles not explicitly identified as such; examples are 1 Tim 2, 3–6; 3, 16; 4, 4–5; 2 Tim 2, 19. In fact, there is a pervasive atmosphere of proverbial wisdom in these letters (e.g., 1 Tim 6, 6–8), which strengthens the impression that they strongly reflect standardized oral teaching practices in the communities among which they circulated (cf. 1 Tim 4, 13. 16; 5, 17; 6, 1–10). One of the ways to keep the faith intact was obviously the cultivation of formulary bits of traditional wisdom taught with apostolic authority.

[4] Ideas are heady stuff; they (and those who teach them) have a way of losing their anchorage in the real world. Teaching—like all intellectual effort (cf. §5, 1)—has a tendency to become self-referent, self-supporting, and self-justifying and to detach itself from conduct as well as worship. When that happens, the precious knowledge (Gk. *gnōsis*) of Christ Jesus (Phil 3, 8; Eph 4, 13; 2 Pet 1, 2; 2, 20; 3, 18) degenerates into ideational self-inflation (1 Cor 8, 1). This in turn fosters conduct unworthy of Christians, as the first Letter to the Corinthians shows in vigorous detail: ascetical and spiritual posturing, tolerance of moral decay, and especially factionalism and lack of considerateness for the community's weaker members. Ominously, therefore, but not surprisingly, the word *hairesis* (literally "choice") already appears in the New Testament, not only in the simple sense of "party" (Acts 5, 17; 15, 5; 26, 5), but also in the pejorative senses of "sect" (applied by Jews to Christians: Acts 24, 5. 14; 28, 22) and "faction" (1 Cor 11, 19; Gal 5, 20). In fact, in one of the early second-century canonical writings, it already emerges as a full-fledged term for "heresy," associated with "false teachers" in the community, modern counterparts of the false prophets in Israel (2 Pet 2, 1).

It was pointed out earlier that common life was a principal focus of the commitment to Christian conduct (§42, 1) and that the reliability of any teaching was determined by the way it *functioned*: if it favored factionalism it had to be rejected; if it enhanced mutual concern it had to be embraced (§41, 2, a). This bears out that *it is an intrinsic function of Christian doctrine to support the community's unity in believing.* Christian teaching is professed *together*—in a community that travels through space and time; hence, Christian doctrine assists in telling the reliable brothers and sisters from the false [*q*].

[*q*] Hence, whatever the original meaning of the standard term for the baptismal creed, *symbolon*, may be (cf. J. N. D. Kelly, *Early Christian Creeds*, pp. 52–61), Augustine was certainly right in interpreting it in *contractual* terms: "Merchants enter into a contract with one another, so that their association may hold together by means of an instrument of good faith" (". . . symbolum inter se faciunt mercatores, quo eorum societas pacto fidei teneatur": *Sermo* 112, 1; *PL* 38, 1058). In keeping with this, the Eastern Churches have considered the *filioque* that the Latins added to the Nicene-Constantinopolitan Creed ("the Holy Spirit, who proceeds from the Father *and the Son*") not so much *theologically* indefensible (cf. DS 850, 853, 1300–1302; CF 321, 24, 322–24) as an attack on the unity of the Church in professing the faith, expressly forbidden at the Council of Ephesus (DS 265). On the other hand it must be remembered that the fact that Constantinople I "had sanctioned a creed was unknown to the West until more than twenty years after Augustine's death. There was therefore no reason why Augustine should hesitate to

Consequently, Christian teaching should never be understood as a mere body of perennial intellectual truths, unrelated to the normative community conduct of which it must be the expression and which in turn it must help shape. This has several important consequences.

[a] First of all, if doctrine is journeying equipment, the ancient tradition has rightly explained Christian doctrine, not as perennial and timeless, but as a *history*: a history of *truth and unity overcoming error and division* (cf. §43, 1–2). The second century will develop the term *hairesis* as a technical term and incorporate it into the teaching tradition; this will produce such large-scale expositions of the faith as Irenaeus' *Against all heresies* and Hippolytus' *Refutation of all heresies*. By the time Gregory of Nyssa writes his "Great Catechetical Oration," in the last quarter of the fourth century, it is clear that there has developed, as a counterpart to the rules of faith, a standard catechetical tradition about heresy. That tradition is as stable and formulary as the tradition of cataloguing sins, which goes back to the New Testament (cf. Rom 13, 13; Gal 5, 19–21; Jas 3, 14–18).

Gregory's *Oration* is a manual written for the use of those who have to instruct catechumens and answer their questions; it plainly sets out to deal with the difficulties of fairly sophisticated late fourth-century Greeks. Yet the preface lists what has obviously become a classic sequence. After pointing out that monotheistic Jews and those born and bred in polytheistic Hellenism must be treated differently, it proceeds to mention further examples of past heresies that require *appropriate* treatment; "the Anomoean, the Manichaean, and the followers of Marcion, Valentinus, and Basilides, and the whole list of those in error according to the several heresies."[40] Thus, present attempts to resolve disagreement and debate and to find unity in understanding take courage and inspiration from the living memory of past intellectual and communitarian victory [r].

---

affirm that the Spirit proceeds from the Father *and the Son*" (Henry Chadwick, *Augustine*, p. 93).

[r] Incidentally, much as Gregory stresses the *therapeutic* purpose of his treatise, his standardized review of the age-old adversaries in the preface is couched in rather more militant terms. This is a characteristic instance of the way in which *agonistic* elements are integral to oral tradition. On this subject, cf. Walter J. Ong, *Interfaces of the Word*, esp. pp. 213–29, and *Fighting for Life*, esp. pp. 15–48, 119–48. Agonistic rehearsal often turned a *succession* of heresies into a *pedigree* of heresies; the history of errors thus came to be viewed as a consistent, unholy tradition, as the worst possible construction came to be put on all errors. A clear example of this tendency is Pope Leo the Great's "second Tome," capably discussed by Alois Grillmeier, who notes that unfair simplification of past error gave rise to doctrinal rigidity (*Jesus Christus im Glauben der Kirche*, 2/1, pp. 196–220; *Christ in Christian Tradition*, II/II, pp. 172–94). This tradition was to be long-lived: in the standard textbooks of philosophy and theology in use in Roman Catholic seminaries till just before Vatican II, every thesis was preceded by a list of "adversaries" whose positions were first unfairly reviewed and then rejected with appropriate scorn. Scholars

[*b*] Secondly, given the intrinsic connection of doctrine with the Christian community's way of life, which is essentially historical, *development of doctrine* is a hallmark of Christian truth. Yet it must be frankly admitted, especially by Roman Catholics, "that Catholic theology has not always found it easy to come to terms with the realities of history" and that the charge that Catholics "remove the Church from the realm of history" are "not wholly unfounded."[41] It was real, and badly mistaken, propositionalist prejudice (cf. §7, 1, a–b) that could come to think of doctrinal development as an awkward problem rather than as a natural, valuable, and necessary property of the Christian tradition of teaching. For all its profession of respect for history, therefore, Bossuet's militant exposé of Protestant deviation from the tradition is as rigidly ideological and as unhistorical as any reformer's dismissal of the Tradition in the name of the *sola scriptura* doctrine.

Owen Chadwick's classic study *From Bossuet to Newman* has given an eloquent account of the difficult debate that preceded Newman's recovery of a conviction that was, in one form or another, implicit in the great Tradition all along: *Christian doctrine remains true to itself by developing*, and this development is accounted for by appealing, neither to raw teaching authority nor to the laws of syllogistic logic but to the dynamics of organic growth (cf. §21, 3, c) [*s*].[42]

[c] Third, one theme in the teaching of the later Newman is highly relevant, both to the thesis that Christian doctrine develops and to the proposition that conduct is an intrinsic component of Christian teaching. Newman came to insist on the need for *virtue* in *all* matters

---

with backgrounds in other Christian traditions, I am sure, could quote analogous examples of heresy hunting.

[*s*] Jossua's proposal to understand development in terms of "successive structurings" (cf. §13, 1, [*e*]) has a twofold advantage. First, it removes from the concept of development the unhistorical connotations of purely linear development and unimpeded progress. Second, it allows for the admission, on the part of the Church, of negative "developments": the great Tradition has also suffered loss of tradition. At the same time, it must be recalled that those successive structurings should not be interpreted, in relativist fashion, as an undifferentiated flow of coequal truths. The doctrinal tradition, including the magisterial tradition, exhibits a *structure*: it must be interpreted with the help of the hierarchy of truths. In one sense, the entire doctrinal tradition should be seen as a highly differentiated commentary on Scripture and the creed, which the authentic teaching office must serve (cf. DV 10). Cf. §23, 4, c; cf. also Grillmeier's fascinating survey of christological sources in use in the patristic Church—a fine example of how fidelity to the core of the tradition was cultivated by means of a living tradition of teaching using a variety of documents of lesser authority (*Jesus der Christus im Glauben der Kirche*, 2/1, pp. 22–103; *Christ in Christian Tradition*, II/I, pp. 20–89). Finally, in all of this it is hard to overstate the importance of *oral tradition*. Before the printed word got invested with final authority, all written doctrinal documents still served to support the *living, spoken* word. And whereas strictly written tradition, by demanding *literal* precision, creates the illusion of changelessness in the handing down of meaning, oral tradition, by subtle, flexible adaptation of the authoritative formulas, guarantees continuity as well as appropriate change.

of judgment, including "questions of truth and falsehood" and "'speculative' questions." He conceives of this virtue, which he calls "Illative Sense," as a "supplement to logic" and describes it in terms of Aristotle's *phronesis*.[43]

In *An Essay on the Development of Christian Doctrine* he had explained that Christian doctrines, while respecting the demands of logic, are the fruit of far broader dynamics, most notably of power of assimilation: they grow by what we might call organic development.[44] Understanding Christian doctrines, therefore, must not be attempted by simply tracing the logic of their manifest elements. He had argued the same proposition almost ten years before the publication of the *Essay on Development* (cf. §15, 3–4); manifest doctrines require *interpretation*.

The later Newman remains true to the insight of his youth. Very much in earnest about the *moral* prerequisites for reliable interpretation, he can write that "our criterion of truth is not so much the manipulation of propositions, as the intellectual *and moral* character of the person maintaining them, and the ultimate silent effect of his arguments or conclusions upon our minds."[45] More specifically, he can insist that there is "a certain *ethical character* . . . which is formally and normally, naturally and divinely, the *organum investigandi* given us for gaining religious truth."[46] In this way, Newman's appreciation of doctrinal development is matched by his sensitivity to the ethical dimensions of the understanding of doctrine [*t*].

[d] There is a final consequence, of a linguistic nature, to the thesis that Christian doctrine is essentially connected with Christian conduct: dogmatic statements are, to use a term favored by Karl Rahner, instances of *language regulation* ("Sprachregelung").[47] This applies both passively and actively: doctrines are pieces of Christian language *authoritatively regulated* in the past, and they go on to *regulate authoritatively* the linguistic *behavior* of the Christian community.

This feature is not a peculiar attribute of Christian doctrine; all language is a matter of *behavior in situations* before it is a matter of cognition,[48] and all language use must avail itself of the normative linguistic structures given in a particular community of discourse. Hence, Christian doctrine cannot be rightly appreciated unless it is seen as a form of normative linguistic *community conduct*: "This is how we speak" [*u*].

[*t*] This analysis of Newman's views would seem to lead to the conclusion that integralism, in its insistence on the absolute normativity of *manifest* doctrine (§19, 1), is at least partly a *moral* failure.

[*u*] Here lies the merit of George Lindbeck's description of doctrine in "cultural-linguistic" or "grammatical" terms (cf. §13, 1, [*f*]; §22, 2, a). Karl Rahner tends to limit the concept of language-regulation to magisterially defined *dogmatic* propositions couched in *terminological* language, which he sharply distinguishes from "true, i.e. kerygmatic,

This must, of course, not be understood in an integralist fashion, as if Christian doctrine consisted in a totally stable, perennial set of propositions completely unrelated to the actual Christian community and its history. Rather, Christian doctrine is *both* authoritative *and* historically determined. This demands, first of all, that the community be open to future doctrinal development. It also demands that doctrine formulated in the past be *interpreted*, by means of an appreciative hermeneutic across space and time; that kind of interpretation is an essential ingredient of the living Tradition of the catholic community (§21, 3; §23, 5).

[5] The intrinsic connection of Christian doctrine with the shared conduct of the Christian community is such an important feature of the catholic tradition that it deserves to be studied by being contrasted with the liberal Protestant tradition, so prominent in North America. Sensitivity to the culture is one of the strengths of American Protestantism, yet uncritical acceptance of the culture would amount to modernism: it could easily amount to the severance of Christian doctrine from the teaching of the historic (§36, 3) Christian faith-community [v].

[a] Friedrich Schleiermacher affords the classical (and influential) example. With regard to what he presents as the central doctrine of the Christian faith, the person and work of Jesus Christ, he proposes that Church doctrines must be critically reviewed on a permanent basis. Only in this way can they be pruned of obsolete and needless determinations. After all, doctrinal developments are exclusively a function of current Christian self-consciousness; for Schleiermacher, faith expresses itself in "the doctrine prevailing in a Christian ecclesiastical society at a given time."[49]

At the roots of this judgment lies Schleiermacher's conviction that "Christian doctrines are the conceptions implicit in the states of the Christian religious affections expressed in language."[50] This is entirely consistent with his propensity to an anthropocentric reduction of the Christian faith (cf. §20; §25; §49, 2, c). In Schleiermacher's view, the Infinite can be attained only indirectly, in the depth-ex-

---

statement[s] of faith" ("Was ist eine dogmatische Aussage?," p. 72; cf. ET, p. 58). The former, in Rahner's view, are specializations of the latter, and they remain dependent on the latter for their meaning. Rahner's view of language-regulation is too narrow. From a linguistic point of view, the "kerygmatic" language, say, of the Scriptures and the liturgy, is as normative and regulatory as defined doctrine. This is not to deny, of course, that the specific problem treated by Rahner is not a real issue, especially in ecumenical matters and in establishing the meaning and function of the magisterium. It could be added that the issue is not just the *meaning* of terminological dogmatic statements but also their *popular use* as ecclesiastical loyalty markers: cf. F. J. van Beeck, "Rahner on *Sprachregelung*: Regulation of Language? of Speech?"

[v] In North America, the liberal Protestant demand for relevance to the culture of the moment is often expressed by means of the demand that the faith be relevant to "history." This seemingly attractive concept of "history" is in fact completely actualist and, hence, profoundly unhistorical, since its dedication to relevance is predicated on forgetting rather than remembering.

perience of the finite self, and any statements about the Infinite are in the nature of inferences drawn from an analysis of the religious self-consciousness. Consequently, doctrines are the *expression*[51] of *piety* ("the states of the religious affections"), *not the introduction to faith*, let alone the introduction to *worship* (cf. §35, 3, a; 4). This fits in with two essential features of Schleiermacher's interpretation of the Christian faith.

First, it is based (to use a traditional term) on an exclusively *incarnational* christology, though one that is interpreted in consistently anthropological terms. What singles Jesus out as the Redeemer is not what he taught, did, and suffered, but his unique, historic God-consciousness—"the abiding power of his God-consciousness, which was a proper being of God in him," as well as being the source of his "sinless perfection."[52] It is into fellowship with this historic, liberating, bliss-imparting, spiritualizing[53] God-consciousness that Christ began to draw, and continues to draw, those who believe in him, starting with the disciples. Present Christian faith thus continues to draw on the continuing spiritual influence of the *historical* Jesus, who is both the example and the prototype of faith.[54] Schleiermacher clinches this with the help of two crucial, related arguments. He implies that "complete assumption into life-communion with Christ" (that is to say, "redemption and reconciliation") was available "before the suffering and death of Christ."[55] He also insists that the disciples "recognized in [Jesus] the Son of God without having any inkling of his resurrection and ascension."[56]

Second, therefore, Schleiermacher can write that "the facts of Christ's resurrection and his ascension, as well as the prediction of his return to judgment, are not proper constituent parts of the doctrine of his person."[57] These "facts" are only believed because they are found in Scripture, and individual Christians are free to take them literally if they find the evidence persuasive;[58] but in Schleiermacher's judgment the essence of Christian faith remains intact even if they are interpreted purely symbolically.

As a result, Schleiermacher's rendition of the Christian faith knows of neither Church community nor eschatology as original, constituent, and, hence, *normative*, elements. At his hands, the Christian faith becomes a matter of an ongoing tradition of *individuals* entering into mystical union with Christ, resulting, at the social level, in an institutionally Christian culture, concretized in a variety of ecclesiastical societies. Christian doctrine is reduced to a series of doctrinal variations played, in a Christian key, on the perennial and universal theme of human religiosity as it is actualized in the course of human history [w].

---

[w] In our day, Gordon D. Kaufman's writings show the family features of the tradition embodied by Schleiermacher in vivid detail. Thus, "contemporary experience" is spon-

[6] The Moravian Friedrich Schleiermacher and the Catholic Karl Rahner share a sharp awareness of the human person's native religiosity as the transcendental precondition for all positive religion (§25, 2, a). Yet unlike Schleiermacher, Rahner refuses to make present religious experience the touchstone of Christian doctrine; he maintains the normativity of the doctrinal tradition. Rahner also agrees with Schleiermacher in viewing defined doctrines as expressions of faith. However, beyond that, in the final analysis, he views all doctrines, even the most terminological, as instances of *inductio in Mysterium*;[59] they refer the believer to the unfathomable mystery of the definitively self-revealing and self-communicating God, who is the ultimate authoritative guarantor of all doctrine (cf. also DS 3008, 3032; CF 118, 126). This point raises the second important issue to be explored in connection with doctrine: its intrinsic connection with *worship*. For besides conduct, it has been explained (§44, 2; § 46, 5), worship is the other inner moment of Christian teaching.

[§52] TEACHING RELATED TO WORSHIP: THE CREEDS

[1] Rules of faith (§43, 4) may have been the first clear result of the Christian *homologia*'s "movement towards fixity,"[60] yet it would be hard to find clearer evidence of established methods of formally *teaching* the Christian faith than *creeds*. As early as the middle and late second century, we find Justin and Irenaeus give evidence both of the Church having "orderly arrangements for instructing converts in Christian doctrine and for satisfying itself that they had properly absorbed it" [x].[61] The practice had irresistible consequences. The early third century saw the beginning of the formation of the so-called declaratory creeds, in

---

taneously alleged as an authoritative witness to argue that Christ's resurrection can reliably be reduced to the disciples' understanding, on the strength of an alleged hallucinatory experience, the significance of the life of Jesus (*Systematic Theology*, p. 426). In the provocative little book *Theology for a Nuclear Age*, Kaufman explains that a complete reconception of God and Christ is mandated by the nuclear threat, described in consistently eschatological terms and called "a historical situation unanticipated either by biblical writers or subsequent theological commentators" (p. 13). At the *empirical level* this last statement is obviously true, and Kaufman is right in arguing that the nuclear threat must stretch the limits of the Christian moral imagination. But at the *level of normative Christian doctrine* the statement fails: in the resurrection of Jesus, Christians accept the revelation of the life beyond all life, and as a result, they profess, in retrospect, that in the death of Jesus they have seen the end of the old, sinful world. In other words, Christian doctrine holds that the death and resurrection of Jesus are the measure of *all* possible challenges to humanity's authenticity and to its relationship with God. There is no good reason—not even a contemporary one!—to assume that Paul could not really mean what he said when he wrote that *nothing* in creation will be able to separate us from the love of God in Christ risen (cf. Rom 8, 38–39). But it is precisely that distinction between empirical experience and normative Christian doctrine that Kaufman, I think, would reject.

[x] In comparison with Irenaeus' far-flung *apologetic* version of the rule of faith already quoted (§43, 5), the version in his *Proof of the Apostolic Teaching* 3–7 (*SC* 62, pp. 31–42; *ACW* 16, pp. 49–52) is much narrower; it suggests, especially by its repeated emphasis on the Trinity, that it has its roots in (pre-)baptismal *catechesis*.

which the principal truths of the Christian faith are put together and introduced by the formula "I believe" in the first person singular. These creeds are increasingly marked by *textual stability*—a feature that highlights (especially in a culture that is still overwhelmingly oral) their *obligatory, normative* character in the community.

[a] There are several basic *types* of creeds; their origins, uses, and mutual affinities and dependencies, capably discussed by J. N. D. Kelly in his *Early Christian Creeds*, remain the subject of animated scholarly discussion. All the classical creeds are basically "tripartite." The simplest, found in both declaratory and interrogatory forms, consist in a trinitarian profession of faith, in which Jesus Christ is professed only as Son of God and Lord and in which the profession of faith in the Holy Spirit is expanded to include mention of the holy catholic Church and, as the case may be, the resurrection of the flesh, life eternal, the unity of God and of Baptism, or the forgiveness of sins (DS 1–5; cf. CF 1).

There is also a more developed form of the "tripartite" creed, found in all the creeds that the tradition has accepted as classic. They all include, within the compass of the basic trinitarian profession of faith, an *expanded christological clause*, detailing not only Christ's sonship and lordship, as well as his birth from the Father and his role in creation, but also, in strong dependence on the christological narrative (cf. §38, 2–4), his birth, death, burial, resurrection, descent to hell, ascension, session, and anticipated return for judgment.

By the mid-fourth century, the texts of the *two great Christian creeds* have become standardized. In the East, the so-called *Nicene-Constantinopolitan Creed*, with its array of theological affirmations (DS 150; cf. 41–42; CF 12; cf. 9–10) is becoming the normative baptismal creed, endorsed and textually fixated at the Council of Ephesus in A.D. 431 (but cf. §51, 4, [q]). Around the same time, the Latin West sees the spread of the "Old Roman Creed" (versions DS 11–16; cf. CF 3)—the prototype of the so-called *Apostles' Creed* (DS 28; CF 5), which will become the West's generally received baptismal creed by the early Middle Ages.

[2] From that same mid-fourth century, in catechetical works by Cyril of Jerusalem, John Chrysostom, and Theodore of Mopsuestia in the East, and Ambrose of Milan in the West,[62] we have evidence that the teaching of the creed never lost touch with worship. "Creeds and credal formulae . . . are part and parcel of the liturgy. They share the fortunes of the prayers and services in which they are embedded."[63]

Towards the end of a full round of prebaptismal catechesis, the baptizands, now fully instructed, often had the creed formally "handed on" to them by the bishop (*traditio symboli*), to whom they were expected to "give it back" by means of a formal rehearsal (*redditio symboli*), thus declaring themselves individually ready and competent to accept the Christian faith. Very importantly, the real acceptance of the creed was *enacted* in worship, as the catechumens underwent and participated in "the awe-inspiring rites of initiation."[64] The creed was one of the elements used *in worship* to impart to the baptizands their full *deputatio ad cultum*, that is to say, their *entitlement to participate in worship*—principally the Eucharist, which would follow immediately upon the rite of baptism. And the central action of that Eucharist, the presidential prayer, would include the solemn rehearsal of the christological narrative inserted, in summary form, into the baptismal creed.

Three classic quotations will convey the creed's function in worship more eloquently than any explanation; they will also show how East and West, despite divergent forms and interpretations, agreed on the substance. Trinitarian creeds, faithful to the Matthaean command to baptize (Mt 28, 19), were the basic shape of the Christians' contract with the Church (cf., again, §51, 4, [q]), but also, and more importantly, they provided the basic shape of their worshipful induction into the mystery of the Triune God—the mystery cherished and celebrated with awe in the community of the Church.

[3] Hippolytus' *Apostolic Tradition* contains the oldest full account of the rites of initiation, dating back to the end of the second century; it comprises the oldest form of the "interrogatory creed," and shows very well how it functioned in the liturgy of baptism. After describing the screening of the applicants and listing the conditions for their acceptance, the three-year catechumenate is mentioned, as well as the prayers, the laying on of hands, and the exorcisms immediately preceding baptism. The oils are blessed, the candidates renounce the devil, and accompanied by a deacon they descend into the water. Hippolytus continues:

When the person baptized has descended into the water, the one who performs the baptism shall lay his hand on him and say, "Do you believe in God the Father Almighty?" And the one who is being baptized shall say in turn, "I believe." And immediately [the one who performs the baptism], holding his hand on his head, shall baptize him once. Then he will say, "Do you believe in Jesus Christ the Son of God, who was born through the Holy Spirit from the Virgin Mary, and crucified under Pontius Pilate, and buried, and who rose alive from the dead on the third day, and ascended to heaven, and is seated at the right hand of the Father, in order to come and judge the living and the dead?" And when he has said, "I believe," he shall be baptized again. And once more he will say, "Do you believe in the Holy Spirit in the Holy Church?" So the one who is being baptized will say, "I believe."

And then, after he has come back up, he shall be anointed with the oil sanctified by thanksgiving, by a priest saying, "I anoint you with holy oil in the Name of Jesus Christ." Then all shall wipe themselves clean and put on their clothes again, and after that they shall enter the church.

The bishop shall lay his hand on them and pray to God with the words, "Lord God, you who have made them worthy of receiving the forgiveness of sins by the bath of rebirth, make them worthy of being filled with the Holy Spirit and send your grace upon them, so that they may serve you according to your will. For to you is the glory, Father and Son with the Holy Spirit, in the Holy Church, now and in the ages of ages. Amen." Then he shall pour the oil sanctified by thanksgiving from his hand on to the head [of the baptizand] and say, "I anoint you with holy oil in God the Father Almighty and in Jesus the Christ and in the Holy Spirit." And after making the sign of the cross on his forehead, he shall give him the kiss and say, "The Lord is with you." And the one who has received the sign shall say, "And with your Spirit."[65] And he shall do so with each one.

And from then on, they will pray with the whole people; they shall not pray with the faithful unless they have undergone all this. And after praying they shall offer the kiss as a sign of peace.[66]

[4] A passage from Theodore of Mopsuestia's third baptismal homily aptly shows the close relationship between the awesomeness of the worship and the precision of the teaching, which, in keeping with the Eastern tradition, concentrates on the Blessed Trinity, the source of divinization (cf. §34, 5, a).

The bishop lays his hand on your head with the words, *"In the name of the Father,"* and while pronouncing them pushes you down into the water. You obediently follow the signal he gives by word and gesture, and bow down under the water. You incline your head to show your consent and to acknowledge the truth of the bishop's words that you receive the blessings of baptism from the Father. *If you were free to speak at this moment you would say "Amen"*—a word which we use as a sign of our agreement with what the bishop says.[67] . . . But since at the moment of baptism you cannot speak, but have to receive the sacrament of renewal in silence and awe, you bow your head when you immerse yourself to show your sincere agreement with the bishop's words.

You bow down under the water, then lift your head again. Meanwhile the bishop says, "And of the Son", and guides you with his hand as you bend down into the water as *before.* You make the sign of consent as before, signifying that you accept the bishop's declaration that it is from the Son that you hope to receive the blessings of baptism. *You raise your head, and again the bishop says, "And of the Holy Spirit," pressing you down into the water again with his hand.* You bend beneath the water again, humbly acknowledging by the same sign that you hope for the blessings of baptism from the Holy Spirit. . . . Then you come up out of the font to receive the completion of the mystery.

Three times you immerse yourself, each time performing the same action, once in the name of the Father, once in the name of the Son, and once in the name of the Holy Spirit. Since each Person is named, you understand that each enjoys equal perfection, and each is able to dispense the graces of baptism. You go down into the font once, but you bend beneath the water three times in accordance with the bishop's words, and you come up out of the font once. This teaches you that there is only one baptism, and that the grace dispensed by the Father, the Son and the Holy Spirit is one and the same. They are inseparable one from the other, for they have one nature. . . . Since their substance is one and their divinity is one, if follows that it is by a single will and a single operation that the Father, Son and Holy Spirit regularly act upon their creatures [cf. Eph 4, 4–6]. So we too can hope for new birth, second creation and in short all the graces of baptism only upon the invocation of the Father, the Son and the Holy Spirit—an invocation which we believe to be the cause of all our blessings.[68]

[5] Ambrose of Milan, finally, with characteristic ardor, interprets the trinitarian rite of Baptism in the direction of *forgiveness*, the characteristic soteriological theme of the West:

You were asked the question, "Do you believe in God the Father Almighty?" You said "I believe," and you were immersed—that is to say, buried. You were asked a second question, "Do you believe in our Lord Jesus Christ and in his cross?" You said, "I believe," and you were immersed. That also means that was together with Christ you were buried [cf. Rom 6, 4], for whoever is buried together with Christ arises together with Christ. You were asked a third question, "Do you also believe in the Holy Spirit?" You said, "I believe"; you were immersed a third time so that the repeated offenses of your former life might be absolved by a threefold confession.

After all—to give you an example—Saint Peter the Apostle, during Christ's passion, had appeared fallen on account of the weakness of the human condition. But afterwards, to wipe out and make amends for that fall, he—the one who had disavowed him before—was asked three times by Christ if he loved Christ. Then he said, "You know, Lord, that I love you." He spoke a third time so as to be absolved a third time.

If, then, the Father forgives sin, so does the Son, and so does the Holy Spirit. But do not be surprised that we are baptized in one name where there is one substance, one godhead, one majesty. This is the name of which it is said, "in which all must be saved" [Acts 4, 12]. In this name you have all been saved, you have been restored to the grace of life.[69]

[6] In view of the creed's home in the baptismal liturgy, it is not out of character, either with the eucharistic liturgy or with the creed, that the latter came to be introduced into the former, both in the East and in the West. Significantly, in both traditions, *the creed is sung* in the setting of the Eucharist—or at least it may be. That, in and of itself, well conveys that the creed involves more than the listing of articles of faith authoritatively taught and obediently accepted. The language of the creed is rightly understood only if it is heard as the articulation of what is, more fundamentally, the sacrifice of praise and thanksgiving, of which the celebration of the Eucharist is the prime instance [y].

---

[y] This has consequences for the interpretation of the creed. A fine discussion of this issue, with an appropriate emphasis on the role of the *imagination* in interpreting the creed, with special reference to F. D. Maurice and John Henry Newman, in John Coulson, *Religion and Imagination*, pp. 33–83.

[a] In the East, the practice started as a local custom in the fifth century; in the West, it spread from Spain, where it was started in the sixth century, to Ireland and the kingdom of the Franks under Charlemagne, until, at the insistence of the saintly but dictatorial Roman emperor Henry II, it was introduced into the Roman liturgy in A.D. 1014. Significantly, in the Eastern liturgy, it occurs immediately after the call for the closing of the doors to all but the faithful, just before the eucharistic prayer: only those who have received the creed can participate in the Eucharist. In the West, it is placed after the homily; in that position it would appear to function as the conclusion of the service of the Word rather than as the introduction to the Eucharist proper.

[7] Finally, any theological discussion of creeds must include a reference to the so-called trinitarian-christological creeds. Creeds of this type start with a very emphatic trinitarian profession of faith, in which the unity and consubstantiality of the three coequal persons of the Blessed Trinity is variously orchestrated; this is followed by a statement of christological faith, ending on an eschatological note. A profession of the *incarnation* usually functions as the bridge between the trinitarian and the christological sections.

[a] Creeds of this type probably did not arise until the fifth century, though they have strong roots in the anti-Arian trinitarian and christological debates of the third and fourth centuries [z]. The original form of the type is found in the so-called *Faith of Damasus* (DS 71–72; CF 14–15) and the *Symbolum Quicumque* ("the Athanasian Creed"; DS 75–76; CF 16–17).

Unlike the tripartite creeds, trinitarian-christological creeds have never been used in the liturgy (except in the fifth-century *Te Deum*— a doxological, abundantly orchestrated version of the trinitarian-christological creed, with appended suffrages). They are really purely *doctrinal*, and often mainly apologetical, professions of *orthodoxy*. This very feature, however, did make them attractive as the model of the authoritative professions of faith of the Latin West, exemplified by the Symbol of the Council of Toledo in A.D. 675 (DS 525–41; CF 308–16, 628–34, 2302).

Not surprisingly, creeds of this type came to be considered the authoritative texts upon which the newly emerging professional theologian had to comment. Peter Lombard's *Sentences*,[70] which became the standard medieval textbook of theology, provides the classical example. In four books, it follows the basic trinitarian-christological

---

[z] But note that Irenaeus' rule of faith (cf. §43, 5) already has a complete trinitarian beginning and then proceeds to an account of the history of salvation, with the *Holy Spirit* functioning as the bridge between the two parts.

pattern as it treats, respectively, the Trinity, creation and sin, incarnation and the life of virtue, and the sacraments and the last things.

Thomas Aquinas' monumental *Summa theologica* exemplifies a further elaboration of the same basic order of treatment. After a first part devoted to God (comprising discussions on God's existence and attributes, on God's Trinity, and on Creation), the second part first deals with God as humanity's ultimate end and, in that context, with the life of virtue, sin, and grace, and then—in a second part—the individual virtues. The third part is devoted to christology, mariology, the sacraments, and the last things.

These theological treatments bring out a characteristic feature of the trinitarian-christological professions of faith: they lend themselves to *expansion*. This already showed in their original form: the *Quicumque* includes two damnatory clauses (2 and 42). However, the true capacity for expansion of creeds of this type lies in the fact that they list the truths of the faith in what can only be interpreted as a descending order of importance. This made them capable of attracting *additional articles* of lesser status, tacked on at the end (cf., for example, DS 800–802).

Room available for additional articles acquired a fateful importance at the time of the Reformation. What separated the churches was not the Nicene-Constantinopolitan Creed or the Apostles' Creed but ecclesiastical *confessions* divided into *articles of religion*, which in turn generated *catechisms* whose only intention was to impart correct doctrine in true propositions (cf. §7, 1, b). With the exception of the Tridentine profession of faith, which at least places the Nicene-Constantinopolitan Creed at the head of its series of additional articles (DS 1862–70; CF 30–38), these confessions entirely consist of doctrinal *propositions*.[71] They start out by replacing the creed by fairly succinct, classical articles of belief in the Trinity, creation, sin, and the incarnation. After that, they proceed to rehearse, in additional articles, often of increasing length and emphasis, all the specialized doctrines that each church subscribes to, often in nervous, discouraging detail.

These specialized professions of faith, of course, have lost all connection with worship. Not surprisingly, they are never sung—who could write music to carry the strains of disharmony? Miserably, they can only be "affirmed," often under oath, (cf., for a Catholic example, DS 3537–50; CF 143, 143/1–13!)—a practice which can at best compel compliance (necessary only in a state of crisis). As a rule, however, articles of faith merely affirmed will encourage conformity without much understanding or conviction; at worst, they will generate more suspicions of heresy.

Ironically, therefore, but not surprisingly, these brave truths turn out to need regular clarification and even modification, in order to meet new crises.[72] Isolated from the stability of the creeds, which reflect, as in a mirror, *God's faithfulness*, they tend to turn into a record of the ongoing ecclesial search for fidelity in believing (cf. §23, 4, c), which seldom moves along straight paths. This, in turn, diminishes their ability to function as carriers of the great Tradition. Since the connection between creed and worship is at best tenuous in all of these confessions and catechisms, it is almost impossible to find in them a clear, theologically responsible sense of the hierarchy of truths.

[8] Theology as a discipline has closer affinities with Christian doctrine than with either conduct or worship (§43, 1, a). The conclusions that the present section leads to, therefore, are likely to be relevant to the further development of the present theological system in the next two volumes. Two points especially suggest themselves.

First of all, it was explained that the official *profession of faith* lost touch with the liturgy, at least in the Christian West. As a result, it became one-sidedly doctrinal. From a theological point of view, therefore, it would appear necessary to state that the renewal of the church demands that the *teaching* of the *Christian faith* retrieve its connection with *community worship*. This can be expected to have two beneficial results. It will restore the *baptismal profession of faith*—and hence, the faith of *all* members of the Church—to the center of the Church's teaching. It will also retrieve an organic understanding, rooted in worship, of *salvation history*, and in the context of that narrative, of the *hierarchy of truths*.

Second, the cause of truly catholic *theology* was not well served by its dependence on the non-liturgical creeds; it lost its organic relationship with the living Church. If the shape of understanding is to be determined by the object to be understood (§8, 6), and if catholic theology must accompany and guide the renewal of the Christian faith, it must do so by focusing on its core. That core is the undivided catholic Church's original, expressive account of its *direct* encounter with the divine condescension: the great christological-soteriological narrative, which has yielded the great creeds and the *regula fidei* (cf. §23, 4, c)— the subject matter of the next volume of *God Encountered*.

Before the next volume of this systematic theology can be undertaken, though, two more issues of an introductory nature remain to be treated, in a final chapter. The former concerns faith—and more specifically, faith-*experience*. The latter concerns theology—and more specifically, its *authority*.

CHAPTER 11

Growth in the Spirit and Theological Authority

THE DYNAMICS OF THE CHRISTIAN FAITH EXPERIENCE

[§53] THREE STAGES OF SPIRITUAL GROWTH

[1] In the course of the last two chapters, a series of six sections (§§47–52) served to fulfill a promise first made long ago, namely, to elaborate an understanding of the Christian faith as a whole by means of an understanding of its three fundamental moments (or "components"): worship, life, and teaching, and of the dynamic hierarchy that prevails among them. The relationships between the three moments, it was stated, involve mutual verification, because in each of the moments the other two must reappear as part of its own inner makeup. This, it was stated, would also enable us to understand the Christian community as a community of spiritual growth and development (§44, 3). It is time to explain this latter issue.

There is, in the great Tradition of the undivided Church, embodied especially in the tradition of ascetical and mystical theology, a consistent tendency, identifiable from the late second century on, to consider the Christian life, not as a reality in which all Christians participate in one identical, undifferentiated fashion, but as dynamic *process* by which Christians are *led* to God.

This is striking, because the Tradition, from the New Testament on, draws a firm line of division between Christians and non-Christians. Neither the New Testament nor the Tradition favor the notion, as widespread in antiquity as it is today, that the religious life is a matter of *natural* process, by which human beings turn "from luxury and self-indulgence and superstition . . . to a life of discipline and sometimes to a life of contemplation, scientific or mystic," thus beginning to actualize their full human and religious potential.[1]

Rather, Christians come to participate in the new life by *sacramental initiation*: by receiving baptism and confirmation, and by participating in the Eucharist for the first time, they become something that they were not thus far. They turn away from the barren life of sin and allow themselves to be drawn into a new, fruitful, and even eternal life, based on the saving knowledge of the true God and of God's Son Jesus Christ in the Holy Spirit, in the community of the Church, which on God's authority holds out the pledge of everlasting life. If the Tradition holds (as indeed it does, for grace builds on nature and perfects it: §26, 2, a) that in the Christian faith the human person's innate potential for human and religious growth is to be actualized, it does so *only on the basis of a total initial conversion* to the Christian faith.

All of this would appear to suggest an important conclusion. Whatever stages of progressive perfection the Christian life of faith will turn out to encompass, the practice of Christian initiation demands that the *whole* of the Christian faith be demonstrated to be somehow actualized at *every* developmental stage.[2]

[2] God praised and loved simply for the sake of God, and neighbor loved, without calculation, for the love of God: the great Tradition has always understood this to be the characteristic, if ideal, way of life in Christ. Yet the sublimity of the ideal has never blinded the Tradition to reality. Remembering Paul's words to the Corinthians (1 Cor 13), and knowing from experience the labyrinthine ways of the human heart—"O unteachably after evil, but uttering truth"[3]—it has never despised fear of punishment or hope for recompense as accessory motives and as the school of realistic love. It comes as no surprise, therefore, to read that "of frequent occurrence in patristic literature is the division of the spiritual life into three stages, according to the virtue predominant in each, [or] into three ways, *all three of which lead to salvation*, either by way of fear, or of hope or of charity."[4]

[a] The *locus classicus* for this tradition is in the fourth book of the *Strōmateis* ("Miscellanies"), written by "the first Christian gentleman," Clement of Alexandria, around the turn of the third century. Clement, availing himself of elements of platonic and stoic philosophy, conceived of and taught the Christian faith as the true *gnōsis*. Accordingly, he recognizes three degrees of spiritual growth: "The first step . . . is instruction with fear, by which we keep away from wrongdoing; the second is hope, by which we come to strive for whatever is best; but what makes perfect is love, which, as is fitting, presently provides training in the gnostic way" [a].[5] Clement puts things a little

---

[a] P. Smulders quotes W. Völker to the effect that knowledge of the gnostic variety is "obviously not mere knowledge, but the full transparency of the pure heart" ("Dogmengeschichtliche und lehramtliche Entfaltung der Christologie," p. 417); hence, Gk. *gnōstikos* is perhaps better rendered by "mystic." Note the word *fitting* (Gk. *prosēikon*), which suggests that love properly "fits" the reality of God, and the word *presently* (Gk.

less neatly elsewhere in the same work: "A divine thing it is, therefore, such a great change: that out of unbelief someone should become a believer, and believe with hope and with fear. This is precisely how faith reveals itself to us as the first move to salvation; after it, fear and hope and repentance, developing along with self-control and endurance, lead us to love as well as *gnōsis*."[6]

On a larger scale, Clement's sequence of treatises *Protreptikos—Paidagōgos—Didaskalos*[7] (Christ, the divine *Logos*, is "Admonisher," "Tutor," and "Master") conveys the same progression: starting with faith and conversion, we must be led through a demanding course of tutored progress in virtue, until we are at last taught without mediation, by the divine *Logos* present to us.

[b] The Tradition uses other images as well, witness the following explanation, much-quoted in the later monastic tradition from Basil the Great's preface to one of the versions of his rule. The metaphors come straight out of the life-experience of the ancient homestead with its various classes of inhabitants: "All in all, I can see these three varieties of disposition toward that inexorable requirement: obedience [to the will of God]. For either we avoid evil because we fear the penalties, and then we are in the servile disposition. Or, in pursuit of the rewards of profit, we fulfill the commandments for the sake of our own advantage, and accordingly we are like wage-earners. Or [we do] what is attractive [*kalon*] for its own sake, and for the love of the One who has given us the law, joyful that we have been judged worthy to serve such a glorious and good God, and thus we are in the disposition of children."[8]

[c] The three phases can also be used more plainly for the purpose or classification: in the Church, there are the beginners, the proficient, and the perfect. The great seventh-century courtier-turned-monk Maximus "the Confessor" ties traditional strands together when he writes: "He called believers [*pistous*] and virtue-seekers [*enaretous*] and gnostics [*gnōstikous*] those who are [just] entering and those who are making progress and those who are perfect, or, alternatively, slaves and wage-earners and children [*hyioi*—"sons"]: the three classes of those who are being saved. For the slaves are the [simple] believers, who fulfill the commandments of the master out of fear of impending threats, and who, in a well-disposed manner, act on what is believed. The wage-earners [are] those who, out of desire for the goods that have been promised, patiently bear the weight of the day and its heat—that is to say, the tribulation that has been implanted and forced upon this present life as a result of our ancestor's sin, and the trials [that befall us] in this life in the interest

---

ēdē), connoting a sense of arrival in the world where the knowledge of God in love is fully actualized.

of [our acquiring] virtue; they are those who wisely, out of self-cho-
sen conviction, trade in life for life—this present life for the life to
come. Finally, the children [are] those who neither out of fear of
impending threats, nor out of desire for the goods that have been
promised, but by the way in which their souls are habitually inclined
and disposed, with conviction, to what is attractive,[9] are never separated from God—just like that son, to whom it was said, 'Child, you
are always with me, and all that is mine is yours' [Lk 15, 31]. Thus
they are, according to deification by grace (as far as this is possible),
what God both is and is believed to be according to nature and cau-
sality."[10]

[d] The tradition is first known in the West through the *Collationes*,
or "conferences," of John Cassian, an energetic monk of obscure origin, who entered a monastery near Bethlehem in the late fourth
century and proceeded to travel, via Egypt and Constantinople, to
Rome; he ended up founding two influential monasteries near Mar-
seilles, in the south of France, in the early fifth century. In a collation
by the Abbot Chaeremon we read: "So you see that there are different degrees of perfection. We are called, by the Lord, from high
places to higher places yet. Thus the man who has become blessed
and perfect in the fear of God, will walk, as it is written, 'from virtue
to virtue' [Ps 84, 7], and, as he ascends with alacrity from perfection
to new perfection—that is, from fear to hope—he is invited to a yet
more blessed state, which is charity: the man who has been a 'faithful
and prudent slave' [Mt 24, 45] passes over into the intimacy of friendship and the 'adoption as children' [Gal 4, 5]. This is, too, how my
words have to be understood. I am not saying that the contemplation
of that eternal punishment or of that most blessed reward is unimportant. No, it is useful, for it introduces those who pursue it to the
initial stages of bliss. But charity inspires a fuller trust and a first
taste of the joy that never ends, and it will take a hold of them and
transport them from servile fear and hope of reward to the love of
God and the adoption as children. Thus, in a way, it makes more
perfect people out of perfect people."[11]

[e] Thomas Aquinas firmly incorporates the tradition into his *Summa*:
"Thus we distinguish different degrees of charity according to the
different endeavors to which a person is led by growth of charity.
For in the beginning the main endeavor incumbent on a person is
to draw away from sin and to resist its beguilements, which move
him in the opposite direction from charity; this is pertinent for beginners, in whom charity is to be nourished and cherished, so that
it might not waste away. There follows the second endeavor: the
person must aim primarily at advancing in goodness; this is pertinent
for the proficient, whose primary object is that charity be strength-

ened in them by growth. The third endeavor consists in this, that a person primarily aims at being one with God and enjoying God; and this is pertinent for the perfect, who wish 'to be freed and be with Christ' [Phil 1, 23] [b].[12]

[f] Finally, the ascetical and mystical tradition has used another set of related terms to clarify the process of union with God. A contemporary master of the spiritual life explains this clearly and succinctly. "Thus, at the point at which the beginner is being purged of his faults, and hence is in what some schemes would call 'the *purgative way*,' he begins to move forward into 'the *illuminative way*' of those who are pressing forward in the service of charity. As this development continues, he normally experiences a crisis in which the whole of the life of his senses is painfully cleansed. Again, when the love of the 'the illuminative way,' which has not been without its self-regarding element, begins to lead into 'the *unitive way*,' in which God is loved for himself alone, the whole spirit undergoes a similar purgation. If we find all this incredible, it is because our notions of God are as unworthy of us as they are of him."[13]

[3] It is not only professional teachers, with their tendency towards systematization, who have noticed these dynamics of growth. The three stages of spiritual development are observable enough for references to them to crop up spontaneously in the writings of people who are not trying to explain anything to others but who do give evidence of reliable personal experience in the art of prayer and self-examination. Two very different examples will serve to make the point.

[a] "May God give to me and to all my brothers and to all men alive and to all women such charity. For I confess I am still far removed from it—from it, I mean, that is, from such *great* charity; for I am not conscious of myself being outside *all* charity, just as I am not outside the grace of Christ the Lord. But Christ means one thing in so far as he is the way, something else in so far as he is the truth, and something else in so far as he is life itself [cf. Jn 14, 6]. And the so-called illuminative [way] is one thing, the perfective [way] is something else. In the same way, some are beginners, others are proficient, and others perfect, even though all of them can be in charity; but then again, so to speak, being in charity is one thing, living in charity another, moving in charity yet another [cf. Acts 17, 28]. Be-

[b] Hence, not surprisingly, the fourteenth-century *Pistle of Preier* opens with the recommendation to start prayer by eliciting dread on account of one's wretchedness, and hope in God's mercy and goodness; thus one can "climb on to the high mountain of perfection, that is to say, the perfect love of God." On a homely note, one could say that "reverence is nothing but dread and love mingled together with a spoon of certain hope" (*Deonise Hid Divinite*, pp. 48–53; quotations pp. 50/13–14, 51/3–4).

ginners have charity inasmuch as they know and hate their sins; the proficient, however, have it by way of a sense of, and a desire for, divine things, that is, Christian virtues, in which they desire to advance and grow every day, etc. But the perfect have and experience it by way of itself, namely, inasmuch as they themselves have come to be moved to search for the knowledge of God and the will of God, in order to accomplish it in every way they can. In the first [group], therefore, charity causes them to go against their sins and to remove them; in the second, it causes them to try hard, with desire, to acquire virtues; but in the last, it causes them to strive, by the immediate knowledge of God, also to grow in the love of that same God."[14]

[b] "That divine Heart is an inexhaustible source, where there are three channels that flow incessantly. First, [there is the channel] of mercy for sinners, upon whom pours down the spirit of contrition and penitence. The second is [the channel] of charity, which stretches itself to help all those wretched people who are in some kind of need, and especially for those who strive for perfection; in it, [they] will find, by the intercession of the holy Angels, the means to overcome all obstacles. From the third [channel] pour down the love and the light for the perfect friends whom he wants to unite with himself, in order to communicate to them his knowledge and his sayings, so that they may consecrate themselves entirely to seeing to it that he is glorified, each in their own way; and the Holy Virgin will be the special protector of these people, in order to make them come to that perfect life. Moreover, this divine Heart will make itself the shelter and the assured haven, at the hour of death, of all those who have honored him while they were alive, and he will defend and protect them."[15]

Thus the ascetical and mystical tradition firmly witnesses to three stages of spiritual growth and development. The question now arises whether these stages are incidental to the fundamental structures of the Christian faith or integral to them.

[§54] STAGES OF GROWTH AND THE MOMENTS OF THE CHRISTIAN FAITH

[1] Ever since Origen, writing in the first half of the third century, it has been apparent, both practically and theoretically, that Scripture requires *interpretation*. The obvious ("literal") sense, Origen observes, sometimes makes no sense at all. Take the Mosaic Law: it includes impossible legislation. For example, failure to have a firstborn son circumcised is punishable, but the punishment is meted out, not to the parents, but to the obviously innocent child (Gen 17, 14). In the same way, the food laws mention nonexistent, fantastic animals: the goat-stag

[Gk. *tragelaphos*] is listed among the clean animals and the griffin [Gk. *gryps*] among the unclean (Deut 14, 5. 13 LXX [*c*]).

Similar difficulties are encountered in some New Testament texts—even in familiar passages in the Gospels: some of them make no sense at all in practice. There is no particular merit in greeting no one on the way (Lk 10, 4), in not wearing two tunics in frigid climates (Mt 10, 10), or in tearing one's eye out (Mt 5, 29).[16] Consequently, such texts must be interpreted at a higher level of meaning to make sense.

But even in passages whose obvious sense does realistically apply there are further, more elevated levels of meaning. And because it is the same God who made both Scripture and the human person and attuned them to each other, those further levels of meaning are consonant with the dynamics of human growth in the Spirit:

Now the road by which it seems we must meet Scripture and understand its meaning is traced by drawing on its own words. From Solomon, in the Proverbs, we learn the following prescription about the divine decrees that are in writing: "And you must copy them in a threefold way, in counsel and knowledge, so as to have words of truth to say in response to what is proposed to you" [Prov 22, 20–21 LXX]. In a threefold way, therefore, the meanings of the holy Scriptures must be copied in the mind, as follows. The simpler people are to be edified by the flesh (so to speak) of the Scriptures—which is what we call the obvious meaning. The people who have climbed a bit higher up [are to be edified] by (to continue the comparison) their soul. Then [there are] the perfect people—those who fit the words of the Apostle: "Among the perfect we utter wisdom, but not the wisdom of this age, nor of the rulers of this age, who are passing away; but we utter God's wisdom hidden in mystery, which God predetermined before the ages for our glorification" [1 Cor 2, 6–7]. [These people are edified] by the spiritual "law which has the shadow of the good things to come" [Heb 10, 1]. For just as the human person consists of body and soul and spirit, so in the same way, does Scripture, since it is the instrument of God's plan, established for the purpose of the salvation of people.[17]

Origen's proposition requires careful attention. He recognizes that there are stages of personal spiritual growth, but the really striking thing is that he thinks these stages are *objectively matched by corresponding levels of reality in the Scriptures*—that is, in one of the central realities in the Church. The Word of God itself, in other words, although thoroughly spiritual (for the Scriptures are essentially the work of the Spirit), is objectively structured in such a way as to guide the Christian, in stages of growth connatural to the human person, to the direct encounter with God in the Spirit [*d*].

[*c*] Both are instances of fanciful translation of words with uncertain reference in Hebrew. In the case of *gryps*, modern editions of the Septuagint read *gyps* ("vulture").

[*d*] For an introduction to the full extent of Origen's theology of Scripture, cf. Hans Urs von Balthasar's splendid anthology, now finally available in English, *Spirit and Fire*, nrs. 150–233, pp. 86–112.

[a] What, after Origen, became a commonplace among the Fathers of the Church (though less so in the Antiochene tradition than in the Alexandrian) also became a commonplace in the early medieval Church.[18] Peter Lombard recapitulates a lot of classical theological opinion when he writes, "The historical sense is easier, the moral sweeter, the mystical sharper; the historical is for beginners, the moral for the advanced, the mystical for the perfect" [e].[19]

[2] These observations lead to a question. The great Tradition has recognized the legitimacy of a truly *theological* (as against a purely psychological or even ascetical) theory about growth in faith, for spiritual growth is reflected in growth in the ability to understand and savor Scripture. In view of this, would it not also appear possible to offer a theological interpretation of the relationships between, on the one hand, the fundamental objective structures of the Christian faith—worship, life, and teaching—and, on the other hand, the classical patterns of spiritual growth and development [f]? In what follows, it will be proposed that the answer to this question must be yes and specified as follows: beginners in the spiritual life are most closely identified with Christian *teaching*, those who are proficient are typically characterized by concern with Christian *life*, and those who are perfect find the center of faith-experience in *worship*. This requires explanation.

[3] If Christian *teaching* conveys anything at all, it conveys that the Church *pre-exists all believers*. All Christians must receive before they can become active: they *are joined* to the body of the Church, and in doing so they allow themselves to be integrated into a reliable, existing Tradition, from which they have everything to learn, and a history of salvation, from which they can draw life.

Beginners, therefore, experience themselves principally as *learners*: they depend on the community and specifically on those in the community who are the bearers of its *authoritative Tradition*. No wonder that Christians who are beginners in the spiritual life—the so-called simple

---

[e] However, theories about interpretation got increasingly involved when complications arose from the *academic study* of the Bible and of the Jewish Scriptures in particular. Theologians began to insist that the Bible, especially the Old Testament, had to be interpreted either literally (i.e., historically) or spiritually (i.e., as prefiguring the New Dispensation). This eventually yielded, not three, but four senses of Scripture: the historical ("literal") sense (which could apply to both the Old Testament and the New) and then, as *subdivisions* of the *spiritual* sense: the allegorical sense (which, in the case of Old Testament passages, explained the "true," i.e., prefigurative, meaning of a passage), the moral sense, and the "anagogical" sense. Thomas Aquinas (*S. Th.*, I, 1, 10, *in c.*; I–II, 102, 2, *in c.*) represents this later tradition, whose indubitable intellectual merits were purchased at great cost to the *lectio divina* tradition.

[f] The question is partly rhetorical, since I have attempted to analyze the postconciliar Catholic faith and identity experience along these lines. Cf. *Catholic Identity After Vatican II*, where I proposed the terminology *pistics—charismatics—mystics* to characterize the three stages of spiritual growth. Much of the remainder of the present section is a *retractatio* of that little book.

faithful, or pistics—are most dependent, for their sense of Christian identity, on teaching, tradition, and authority. They cherish the reliability of impressive as well as familiar patterns and formulas of worship and prayer, the challenge involved in firm, straightforward, shared moral requirements, and the stability of well-defined traditional doctrine.

As a class, pistics are typified by an impressive *faith*—even though this faith may be a bit guileless and at times even naive and not infrequently shot through with fearfulness toward God and human respect in relation to others. No wonder that pistics prize the *unity of the Church* and depend, for their sense of identity, on firm limits to demarcate the Church from the world. No wonder, finally, that they reverence the *past*—the faith of their ancestors (even if, from an historical point of view, they project on to the past a uniformity and a lack of development that never existed).

[a] There is no sound theological reason to despise the pistic type of faith. Rather, the contrary is true. Among the New Testament authors, Paul frankly recognizes that the simple faithful are weak in faith and, hence, susceptible to scandal. But more importantly, he regards the pistic believer as "the brother [and sister] for whom Christ died" (1 Cor 8, 11). Hence, in Paul's eyes, the weak qualify as a test of the community's spiritual mettle: as judges, to shame the pride of those who think of themselves as spiritual (1 Cor 6, 4), and as the concrete test of real love and concern in the community (1 Cor 8, 7–13; 12, 22–25). The synoptics and the Letter of James do likewise (Mk 9, 42 parr.; Jas 2, 1–7). Finally, no historical accounts of the life in the early Christian communities justify the claim that the presence of the simple faithful in the Church is simply a corruption brought on by mass conversions or indiscriminate baptismal practices. If anything, the record suggests that "beginners" have always constituted a majority in the community—a suggestion which centuries of missionary experience can well be taken to confirm.

[b] One of the strengths of mainstream catholicism has been its reluctance to adopt very strict requirements for membership in the Church in the area of class, sophistication, or even moral behavior. In the catholic tradition, Donatism, Montanism, puritanism, and related forms of scorn for the uncouth and the less-than-perfect have not won the day. However, there is a dark side to this, too. It is not unreasonable to think that there has prevailed, especially in the Roman Catholic Church, a questionable (and rather clerical) tradition of *idealizing* this type of faith—a tendency to misrepresent pistic faith as *normative*, especially for lay people. This has always been dubious, but it is especially so in our day. The modern need for openness, not to mention the Church's responsibility to the world (GS 43) and

the universal vocation of all Christians to personal holiness (LG 39-42), make it critically important for the Catholic community to develop a shared sense of identity that is not so predominantly predicated on dependency on authoritative limits and definitions.

[c] The pistic experience, if allowed to predominate, will show its inherent weaknesses, which must be recognized if they are to be healed and overcome. Some must be mentioned. Reliance on the teaching of the Church may degenerate into dull, dutiful passivity and loss of the spiritual freedom that is integral of the gospel, in the form of *inappropriate lay dependency* on clerical assurance. Furthermore, while beginners rightly appreciate the gift of salvation, this may degenerate into an almost exclusive *concern with one's own salvation*, at the expense of Christian responsibility for others. Finally, the pistic stance is incapable of engaging the world in a true *missionary* dialogue; a Church that allows its life to be dictated by the agenda of the simple faithful (or of a clergy intent on maintaining their jurisdiction over the simple faithful!) becomes *structurally impatient and inhospitable*, and even *judgmental* in its relations with the surrounding culture, with tendencies towards integralism.

[d] A final observation on the relationship between the pistic type of faith and the central mystery of Christianity. It would appear that the typically pistic experience of *faith in Jesus Christ* is most strongly thematized by its *past* as well as its most strongly *creedal* aspects: the incarnation of the Word (and in that connection, the motherhood of the Blessed Virgin) and Christ's redeeming, vicarious suffering and death. Thankful acceptance, in faith, of the objective order of salvation once for all accomplished by God in Jesus Christ is the characteristic feature. But this very devotion to the Word Incarnate has its negative features: among pistics, there is a tendency towards "crypto-monophysitism"—a hidden tendency to see in Jesus only God, and to downplay the full reality of his humanity. Not surprisingly, conscious commitment to discipleship and profound appreciation of the depth of the paschal mystery are often underdeveloped in pistics.

[4] If Christian *living* means anything, it is that the Church is *God's people on the way* to the eschatological kingdom, with which the Church is not simply identical. Having accepted and professed the creed and having been joined to the body of Christ, Christians are to *carry the great Tradition forward* and to share in *shaping the history of salvation* in every *present moment*, both by helping build the community and by being part of the Church's mission to the world (cf. §42, 1).

With "*proficient*" Christians, the faith they have received will become a personal issue. They will want to distinguish themselves as Christians, not so much by virtue of ecclesial authorization as by virtue of *conduct based on inner motivation*; they will seek to exercise their special, distinctive gifts, or *charisms*, by involving themselves in special commitments. In this sense, they are "charismatics" [g]. Christians who are thus advancing in the way of the Spirit tend to be *doers*; they wish to lead lives of active, disciplined virtue on the strength of a personal appropriation of the gift of faith and on the basis of a real readiness to sacrifice personal comfort in the practice of faith. This implies that they tend to act on an inner call to *service*; in obeying that call, they enrich the *variety of ministries* needed in the life of the Church, both to give it a dynamic inner unity and to help attune it to the surrounding world it must address.

As a class, charismatics see room for improvement (almost) everywhere. They are typified by an impressive *hope*—even though this hope may at times look like a bland optimism very much in need of testing; in times of frustration, hope of this kind may even turn out to be laced with a surprising amount of underlying negative affect. No wonder, though, that charismatics appreciate *openness in the Church* and strongly depend, for their sense of identity, on integrity, authenticity, and personal responsibility. No wonder, either, that such motivated Christians, paradoxically, require more, not less, ministerial care; yet understandably, they tend to resist and resent even the suspicion of clerical, institutional supervision or tutelage. Hence they tend to do what motivated lay people have done ever since conscientious Christian lay folk started moving into the desert monasteries near Alexandria in the third century: they create inspirational communities of support and direction—not infrequently of the kind that local bishops find hard to oversee. And since they have also come to respect the world, they tend to appreciate the unity of the Church only to the extent that it is *open*— open to the deeper reaches of the life-experience of its own members and open to what is best and noblest, as well as what is most dubious and most offensive, in the world that it must serve.

[a] That faith without works is dead (Jas 2, 26) is a maxim found everywhere in the New Testament, if not always in this form. Exhortations to active discipleship are everywhere in the accounts of Jesus' journey to Jerusalem in Mark (esp. Mk 10, 1–52; Lk 9, 51–19, 48), and the fourth Gospel is especially emphatic on the connection between discipleship and imitation (Jn 12, 26; 13, 12–17). While Paul, in the first Letter to the Corinthians, makes a point of demanding that the community's weaker members be especially re-

---

[g] The term *charismatics* as used here does not necessarily refer to Christians involved in the charismatic renewal movement, prominently characterized by a relatively spontaneous style of common prayer. Rather, it refers to Christians, who whether acting individually or in groups, are primarily characterized by personal motivation and initiative in the active practice of the faith. Many of such Christians are indeed found in the renewal movement, but the two classes only overlap; they do not coincide.

garded, he also makes a point of encouraging the community to active love, while casting himself as a man in ceaseless, single-minded pursuit of the perfection demanded by his call (1 Cor 9, 19–27; cf. Phil 3, 8–14), even to the point of urging the Corinthians to imitate him in his imitation of Christ (1 Cor 4, 16; 11, 1; cf. Phil 3, 17). The freedom from the old slavery must inspire the Christian to live by the Spirit and to bear its fruits (Gal 5, 25. 22) and to live a life of service (Gal 5, 13; cf. 1 Pet 2, 16)—a service that can never be viewed as completed (Lk 17, 10) since its measure is God's own perfection, which is the perfection of compassion (Mt 5, 48; Lk 6, 36).

[b] The Churches of the Reformation can point to a long and honorable tradition of cultivating, as a matter of principle, a participative, evangelical, "charismatic" style of faith experience and expression on the part of all members of the Church and one which is relatively independent of clerical assurance. This must be appreciated as part of the historic heritage of Protestantism. One of the sharpest protests against Catholicism heard at the time of the Reformation concerned the unconcern of a systematically self-centered clerical establishment and the exclusion of the laity—and the emancipated laity in particular—from the fullness of their birthright as baptized Christians [h]. Much as the charge has been exaggerated at times, the warning remains salutary, even after the explicit recognition of the common priesthood of all the faithful by the Second Vatican Council (LG 10).

In this light, the impulse that the council gave both to the *aggiornamento* of the Church and to the personal responsibility of all of the Church's members is of historic importance, both for the self-awareness of the laity in the Catholic Church and for the cause of a truly comprehensive ecumenism [i].

[c] Like the pistic experience, the charismatic experience has inherent weaknesses, which must be frankly acknowledged. Again, a few must be mentioned. Openness in the Church and involvement in dialogue with the surrounding culture can lead to *diffuseness* and unconscious *compromise* in doctrinal matters, especially since charismatic *actualism*

---

[h] Fyodor Dostoyevsky's dramatic "Legend of the Grand Inquisitor," in *The Brothers Karamazov* (V, 5) draws the final conclusion: the "most fundamental feature" of Roman Catholicism is the belief that Christ has handed over everything to the pope and to the hierarchy. This has deprived the faithful of direct access to Christ and left nothing but a debased version of the Christian faith, accommodated to the needs of an irresponsible populace craving for assurance. Thus the Church of Christ is replaced by a totalitarian theocracy run by a clergy that has itself lost all faith. Ivan, the atheist who tells the story in *The Brothers Karamazov*, implicitly agrees that this is the only form of Christianity that is practical, thus making the charge against the Catholic Church even more devastating.

[i] On the complementarity of Catholicism and Protestantism, see the interesting discussion in Avery Dulles' *The Catholicity of the Church*, pp. 147–66. One telling limitation of that discussion, it would seem, is the absence of any reference to the Oriental Churches. It is arguable that the disintegration that occurred at the Reformation was not unrelated to the West's loss of contact with the doxological traditions of the East.

has a tendency to ignore the Tradition in the name of "contemporary experience"—which is not infrequently canonized without discernment. As a result, the great variety of chosen agendas and ministries can lead to factionalism in the Church. The good thing is, of course, that charismatics *choose*; the problem is that in doing so they often *select*. This is compounded by the fact that charismatics tend to be better doers than sufferers. Action—including generous, highly motivated action—is inherently bracing and exciting and thus harbors a strongly self-conscious, self-regarding, and, hence, self-justifying element. Whereas the characteristic self-righteousness of the pistic is predicated on passive obedience, the charismatic brand is activist: precisely because we experience our causes as worthy and our intentions as the very best, we will do justice with a vengeance. Adopting political action models in doing battle for "the cause," therefore, is not uncharacteristic of charismatics, both on the Left and on the Right. This, of course, easily leads to contempt for weaker brothers and sisters in the community—in the form of either disregard or paternalism.

[d] Even more importantly, however, the charismatic stance may in practice lead to a misinterpretation of the person and the work of Christ. Charismatics are serious about conduct and, hence, about the *imitation of Christ*; typically, they take a profound—and not seldom prayerful—interest in the historical Jesus' ministry. In so doing, however, they run the serious risk of adopting a completely *moralistic version of the Christian faith* and of *reducing the person of Jesus Christ* to that of a teacher, a prophetic advocate, or even a social revolutionary, and his ministry to little more than the original example of Christian dedication to the cause of justice. To grow further in the Spirit, therefore, charismatics will have to agree to have their activism chastened and their ego curbed. What they could profitably discover is the meaning and use of *patience*, and discover it they must at the source by learning to interpret Jesus' ministry as a *mystery*, not so much of action as of compassion (Mt 8, 16–17!) and, ultimately, of total abandon to God, down to the acceptance of death on the cross. In the long run, only entrance into the paschal mystery will keep charismatics—and their moral conduct along with them—Christian.

[5] If Christian *worship* conveys anything, it conveys that God is the central focus as well as the all-encompassing reality of the Christian faith: God approached with awe as well as confidence and praised, thanked, and implored in the Spirit, under invocation of Jesus Christ and in union with him. Without worship, Christianity ceases to be faith in God, that is to say, it ceases to be *religious* faith, except in the most theoretical of senses (cf. §25, 4, b; §30, 5). But by the same token, it also ceases to span the whole world—not only its past and its present,

but also, and especially, its *future*; for it is in worship that Christians come to participate in the divine *comprehensiveness*. The glory that is given to the Father, the Son, and the Holy Spirit is, of its nature *universal*: glory given from the beginning, being given now, and ever to be given, by all that has been, is, and will be, world without end. God and only God can fill all that is with the majesty and the loveliness of the divine presence.

In worship, too, Christians celebrate and believe in actuality—if in anticipation (cf. §38, 5)—the full meaning of all Christian teaching as well as the fulfillment of all Christian moral life: *holiness*. In worship they also anticipate the eschatological communion of the saints, the remission of all sin, the establishment of final justice in the resurrection, and the life that lasts forever. In worship, finally, Christians learn to participate in the divine *intensity*: they share in actuality—if, again, in anticipation—the divine nature (2 Pet 1, 4). Divine comprehensiveness and intensity: these two sum up the reality of the Holy Spirit (cf. § 34, 5). This means that Christian worship and all Christian prayer is ultimately a matter of participating in an all-penetrating and all-encompassing *love*. Only God can absorb and outsuffer, by a welcoming love, the violence that sickens the world, and only God is capable of gathering in the whole world by love and of gathering it in in freedom, without compulsion. For only God can touch the heart of all created reality, and *those who feel that touch will entirely live by it*.

They are those whom the Tradition has called the *"perfect"*; their faith-experience is characterized by *mystical union with God in love* [j]. Participation in this long-suffering and most compassionate love is learned in the school of Jesus Christ.

Mystics no longer believe and live by relying on the authority of the Church of God (though they very much tend to cherish and respect the Church, even when misunderstood by it). Nor do they believe and live by appealing to the authority of the inner call of grace in the conscience (though they do tend to live out of an inner conviction typical of the truly conscientious person). Rather, the ground that sustains the Christian mystic in everything is *union with Christ*. With and through and in Christ, they acquire their own identity by *mortification* of the self-conscious self. Paradoxically, that mortification consists in removing what maintains and defends and justifies the self, and there is much pain in the removing. But in this way they succeed in allowing the

---

[j] An important caution. This portrayal of the state of the "perfect" is offered by way of a broad *theological* characterization of the *nature* of their experience; it is *not* offered by way of a *descriptive report* on their *experienced states of (self)-consciousness*. Anyone even remotely familiar with the literature of mysticism knows, first of all, that there is a great variety of mystical states of consciousness and, second, that these states (unlike some of the descriptions of them) are characterized, not by self-consciousness, but by a unifying focus on God. Among the many dependable books on the subject, A. Poulain's *The Graces of Interior Prayer* remains an authoritative, if somewhat prosaic, guide.

aggressive barbed-wire defenses, behind which people stay distant from God, from others, and from themselves, to be removed—at times rudely and smartingly, but more often gently and gradually.

> With an anvil-ding
> And with fire in him forge thy will
> Or rather, rather then, stealing as Spring
> Through him, melt him but master him still:
> Whether at once, as once at a crash Paul,
> Or as Austin, a lingering-out sweet skill,
> Make mercy in all of us, out of us all
> Mastery, but be adored, but be adored King.[20]

In the process, mystics gain fresh, and much less inhibited, access to their deeper selves, to God, and to others. Their egos lose their bristle. As they become interiorly mortified, they become transparent, first toward God, from whom they come to expect everything. Identified by God, they will identify with others. Others will sense a curious attraction to them and often find their cares and concerns radically understood and fathomed by them, with the empathy of gracious (and frequently shrewd) love.

Thus dispossessed, divested, and disarmed, their souls more and more live beyond the ecclesiastical dilemmas and the judgments necessarily implied in them; they find identity neither in the limits nor in the openness of the Church but, most importantly, in its depth. Thus *they take on the Church's essential inner form* [k]: mystics are the heart of the Church—both on fire and at peace, by the Spirit. Thus they bear out the mystery shared by all, namely that with Christ dead and risen, we ultimately walk in this world as on water, in complete abandon to the providential care of his Father dear, whether in light or in dark, whether in acceptance or in rejection, whether in life or in death:

> None of us live for ourselves
> and none of us die for ourselves.
> For if we live, it is for the Lord that we live;
> if we die, it is for the Lord that we die.
> So whether we live,
> whether we die,
> we are the Lord's.
> For to this purpose Christ died and lived:
> to be of both the dead and the living
> the Lord.
>
> (Rom 14, 7–9)

[a] While the New Testament as it has come down to us is mostly the direct record of the early communities' practice of teaching and

---

[k] On the concept of *anima ecclesiastica*, cf. *In der Fülle des Glaubens*, p. 226 (ET *The von Balthasar Reader*, p. 228).

exhortation, the practice of worship and prayer is immediately below the surface almost everywhere. Overlooking or disregarding this amounts to misreading the New Testament (cf. §§33–34).

[b] It has been one of the signal strengths of the Oriental Churches to have cultivated practices of worship that convey and breathe this mystical spirit so integral to the Christian faith-experience. Without that spirit, Christian conduct and Christian doctrine degenerate into righteous moralism and opinionated orthodoxy. Consequently, it is arguable that one of the greatest recent blessings of the Church has been the liturgical movement, which—in concert with the ecumenical movement—has swept across the Christian West over the past century. The Second Vatican Council's inspired decision to place the reform of the liturgy at the top of its agenda has profoundly affected, in a deeply positive direction, the faith-experience of Catholics around the world. The recovery of liturgy in many Protestant Churches is having comparable beneficial effects. Both developments, if cherished and fostered, may succeed in gradually repelling the atmosphere of prayerlessness that so often pervades the Churches.

[c] The Tradition of the undivided Church has recognized "perfection," not only as the culmination of the life of faith of *every Christian* [*l*], but also as a possible, and even desirable, *state of life*—the "state of perfection." Two forms of this state have been recognized in the course of Church history. The first is *episcopacy*: many theologians have taught that being at the head of a local Church entails the obligation of practicing in one's ministry what the Church most deeply *is*: the Body of Christ mystically united with its Head. The second is *religious life*: the institutional, communal pursuit [*m*] of evangelical perfection, in a life marked by freely chosen renunciation of property, sexual continence, and obedience to superiors [*n*].

[d] The mystic stance has its own inherent weaknesses. The obvious one is self-isolation, in spiritual pride, from the imperfect, which tends to give rise to masked immorality and to contempt for the

---

[*l*] Note Calvin's insistence on this, in his criticism of false claims made in behalf of religious life: *Instit.*, IV, 13, 11.

[*m*] An essential word: what is institutionalized is not the perfection but its pursuit. Religious life is the *status perfectionis acquirendæ*.

[*n*] It is important to point out that *mysticism*—or "contemplation"—is at the heart of religious life, not to be replaced by anything else. This does not mean that religious must not be active—far from it. It does mean, however, that the life of active religious men and women must be rooted in the pursuit of union with God; it must be based on a "loving service mysticism" (H. Egan, *Christian Mysticism*, p. 41). Is it foolish to suggest that the recent numerous departures from religious life and its continuing crisis have exposed the fact that many religious communities, for all the generous, hard, and often unrewarding work "charismatically" done by its members, have been lacking in lived experience in the mystical life?

Church in the name of private illumination. Yet the most serious weakness that threatens the mystic—and the one to be feared above all else—is what the ascetical tradition has called *abandonment*—separation from God brought on by negligence or pride.

To clarify the issue, an important preliminary remark is in order. Spiritual growth and development is not simply progressive or cumulative. Rather, it is *dialectical*: the more someone advances, the greater the risk of loss of faith. The main liabilities of the *pistic* are overconcern with one's own salvation, fearfulness in professing one's faith, pusillanimity in prayer, and lack of a generously ministerial attitude toward others. The *charismatic*'s faith is in greater jeopardy: it is threatened by temptations to disregard the weaker brothers and sisters, to cultivate factions to the point of fanaticism, and to cast Jesus in the image of a favorite prejudice. The *mystic*'s faith is at still greater risk: intimate union with God is in danger of being forfeited and turned into its dreaded opposite: a state of *egkataleipsis*[21] ("abandonment" or "dereliction"). This requires some explanation. The sixth-century desert monk Dorotheus of Gaza is a reliable authority here.

States of profound spiritual desolation, Dorotheus explains, will befall persons who have advanced in the life of the Spirit, but if endured, such episodes can dramatically enhance their union with God [o]. However, if they are not endured but avoided, the opposite will happen: "We have said that what has been sown, *even after it has sprouted and grown and borne fruit*, withers and is lost if the rain does not regularly come down again. This also applies to persons. If, after all they have done, God takes away his protection for a while, they are lost. *But abandonment befalls persons when they do something that goes against their condition.* Let me give an example. Someone is devout and falls into carelessness, or he is humble and falls into presump-

---

[o] Dorotheus' account of his own deliverance of such a state of desolation, in the course of an experience that is curiously hallucinatory, is found in the fifth of his *Instructions* (SC 92, §67, pp. 260–65). A particularly vivid piece of advice to people suffering from desolation, ultimately encouraging them to abandon themselves to God, is found in the thirteenth instruction: "There are people whose occupation forces them to swim in the sea. Now if they know the art of swimming, when a wave comes down upon them, they plunge before it and allow themselves to go underneath it until it passes by, and thus they continue swimming without harm. But if they want to offer resistance to the wave, it pushes them out of their way and throws them back a good distance. As soon as they start swimming again, another wave comes down upon them; if they resist again, it pushes them again and tosses them out of their way, and all they do is tire themselves out without advancing any. But if, as I said, they plunge before the wave and humble themselves underneath it, it passes by without harming them, and they continue to swim as much as they want, and thus they do their work. The same is true with regard to temptations: if someone bears his temptation with patience and humility, it passes him by without causing difficulty. But if he continues to let himself get irritated and troubled, and to blame everybody, he punishes himself by making his temptation weigh down more heavily on himself, and from that he will draw no profit; in fact, it will even harm him" (SC 92, §140, pp. 406–7; cf. Aelred Squire, *Asking the Fathers*, pp. 214–15).

tuousness. Now *God does not abandon the careless man when he acts care-lessly, or the presumptuous man when he acts presumptuously, so much as he abandons the devout man when he acts carelessly, and the humble man when he acts presumptuously. That is what is meant by 'someone sinning against his condition'; that is where abandonment comes from.* That is why Saint Basil judges the sin of the devout man one way, and the sin of the careless man another way."[22]

The nearer one draws to God, the sharper the consciousness of God as the ever-receding standard of excellence (cf. §49, 2, c) and, hence, the sharper the consciousness of the precariousness of faith. United with God, mystics are utterly aware of their inability to bridge the gap that separates them from God. Life is union with the Source of life, maintained only by holding on to the Source, and even the holding on is pure gift. Those united with God live where union with Life itself and the threat of imminent fall into death coincide. Taught by deeper experience than either the pistic or the charismatic, the mystic has more reason than both to pray, "Let me never be sepa-rated from you."

[6] One of the constant teachings of Thomas Aquinas, from his com-mentary on Peter Lombard's *Sentences* on, is that "a goal is first in intention and last in execution."[23] This means that the work finished and the goal accomplished best indicate what the whole work was about in the first place.

The principle is very much applicable to the present discussion. All Christians participate in the doxological essence of the Christian faith, which consists in encounter with the living God (cf. §36, 1, a). But this encounter occurs in different degrees—degrees made possible by the fact that the faith's doxological essence is played out in a soteriological dynamism consisting in three moments: worship, life, and teaching (cf. §38, 1; §44, 3).

It is in the *mystic* that the faith's doxological essence is shown to best advantage, for mystics are most characterized by worship and prayer. But mystics never outgrow the requirements of Christian conduct and teaching: they do not leave the commandments behind, and it is from the Church that they continue to receive the faith that is the love of their lives.

Charismatics will have their doxological experience, too; they are not just moral drudges. But they do tend to discover that the road of virtue is endless and ultimately wearying and that only God, approached in worship, is capable of fulfilling their thirst for more. They also tend to discover, as in a second innocence, that it is the faith of the Church, not their own, that they have been trying to appropriate more fully.

The *pistic*, finally, is far from being simply a passive believer. First of all, pistics are charismatics in that they are called to live by the commandments. More importantly, however, they are capable of worship in Spirit and truth. Having been initiated in Christ's death and resurrection by Baptism, they are qualified, as members of the Body, to be mystically united with God by the eucharistic Body and Blood of Christ, as the Church gives praise and thanksgiving to God.

Thus all individual Christians profess the whole faith, but, to use Origen's image, they experience it at various levels. The pistics believe by the flesh—but it is the flesh that the Word has taken on. The charismatics live by the soul—but it is the soul that animated the flesh of Christ to enable it to obey the divine will in freedom (DS 556; CF 635). The mystics worship by the spirit—but it is the spirit in which Christ abandoned himself, in his human body and soul, to the Father.

[a] A final comment on this fundamental *unity* of the Christian faith-experience. It was suggested earlier that whatever stages of progressive perfection of the Christian life of faith will turn out to encompass, the practice of Christian initiation demands that the *whole* of the Christian faith be demonstrated to be somehow actualized at *every* developmental stage (§53, 1).

The New Testament bears this out, in that it treats *apostasy* in the severest terms—that is to say, it judges it by the standard of the *central mystery* that former Christians have renounced. The Letter to the Hebrews evokes with horror the irredeemable, dead-end situation of those "who have been enlightened once for all, and tasted the heavenly gift, and shared the Holy Spirit, and tasted the good word of God and the powers of the age to come, and lapsed." They have "on their own account re-crucified and pilloried the Son of God"; they have "trampled the son of God, and made light of the blood of the Covenant in which they were sanctified, and outraged the Spirit of grace" (Heb 6, 4–5; 11, 29). There is a very sobering way in which the Gospel of Matthew expresses this theme: it conveys its awe at the gift of participation in God's kingdom by holding up the terror of the alternative: rejection and exclusion from the kingdom (Mt 8, 12; 13, 42. 50; 24, 51; 25, 30; cf. Lk 13, 28).

This shows that apostasy is considered a falling away, not from a *stage* of faith-experience, but from the doxological essence of the Christian faith itself—that is to say, from the encounter with the living God, in which all Christians participate at every stage of development.

[b] A final comment, too, on the developmental stages. The three stages of spiritual growth, it would seem, bear a resemblance to the three steps by which the human mind naturally ascends to the knowledge of God. Throughout his career, from his commentaries on Pseudo-Dionysius' *On the Divine Names* and Peter Lombard's *Sentences*

right up to the *Summa*, Aquinas kept insisting on this triple way. We can make affirmative statements about God in so far as God is the cause of all finite things. We must also speak negatively, by way of removal (*remotio*), lest we attribute to God what is proper only to the creature. Thus we come to a sense of God's absolute *eminence* in which affirmation and negation, speech and silence, are synthesized.[24] It would seem that the pistic typically believes by affirmation; as charismatics advance, they tend to shed naively affirmative conceptions of God and begin—often painfully—to believe and pray by negation;[25] the mystic realizes, both in speech and in silence, that all language fails to do justice to the God in whom we believe but also that God's glory and love forbid that we should remain completely silent.

[7] The method of understanding must be determined by the matter to be understood (§8, 6). The past three chapters have unfolded the unity of the Christian faith by means of an exploration of its intrinsic, structural components: teaching, life, and worship. In accordance with this, the *teaching* tradition gives rise to *systematic* theology (in its *dogmatic*, *constructive*, and *fundamental* functions: §14, 4); theological reflection on Christian *conduct* gives rise to Christian *ethics*, or *moral* theology; and the *worship* tradition generates *liturgical* and *sacramental* theology. The inner diversity of the Christian faith both requires and justifies this differentiation of theological disciplines. But the unity of the Christian faith demands that the disciplines not be allowed to drift apart but be pursued in an integrated manner. This has consequences for all branches of theology.

This integration should be effected in at least two ways.

First of all, a truly catholic *systematic* theology should cease being a most exclusively concerned with the teaching of *doctrine* and reintegrate *ethics* and the *theology of prayer*—at least in a fundamental fashion, by exploring the inner connections of doctrine with conduct and worship. *God Encountered* proposes to do this under the rubric of the divine *reditus*, in the third part.

But second, *all* theological disciplines should give up their almost exclusive concern with the *pistic* variety of faith: theology should deal, not only with the life of faith insofar as it remains tied to its initial stage, but also with progress in virtue and with union with God as it is experientially attainable in the Christian life. Hence, systematic theology should not be divorced from *ascetical* theology (which deals with the experiences of the "proficient" or "charismatics") and *mystical* theology (which deals with the experiences of the "perfect"). Analogous connections between the disciplines could probably be established by ethicists and moralists, and by sacramental theologians and liturgiologists. In any case, the entire enterprise of catholic theology could, by means of a coherent exercise of its legitimate specialties, come to do justice, both to the unity of the faith and to its integral components (cf. §44, 1–3).

TEACHING WITH AUTHORITY

[§55] THE AUTHORITY OF THEOLOGY

[1] At the close of this introductory volume of systematic theology, a much-debated contemporary question of a *normative* nature (cf. §12, 2) presents itself for acknowledgment and brief treatment: Does theology have *theological*—that is to say, *ecclesial*—authority? Can a theologian claim the attention of the Christian community? The question has recently been the subject of much animated discussion in the Catholic Church, mainly in the form of the question about the relationship between the theologian and the magisterium.[26] Yet the issue of the theology's ecclesial authority is very much alive elsewhere as well, especially in Churches that do not recognize (or emphasize) a highly visible, institutional teaching authority. In fact, in these Churches the question is often asked with greater urgency. If it is granted that the Church owes allegiance to a profession of faith, does theology qualify as a tribunal?

An observation of a principled nature must open this discussion. Christian theology, it was stated long ago, is a form of disciplined intellectual understanding related to the Christian faith. That relationship, it was further explained, is far from extrinsic. Even at the natural level, acts of human *understanding*, in and of themselves, encompass a basic aspiration to worship (§8, 8); on the other hand, acts of Christian *faith*, being structured and hence amenable to understanding (§§9–10), in and of themselves give rise to thought (§12, 1). There is, in other words, a fundamental legitimacy—and hence, an intrinsic authority—to theology, predicated on the nature of human understanding, on the one hand, and the intelligibility of the Christian faith as a positive religion, on the other. There is no good reason to deny ecclesial authority to theology solely on the ground that it is very much an exercise in human intelligence.

[a] As a consequence of the fundamental relatedness between faith and understanding, theology can arrive at a true and fruitful understanding of the Christian faith in itself (cf. §12, 1, a), without "sticking determinateness on to [it] in a merely extrinsic fashion" (cf. §8, 6, a; §13, 1).

To be *theologically* and *ecclesially* authoritative, theology must, of course, be *competently done*. This is often misunderstood. To ascribe no more than an "academic," or "scholarly," authority to theology competently done amounts to saying that understanding is unrelated to *subject matter*. The opposite is true, of course: understanding is competent according to how it accommodates itself to, and thus participates in, the subject matter (cf. §8, 6). True theological reason is "reason illuminated by the faith" it studies (DS 3016; CF 132). The authority of theology competently done, therefore, derives *proximately* from the theologian's appropriate use of intellectual talent—that is to say, the theologian's ability to attune mind to subject matter, which is at least partly a matter of virtue (cf. §8, 7, a). Ultimately, however, and decisively, it comes from the authority resident in the Christian faith itself, competently mediated by the theologian. For this reason it comes as no surprise that Thomas Aquinas derives the teaching authority of the *cathedra magistralis* (that is, the theologians, as distinct from the bishops' *cathedra pastoralis*) simply by reference to "sufficiency of learning." It is *learning* that earns the theologian the *license* to train others in the understanding of the faith; however, the *exercise* of that license, according to Aquinas, is an office of *charity*, or, in modern ecclesiological idiom, a charism shared with the community.[27]

[2] The Christian faith is *historical* and not just in the workaday sense that, like everything else in the world, it is *set in* history. The Christian takes its origin from, and encompasses, historic events of divine origin. In virtue of the eschatological perspective involved in these events, the Christian community commits itself in every *present* moment to the *future* as a continuing history of salvation. But the historic origins of the Christian faith also involve the reinterpretation of the entire *past* history of Israel and the world; moreover, according as the account of the continuing history of salvation becomes part of the original narrative, the Christian community's commitments also include a commitment to its own historic past (cf. §36, 3; §38, 1; §40, 2–3; §42, 1; §43, 2).

On the one hand, therefore, *all* reliable teaching of the Christian faith must be rooted in a participatory understanding of the historic Christian teaching Tradition. On the other hand, however, that very Tradition demands that both understanding and teaching be done integrally—that is to say, that *the present and future dynamics* of the Tradition be recognized. To the extent that the Christian faith is oriented to the *past*, the theologian-teacher needs the gift of fidelity in understanding, to do justice to the great Tradition ("Hold fast to what is good": 1 Thess 5, 21). To the extent that it is actualized in the *present*, the theologian-teacher needs the gift of prophetic discernment, to read the given situation correctly and to choose what is right ("Do not quench the Spirit, do not despise prophesying but test everything": 1 Thess 5, 19–21). To the extent that Christian doctrine must be open to the *future*, the theologian-teacher needs the gift of prayer and thanksgiving, to expect everything from God ("Rejoice always, pray constantly, give thanks in all circumstances, for this is the will of God for you": 1 Thess 5, 16–18).

Competent, authoritative teaching based on true, participatory understanding of the Christian faith, therefore, has three aspects. The indispensable *primary competence* required in the theologian is *magisterial*: theology must draw on the authoritative past. Theology's greatest *challenge* consists in the *service* it has to render *to the Church now*: it must provide the search for a new configurative balance between the Tradition and the culture with pastoral guidance, so as to keep the great Tradition alive. Finally, to maintain the reference to the mystery—that is to say, to remain *theology*—theology must be *mystagogical*: it must seek to keep open the Tradition's eschatological perspective. It must do the latter, not only by referring the *Church*'s teaching tradition to worship, but also by respecting the *culture*'s unrealized potential for integration into the living Tradition as it points to its own fulfillment (cf. §14, 1– 4) [*p*].

[3] From the preceding it follows that *pastoral and mystagogical elements are inseparable from the practice of theology* understood in its broadest sense: the understanding and teaching of the living Christian faith-tradition. No wonder the magisterium and the theologians have a number of *ecclesial* tasks and responsibilities in common, not only in the area of teaching, but also in the pastoral and liturgical areas.[28] It is bad *theology* for theologians to be mewed up in their academies—whether by their own choice or by ecclesiastical design. In particular, it is a mistake to disavow the theologian's pastoral and spiritual responsibility, for instance, by claiming that bishops are the only "real" teachers in the Church, with "real" responsibility for Christian conduct and prayer.

There are, obviously, decisive differences between the tasks and responsibilities of the episcopal magisterium and the theologians. The two principal ones, it would seem, are the following. First, the bearers of the ecclesiastical magisterium are *authentic teachers*—that is to say, they enjoy an authority that is directly connected with Christ's (LG 25).[29] Hence, for the sake of Christ, they are entitled to a respectful hearing on the part of their Churches as a whole; theologians are not. Second, these authentic teachers are also *leaders* (LG 27) and *priests* (LG 26): they have full *ecclesial authority* in the pastoral and liturgical areas, whereas theologians have only such authority as is inseparable from their far more limited authority as teachers.

But then again, there are significant, and very fundamental, ways in

---

[*p*] Consequently, apologetics, from a Christian perspective, is not a merely political act of studied deference to the culture understood as an *authority* (cf. §14, 3). It is also an act of patient, critical empathy with the world (cf. F. J. van Beeck, *Christ Proclaimed*, pp. 486–501) and, ultimately, a vicarious gesture of eschatological aspiration, on the unevangelized world's behalf, for its integration into the worship of the new heaven and the new earth.

which the magisterium and the theologians share a common lot—so much so that cooperation rather than antagonism would appear to be the obvious thing to attempt. Two important ones come to mind.

First, to arrive at an authoritative understanding of the Tradition, the bearers of the authentic teaching office and the theologians have at their disposal *no means other than those also accessible, in principle, to all Christians.* These means are: the present life of the Church; the record of the great Tradition of the undivided Church, laid down in Scripture and further authoritative documents; and further down the line, any broad, substantial, sustained, documented agreement on doctrinal, moral, and liturgical issues on the part of Church Fathers, popes, councils, synods, saints, and theologians ("*consensus theologorum*"). To attune themselves to this wealth of sources, they can profitably cultivate a willingness to learn and to be taught,[30] and a discerning attitude, guided by worship and prayer, vis-à-vis the Church community and the surrounding culture.

Second, both the bearers of the authentic teaching office and the theologians would do well to realize that *no one in the Church can claim control over the living Tradition.* Both the members of the magisterium and the theologians are the *servants* of the Tradition, not its masters. Very concretely, this means that all teaching is subject, in one way or another, to the dynamics of *reception.* It is true that authentic magisterial teaching can command *acceptance* and, in cases of infallible pronouncements, even unconditional acceptance (LG 25); but acceptance is not identical with reception. Just *how* magisterial teaching—even of the unconditionally and universally obligatory kind—is going to function in the Church's living Tradition remains a matter of the *sensus fidelium. Only the Church community as a whole is the integral subject of the Tradition.* The occupants, both of the *cathedra pastoralis* and the *cathedra magistralis,* have fundamental theological reasons to be respectful.

[a] The relationships between bishops and theologians in the Christian West have been profoundly affected by historic developments since the first millennium [q]. On the one hand, the ecclesial profession of the Christian faith, which provided the theologians with their systematic framework, had become strongly dependent on a non-liturgical type of creed (§52, 7–8). But on the other hand, from the thirteenth century on, theology also increasingly left the precincts of the monasteries and the cathedral schools, and, in a move with incalculable consequences, migrated to the university. There it grad-

---

[q] The situation of the Church in the first millennium is sometimes idealized. While it is true that "most theologians were also bishops, and many of the more influential bishops were theologians" (Francis A. Sullivan, *Magisterium,* p. 181), it must not be forgotten that many local bishops were quite poorly educated. Theological talent was rare, then as always. The bishop of Hippo did everything to keep Augustine in town, to prevent him from being drafted by some rural Church and thus being lost to the see.

ually lost its familiarity with the *lectio divina* tradition of reading and interpreting Scripture as well as much of its respect for the positive theology of the fathers and became strongly indebted to philosophical speculation (cf. §14, 4, a). Both developments tended to estrange both the profession of faith and the practice of theology from the liturgy as well as from the pastoral office. All this prepared the ground for the doctrinal propositionalism of the sixteenth and seventeenth centuries (cf. §52, 7, a; also, cf. §7, 1, a–b; §19, 1), which operated in an atmosphere in which formulating a proposition was taken to be tantamount to understanding its meaning and teaching it.

The modern issue between the magisterium and the theologian arises in the aftermath of these developments. In the critical atmosphere of the Enlightenment, catholic orthodoxy became more and more a matter of unhistorical, authoritative affirmativeness on the part of a hierarchy determined to resist the leveling influences of rationalism (cf. §51, 4, b).

In this situation, the Romantic inspiration—with its strong anti-rationalist bias and its affinity with Catholicism [r]—provided a new idea: the true tradition could be recovered only by *individual talent*. The theologian was no longer seen as *"representing* an objective revelation but as imaginatively *constructing* the immediate, though historical, experience of salvation."[31]

This had enormous consequences. In Catholicism, the "magisterium"—a term used with increasing insistence by the magisterium itself[32]—set itself up as the guardian of the Tradition, understood more and more in a retrospective sense [s]. Over against this magisterium (or, in the case of Protestantism, over against the official Church confessions), the individual theologian, supported by the Romantic infatuation with originality, became an *author*—that is to say: a lonely, even heroic witness to the truth, an "ecclesial diviner,"[33] possessed of a mantic force attuned, by definition, to "living reality"—almost an oracle [t]. "Thus the Romantic paradigm understands

---

[r] The names of Joseph de Maistre and Friedrich Schlegel come to mind, as well as, of course, the latter's friend and protégé, the German poet Novalis (Friedrich Leopold Freiherr von Hardenberg), whom Schleiermacher memorialized (*On Religion*, pp. 41, 104, 184) and whose strong leanings toward Catholicism remained in suspended animation when he died in 1801, at the age of twenty-nine.

[s] These nineteenth-century professions of loyalty to the Tradition, however, are often about as well supported by real knowledge of the Tradition as neo-Gothic architecture was by the medieval cathedrals. Much neo-scholasticism of late nineteenth-century inspiration was naively restorationist and was much more indebted to eighteenth-century rationalism than it was aware of. Cf. M.-D Chenu, "Vérité évangélique et métaphysique wolffiennne à Vatican II."

[t] Schleiermacher, again, is the original example here. Consistent with his contention that faith expresses itself in "the doctrine prevailing in a Christian ecclesiastical society at a given time" (cf. §51, 5, a), he attributes to the individual theologian the ability to

the theologian to be primarily responsible to the developing experience of the Church at large, but ascribes a remarkable degree of power to the talent, discretion, and authority of the individual theologian."[34] Even in cases in which these authors themselves were not writing as self-consciously influential theologians, they frequently came to be held in veneration by devoted disciples, who fashioned highly self-conscious, self-cultivating schools of thought, devoted, in more than one case, to a rigid orthodoxy where the master had merely followed his theological insights. In many ways, the history of Christian theology of the past two centuries has been the history of the debates conducted by (and about) great theological authors and schools. Names, too many to mention, come to mind, not to mention dissertation titles.

This situation has created the awkward situation in which reductive and selective renditions of the great Tradition, elaborated by individual authors or schools of theology, have gotten accustomed to presenting themselves as authoritative interpretations of the Christian faith (§15, 4, [n]). This amounts to a systemic manipulation of the great Tradition, by means of attempts to replace it by *theological opinion presented as matter for belief* (cf. §19, 1, [d]), both on the Left and the Right. There are those who, often with minimal reference to the great Tradition, treat it simply as a well-known history of past ideas and proceed self-consciously to develop "new ideas," "paradigm shifts," and the like [u]. Others will sound the loyalty trumpet and side with the Tradition, apparently oblivious of the fact that one is carried by the Tradition. Siding with the Tradition or otherwise sitting in judgment on it necessarily means distorting it; traditions are there to be understood and pondered in their historic and empirical integrity [v].

---

keep the tradition "mobile" by means of necessary "heterodoxy." The Catholic Tübingen theologian Johann Sebastian Drey agrees that "the further development of [the] spirit [of Christianity] and the clearer determination of its doctrinal tradition 'can only proceed from individuals' " (John E. Thiel, "Theological Responsibility," p. 583). In this context, an article by Robert Preyer deserves mention: "Tennyson as an Oracular Poet." Preyer describes how Tennyson, in his twenties, dressed à la Byron and Berlioz and wrote as a self-consciously original, oracular poet; but much of the poetry he wrote falsely suggested access to depths of meaning inaccessible to the ordinary mind. In the Romantic world, it is not good poetry that identifies the capable poet, but the poet who self-consciously postures as an individual talent that guarantees admirable poetry.

[u] For a recent example of this, cf. Paul Knitter's preface to *The Myth of Christian Uniqueness* (pp. vii–xii), a collection that self-consciously presents itself as "the crossing of a theological Rubicon." Could this kind of judgment be left up to history?

[v] Here lies the merit of Bernard Lonergan's protest against "the abstract logic of classicism" and his plea in favor of "the concreteness of method," which respects reality in its historic, empirical integrity (*Method in Theology*, p. 338; cf. *A Second Collection*, pp. 1–9). It should be pointed out, however, that the "classicism" Lonergan inveighs against is itself somewhat of an abstraction; in context, Lonergan uses it mainly as an ideal-typical foil to aid him in developing his thought. From a historical point of view, I suggest,

[4] In this situation, is it possible for a theologian to escape the pull towards self-conscious claims to authority and the temptation to partisanship and polarization, so as to be authoritative in a genuine ecclesial sense? A constructive answer, it would seem, is yes, but only by the practice of an appreciative hermeneutic across space and time (§21, 3). This means: by attempting to understand the great Tradition with the objectivity of love, so as to become a better mediator, capable of interpreting the great Tradition to the present Church.

This is best done by *not* looking to the present moment for clues as to what authoritative, let alone original, things to say. For authority belongs solely to the Tradition, and originality is not a matter of intention; and all the present moment has to offer is the urgency of a world ever in travail. If a theologian should turn out to be fortunate enough to become the medium of a constructive encounter between the authority of the great, ever so intractable Tradition and the urgency of the equally intractable present, and if new understanding should emerge from this (cf. §14, 2), then the Tradition *as a whole* stirs and is aroused, and it advances by one short but *intrinsically authoritative* step. T. S. Eliot's words about the poet's relatedness to the tradition apply to the theologian and the great Tradition as well:

The existing order is complete before the new work arrives; for order to persist after the supervention of novelty, the *whole* existing order must be, if ever so slightly, altered; and so the relations, proportions, values of each work . . . toward the whole are readjusted; and this is conformity between the old and the new. Whoever has approved this idea of order, . . . will not find it preposterous that the past should be altered by the present as much as the present is directed by the past. And the poet who is aware of this will be aware of great difficulties and responsibilities.[35]

"classicism" should be taken to refer to the whole complex of propositionalist thinking-patterns dominant in the West since the mid-sixteenth century.

Notes

Introduction

1. Avery Dulles, *The Catholicity of the Church*, pp. 24, 101, 133.
2. ". . . anima hominis fit omnia quodammodo secundum sensum et intellectum, in quo cognitionem habentia ad Dei similitudinem quodammodo appropinquant, in quo omnia præexistunt . . ." (*S. Th.*, I, 80, 1, *in c.*).
3. *Spiritual Exercises*, [22]. The Spanish original would also allow the last phrase to be translated as follows: ". . . let him look for all the means proper to get it understood rightly and thus salvaged."
4. J. Verhaar, "Language and Theological Method," pp. 22, 25–26.

Chapter 1

1. Richard Freeborn, *Turgenev*, p. 186. Also quoted by Aelred Squire, *Summer in the Seed*, p. 53.
2. Cf. Beryl Smalley, *The Study of the Bible in the Middle Ages*, pp. 112–95.
3. On the subject of this entire paragraph, cf. Walter J. Ong, *Ramus, Method and the Decay of Dialogue*, as well as the following works by the same author: *The Presence of the Word; Rhetoric, Romance, and Technology* (which contains some excellent essays on the mechanistic interpretation of the human mind); *Orality and Literacy*. Cf. also J. H. van den Berg, *Leven in meervoud*, esp. pp. 133–56. On the tendency towards definition, cf. F. J. van Beeck, "Reflections on a Dated Book," pp. 55–56; *Catholic Identity after Vatican II*, pp. 28–29.
4. "Die Wissenschaft darf sich nur durch das eigne Leben des Begriffs organisieren; in ihr ist die Bestimmtheit, welche aus dem Schema äusserlich dem Dasein aufgeklebt wird, die sich selbst bewegende Seele des erfüllten Inhalts" (G. W. F. Hegel, *Phänomenologie des Geistes*, Vorrede, p. 44).
5. K. Rahner, *Foundations of Christian Faith*, p. 4 (*Grundkurs*, p. 16).
6. *Q. D. de Ver.* 22, 2, *ad* 1: "Omnia cognoscentia cognoscunt implicite Deum in quolibet cognito."
7. For the arguments that this passage should not be interpreted in a general way, but read as dealing with the *actuality* of the [nations'] relationship with God, and for a comparison with Is 64, 8, cf. W. A. M. Beuken, '*Abraham weet van ons niet*' (*Jesaja 63:16*).
8. *S. Th.*, I, 60, 5, *in c.*: "Omnis creatura naturaliter secundum id quod est, Dei est." In context, Thomas is arguing that the love of God, for God's own sake, naturally takes priority over self-love.
9. Friedrich Schleiermacher, *On Religion*, pp. 26–101; on the quotation, cf. §35, 3, a,

where John Oman's translation (*On Religion*, p. 37) is corrected. Cf. also F. J. van Beeck, *Christ Proclaimed*, pp. 548–66, and the literature referred to there.

10. Cf. esp. the early accounts of this position in *Hörer des Wortes* (1969 ET *Hearers of the Word*, by M. Richards, unusable; partial translation available in G. McCool's *A Rahner Reader*) and *Spirit in the World*, and the mature account in the opening chapters of *Grundkurs des Glaubens* (ET *Foundations of Christian Faith*).

11. A classic account, though one limited by its empirical-experiential bias, is William James, *The Varieties of Religious Experience*. For a sensitive and learned, as well as far-ranging, discussion, cf. Louis Dupré, *The Other Dimension*.

12. Again, a piece of Aquinas' constant teaching, from his commentary on Aristotle's *Perihermeneias* to the *Summa theologica*. Cf. one out of countless examples in *S. Th.* I, 85, 5.

13. Cf. also F. J. van Beeck, *Christ Proclaimed*, pp. 185–88.

14. For a suggestive thumbnail sketch of one instance of the role of merchants in the spread of religion, cf. Peter Brown, "The Diffusion of Manichaeism in the Roman Empire," p. 102. Also, cf. Alois Grillmeier, *Jesus der Christus im Glauben der Kirche*, vol. 2/1, p. 218; *Christ in Christian Tradition*, vol. 2, pt. 1, p. 191. Finally, cf. Randolph F. Lumpp, "Literacy, Commerce, and Catholicity: Two Contexts of Change and Invention."

Chapter 2

1. Cf. F. J. van Beeck, *Catholic Identity After Vatican II*, pp. 9–10.

2. Readers of my book *Christ Proclaimed* will recognize in this series the "triple rhetoric" of inclusion, obedience, and hope set forth there.

3. Cf. F. J. van Beeck, *Catholic Identity After Vatican II*, pp. 9–10.

4. *Spiritual Exercises*, [363].

5. "System is schon an sich ein Hindernis der Wahrheit": quoted by E. Jansen Schoonhoven, *Jodendom Christendom Verlichting*, p. 124.

6. Published in *Essays Critical and Historical*, vol. 1, pp. 30–99. I have much benefited from John Coulson's *Religion and Imagination*.

7. John Henry Newman, *Essays Critical and Historical*, vol. 1, pp. 40–42.

8. Cf. F. J. van Beeck, *Catholic Identity After Vatican II*, pp. 5–6.

9. *Mystery and Manners*, p. 167. Cf. also, for a related insight, pp. 226–27.

10. "Das Katholische tilgt nicht, aber verwandelt die Angst" (*Katholisch*, p. 12).

Chapter 3

1. Cf. the second and third of Descartes' *Meditationes de Prima Philosophia*, [*23*, 20–52, 20], pp. 24–52.

2. Cf. *Gott als Geheimnis der Welt*, §§8–10, pp. 138–203 (ET *God as the Mystery of the World*, pp. 105–52).

3. Cf. Francis A. Sullivan, *Magisterium*.

4. Cf. Avery Dulles, *The Survival of Dogma*.

5. Flannery O'Connor, *The Habit of Being*, p. 92.

6. Johannes Feiner, "Commentary on the Decree [on Ecumenism]," in *Commentary on the Decrees of Vatican II*, vol. 2, esp. pp. 114–21, quotation p. 119; cf. F. J. van Beeck, *Catholic Identity After Vatican II*, pp. 91–92.

7. On the whole issue, P. T. R. Gray, *The Defense of Chalcedon in the East (451–553)*; Alois Grillmeier, *Jesus der Christus im Glauben der Kirche*, vol. 2/1, *Das Konzil von Chaldedon (451): Rezeption und Widerspruch (451–518)*; quotation (*ta en Chalkēdoni kalōs dogmatisthenta*) pp. 303–4 (*Christ in Christian Tradition*, vol. 2, *From the Council of Chalcedon (451) to Gregory the Great (590–604)*, pt. 1, *Reception and Contradiction: The development of the discussion about Chalcedon from 451 to the beginning of the reign of Justinian*; quotation p. 268).

8. Cf. Gerald O'Collins, *The Case Against Dogma.*
9. Cf. John Henry Newman, *An Essay on the Development of Christian Doctrine,* chap. 5, sec. 3; chap. 8.
10. *The Brothers Karamazov,* bk. 5, chap. 5.
11. Cf. Oscar L. Arnal, *Ambivalent Alliance.*
12. J. H. Newman, *An Essay on the Development of Christian Doctrine,* chap. 5, sec. 3; chap. 8.
13. The original: "Ça m'est bien égal d'être tué en guerre. De ce que j'ai aimé, que restera-t-il? Autant que des êtres, je parle des coutumes, des intonations irremplaçables, d'une certaine lumière spirituelle. Du déjeuner dans la ferme provençale sous les oliviers, mais aussi de Haendel. Les choses, je m'en fous, qui subsisteront. Ce qui vaut, c'est un certain arrangement des choses. La civilization est un bien invisible puisqu'elle porte non sur les choses, mais sur les invisibles liens qui les nouent l'une à l'autre, ainsi et non autrement. Nous aurons de parfaits instruments à musique distribués en grande série, mais où sera le musicien?" (*Un Sens à la Vie,* p. 230; italics in the translation added). The quotation is from "Lettre au Général 'X,' " written at La Marsa near Tunis, in July, 1943, published in *Un Sens à la Vie,* pp. 219–31; cf. *Le Figaro Littéraire,* n° 103, April 10, 1948; also quoted by Aelred Squire (*Summer in the Seed,* p. 136), who adds: "This is a variant on his conviction that the fullness of being human, even in one's solitude, consists in one's sense of one's debt to and link with others."
14. *The Habit of Being,* pp. 230–31; italics added.
15. *Loci Communes Theologici* (1521), p. 21; cf. *Loci communes von 1521,* p. 7: ". . . hoc est Christum cognoscere beneficia eius cognoscere. . . ."
16. Irenaeus, *Adv. Hær.* V, *Præf.,* PG 7, 1120.
17. Thus Hans Engelland in *Melanchthon on Christian Doctrine: Loci Communes 1555,* p. xxxii.
18. *Melanchthon on Christian Doctrine: Loci Communes 1555,* p. xlvi. Cf. F. J. van Beeck, "Fackre's *Christian Story*: A Review Article."
19. John Henry Newman, *Essays Critical and Historical,* vol. 1, pp. 47–48.
20. *The Christian Faith,* §95, pp. 389–90.
21. Cf. F. J. van Beeck, *Catholic Identity After Vatican II.*
22. Flannery O'Connor, *Mystery and Manners,* p. 192.
23. Cf. Max Weber, *The Protestant Ethic and the Spirit of Capitalism.*
24. Cf., for instance, Norman Vincent Peale, *The Power of Positive Thinking,* and his anthology *Faith Made Them Champions.* Cf. also Robert H. Schuller's take-off on the Beatitudes *The Be (Happy) Attitudes.*
25. For example, Robert H. Schuller, *Self Esteem: The New Reformation.*
26. E.g., the Moral Majority movement led by the Reverend Jerry Falwell, discussed by Gabriel Fackre, *The Religious Right and Christian Faith.*
27. Cf. Neal Punt, *Unconditional Good News: Toward an Understanding of Biblical Universalism.*

Chapter 4

1. Avery Dulles, *The Catholicity of the Church,* pp. 24, 133, 202.
2. "Quæ Ecclesiarum localium in unum conspirans varietas indivisæ Ecclesiæ catholicitatem luculenter demonstrat" (*Vat II,* p. 137).
3. Cf. Patrick Granfield, *The Limits of the Papacy,* esp. pp. 78ff., 114ff.
4. Cf. Avery Dulles, *The Catholicity of the Church,* p. 88.
5. Cf. Johannes Feiner, "Commentary on the Decree [on Ecumenism]," in *Commentary on the Decrees of Vatican II,* vol. 2, pp. 90–93; Charles Moeller, "Conclusion [on the Pastoral Constitution on the Church in the Modern World]," in *Commentary on the Decrees of Vatican II,* vol. 5, pp. 371–73. Also, F. J. van Beeck, *Catholic Identity After Vatican II,* pp. 71–78.

6. Cf. F. J. van Beeck, *Catholic Identity After Vatican II*, pp. 76–78.

7. On this issue, and on the crucial role played by Cardinal Augustin Bea in this respect, cf. Norbert Lohfink, "Augustin Bea und die Freiheit der biblischen Forschung." Cf. also Raymond E. Brown, *Biblical Exegesis and Church Doctrine*.

8. Cf. also the Ecumenical Directory, DocVatI, p. 517.

9. "Id teneamus quod semper, quod ubique, quod ab omnibus creditum est" (chap. 2; *PL* 50, 640; R 2168).

10. Cf. chaps. 13–16 (*PL* 50, 655–60; cf. R 2170–71).

11. Cf. chap. 23 (*PL* 50, 667–69; cf. R 2174).

12. "In omnibus divinæ legis quæstiunculis" (chap. 28, *PL* 50, 675; R 2175).

13. Cf. Francis A. Sullivan, *Magisterium*, pp. 153–73, for a careful analysis.

14. Francis A. Sullivan, *Magisterium*, p. 173.

15. Saying attributed to St. Ignatius Loyola by the *Thesaurus spiritualis Societatis Iesu*, p. 480, VIII.

16. *Die Wahrheit ist symphonisch*: title of a small book by Hans Urs von Balthasar.

17. M.-D. Chenu ("Vérité évangélique et métaphysique wolffienne à Vatican II") has convincingly made this point by showing that many features of traditional Roman Catholic seminary theology derived, not from, say, Aquinas, but from mid-eighteenth century rationalism.

18. Robert Bolt, *A Man for All Seasons*, p. 126 (Thomas More to Roper).

19. Cf. F. J. van Beeck, *Christ Proclaimed*, pp. 202–13 (on p. 203, in the quotation from Tillich's *Systematic Theology*, read "Philosophy formulates the *questions* implied in human existence," etc.).

20. Cf., for example, *Foundations of Christian Faith*, pp. 138–75 (*Grundkurs*, pp. 143–77).

21. Cf. F. J. van Beeck, *Catholic Identity After Vatican II*, p. 15.

22. Cf. F. J. van Beeck, *Christ Proclaimed*, p. 220.

23. Bernard Lonergan, *Method in Theology*, pp. 125–368.

24. *Der christliche Glaube* (ET *The Christian Faith*), *passim*, but esp. §§5, 6, 29, 32.

25. Cf. Tillich's *Systematic Theology*, esp. vols. 1 and 2.

26. *The Mysteries of Christianity*.

27. Cf. esp. *Sanctorum Communio* and *Christ the Center*, and the connections between them, but also the seventh thesis that Bonhoeffer offered to defend at his doctoral "promotion" in 1927: "According to her sociological structure, the Church includes within herself each and every possible type of social relatedness and raises (*überhöht*) them in the 'community of the Spirit'; the latter is based on the fundamental sociological law of representation" (*Gesammelte Schriften*, vol. 3, p. 47; *No Rusty Swords*, p. 28).

28. Cf. the five volumes of *A Theology for Artisans of a New Humanity*.

29. Cf. esp. his *Catholicism*.

30. In *Doxology: The Praise of God in Worship, Doctrine, and Life*.

31. Esp. in *Jesus: An Experiment in Christology* and in his two books on ministry, *Ministry* and *The Church with a Human Face*.

32. Especially in *Infallible?* and *On Being a Christian* but also in *The Church* and other works.

33. Cf. his *Systematic Theology: A Historicist Perspective*.

34. *Transforming Grace: Christian Tradition and Women's Experience*.

35. Cf. also F. J. van Beeck, *Christ Proclaimed*, pp. 299–303.

36. The *word* "exchange" (*antallagē*) first occurs in *Ep. ad Diogn.*, 9, 5: *O tēs glykeias antallagēs!*—"What sweet exchange!" Chapter 10 then exhorts Christians to match God's goodness shown in Christ by becoming "imitators (*mimētai*) of God."

37. Irenaeus, *Adv. Hær.*, V. *Præf.*, *PG* 7, 1120B (*SC* 153, p. 14f.; R 248); ET ed. J. Keble (Oxford, 1872), p. 449. A large number of references to patristic *loci* on this theme in Yves Congar, *Jesus Christ*, p. 20, n. 17. Cf. also Henri de Lubac, *The Mystery of the Supernatural*, pp. 174–75.

38. *Adv. Marc.* II, 27, 7; *CC* (*Ser. Lat.*) 1, p. 507; ed. E. Evans (Oxford, 1972), pp. 162–63.

39. *Elench.* X, 33, 7; *GCS* 26, 290; *ANF* 5, 151 (= X, 29; translation slightly revised).

40. *Protr.* I, 8, 4; *SC* 2, p. 63: "... *ho logos ho tou theou anthrōpos genomenos, hina dē kai sy para anthrōpou mathēis, pēi pote ara anthrōpos genētai theos."* C. Mondésert, the editor, tampers with the natural meaning of the Greek by translating: "... the Logos of God [that has] become man, so that it would be a man that would teach you in your turn how a God has become man" ("le Logos de Dieu devenu homme, afin qu'à vous encore ce soit un homme qui apprenne comment un Dieu est devenu homme"). This translation reduces the meaning of the subclause to a redundancy. Is this an example of theological trepidation before the boldness of the exchange principle?

41. Cf. P. Smulders, "Dogmengeschichtliche und lehramtliche Entfaltung der Christologie," pp. 408–10, 416, 418, 429–30.

42. "Mirum proinde nobiscum egit mutua participatione commercium: nostrum erat, unde mortuus est; illius erit unde vivamus. Verumtamen carnem, quam de nobis unde moreretur assumpsit, etiam ipsam quoniam creator est, dedit; vitam vero, qua in illo et cum illo victuri sumus, non a nobis accepit" (*Sermo Morin Guelferbytanus* 3, *PLS* 2, 545–46; cf. Roman breviary, Monday in Holy Week, Office of Readings).

43. "Quia igitur homo Christus summam plenitudinem gratiae obtinuit quasi Unigenitus a Patre, consequens fuit ab ipso in alios redundaret, ita quod Filius Dei factus homo, homines faceret deos et filios Dei, ..." (*Comp. Theol.*, cap. 214, ed. Marietti, n. 429).

44. "Unigenitus siquidem Dei Filius suæ Divinitatis volens nos esse participes, naturam nostram assumpsit, ut homines deos faceret factus homo" (*Off. de Festo Corporis Christi, In primo Nocturno, Lectio I*, ed. Marietti).

45. *Apol.* I, 46, 2–4; Goodspeed, pp. 58–59; *FC* 6, pp. 83–84 (Bettenson, p. 5).

46. *Apol.* II, 13, 3–6; Goodspeed, pp. 88–89 (ET Bettenson, p. 5).

47. *Elench.*, X, 30; cf. *ANF* 5, 153.

48. Cf., for example, Athanasius' *Or. contra Arianos*, II, 78–82; *PG* 26, 312B–321A.

49. Cf., for instance, Friedrich Schleiermacher, *Der christliche Glaube*, (ET *The Christian Faith*), §94, 3.

50. *The Divine Trinity*, esp. pp. 3–158.

51. On *perichōrēsis*, cf. M. J. Scheeben, *Handbuch der katholischen Dogmatik*, 5/1, nn. 584–97, pp. 267–74.

52. Cf. Harry A. Wolfson, *The Philosophy of the Church Fathers*, vol. 1, pp. 418–28. Also, cf. the second half of the quotation from Augustine, in §23, 3, b.

53. Cf. the Ecumenical Directory *Spiritus Domini*, nr. 74 (DocVatI, p. 522), and the "Reflections and Suggestions Concerning Ecumenical Dialogue," nr. 4b (DocVatI, p. 454). Also, cf. the observations and the bibliographical materials in Yves Congar, *Diversity and Communion*, pp. 126–33.

54. John Coventry, *Reconciling*, p. 37.

55. Alois Grillmeier, *Jesus der Christus im Glauben der Kirche*, vol. 2/1, pp. 238–60, 376–78; *Christ in Christian Tradition*, vol. 2, part 1, pp. 210–30, 333–35.

56. Cf. F. J. van Beeck, *Catholic Identity After Vatican II*, esp. pp. 1–11.

57. Cf. also F. J. van Beeck, *Catholic Identity After Vatican II*, pp. 76–78.

58. James Hennesey, s.v. "History," in *The New Dictionary of Theology*, pp. 469–72; quotation p. 472.

59. Cf. the important study of sacramental theology by L.-M. Chauvet, *Du symbolique au symbole*, esp. 13–122.

60. Cf. F. J. van Beeck, *Catholic Identity After Vatican II*.

Chapter 5

1. "Zurück also, wenn es Euch Ernst ist, die Religion in ihren bestimmten Gestalten zu betrachten, von dieser erleuchteten zu den verachteten positiven Religionen, wo alles wirklich, kräftig und bestimmt erscheint, wo jede einzelne Anschauung ihren bestimmten Gehalt und ein eignes Verhältnis zu den übrigen, jedes Gefühl seinen eignen Kreis und seine besondere Beziehung hat; wo Ihr jede Modifikation der Religiosität irgendwo antrefft, und jeden Gemütszustand, in welchen nur die Religion

den Menschen versetzen kann; wo ihr jeden Teil derselben irgendwo ausgebildet und jede ihrer Wirkungen irgendwo vollendet findet; wo alle gemeinschaftlichen Anstalten und alle einzelnen Äußerungen den hohen Wert beweisen, der auf die Religion gelegt wird bis zum Vergessen alles übrigen; wo der heilige Eifer, mit welchem sie betrachtet, mitgeteilt, genossen wird, und die kindliche Sehnsucht, mit welcher man neuen Offenbahrungen himmlischer Kräfte entgegensieht, Euch dafür bürgen, daß keines von ihren Elementen, welches von diesem Punkt aus schon wahrgenommen werden konnte, übersehen worden und keiner von ihren Momenten verschwunden ist, ohne ein Denkmal zurückzulassen" (*Über die Religion*, pp. 186–87 (cf. *KGA*, p. 311; *On Religion*, pp. 234–35).

2. Quoted by G. Meckenstock, in F. Schleiermacher, *Schriften aus der Berliner Zeit, 1796–1799,* (*KGA* I, 2), p. LIX.

3. Cf. the discussion of Schleiermacher's hermeneutics in Hans Frei, *The Eclipse of Biblical Narrative*, pp. 282–324.

4. F. Schleiermacher, *Über die Religion*, pp. 41–99 (ET *On Religion*, pp. 26–101); *Der Christliche Glaube* (ET *The Christian Faith*), §§3–4. Cf. Richard R. Niebuhr, *Schleiermacher on Christ and Religion*, pp. 116–34; F. J. van Beeck, *Christ Proclaimed*, pp. 548–66.

5. K. Rahner, *Foundations of Christian Faith*, p. 150 (slightly altered; cf. *Grundkurs*, pp. 154–55). Cf. also, in G. McCool's *A Rahner Reader*, the passages taken from *Hörer des Wortes* (ET *Hearers of the Word*).

6. *Foundations of Christian Faith*, p. 208 (*Grundkurs*, pp. 207–8).

7. Cf., for example, *Foundations of Christian Faith*, pp. 140–42; 178–203 (*Grundkurs*, pp. 145–47; 180–202).

8. *The Autobiography of Benjamin Franklin*, pp. 100–22.

9. Cf. James Hennesey, "Séparation de l'Église et de l'État: États-Unis et France."

10. Willem Kloos' sonnet "Ik ben een god in 't diepst van mijn gedachten."

11. "Nur das Metaphysische, keineswegs aber das Historische, macht selig" (cf. E. Jüngel, *Gott als Geheimnis der Welt*, pp. 170 ff.; quotation pp. 170–71. ET *God as the Mystery of the World*, pp. 128 ff.; quotation p. 129, slightly altered).

12. R. Otto, "Zur Einführung," in F. Schleiermacher, *Über die Religion*, pp. 11–12 (author's translation); cf. ET *On Religion*, pp. xv–xvi.

13. Esp. pp. 24–89 (*Grundkurs*, pp. 35–96).

14. Cf. "Vergegenwärtigung neutestamentlicher Texte," in *Gesammelte Schriften*, III, esp. 304–5 (*No Rusty Swords*, pp. 303–4). Cf. F. J. van Beeck, *Christ Proclaimed*, p. 248.

15. *The Habit of Being*, pp. 427, 479, (italics added).

16. *S. Th.*, I, 1, 8, *ad* 2: "Since grace does not cancel nature, but perfects it, natural reason must pay homage to faith" ("cum enim gratia non tollat naturam, sed perficiat, oportet quod naturalis ratio subserviat fidei"). *S. Th.*, I, 2, 2, *ad* 2: "Faith presupposes natural knowledge, just as grace does nature, and a perfection something capable of being perfected" ("sic enim fides præsupponit cognitionem naturalem, sicut gratia naturam, et ut perfectio perfectibile").

17. *S. Th.*, I–II, 112, 1, *in c.* ("donum . . . gratiæ excedit omnem facultatem naturæ creatæ"); cf. *S. Th.*, I–II, 114, 2, *in c.*, and 5, *in c.* Note, too, the clarity and ardor with which Aquinas draws his conclusion in *S. Th.* I–II, 113, 9, *ad* 2: "The goodness involved in the grace of one person is greater than the natural goodness involved in the whole universe" ("bonum gratiæ unius majus est quam bonum naturæ totius universi").

18. Cf. Norman Cohn, *The Pursuit of the Millennium*.

19. Cf., for example, Emmanuel Le Roy Ladurie, *Montaillou, The Promised Land of Error*.

20. Cf., for example, C. S. Lewis, *The Allegory of Love*.

21. Cf., for instance, E. L. Fortin, *Dissidence et philosophie au Moyen Age: Dante et ses antécédents*.

22. *Gottesfinsternis* (ET *Eclipse of God*).

23. J. Bots, *Tussen Descartes en Darwin*.

24. Cf. A. D. Nock, *Conversion*, pp. 164–86, 138–55; on the Isis religion, cf. also F. Solmsen, *Isis among the Greeks and Romans*, esp. pp. 49ff., 57ff., 87–113.
25. Celsus' work is lost, but his positions can be retrieved from the numerous quotations in Origen's *Contra Celsum*. Henry Chadwick's fine edition helpfully prints the quotations in italics.
26. Cf. *C. Celsum* I, 14.
27. Cf. *C. Celsum* VIII, 65.
28. Cf., for example, *C. Celsum* V, 34ff.
29. *C. Celsum* VII, 68.
30. Cf., for example, *C. Celsum* VIII, 33; VIII, 55.
31. *C. Celsum* I, 14.
32. Cf., for instance, *C. Celsum*, IV, 31–48.
33. Cf. *C. Celsum* VI, 12; H. Chadwick, in a note, refers to I, 27; III, 44, 50, 55, 59, 74, 75; VI, 13–14.
34. *C. Celsum* IV, 14.
35. Cf. *C. Celsum* IV, 2–3.
36. *C. Celsum* IV, 5–6.
37. *C. Celsum* II, 32.
38. *C. Celsum* VI, 78; cf. IV, 36; V, 50 ("one corner in the land of Judaea").
39. *C. Celsum* VI, 78.
40. *C. Celsum* IV, 99.

Chapter 6

1. Cf. Gerald O'Collins, *The Case Against Dogma*, esp. pp. 7–13, 20–22, 49–52.
2. "The Call," in *The Works of George Herbert*, p. 156 (italics added).
3. A fine and very full account of the process in England is John Redwood's *Reason, Ridicule and Religion*.
4. *Christianity not Mysterious*, p. ix.
5. *Christianity not Mysterious*, p. x.
6. *Christianity not Mysterious*, p. xviii.
7. *Christianity not Mysterious*, p. xiii. The reference is to Jas 1, 17.
8. *Christianity not Mysterious*, p. xv.
9. *Christianity not Mysterious*, p. vii.
10. *Christianity not Mysterious*, p. xiv.
11. Cf. *Christianity not Mysterious*, p. xxvi.
12. *The Divine Poems*, p. 15.
13. *Christianity not Mysterious*, pp. xiv, xxviii. The reference—in the singular—is to Heb 12, 2.
14. *Christianity not Mysterious*, pp. xxvi–xxviii.
15. *Christianity not Mysterious*, pp. xxvi–xxvii.
16. *Pantheisticon, or, The Form of Celebrating the Socratic-Society*.
17. Günter Gawlick, "Einführung," in John Toland, *Christianity not Mysterious*, p. 28*.
18. Walter J. Ong, "Psyche and the Geometers," in *Rhetoric, Romance, and Technology*, pp. 213–36; quotation p. 220.
19. Quoted by Henry Chadwick, in *Lessing's Theological Writings*, p. 13.
20. Cf. Henry Chadwick, in *Lessing's Theological Writings*, pp. 44–45.
21. Cf. G. E. Lessing, "On the Origin of Revealed Religion," theses 5, 7, and 8; the full text in *Lessing's Theological Writings*, pp. 104–5.
22. *Émile, ou De l'éducation*, in *Oeuvres completes*, III, pp. 565–635. In the English translation, *Emile; or, Education*, by Barbara Foxley, the "Creed of a Savoyard Priest" is found on pp. 228–78; the translation is to be used with caution.
23. "Dans la juste défiance de moi-même la seule chose que je lui demande ou plustôt que j'attends de sa justice est de redresser mon erreur, si je m'égare et si cette erreur m'est dangereuse. Pour être de bonne foi je ne me crois pas infaillible. Mes opinions

302 / NOTES [124–133]

qui me semblent les plus vraies sont peut-être autant de mensonges, car quel homme ne tient pas aux siennes, et combien d'hommes sont d'accord en tout? L'illusion qui m'abuse a beau me venir de moi, c'est lui seul qui m'en peut guérir. J'ai fait ce que j'ai pu pour atteindre à la vérité mais sa source est trop élevée: quand les forces me manquent pour aller plus loin de quoi puis-je être coupable? C'est à elle à s'approcher" (*Émile*, pp. 605–6; cf. ET, pp. 257–58). The last, bracketed sentence reads: "En attendant je suis heureux, parce que je compte pour peu tous les maux de la vie et que le prix qui les rachette est en mon pouvoir" (*Émile*, p. 1569, note *(a)*); while it was deleted by Rousseau, it proves that he was thinking of the Incarnation and the Atonement.

24. "Je regarde toutes les réligions particulieres comme autant d'institutions salutaires qui prescrivent dans chaque Pays une maniére convenable d'honorer Dieu par un culte public. . . . Je les crois toutes bonnes quand on y sert Dieu convenablement: le culte essenciel est celui du coeur" (*Émile*, p. 627; cf. ET, p. 273).

25. The account, in the course of the vicar's confession (!), of how he descended into himself (*Émile*, p. 569), for instance, recalls a famous passage in *Confessions* VII, 10 (*CSEL* 33, p. 157). The association with Augustine is not surprising in an author who entitled his autobiography *Les Confessions* (*Oeuvres completes*, I, pp. 1–656); cf. Ann Hartle, *The Modern Self in Rousseau's Confessions: A Reply to St. Augustine*.

26. "J'appris ce qu'on vouloit que j'apprisse, je dis ce qu'on vouloit que je disse; je m'engagai comme on voulut, et je fus fait prêtre. Mais je ne tardai pas à sentir qu'en m'obligeant de n'être pas homme j'avois promis plus que je ne pouvois tenir" (*Émile*, p. 566; cf. CT, pp. 228–29).

27. "Ce qui redoubloit mon embarras étoit qu'étant né dans une Eglise qui décide tout, qui ne permet aucun doute, un seul point rejetté me faisoit rejetter tout le reste, et que l'impossibilité d'admettre tant de décisions absurdes me détachoit aussi de celles qui ne l'étoient pas. En me disant: croyez tout, on m'empêchoit de rien croire, et je ne savois plus où m'arrêter" (*Émile*, p. 19; cf. ET, p. 230).

28. Quoted by J. H. van den Berg, *Leven in meervoud*, pp. 107–10.

29. On this subject, cf. T. S. Eliot's classic essay "The Metaphysical Poets," in *Selected Essays*, pp. 241–50. Cf. also J. H. van den Berg's *Leven in meervoud* and the copious literature cited there; van den Berg's analyses of Diderot's *Le neveu de Rameau* and *Le rêve de d'Alembert* and of the sensibility behind the *Encyclopédie* provide particularly insightful introductions to the chaotic tendencies of the civilized eighteenth-century mind.

30. J. H. van den Berg, *Leven in meervoud*, pp. 162–65; cf. *'s Morgens jagen, 's middags vissen*, pp. [14–15].

31. J. H. van den Berg, *'s Morgens jagen, 's middags vissen*, pp. [8–9].

32. Thus Henry Chadwick in *Lessing's Theological Writings*, p. 28.

33. I have, regretfully, found no satisfactory alternative to translate the inclusive German word *Mensch*, which is in many ways the key word in the text.

34. Cf. Erich Schenk, *Mozart*, pp. 455, 559–63.

35. Cf. chap. 8 ("The Church in Danger—Ridicule Runs Riot"), in John Redwood, *Reason, Ridicule and Religion*. A quick review of eighteenth-century literature will also bear out the point.

36. *The Analogy of Religion*, p. 5.

37. Cf. F. J. van Beeck, "Professing the Uniqueness of Christ," esp. pp. 20–22, 31–33.

38. Cf. Nicholas Lash, *Voices of Authority*.

39. Thus Sir Julian Huxley in his introduction to Pierre Teilhard de Chardin's *The Phenomenon of Man*, p. 11—a fine example of a constructive encounter between a modern agnostic with impeccable rationalist credentials and a modern Christian devoted to orthodoxy.

40. For the former, cf. esp. *Letters and Papers from Prison* under July 16, 1944; for the latter, cf., for example, the entry under June 8, 1944. Cf. also F. J. van Beeck, *Christ Proclaimed*, pp. 232–51, and the literature quoted there.

41. *L'Activation de l'Énergie*, p. 375 (ET *Activation of Energy*, p. 356).

42. Cf. F. J. van Beeck, *Catholic Identity After Vatican II*, esp. pp. 11–21, 23–24.
43. *Lessing's Theological Writings*, p. 44.
44. *Doxology*, p. 57.
45. *C. Celsum*, I, 2; 62; III, 68; VI, 2.
46. Cf. Henry Chadwick, in *Lessing's Theological Writings*, pp. 34–35. The references, listed by Chadwick, are to *C. Celsum* I, 28; 38; II, 28; 48 ff.
47. Dietrich Bonhoeffer, *Letters and Papers from Prison*, under August 3, 1944 ("Chapter I, b"). Cf. also the quotation from Pascal, §28, 7, [h].
48. *Lessing's Theological Writings*, pp. 51–56.
49. *Lessing's Theological Writings*, p. 52 (slightly adapted, after the original, ed. Lachmann-Muncker, vol. 13, p. 4, lines 22–24).
50. William Wordsworth's sonnet "It is a beauteous evening, calm and free (*The Poetical Works of William Wordsworth*, vol. 3, p. 17).
51. *S.c.G.* I, 2 (*Assumpta igitur*).
52. *S. Th.*, I, 1, 1, *in c.*
53. "Eine transzendentale Christologie als solche kann sich nicht Aufgabe und Möglichkeit anmaßen, zu sagen, daß dieser absolute Heilbringer, den die radikale Hoffnung auf Gott selbst als die absolute Zukunft in der Geschichte sucht, schon darin zu finden ist un daß er gerade in Jesus von Nazareth gefunden worden ist. Beides gehört zur unableitbaren Erfahrung der Geschichte selbst. *Heute* aber würde man dieser faktischen Geschichte gegenüber blind, träte man ihr nicht gegenüber mit jener reflektierten und artikulierten Heilshoffnung, die sich in einer transzendentalen Christologie reflektiert. Diese läßt suchen und suchend verstehen, was man in Jesus von Nazareth schon immer... gefunden hat." (Karl Rahner and Wilhelm Thüsing, *Christologie: systematisch und exegetisch*, p. 24; the English translation *A New Christology*, for which Rahner wrote an adapted version of his contribution, does not contain this passage.) For the same thought, cf. *Foundations of Christian Faith*, pp. 206–7 (*Grundkurs*, pp. 206–7).
54. Cf. F. J. van Beeck, *Catholic Identity After Vatican II*, pp. 61 ff.
55. *Gesammelte Schriften*, vol. 3, pp. 304–5 (cf. ET in *No Rusty Swords*, pp. 303–4).
56. Cf., for a good example of an important European bishop who operates from this premises, a fine article by Steven Englund, "The force of Cardinal Lustiger."

Chapter 7

1. *Epist.* X, 96. Text in *C. Plini Cæcili Secundi Epistularum Libri Decem*, pp. 338–40. Also in K 28–30; ET in Bettenson, pp. 3–4; Barry, pp. 75–76.
2. The complete text: "Adfirmabant autem hanc fuisse summam uel culpæ suæ uel erroris, quod essent soliti stato die ante lucem conuenire, carmenque Christo quasi deo dicere secum inuicem seque sacramento non in scelus aliquod obstringere, sed ne furta ne latrocinia ne adulteria committerent, ne fidem fallerent, ne depositum adpellati abnegarent. Quibus peractis morem sibi discedendi fuisse rursusque coeundi ad capiendum cibum, promiscuum tamen et innoxium; quod ipsum facere desisse post edictum meum, quo secundum mandata tua hetærias esse vetueram."
3. Robert L. Wilken, *The Christians as the Romans Saw Them*, pp. 10–15; note, however, the exception extended, by imperial indult, to a benefit society (pp. 14–15).
4. Robert L. Wilken, *The Christians as the Romans Saw Them*, pp. 35–40.
5. Cf. *The Study of Liturgy*, pp. 51–52 (Bibliography).
6. The word *sacramentum* did not become a technical term until the twelfth century, when Peter Lombard first subsumed the seven sacraments under this common heading. The term attained authoritative, doctrinal status in the West only at the second Council of Lyons (A.D. 1274; DS 860). Cf., for instance, Wendelin Knoch, *Die Einsetzung der Sakramente durch Christus*, pp. 145 ff.
7. Cf. esp. chap. 67; also chaps. 65–66; *FC* 6, pp. 104–7 (Bettenson, pp. 66–67; Barry, pp. 35–36).

8. Chapters 9–10; *AF* I, pp. 322–25 (K 2–3; ET Bettenson pp. 64–65; Barry p. 27).

9. G. Dix, *The Shape of the Liturgy*, pp. 79–80. Cf. J. Jeremias, *Die Abendmahlsworte Jesu*, pp. 104, 109–10 (Bibliography), and n. 2 (ET *The Eucharistic Words of Jesus*, pp. 110, 116–17 [Bibliography], and n. 2).

10. Cf. Cyprian Vagaggini, *Theological Dimensions of the Liturgy*, pp. 159–60.

11. Hans-Peter Bütler, *Die geistige Welt des jüngeren Plinius*, pp. 10–20, esp. 13.

12. *Annals*, XV, 44.

13. *De vita Cæsarum*, VI, 16, 2; A. D. Nock, *Conversion*, p. 207.

14. A. D. Nock, *Conversion*, p. 162; cf. p. 203: "The impression made on an educated pagan would probably be that this was of the nature of superstition, that is ungentlemanly popular religion."

15. Cf. Robert L. Wilken, *The Christians as the Romans Saw Them*, pp. 38–67.

16. *Epist.*, X, 97 (*C. Plini Cæcili Secundi Epistularum Libri Decem*, p. 340). Also K 31 (ET Bettenson, p. 4; Barry, p. 76).

17. This will have to be elaborated in the context of soteriology. For present reference, cf. Dorothee Sölle, *Stellvertretung* (ET *Christ the Representative*). Also, F. J. van Beeck, "Ten Questions on Soteriology and Christology," p. 277.

18. Cf. F. Malmberg, "Het middellijk-onmiddellijke contact met God in onze geloofsact."

19. Cf. Raymond E. Brown, *The Gospel According to John*, pp. 180–81.

20. *The Living Flame of Love*, st. 3, n. 78. *The Collected Works*, p. 641, gives the literal translation: '. . . the soul . . . gives to God, God Himself in God" (cf. *Obras*, p. 724; "[el alma] está dando a Dios al mismo Dios en Dios"). This preserves the underlying trinitarian order of the expression, according to which the soul gives, to the Father, the Son in the Spirit. In the interest of clarity and elegance, I have reversed this order.

21. Still, the insertion of "with him" antedates the Arian controversy by at least a century and a half: cf. the doxology in the *Martyrdom of St. Polycarp*, 14, 3 (*AF* II, pp. 332–33). For the later, mainstream explanation of the usage, cf. esp. Basil the Great, *On the Holy Spirit*, esp. VII, 16–VIII, 21 (*PG* 32, coll. 93B–106C; ET pp. 33–42). Cf. also Joseph A. Jungmann, *The Place of Christ in Liturgical Prayer*, pp. 127–212.

22. On naming, cf. F. J. van Beeck, *Christ Proclaimed*, pp. 88–93, 112–15, 146–52. In that book, however, while the naming of Christ insofar as it establishes the relationship between him and the Church is well elaborated, insufficient attention is paid to christological titles that derive from Israel's tradition of naming God.

23. Cf., among the massive literature on the subject, Vincent Taylor, *The Names of Jesus*; Ferdinand Hahn, *The Titles of Jesus in Christology*.

24. "Der Unbekannte Jenseits des Wortes," in *Spiritus Creator*, p. 97.

25. For a fundamental treatment of this, cf. Donald D. Evans, *The Logic of Self-Involvement*.

26. Basil the Great, *On the Holy Spirit*, XXVI, 64 (*PG* 32, coll. 185–86B; ET, p. 97).

27. Cf. esp. P. Carnley, *The Structure of Resurrection Belief*, pp. 249–59, esp. pp. 253–56.

28. Odo Casel, "Die *Logikē thysia* der antiken Mystik in christlich-liturgischer Umdeutung."

29. *The Idea of the Holy*, pp. 12–40.

30. On responsive (or relational) identity, cf. F. J. van Beeck, *Christ Proclaimed*, esp. pp. 245–51, 270–72, 327–29, 412–15, 423–27.

31. *Guide to the Debate About God*, p. 38.

32. Cf. *LThK*, IX, coll. 239f. (K. Rahner); VII, coll. 829f. (O. Semmelroth).

33. *Gottesfinsternis*, pp. 511, 523 (cf. *Eclipse of God*, pp. 13, 28; translation corrected).

34. *The Idea of the Holy*, p. 3.

35. Cf. *The Idea of the Holy*, pp. 5–6; quotation p. 6.

36. Cf. F. Schleiermacher's second Speech: *Über die Religion*, pp. 41–99 (*On Religion*, pp. 26–118).

37. *On Religion*, p. 39; cf. *Über die Religion*, p. 51: "Religion ist Sinn und Geschmack fürs Unendliche."

38. *On Religion*, pp. 36, 103.

39. Cf. F. J. van Beeck, *Christ Proclaimed*, pp. 548–66.
40. David Jenkins, *Guide to the Debate About God*, p. 30.
41. *The Idea of the Holy*, pp. 8–11; quotation p. 10 (italics added).
42. *The Varieties of Religious Experience: A Study in Human Nature*, p. 62; quoted by R. Otto, *The Idea of the Holy*, p. 10, n. 1.
43. *The Idea of the Holy*, p. 11, note.
44. ". . . [die Frömmigkeit] hat auch eine leidende Seite, sie erscheint auch *als ein Hingeben*, ein sich bewegen lassen von *dem Ganzen welchem der Mensch gegenüber steht*" *(Über die Religion* [3d ed., 1821], p. 63 [italics added]). Cf. ET *On Religion*, p. 37 (J. Oman's translation inaccurate).
45. Cf., on the *actus directus* and the *actus reflexus*, F. J. van Beeck, *Christ Proclaimed*, esp. pp. 232–53.
46. Cf. the English translation of Odo Casel's principal work, supplemented by an anthology of his other writings: *The Mystery of Christian Worship and Other Writings*. The present paragraph serves to make the same points as chap. 2 of Casel's book (pp. 9ff.).
47. Cf. Arno Schilson, "Vergessener und dennoch aktueller Erneuerer: Zum 100. Geburtstag von Odo Casel," quotations p. 436 (italics added). Cf. also Schilson's *Theologie als Sakramententheologie*, esp. pp. 141, 182, 226, 272, 279, for some detailed comparisons between Casel and Rahner.
48. Cf. esp. *Foundations of Christian Faith*, pp. 44–89, 116–75 (*Grundkurs*, pp. 54–96, 122–77).
49. Cf. also Wolfhart Pannenberg, "Analogy and Doxology," in *Basic Questions in Theology*, vol. 1, pp. 212–38.
50. Cf. Lessing's one hundred theses under that heading, amounting to a completely secularized rendition of Christianity, in *Lessing's Theological Writings*, pp. 82–98.
51. For this central theme in the thought of Hans Urs von Balthasar, cf., for example, *Die Wahrheit ist symphonisch*, pp. 32–41.
52. *The Cloud of Unknowing*, chap. 34, pp. 69–71.
53. *Ad Eph.* 20 (*AF* I, pp. 192–93).
54. Gabriele Giamberardini, "Il «Sub tuum praesidium» e il titolo «Theotokos» nella tradizione egiziana," pp. 350–62.
55. Gabriele Giamberardini, "Il «Sub tuum praesidium» e il titolo «Theotokos» nella tradizione egiziana," p. 330. The author gives the following Italian translation of his reconstruction of the Greek text: *Sotto la tua / Misericordia / Ci rifugiamo, / Genitrice di Dio. Le nostre / Suppliche tu non le respingere nella / Necessità, / Ma dal pericolo / Libera noi: / Sola casta, so- / la benedetta.* The text is the oldest known version of the antiphon *Sub tuum præsidium*; cf. Michael O'Carroll, *Theotokos*, p. 336.
56. Cf. Pieter Smulders, "Dogmengeschichtliche und lehramtliche Entfaltung der Christologie," p. 451–57.
57. *Dial. c. Tryph.*, 100, 3–5 (Goodspeed, pp. 214–15).
58. *Adv. Hær.*, III, 21, 10–22, 4 (*SC* 211, pp. 426–45).
59. *S. Th.* II–II, 103, 4, 2 and *ad* 2.
60. *De natura et gratia*, XXXVII, 42 (*CSEL* 60, pp. 263–64; italics added). The original: "Deinde commemorat eos, 'qui non modo non peccasse, uerum etiam iuste uixisse referuntur: . . .' ipsam etiam domini ac saluatoris nostri matrem, 'quam' dicit 'sine peccato confiteri necesse esse pietati'. excepta itaque sancta uirgine Maria, de qua propter honorem domini nullam prorsus, cum de peccatis agitur, haberi uolo quaestionem—unde enim scimus quid ei plus gratiae conlatum fuerit ad uincendum omni ex parte peccatum, quae concipere ac parere meruit, quem constat nullum habuisse peccatum?—hac ergo uirgine excepta, si omnes illos sanctos et sanctas, cum hic uiuerent, congregare possemus et interrogare, utrum essent sine peccato, quid fuisse responsuros putamus? . . . *si dixerimus quia peccatum non habemus, nos ipsos decipimus et ueritas in nobis non est.*"
61. Cf. St. Augustine, *Tract. in Joh.*, IV, 10: "He was not conceived in iniquity, for he was not conceived of mortality; nor did his mother sustain him in her womb in sins

[Ps 51, 5]: he was conceived by a virgin, and born of a virgin; for it was by faith that she conceived, and by faith that she welcomed him."

62. *De sancta virginitate*, III, 3 (*CSEL* 41, p. 237; italics added). The original: "Scriptum est in euangelio, quod mater et fratres Christi, hoc est consanguinei carnis eius, cum illi nuntiati fuissent et foris expectarent, quia non possent eum adire prae turba, ille respondit: quae est mater mea aut qui sunt fratres mei? extendens manum super discipulos suos ait: hi sunt fratres mei; et quicumque fecerit voluntatem patris mei, ipse mihi frater et mater et soror est, quid aliud nos docens nisi carnali cognationi genus nostrum spiritale praeponere nec inde beatos esse homines, si iustis et sanctis carnis propinquitate iunguntur, sed si eorum doctrinae ac moribus oboediendo atque imitando cohaerescunt? beatior ergo Maria percipiendo fidem Christi quam concipiendo carnem Christi. nam et dicenti cuidam: beatus venter qui te portavit, ipse respondit: immo beati qui audiunt uerbum dei et custodiunt. denique fratribus eius, id est secundum carnem cognatis, qui non in eum crediderunt, quid profuit illa cognatio? sic et materna propinquitas nihil Mariae profuisset, nisi felicius Christum corde quam carne gestasset."

Chapter 8

1. Cf. Amos Wilder, *Early Christian Rhetoric*, esp. p. 28.
2. On *parrhēsia*, cf. F. J. van Beeck, *Christ Proclaimed*, esp. pp. 349–52.
3. Cf. J. Jeremias, *The Prayers of Jesus*, pp. 112–15.
4. Joachim Jeremias, *The Prayers of Jesus*, p. 78.
5. On Israel's *b'rakhôt*, cf. Louis Bouyer, *Eucharist*, pp. 15–90.
6. Cf. Cross, s.v. "Alleluia," p. 38.
7. *Contra Noëtum*, 14; *Contre les hérésies*, ed. Nautin, p. 257; cf. ET *ANF* 5, p. 228.
8. J. B. Metz, *Glaube in Geschichte und Gesellschaft*, esp. pp. 136–48, (ET *Faith in History and Society*, pp. 154–68).
9. Cf. esp. H. Weinrich, "Narrative Theologie," and J. B. Metz, "Kleine Apologie des Erzählens." Also, Hans Frei, *The Eclipse of Biblical Narrative*, pp. 202–32, 267–324, and *The Identity of Jesus Christ*, pp. xiii–xvii. Again, J. B. Metz, *Glaube in Geschichte und Gesellschaft*, esp. pp. 143–58, 181–94 (ET *Faith in History and Society*, pp. 161–79, 205–18).
10. Cf., for instance, John Shea, *Stories of God: An Unauthorized Biography*, and Anthony de Mello, *Song of the Bird*.
11. Peter Carnley, *The Structure of Resurrection Belief*, pp. 358–60, has an analogous point to make. The entire issue of narrative theology is well discussed in Eberhard Jüngel, *Gott als Geheimnis der Welt*, pp. XV–XVIII, 409–30 (ET *God as the Mystery of the World*, pp. xi–xii, 299–314).
12. Cf. F. J. van Beeck, "Fackre's *Christian Story*: A Review Article," esp. pp. 126–27, 130–32.
13. Cf. F. J. van Beeck, "Professing the Uniqueness of Christ," pp. 17–19.
14. Cf. Yves M.-J. Congar, *La Tradition et les traditions*, vol. 2, pp. 149–66 (ET *Tradition and Traditions*, pp. 391–409) for related suggestions. For a listing of the *content* of non-Scriptural Tradition according to a variety of Church fathers and theological authors, cf. *La Tradition et les traditions*, vol. 1, pp. 64–76 (ET *Tradition and Traditions*, pp. 50–64).
15. On this double function of metaphor, cf. F. J. van Beeck, *Christ Proclaimed*, pp. 88–92.
16. Cf., e.g., Gerard O'Collins, *Jesus Risen*, pp. 90, 109, and 138 (quoting W. Pannenberg); Pheme Perkins, *Resurrection*, pp. 75, 102, 317.
17. Pheme Perkins' *Resurrection* provides a good survey of the related concerns and themes that have been integrated—some more, some less—into the resurrection theme.
18. Quoted by L. Bouyer, *Eucharist*, p. 72 (translation modified).

19. On the primacy of the future in the Christian experience of the present, cf. F. J. van Beeck, *Christ Proclaimed*, pp. 265–93; 331–42.
20. Cyril of Jerusalem, *Catech.* XIII, iv; *PG* 33, 777A. Cf. Aelred Squire, *Fathers Talking*, p. 26.
21. Cf. Martin Hengel, *Der Sohn Gottes* (ET *The Son of God*).
22. Cf. F. J. van Beeck, *Christ Proclaimed*, pp. 461–63.
23. *Jezus*, pp. 386–92; ET *Jesus*, pp. 472–80.
24. Cf. Harvey H. Guthrie, Jr., *Theology as Thanksgiving*, pp. 1–70.
25. Cf. Franz Joseph Schierse, *Verheissung und Heilsvollendung*.
26. Cf. James D. G. Dunn, *Christology in the Making*, for a careful account of the origins of pre-existence christology.
27. *Ad Magn.* 10 (*AF* I, pp. 206–7).
28. Translations of the canon from the *Apostolic Tradition* in Bettenson, pp. 75–76; Barry, p. 48. A translation of the complete *anaphora* from the Liturgy of St. Basil in *Prayers of the Eucharist: Early and Reformed*, pp. 97–104.
29. Cf., on the subject of myth as well as the Christian "valorization of time," Mircea Eliade's *Myth and Reality*; cf. also his *The Myth of the Eternal Return*, and *The Sacred and the Profane*.
30. Cf. F. J. van Beeck, *Christ Proclaimed*, pp. 328–29.
31. C. H. Dodd's *The Apostolic Preaching and its Developments* remains a valuable resource on this subject.
32. F. J. van Beeck, *Christ Proclaimed*, pp. 336–37, 344, 510.
33. Cf. F. J. van Beeck, *Christ Proclaimed*, pp. 150–53, 163–64. Also, cf. Vincent Taylor, *The Names of Jesus*.
34. M. Kähler, quoted by Peter Carnley, *The Structure of Resurrection Belief*, p. 349.
35. Cf. F. J. van Beeck, *Christ Proclaimed*, pp. 341–44.
36. Cf. F. J. van Beeck, *Christ Proclaimed*, pp. 146–48, 182–83.
37. Cf. F. J. van Beeck, *Christ Proclaimed*, p. 510.
38. Cf. J. N. D. Kelly, *Early Christian Creeds*, esp. pp. 76ff.
39. Cf. J. N. D. Kelly, *Early Christian Creeds*, pp. 62–76.
40. *Adv. Hær.* I, 10, 1–2 (*SC* 264, pp. 155–59; italics added); cf. K 191–92; ET Barry, p. 44. Cf. J. N. D. Kelly, *Early Christian Creeds*, p. 79.
41. *CC* 1, pp. 185–224; italics added.
42. *De præscr. hær.*, VII, 12–13 (*CC* 1, p. 193); K 288.
43. Cf. J. N. D. Kelly, *Early Christian Creeds*, pp. 86–88.
44. *De præscr. hær.*, XIII, 1–6 (*CC* 1, pp. 197–98); K 290.

Chapter 9

1. "Jeder der Teile der Philosophie ist ein philosophisches Ganzes, ein sich in sich selbst schließender Kreis, aber die philosophische Idee ist darin in einer besonderen Bestimmtheit oder Elemente. Der einzelne Kreis durchbricht darum, weil er in sich Totalität ist, auch die Schranke seines Elements und begründet eine weitere Sphäre; das Ganze stellt sich daher als ein Kreis von Kreisen dar, deren jeder ein notwendiges Moment ist, so daß das System ihrer eigentümlichen Elemente die ganze Idee ausmacht, die ebenso in jedem einzelnen erscheint" (*Enzyklopädie* [1830], §15).
2. Cf. esp. *Jenaer Systementwürfe II*, pp. 241–50 (the discussion of the lever), 105–25 (the final pages of the Jena *Logik*).
3. "Das Moment ist ein wesensnotwendiger Bestandteil des Ganzen als ruhenden Systems und ein notwendiges Durchgangsstadium im Ganzen als dialektischer Bewegung" (Johannes Hoffmeister, *Wörterbuch der philosophischen Begriffe*, p. 408).
4. On the general problem, cf. James Barr's important book *The Semantics of Biblical Language*.
5. Cf. *PGL*, pp. 499–500, 957–58.
6. Cf. J. Ratzinger, "Originalität und Überlieferung in Augustins Begriff der *confessio*," pp. 378–84.

7. In the fourteenth century, especially in English versions of the Psalms, it was attempted to carry the full meaning of *confiteri/confessio* forward in English by means of the verb *schrive*, used to translate *confiteri* of the Vulgate, with the meaning "to ascribe praise and glory to God." Thus the translation of Richard of Saint Victor's *Benjamin Minor* contains the phrase "Now schal I schryue to oure Lorde," to render "Modo confitebor Domino" in Gen 29, 35 according to the Vulgate. The more common meaning of the verb, however, and the only one eventually to carry the day, was "to make one's confession and receive absolution and penance." Cf. *Deonise Hid Divinite*, pp. 26 (line 6), 131 (notes 21/3–4 and 21/4).

8. "audio uulgus: cum ad cælum manus tendunt, nihil aliud quam 'Deum' dicunt et 'Deus magnus est' et 'Deus verus est' et 'si Deus dederit.' uulgi iste naturalis sermo est an christiani confitentis oratio? et qui Iovem principem uolunt, falluntur in nomine, sed de una potestate consentiunt" (*Octavius*, 18, 11; *CSEL*, II, p. 25; cf. K 270).

9. Peter Brown, *Augustine of Hippo*, p. 175.

10. H. Böhmer, "Die Lobpreisungen des Augustinus," p. 423.

11. *Confessiones*, IV, 1 (*CSEL* XXXIII, p. 64). H. Böhmer ("Die Lobpreisungen des Augustinus," pp. 422–23) lists parallel passages.

12. *Confessiones*, I, 15. Cf. Maurice Jourjon, "Minuties augustiniennes: *Etiam peccata*."

13. J. Ratzinger, "Originalität und Überlieferung in Augustins Begriff der *confessio*," pp. 388–89.

14. Cf. Goulven Madec, "Connaissance de Dieu et action de grâces," esp. pp. 302–7.

15. *Confessiones*, X, 1 (*CSEL* XXXIII, p. 226); cf. Peter Brown, *Augustine of Hippo*, p. 181.

16. *Confessiones*, I, 1 (*CSEL* XXXIII, p. 1).

17. *Confessiones*, XI, 1 (*CSEL* XXXIII, p. 280).

18. Cf. *TDNT* under *homologeō*, V, pp. 212, 217.

19. F. J. van Beeck, *Christ Proclaimed*, p. 328. The expression "historical atavism" (cf. §4, 1), to convey the unquestioning use of traditional formulas of worship and witness, is Karl Rahner's.

20. The present analysis of witness is indebted to Martin Buber's *Ich und Du* (ET *I and Thou*).

21. F. J. van Beeck, *Christ Proclaimed*, p. 328.

22. Joseph A. Jungmann, *The Mass of the Roman Rite*, vol. 1, esp. pp. 78–80.

23. On this subject, cf. *LThK*, vol. 6, coll. 1001–2.

24. ". . . obsecrationum quoque sacerdotalium sacramenta respiciamus, quæ ab Apostolis tradita in toto mundo atque in omni Ecclesia catholica uniformiter celebrantur, ut legem credendi statuat lex supplicandi."

25. Cf. Augustine, *De dono perseverantiæ*, 23, 63–64 (*PL* 45, 1031–32); *Ep.* 217, esp. VII, 28–30 (*SCEL* 57, pp. 423–25).

26. Hippolytus, *Trad. Apost.* 21 (*SC* 11bis, pp. 90–91).

27. F. J. Dölger, *Antike und Christentum*, vol. 2, pp. 204, 318–19.

28. Hippolytus, *Trad. Apost.* 4 (*SC* 11bis, pp. 48–49).

29. W. C. van Unnik, "*Dominus vobiscum*: The Background of a Liturgical Formula."

30. Alban Dold, "Das 'Dominus vobiscum' der heiligen Messe als Mittel unserer Verbindung mit Gott."

31. Joseph Pascher, "Der Friedensgruß der Liturgie."

32. *Hom. de S. Pentecoste* I, *PG* 50, coll. 458–59; cf. *Hom. in Ep. II ad Tim.*, X, 4 (*PG* 62, coll. 659–60). Elsewhere, Chrysostom explains how the presider, in giving the greeting of peace to the congregation, is the type of Christ (*In Matth. Hom.* 32 [*al.* 33]; *PG* 57, col. 384). Cf. also Theodore of Mopsuestia's fourth Baptismal Homily (Edward Yarnold, *The Awe-Inspiring Rites of Initiation*, pp. 232–33): "These words do not refer to the bishop's soul, but to the grace of the Holy Spirit by which his people believe he is called to the priesthood. [There follows an explanation of Rom. 1:9.] This is the reason for the ancient custom of the Church that the congregation should reply to the bishop: 'And with your spirit'. When all is well with the bishop, the whole body of the Church feels the benefit, but when he is ailing, the whole community suffers. So all pray that this 'peace' will bring him the grace of the Holy

Spirit to enable him to fulfill his duties and perform liturgy worthily on behalf of the community. Conversely, the abundance of the grace of the Holy Spirit will give the bishop peace, make it easier for him to perform the prescribed ceremonies when in all his affairs and especially in the liturgy he shows that he has a clear conscience." Cf. "Theodore on Eucharist and Liturgy," *Woodbrooke Studies*, vol. 6, pp. 90–92, for a similar passage. Finally, cf. J. Jungmann, *The Mass of the Roman Rite*, vol. 1, p. 365.

33. Joseph Jungmann, *The Place of Christ in Liturgical Prayer*, p. xx.
34. Cf. Joseph Jungmann, *The Place of Christ in Liturgical Prayer*, pp. 1–171; Cyprian Vagaggini, *Theological Dimensions of the Liturgy*, pp. 207ff. ("Cum altari assistitur, semper ad Patrem dirigatur oratio": p. 210, n. 27).
35. Joseph A. Jungmann, *The Mass of the Roman Rite*, vol. 1, p. 380–82.
36. Joseph A. Jungmann, *The Mass of the Roman Rite*, vol. 1, p. 80.
37. Cf. Joseph A. Jungmann, *The Mass of the Roman Rite*, vol. 1, p. 371, where Origen's *De oratione*, chap. 33 (*PG* 11, 557f.), is very appropriately referred to.
38. *"Ut qui sine te esse non possumus, secundum te vivere valeamus"* (collect for Thursday in the first week of Lent in the postconciliar Roman missal).
39. Cf. Joseph Jungmann, *The Place of Christ in Liturgical Prayer*, pp. 172–212 (quotation p. 212); Cyprian Vagaggini, *Theological Dimensions of the Liturgy*, pp. 209–23.
40. On this and related issues, cf. also F. J. van Beeck, "Intercommunion: A Note on Norms."
41. Heinrich Fries and Karl Rahner, *Unity of the Churches*, p. 7.
42. Cf. Heinrich Fries and Karl Rahner, *Unity of the Churches*, pp. 25–41.
43. F. J. van Beeck, *Christ Proclaimed*, pp. 328–29.

Chapter 10

1. Cf. Jürgen Moltmann, "Die Zukunft als neues Paradigma der Transzendenz." Also, F. J. van Beeck, *Christ Proclaimed*, esp. pp. 286, 293, 331.
2. "Desiderium sinus cordis": St. Augustine, *Tract. in Joh.* 40, 10; quoted in Peter Brown, *Augustine of Hippo*, p. 156. On the subject of the priority of the future over the past, cf. F. J. van Beeck, *Christ Proclaimed*, pp. 265–93.
3. Augustine, *In Ep. Joan. ad Parthos Tract.*, IV, 6 (*SC* 75, pp. 230–31): "Tota vita Christiani boni, sanctum desiderium est."
4. John L. White, "New Testament Epistolary Literature in the Framework of Ancient Epistolography," esp. pp. 1746–48.
5. I am much indebted to my friend and colleague John L. White for the New Testament backgrounds of some of the insights in this paragraph.
6. *De Civ. Dei* X, 6 (*CC* 47, p. 278): "omne opus, quo agitur, ut sancta societate inhæreamus Deo, relatum scilicet ad illum finem boni, quo veraciter beati esse possimus."
7. "Hoc est sacrificium Christianorum: multi unum corpus in Christo" (*De Civ. Dei* X, 6; *CC* 47, p. 279).
8. Cf. F. J. van Beeck, *Christ Proclaimed*, pp. 365–70.
9. On martyrdom, cf. F. J. van Beeck, *Christ Proclaimed*, pp. 479–86; quotation p. 483.
10. *S. Th.* II–II, 23, 2, *ad* 1, and 3, *ad* 3; 24, 2, *ad* 1, and 7, *in c.*
11. Cf. for instance, *S. Th.* I–II, 62, 4, *in c.*; I–II, 62, 4, *in c.*; II–II, 4, 3; 23, 8; 24, 12, *ad* 4.
12. *S. Th.* I–II, 65, 2, 4; 71, 4, *in c.*; II–II, 23, 7; 51, 2, *in c.*; 108, 2, *ad* 2.
13. *S. Th.* I–II, 65, 3 and 5.
14. II–II, 24, 12, *ad* 4; 45, 4, *in c.*; 136, 3, *in c.*; III, 79, 1, *in c.*
15. Augustine, *Confessiones* X, 29: "o amor, qui semper ardes et numquam extingueris, caritas, deus meus, accende me! continentiam iubes: da quod iubes et iube quod vis" (*CSEL* 33, p. 256).
16. *University Sermons*, pp. 18–19 (italics added).
17. "Tales nos amat Deus, quales futuri sumus ipsius dono, non quales sumus nostro merito." (Italics added.)

18. *La peste*, p. 220 (cf. ET *The Plague*, p. 124): "... en donnant trop d'importance aux belles actions, on rend finalement un hommage indirect et puissant au mal. Car on laisse supposer alors que ces belles actions n'ont tant de prix que parce qu'elles sont rares et que la méchanceté et l'indifférence sont des moteurs bien plus fréquents dans les actions des hommes."

19. Cf. Pheme Perkins, *Love Commands in the New Testament*, p. 1.

20. *The Epistle to Diognetus*, V, 1–4. 6–7. 10 (*SC* 33, pp. 62–65; italics added).

21. James Hennesey, *American Catholics*, pp. 38–41.

22. Cf. DocVatAb, pp. 672–74.

23. Cf. F. J. van Beeck, *Christ Proclaimed*, pp. 267, 278, 291.

24. *S. Th.* I–II, 94, 2, *in c.*

25. *S. Th.* II–II, 154, 12, *ad* 2 ("ordo naturæ humanæ inditus est prior et stabilior quam quilibet alius ordo superadditus").

26. *S. Th.* II–II, 154, 12, *ad* 1 ("sicut ordo rationis rectæ est ab homine, ita ordo naturæ est ab ipso Deo"). Cf. also *S. Th.* III, *Suppl.*, 65, 1, *ad* 4.

27. *S. Th.* II–II, 57, 3, *in c.*

28. *S. Th.* I–II, 91, 2, *in c.*; note the expressions "ex *impressione* ejus [viz. legis eternæ] habent inclinationes in proprios actus et fines" and "*excellentiori* quodam *modo.*"

29. The expression "*ius gentium*" (*S. Th.* II–II, 57, 3, *in c.*) sums up the legal-moral systems of non-Christian nations.

30. Cf. *S. Th.* I–II, 94, 4, *ad* 1: "... ea quæ sunt de lege naturæ, plenarie ibi [= in Evangelio] traduntur." Aquinas then proceeds to appeal to Gratian, who treats the golden rule as the summary of the natural law.

31. On this issue, cf. Francis A. Sullivan, *Magisterium*, pp. 136–52.

32. Cf. Karl Rahner, "Towards a Fundamental Theological Interpretation of Vatican II."

33. P. Schoonenberg, *Hij is een God van mensen*, p. 30 (ET *The Christ*, p. 36). Cf. F. J. van Beeck, *Christ Proclaimed*, pp. 286–92.

34. "Sed Dominus noster Christus ueritatem se, non consuetudinem, cognominauit": *De Virg. Vel.* I, 1 (*CC* 2, p. 1209).

35. Cf. Norman Perrin, *Rediscovering the Teaching of Jesus*, esp. pp. 15–53.

36. Cf. W. Pannenberg, *Jesus—God and Man*, pp. 53–66.

37. Cf. C. H. Dodd, *The Apostolic Preaching and its Developments*, p. 10.

38. Cf. C. H. Dodd, *The Apostolic Preaching and its Developments*, pp. 7–35.

39. Cf. F. J. van Beeck, *Christ Proclaimed*, pp. 474–77.

40. Gregory of Nyssa, *Logos katēchētikos* ["*Oratio catechetica magna*"], *Prol.* (*PG* 45, coll. 9–114; quotation 9A; Srawley, pp. 1–2).

41. Avery Dulles, *The Catholicity of the Church*, p. 99.

42. Cf. *From Bossuet to Newman*, esp. pp. 1–48.

43. *An Essay in Aid of a Grammar of Assent*, chap. 9, §2 (p. 277); chap. 8, §2, 3 (p. 251).

44. *An Essay on the Development of Christian Doctrine*, chap. 1; chap. 5, §3 and 4; chaps. 8 and 9 (pp. 57–75, 189–97, 337–75).

45. *An Essay in Aid of a Grammar of Assent*, chap. 8, §2, 2 (p. 240); italics added.

46. *An Essay in Aid of a Grammar of Assent*, n. 2 (p. 386); italics added in the English words.

47. For a survey of Rahner's discussions of this issue, cf. F. J. van Beeck, "Rahner on *Sprachregelung*: Regulation of Language? of Speech?"

48. Cf. F. J. van Beeck, *Christ Proclaimed*, pp. 93–98.

49. *Der christliche Glaube* (ET *The Christian Faith*), §95 (cf. F. J. van Beeck, *Christ Proclaimed*, pp. 566–75); §19 (title).

50. "Christliche Glaubenssätze sind Auffassungen der christlich frommen Gemütszustände in der Rede dargestellt": title of §15 of *Der Christliche Glaube* (ET *The Christian Faith*); cf. its elaboration in §15 and the conclusions that follow for the nature of dogmatic propositions in §§16–17.

51. Cf. the footnote on p. 105 of vol. 1 of the Redeker edition of *Der Christliche Glaube*: "The propositions are only derived and the internal state of affection (is) the orig-

inal" ("die Sätze [sind] nur das Abgeleitete und der innere Gemütszustand das Ur-
sprüngliche").

52. *Der christliche Glaube* (*The Christian Faith*), §94; §88; cf. §98
53. *Der christliche Glaube* (*The Christian Faith*), §101; §113; §94, 3.
54. *Der christliche Glaube* (*The Christian Faith*), §93.
55. *Der christliche Glaube* (*The Christian Faith*), §101, 4.
56. *Der christliche Glaube* (*The Christian Faith*), §99, 1.
57. *Der christliche Glaube* (*The Christian Faith*), §99, title.
58. *Der christliche Glaube* (*The Christian Faith*), §99, 2.
59. Cf. "Was ist eine dogmatische Aussage?," pp. 72–81; cf. ET "What is a Dogmatic
    Statement?" pp. 58–66. Cf. also "Überlegungen zur Methode der Theologie," pp.
    113–26; ET "Reflections on Methodology in Theology," pp. 101–14.
60. J. N. D. Kelly, *Early Christian Creeds*, pp. 62–99.
61. J. N. D. Kelly, *Early Christian Creeds*, p. 43.
62. Cf. the full treatment provided in Edward Yarnold, *The Awe-Inspiring Rites of Initi-
    ation*, and in Hugh M. Riley, *Christian Initiation*.
63. J. N. D. Kelly, *Early Christian Creeds*, p. 98.
64. Edward Yarnold, *The Awe-Inspiring Rites of Initiation*, p. x.
65. Cf. §48, 2, a.
66. *Trad. Apost.* 21 (*SC* 11bis, pp. 84–91); the translation follows Dom Bernard Botte's
    emendations of the text.
67. Cf. §48, 2, e.
68. *Hom. Bapt.* III, 18–20, in Edward Yarnold, *The Awe-Inspiring Rites of Initiation*, pp.
    201–2.
69. *De sacr.* II, 20–22 (*SC* 25, pp. 68–69). For a similar passage, cf. *De sacr.* VI, 5–8 (*SC*
    25, pp. 99–100), where, however, the emphasis is more on the gift of the Spirit and
    the sign of the cross.
70. *PL* 192, coll. 519–964.
71. Cf. *CrC*, pp. 61–323, 440–42.
72. For an enlightening example, cf. E. J. Bicknell, *The Thirty-Nine Articles*, rev. ed., H.
    J. Carpenter.

Chapter 11

1. Cf. A. D. Nock, *Conversion*, esp. pp. 164–86; quotation p. 179.
2. Cf. Hegel's thesis that the philosophic Idea is present in each part of philosophy in
   a particular determinacy or element (§44, 1).
3. Gerard Manley Hopkins, *The Wreck of the Deutschland*, stanza 18 (*Poems*, p. 57).
4. *DictSpir* II, 535 (italics added).
5. *Strom.*, IV, 7 (*PG* 8, 1264C–1265A). For references to related passages in Clement's
   works, cf. *DictSpir* II, 535.
6. *Strom.* II, 6, 31 (*SC* 38, p. 57; *PG* 8, 965B).
7. We can prescind from the question whether the *Strōmateis* are, in whole or in part,
   identical with the (lost) *Didaskalos*.
8. *Prooemium in Regulas fusius tractatas*, 3 (*PG* 31, 896B). Cf. Dorotheus of Gaza, *Instructions*, IV, §48; cf. XIV, §157 (*SC* 92, pp. 222–23, 440–41). For a similar passage, cf.
   Gregory of Nyssa, *Hom. in Cant.*, I (*PG* 44, 765BC; Jaeger VI, pp. 15–16).
9. Lit.: "by matter and habit of inclination as well as disposition of soul towards the
   attractive by conviction" (*tropōi kai hexei tēs pros to kalon kata gnōmēn tēs psychēs ropēs te
   kai diatheseōs*).
10. *Myst.* XXIV (*PG* 91, 709D–712A).
11. *Coll.* XI, 12 (*SC* 54, p. 114).
12. *S. Th.*, II–II, 24, 9, *in c.*
13. Aelred Squire, *Asking the Fathers*, pp. 206–7 (italics added).
14. Blessed Peter Faber, S. J., *Memoriale*, 67 [August 6, 1542] (*Fabri Monumenta*, pp. 525–
    26); italics added for emphasis.

15. Margaret-Mary Alacocque, *Lettre* 132 (125 or 127 in other editions), *Vie et Oeuvres, Novelle Édition authentique*, vol 2, p. 558.

16. *De princ.*, IV, 17–18 (*PG* 11, 380A–384A).

17. *De princ.*, IV, 11 (*PG* 11, 364B–365A).

18. Cf. Beryl Smalley, *The Study of the Bible in the Middle Ages*, pp. 1–36.

19. Quoted by Beryl Smalley, *The Study of the Bible in the Middle Ages*, p. 245.

20. Gerard Manley Hopkins, *The Wreck of the Deutschland*, stanza 10 (*Poems*, p. 54).

21. Cf. *DictSpir*, II, 344–57.

22. *Instructions*, XII, §136, (*SC* 92, pp. 398–401); italics added. The reference is to Basil's *Homilia in Ps. 7*, 5 (*PG* 29, 240; ET *FC* 46, p. 172) and to his homily *In princ. Proverbiorum*, 9 (*PG* 31, 404BC).

23. "Finis est prior in intentione, et posterior in executione": *Quodlib.* IV, 12, 2, 1. Occurrences in other late works, with slight variations of expression: *S. Th.* I–II, 1, 1, *ad* 1; 18, 7, *ad* 2; 20, 1, *ad* 2; 20, 1, *in c*.

24. A very select anthology of references: *In libros Sent.*, I, 3, *praef.*, *div. text.*; *S. c. G.*, I, 14; *S. Th.* I, 12, 12, *in c.*; 84, 7, *ad* 3.

25. Ralph Keifer has rightly repeated this in our own day by pointing out that an uncritical use of the affirmative language borrowed from personal relationships may be an obstacle to growth in the life of the Spirit: "A Spirituality of Mystery," esp. p. 100.

26. Cf. Francis A. Sullivan, *Magisterium*, pp. 174–218.

27. *Quodlib.* III, 4, 1; the *cathedra pastoralis* is also called *cathedra pontificalis* and *cathedra episcopalis* in the same article.

28. Francis A. Sullivan, *Magisterium*, pp. 185–89.

29. "Episcopi sunt . . . doctores authentici seu auctoritate Christi præditi." The word *authentic*, repeated twice in the course of LG 25, means "authoritative" in virtue of Christ's charge.

30. Francis A. Sullivan, *Magisterium*, pp. 217–18.

31. John E. Thiel, "Theological Responsibility," pp. 578–79.

32. Francis A. Sullivan, *Magisterium*, pp. 25ff. (cf. notes).

33. John E. Thiel, "Theological Responsibility," p. 582.

34. John E. Thiel, "Theological Responsibility," p. 582. Cf. p. 584 for more interesting claims.

35. "Tradition and the Individual Talent," in *Selected Essays 1917–1932*, pp. 3–11; quotation, p. 5.

Bibliography

[Alacocque, St. Margaret-Mary]. *Vie et Oeuvres de Sainte Marguerite-Marie Ala-cocque*. Vol. 2, *Oeuvres: Nouvelle Édition authentique*. Paris: Ancienne librairie Poussielgue, 1920.

[Anselm of Canterbury, St.]. *St. Anselm's Proslogion, with A Reply on Behalf of the Fool by Gaunilo and The Author's Reply to Gaunilo*. Translated by M. J. Charlesworth. London: Oxford University Press; Notre Dame, IN: University of Notre Dame Press, 1965–79.

[Aristotle]. *The Basic Works of Aristotle*. Edited by Richard McKeon. New York: Random House, 1941.

Arnal, Oscar L. *Ambivalent Alliance: The Catholic Church and the Action Française 1899–1939*. Pittsburgh, PA.: University of Pittsburgh Press, 1985 (bibliography).

Baillie, D. M. *God Was in Christ: An Essay on Incarnation and Atonement*. New York: Scribner's, 1948.

[Balthasar, Hans Urs von]. *In der Fülle des Glaubens: Hans Urs von Balthasar-Lesebuch*, 2d ed. Edited by Medard Kehl and Werner Löser. Freiburg, Basel, and Vienna: Herder, 1981 (ET *The von Balthasar Reader*. Edited by Medard Kehl and Werner Löser; translated by Robert J. Daly, S.J. and Fred Lawrence. Edinburgh: T. & T. Clark; New York: Crossroad, 1985).

Balthasar, Hans Urs von. *Katholisch: Aspekte des Mysteriums (Kriterien, 36)*. Einsiedeln: Johannes Verlag, 1975.

―――. *Neue Klarstellungen (Kriterien, 49)*. Einsiedeln: Johannes Verlag, 1979.

―――. See Origen.

―――. *Spiritus Creator (Skizzen zur Theologie, III)*. Einsiedeln: Johannes Verlag, 1967.

―――. *Die Wahrheit ist symphonisch: Aspekte des christlichen Pluralismus (Kriterien, 29)*. Einsiedeln: Johannes Verlag, 1972.

Barr, James. *The Semantics of Biblical Language*. Oxford University Press, 1961.

Basil the Great, St. *On the Holy Spirit*. Translated by David Anderson. Crestwood, NY: St. Vladimir's Seminary Press, 1980.

Bede, [The Venerable]. *Ecclesiastical History of the English Nation*. In *Bædæ Opera Historica*, translated by J. E. King. 2 vols. Loeb Classical Library. London and New York: William Heinemann, 1930 (Modern ET: *A History of the English Church and People*. Translated by Leo Sherley-Price. Harmondsworth: Penguin Books, 1955).

Beeck, Frans Jozef van. *Catholic Identity After Vatican II: Three Types of Faith in the One Church*. Chicago: Loyola University Press, 1985.

————. *Christ Proclaimed: Christology as Rhetoric.* New York, Toronto, Ramsey, NJ: Paulist Press, 1979.

————. "Fackre's *Christian Story*: A Review Article." *Andover Newton Theological Quarterly* 20(1979):122–32.

————. "Intercommunion: A Note on Norms." *One in Christ* 12(1976):124–41.

————. "Professing the Uniqueness of Christ." *Chicago Studies* 24(1985):17–35.

————. "Rahner on *Sprachregelung*: Regulation of Language? of Speech?" *Oral Tradition* 2(1987):323–36.

————. "Reflections on a Dated Book." *The Heythrop Journal* 24(1983):51–57.

————. "Ten Questions on Soteriology and Christology." *Chicago Studies* 25(1986):269–78.

Berg, J. H. van den. *Leven in meervoud: Een metabletisch onderzoek*, 5th ed. Nijkerk: G. F. Callenbach, 1967.

————. *'s Morgens jagen, 's middags vissen.* Nijkerk: Callenbach, 1971.

Beuken, W. A. M. *'Abraham weet van ons niet' (Jesaja 63:16): De grond van Israels vertrouwen tijdens de ballingschap.* Nijkerk: G. F. Callenbach, 1986.

Bicknell, E. J. *A Theological Introduction to the Thirty-Nine Articles of the Church of England.* Rev. ed. edited by H. J. Carpenter. London, New York, and Toronto: Longmans, Green, 1955.

Böhmer, H. "Die Lobpreisungen des Augustins." *Neue kirchliche Zeitschrift* 26(1915):419–38.

Bolt, Robert. *A Man for All Seasons: A Play in Two Acts.* New York: Vintage Books, 1962.

Bonhoeffer, Dietrich. *Christ the Center.* New translation by Edwin H. Robertson. San Francisco: Harper & Row, 1978.

————. *Gesammelte Schriften.* Edited by Eberhard Bethge. Vol. 3, München: Chr. Kaiser Verlag, 1966.

————. *Letters and Papers from Prison.* Rev. ed. edited by Eberhard Bethge. New York: Macmillan, 1967.

————. *No Rusty Swords.* Vol. I, Edited by Edwin H. Robertson. Revised by John Bowden and [Eberhard] Bethge. London: Collins, 1970.

————. *Sanctorum Communio: Eine dogmatische Untersuchung zur Soziologie der Kirche*, 4th ed. München: Chr. Kaiser Verlag, 1969.

Bots, J. *Tussen Descartes en Darwin: Geloof en natuurwetenschap in de achttiende eeuw in Nederland.* Assen: Van Gorcum & Comp. N.V., 1972.

Bouyer, Louis. *Eucharist: Theology and Spirituality of the Eucharistic Prayer.* Translated by Charles Underhill Quinn. Notre Dame and London: University of Notre Dame Press, 1968.

Brown, David. *The Divine Trinity.* London: Duckworth, 1985.

Brown, Peter. *Augustine of Hippo: a Biography.* Berkeley, Los Angeles, and London: University of California Press, 1969.

————. "The Diffusion of Manichaeism in the Roman Empire." *Journal of Roman Studies* 59(1969):92–103.

Brown, Raymond E. *Biblical Exegesis and Church Doctrine.* New York and Mahwah, NJ: Paulist Press, 1985.

[————]. *The Gospel According to John. Anchor Bible.* Translated by Raymond E. Brown. Garden City, NY: Doubleday, 1966.

Buber, Martin. *Gottesfinsternis: Betrachtungen zur Beziehung zwischen Religion und Philosophie.* In *Werke*, vol. 1, *Schriften zur Philosophie.* Munich: Kösel;

Heidelberg: Lambert Schneider, 1962, pp. 503–603 (ET *Eclipse of God: Studies in the Relation Between Religion and Philosophy*. New York: Harper & Row, 1957).

———. *Ich und Du*, 2nd ed. Cologne: Verlag Jakob Hegner, 1966 (ET *I and Thou*. Translated by Walter Kaufmann. New York: Charles Scribner's Sons, 1970).

Busch, Eberhard. *Karl Barth: His life from letters and autobiographical texts*. Translated by John Bowden. Philadelphia, Fortress Press, 1976.

Butler, Joseph. *The Analogy of Religion, Natural and Revealed, to the Constitution and Course of Nature*. New York: Jonathan Leavitt; Boston: Crocker and Brewster, 1833.

Bütler, Hans-Peter. *Die geistige Welt des jüngeren Plinius: Studien zur Thematik seiner Briefe*. Heidelberg: Carl Winter Universitätsverlag, 1970.

Calvin, John. *Institutes of the Christian Religion* [ed. of 1559]. Translated by Henry Beveridge. Grand Rapids, MI: Wm. B. Eerdmans, 1983.

Camus, Albert. *La Peste*. In *Oeuvres completes*. Vol. 1, Récits et Romans—*L'étranger, La peste, La chute*. Paris: Imprimerie nationale, 1962 (ET *The Plague*. Translated by Stuart Gilbert. New York: Random House, Vintage Books, 1972).

Carnley, Peter. *The Structure of Resurrection Belief*. Oxford: Clarendon Press, 1987.

Carr, Anne E. *Transforming Grace: Christian Tradition and Women's Experience*. San Francisco: Harper & Row, 1988.

Casel, Odo. "Die *Logikē thysia* der antiken Mystik in christlich-liturgischer Umdeutung." *Jahrbuch für Liturgiewissenschaft* 4(1924):37–47.

———. *The Mystery of Christian Worship and Other Writings*. Edited by Burkhard Neunheuser. Westminster, MD: Newman Press; London: Darton Longman & Todd, 1962.

Chadwick, Owen. *From Bossuet to Newman*, 2d ed. Cambridge: Cambridge University Press, 1987.

Chauvet, Louis-Marie. *Du symbolique au symbole: Essai sur les sacrements*. Paris: Editions du Cerf, 1979.

Chenu, M.-D. "Vérité évangélique et métaphysique wolffiennne à Vatican II." *Revue des Sciences philosophiques et théologiques* 57(1973):632–40.

The Cloud of Unknowing and the Book of Privy Counselling. Edited by Phyllis Hodgson. Early English Text Society, 218. London, New York, and Toronto: Oxford University Press, 1944 (for 1943), rev. 1958, reprinted 1981.

Cohn, Norman. *The Pursuit of the Millennium: Revolutionary Millenarians and Mystical Anarchists of the Middle Ages*. Rev. ed. New York: Oxford University Press, 1970.

Collins, John J. "Introduction: Towards the Morphology of a Genre." In *Apocalypse: The Morphology of a Genre*, edited by John J. Collins. Semeia, 14, 1979.

Commentary on the Decrees of Vatican II. Edited by Herbert Vorgrimler. New York: Herder and Herder, vol. 2, 1968; vol 5, 1969.

Congar, Yves M.-J. *Diversity and Communion*. Translated by John Bowden. Mystic, CT: Twenty-Third Publications, 1985.

————. *A History of Theology.* Translated by Hunter Guthrie. Garden City, NY: Doubleday, 1968.

————. *La Tradition et les traditions.* Vol. 1, *Essai historique*; vol. 2, *Essai théologique.* Paris: Librairie Arthème Fayart, 1960, 1963 (ET *Tradition and Traditions: An historical and a theological essay.* New York: Macmillan, 1966).

————. *Jesus Christ* Translated by Luke O'Neill. New York: Herder and Herder, 1966.

Coulson, John. *Religion and Imagination: 'in aid of a grammar of assent.'* Oxford: Clarendon Press, 1981.

Coventry John. *Reconciling.* London: SCM Press, 1985.

Cragg, Gerald R. *The Church and the Age of Reason 1648–1789.* Vol. 4 of *The Pelican History of the Church.* Rev. ed. Harmondsworth: Penguin Books, 1970.

Dalrymple, John, et al. *Authority in a Changing Church.* London and Sydney: Sheed and Ward, 1968.

Damiani, Petrus. *Das Büchlein vom Dominus vobiscum: Vom Geiste, der den einsamen Beter des Stundengebets erfüllen soll.* Translated by Adolf Kolping. Düsseldorf: Patmos-Verlag, 1949.

Defoe, Daniel. *The Life and Strange Surprizing Adventures of Robinson Crusoe of York, Mariner.* London: Folio Society, 1972.

————. *The Shortest-Way with the Dissenters: or Proposals for the Establishment of the Church.* Vol. 6 of *The Shakespeare Head Edition of the Novels and Selected Writings of Daniel Defoe.* Oxford: Basil Blackwell, 1927.

Descartes, [René]. *Meditationes de Prima Philosophia: Méditations métaphysiques.* Edited by Geneviève Rodis-Lewis. Paris: J. Vrin, 1970.

Deonise Hid Divinite and Other Treatises on Contemplative Prayer Related to The Cloud of Unknowing. Edited by Phyllis Hodgson. Early English Text Society, 231, Reprint. London, New York, and Toronto: Oxford University Press, 1958.

Dix, Dom Gregory. *The Shape of the Liturgy.* New York: Seabury, 1982.

Dodd, C[harles] H[arold]. *The Apostolic Preaching and its Developments: Three Lectures with an Appendix on Eschatology and History.* New York: Harper, 1936.

Dölger, F. J. *Antike und Christentum,* vol 2. Münster: Aschendorff, 1930.

Dold, Alban. "Das 'Dominus vobiscum' der heiligen Messe als Mittel unserer Verbindung mit Gott." *Benediktinische Monatschrift* 26(1950):261–64.

Donne, John. *The Divine Poems,* 2d ed. Oxford: Clarendon Press, 1978.

Dostoyevsky, Fyodor. *The Brothers Karamazov.* Translated by David Magarshak. Harmondsworth: Penguin Books, 1958.

Dulles, Avery. *The Catholicity of the Church.* Oxford: Clarendon Press, 1985.

————. *The Survival of Dogma.* Garden City, NY: Doubleday, 1971.

Dunn, James D.G. *Christology in the Making: A New Testament Inquiry into the Origins of the Doctrine of the Incarnation.* Philadelphia: Westminster Press, 1980.

Dupré, Louis. *The Other Dimension: A Search for the Meaning of Religious Attitudes.* Garden City, NY: Doubleday, 1972.

Egan, Harvey D. *Christian Mysticism: the future of a tradition.* New York: Pueblo Publishing, 1984.

Eliade, Mircea. *The Myth of the Eternal Return, or, Cosmos and History.* Translated by Willard R. Trask. Bollingen Series XLVI. Princeton, NJ: Princeton University Press, 1971.

_____. *Myth and Reality.* Translated by Willard R. Trask. New York and Evanston: Harper and Row, Torchbook, 1968.

_____. *The Sacred and the Profane: The Nature of Religion.* Translated by Willard R. Trask. New York: Harcourt, Brace & World, Harvest Book, 1959.

Eliot, T. S. *Selected Essays 1917–1932.* New York: Harcourt, Brace and Company, 1932.

Englund, Steven. "The force of Cardinal Lustiger." *Commonweal* 108 (1986):242–48.

Evans, Donald D. *The Logic of Self-Involvement.* New York: Herder and Herder, 1963.

[Faber, Blessed Peter]. *Fabri Monumenta: Beati Petri Fabri Primi Sacerdotis e Societate Jesu Epistolae, Memoriale et Processus. Monumenta Historica Societatis Jesu.* Madrid: Gabriel Lopez del Horno, 1914.

Fackre, Gabriel. *The Christian Story.* Grand Rapids, MI: Wm. B. Eerdmans, 1978.

_____. *The Religious Right and Christian Faith.* Grand Rapids, MI: Wm. B. Eerdmans, 1982.

Fortin, E. L. *Dissidence et philosophie au Moyen Age: Dante et ses antécédents. Cahiers d'études médiévales, 6.* Paris: J. Vrin, 1981.

[Franklin, Benjamin]. *The Autobiography of Benjamin Franklin.* Edited by Richard B. Morris. New York: Washington Square Press, 1955.

Freeborn, Richard. *Turgenev: The Novelist's Novelist.* London: Cambridge University Press, 1960.

Frei, Hans W. *The Eclipse of Biblical Narrative: A Study in Eighteenth and Nineteenth Century Hermeneutics.* New Haven and London: Yale University Press, 1974.

_____. *The Identity of Jesus Christ: The Hermeneutical Bases of Dogmatic Theology.* Philadelphia: Fortress Press, 1975.

Fries, Heinrich, and Karl Rahner. *Unity of the Churches: An Actual Possibility.* Translated by Ruth C. L. Gritsch and Eric W. Gritsch. Philadelphia: Fortress Press; New York and Ramsey, NJ: Paulist, 1985.

Frye, Northrop. *The Great Code: The Bible and Literature.* San Diego, New York, and London: Harcourt Brace Jovanovich, 1982.

Giamberardini, Gabriele. "Il «Sub tuum praesidium» e il titolo «Theotokos» nella tradizione egiziana." *Marianum* 31(1969):324–62.

Granfield, Patrick. *The Limits of the Papacy: Authority and Autonomy in the Church.* New York: Crossroad, 1987.

Gray, Patrick T. R. *The Defense of Chalcedon in the East (451–553).* Leiden: Brill, 1979.

Gregory of Nyssa, St. *The Catechetical Oration.* Edited by James Herbert Srawley. Cambridge Patristic Texts. Reprint. Cambridge: Cambridge University Press, 1956.

Grillmeier, Alois. *Jesus der Christus im Glauben der Kirche.* Vol. 2/1, *Das Konzil von Chaldedon (451): Rezeption und Widerspruch (451–518).* Freiburg, Basel, and Vienna: Herder, 1986 (ET *Christ in Christian Tradition.* Vol. 2, *From the Council of Chalcedon (451) to Gregory the Great (590–604).*

Part 1, *Reception and Contradiction: The development of the discussion about Chalcedon from 451 to the beginning of the reign of Justinian*. Translated by Pauline Allen and John Cawte. Atlanta, GA: John Knox Press, 1987).

Gustafson, James M. *Ethics from a Theocentric Perspective*. Vol. 1, *Theology and Ethics*. Vol. 2, *Ethics and Theology*. Chicago and London: University of Chicago Press, 1981, 1984.

Guthrie, Harvey H., Jr. *Theology as Thanksgiving: From Israel's Psalms to the Church's Eucharist*. New York: Seabury, 1981.

Hahn, Ferdinand. *The Titles of Jesus in Christology: Their History in Early Christianity*. New York and Cleveland, OH: World Publishing, 1969.

Hartle, Ann. *The Modern Self in Rousseau's Confessions: A Reply to St. Augustine*. Notre Dame, IN: University of Notre Dame Press, 1983.

Hegel, G. W. F. *Enzyklopädie der philosophischen Wissenschaften im Grundrisse (1830)*. Vol. 8 of *Werke*. Frankfurt am Main: Suhrkamp Verlag, 1970.

———. *Jenaer Systementwürfe II*. Edited by Rolf-Peter Horstmann and Johann Heinrich Trede. Vol. 7 of *Gesammelte Werke*. Hamburg: Felix Meiner Verlag, 1971.

———. *Phänomenologie des Geistes*, Edited by J. Hoffmeister. Vol. 114 of *Philosophische Bibliothek*. Hamburg: F. Meiner, 1952.

Heim, S. Mark. "D. C. MacIntosh and the Evangelical Roots of Liberal Theology." Ph.D. diss., Boston College, Andover Newton Theological School; cf. *Diss. Abstr. Internat.*, vol 42, N° 10, 10 April 1982.

Hengel, Martin. *Der Son Gottes: Die Entstehung der Christologie und die jüdisch-hellenistische Religionsgeschichte*. Tübingen: J. C. B. Mohr (Paul Siebeck), 1975 (ET *The Son of God: The Origin of Christology and the History of Jewish-Hellenistic Religion*. Translated by John Bowden. Philadelphia: Fortress Press, 1976).

Hennesey, James. *American Catholics: A History of the Roman Catholic Community in the United States*. New York & Oxford: Oxford University Press, 1981.

———. "Séparation de l'Église et de l'État: États-Unis et France." In *Concilium* 114 (Théologie pratique). Paris: Beauchesne, 1976, pp. 65–76.

Henrichs, Albert. "Pagan Ritual and the Alleged Crimes of the Early Christians: A Reconsideration." In *Kuriakon: Festschrift Johannes Quasten*, edited by Patrick Greenfield and Joseph A. Jungmann, vol. 1, Münster: Verlag Aschendorf, 1970, pp. 18–35.

[Herbert, George]. *The Works of George Herbert*. Edited by F. E. Hutchinson. Oxford: Clarendon Press, 1941.

Hick, John, and Paul F. Knitter, eds. *The Myth of Christian Uniqueness: Toward a Pluralistic Theology of Religions*. Maryknoll, NY: Orbis Books, 1987.

Hoffmeister, Johannes. *Wörterbuch der philosophischen Begriffe*. Hamburg: Felix Meiner, 1955.

[Hopkins, Gerard Manley]. *The Poems of Gerard Manley Hopkins*. 4th ed. Edited by W. H. Gardner and N. H. MacKenzie. London, Oxford, and New York: Oxford University Press, 1975.

James, William. *The Varieties of Religious Experience: A Study in Human Nature*, 9th ed. New York and London: Collier and Macmillan, 1974.

Jansen Schoonhoven, E. *Jodendom Christendom Verlichting: Johan Georg Hamann en Moses Mendelssohn, een achttiende eeuws dispuut als bijdrage aan he-dendaagse discussie.* Nijkerk: Uitgeverij G. F. Callenbach, 1986.

Jenkins, David. *Guide to the Debate About God.* London: Lutterworth Press, 1966.

Jeremias, Joachim. *Die Abendmahlsworte Jesu,* 4th ed. Göttingen: Vandenhoeck & Ruprecht, 1967 (ET of the 3d ed. *The Eucharistic Words of Jesus.* Translated by Norman Perrin. London: SCM Press, 1966).

––––––. *The Prayers of Jesus.* Studies in Biblical Theology, second series, 6. London: SCM Press, 1967.

[John of the Cross, St.]. *The Collected Works of Saint John of the Cross.* Translated by Kieran Kavanaugh and Otilio Rodriguez. Washington, DC: Institute of Carmelite Studies, 1979 (Spanish ed.: *Obras de San Juan de la Cruz.* Edited by Silverio de Santa Teresa. Burgos, Spain: Tipografia de "El Monte Carmelo," 1943).

Jossua, J. P. "Immutabilité, progrès ou structurations des doctrines chrétiennes?" *Revue des sciences philosophiques et théologiques* 52(1968):173–200.

––––––. "Rule of Faith and Orthodoxy." *Concilium* 51(1970):56–67.

Jourjon, Maurice. "Minuties augustiniennes: *Etiam peccata.*" *Vigiliae Christianae* 9(1955):249–51; 10(1956):64.

Jüngel, Eberhard. *Gott als Geheimnis der Welt: Zur Begründung der Theologie des Gekreuzigten im Streit zwischen Theismus und Atheismus,* 3d ed. Tübingen: J. C. B. Mohr (Paul Siebeck), 1978 (ET *God as the Mystery of the World: On the Foundation of the Theology of the Crucified One in the Dispute Between Theism and Atheism.* Translated by Darrell L. Guder. Grand Rapids, MI. Wm. B. Eerdmans, 1983).

Jungmann, Joseph [Andreas]. *The Mass of the Roman Rite: Its Origins and Development (Missarum Sollemnia).* Translated by Francis A. Brunner. 2 vols. New York: Benziger Brothers, 1951–1955.

––––––. *The Place of Christ in Liturgical Prayer.* Translated by A. Peeler. 2d rev. ed. Staten Island, NY: Alba House, 1965.

Kaufman, Gordon D. *Systematic Theology: A Historicist Perspective.* New York: Charles Scribner's Sons, 1968.

––––––. *Theology for a Nuclear Age.* Manchester: Manchester University Press; Philadelphia: Westminster Press, 1985.

Keifer, Ralph A. "A Spirituality of Mystery." *Spirituality Today* 33(1981):100–109.

Kelly, J. N. D. *Early Christian Creeds,* 2d ed. New York: David McKay, 1960.

Knitter, Paul F. See Hick, John.

Knoch, Wendelin. *Die Einsetzung der Sakramente durch Christus: Eine Untersuchung zur Sakramententheologie der Frühscholastik von Anselm von Laon bis zu William von Auxerre, (Beiträge zur Geschichte der Philosophie und Theologie des Mittelalters,* Neue Folge, vol. 24). Münster: Aschendorff, 1983.

Knox, Ronald A. *Enthusiasm: A Chapter in the History of Religion.* New York: Oxford University Press, Galaxy Book, 1961.

Küng, Hans. *Christ sein,* Munich and Zurich: R. Piper & Co. Verlag, 1974 (ET *On Being a Christian.* Garden City, NY: Doubleday, 1976).

––––––. *Die Kirche.* Freiburg: Herder Verlag, 1967 (ET *The Church.* Garden City, NY: Doubleday, 1976).

––––––. *Rechtfertigung: Die Lehre Karl Barths und eine katholische Besinnung.* Introduction by Karl Barth (*Horizonte*, 2). Einsiedeln: Johannes Verlag 1957 (ET *Justification: The Doctrine of Karl Barth and a Catholic Reflection*. Translated by Thomas Collins, Edmund E. Tolk, and David Granskau. London: T. Nelson, 1964).

————. *Unfehlbar?: Eine Anfrage*, Einsiedeln, Zurich, and Cologne: Benziger Verlag, 1970 (ET *Infallible?: An Inquiry*. Garden City, NY: Doubleday, 1971).

Lash, Nicholas. *Voices of Authority*. Shepherdstown, WV: Patmos Press, 1976.

Lecler, Joseph. "A propos d'une maxime citée par le Pape Jean XXXIII: *In necessariis unitas, in dubiis libertas, in omnibus caritas.*" *Recherches de science religieuse* 49(1961):549–60.

————. "Note complémentaire sur la maxime: *In necessariis unitas, in non necessariis libertas, in omnibus caritas.*" *Recherches de science religieuse* 52(1964):432–38.

Le Roy Ladurie, Emmanul. *Montaillou, The Promised Land of Error*. New York: Vintage Books, 1979.

Lessing, G. *Axiomata*, Vol. 13 of *Sämtliche Schriften*, edited by Karl Lachmann, revised by Franz Muncker. Berlin: Walter de Gruyter, 1968, pp. 105–137.

————. "Über den Beweis des Geistes und der Kraft." Vol. 13 of *Sämtliche Schriften*, edited by Karl Lachmann, revised by Franz Muncker. Berlin: Walter de Gruyter, 1968, pp. 1–8.

————. *Nathan the Wise*. Translated by Bayard Quincy Morgan. In *College Translations, Translations from German Literature*, edited by Bayard Quincy. New York: Frederick Ungar Publishing, 1955.

[————]. *Lessing's Theological Writings*. Selected by Henry Chadwick. Stanford, CA: Stanford University Press, 1957.

Lewis, C. S. *The Allegory of Love: A Study in Medieval Tradition*. London: Oxford University Press, Geoffrey Cumberlege, 1936.

Lindbeck, George A. *The Nature of Doctrine: Religion and Theology in a Postliberal Age*. Philadelphia: Westminster Press, 1984.

Liturgisch woordenboek. Edited by L. Brinkhoff, G. Laudy, A. Verheul, Th. Vismans. Roermond and Maaseik: J. J. Romen & Zonen, 1958–62.

Lohfink, Norbert. "Augustin Bea und die Freiheit der biblischen Forschung." *Orientierung* 45(1981):129–34.

Lonergan, Bernard. *A Second Collection*. Edited by William F. J. Ryan and Bernard J. Tyrrell. Philadelphia: Westminster Press, 1974.

————. *Method in Theology*, 2d ed. New York: Herder and Herder, 1973.

Long, A. A. *Hellenistic Philosophy: Stoics, Epicureans, Sceptics*. New York: Charles Scribner's Sons, 1974.

de Lubac, Henri. *The Mystery of the Supernatural*. New York: Herder and Herder, 1967.

Lumpp, Randolph F. "Literacy, Commerce, and Catholicity: Two Contexts of Change and Invention," *Oral Tradition* 2(1987):337–56.

Madec, Goulven. "Connaissance de Dieu et action de grâces." *Recherches augustiniennes* 2(1962):273–309.

Malmberg, F. "Het middellijk-onmiddellijke contact met God in onze geloofsact." *Jaarboek van het Werkgenootschap van katholieke theologen in Nederland* (1952):47–58.

Maslow, Abraham H. *Religions, Values, and Peak Experiences.* Columbus, OH: Ohio State University Press, 1964.

———. *Towards a Psychology of Being,* 2d ed. New York: Van Nostrand Reinhold, 1968.

McBrien, Richard P. *Catholicism.* Study edition. Minneapolis, MN: Winston Press, 1981.

Melanchthon, Philip. *Loci Communes Theologici.* Translated by Lowell J. Satre, edited by Wilhelm Pauck. In *Melanchthon and Bucer,* edited by Wilhelm Pauck. Vol. 19 of *The Library of Christian Classics.* Philadelphia: Westminster Press, 1969, pp. 1–152.

———. *Loci communes von 1521.* Edited by Hans Engelland. Vol. 2, pt. 1 of *Melanchthons Werke,* edited by Robert Stupperich. Gütersloh: C. Bertelsmann Verlag, 1952, pp. 3–163.

[———]. *Melanchthon on Christian Doctrine: Loci Communes 1555.* Translated by Clyde L. Manschrek. New York: Oxford University Press, 1965.

Mello, Anthony de. *The Song of the Bird.* Series VII: *Pastoral,* 6. Anand, India: Gujarat Sahitya Prakash, 1982.

Metz, Johann Baptist. *Glaube in Geschichte und Gesellschaft: Studien zu einer praktischen Fundamentaltheologie.* Mainz: Mathias-Grünewald-Verlag, 1977 (ET *Faith in History and Society: Toward a Practical Fundamental Theologie.* Translated by David Smith. New York: Seabury Press, Crossroad Book, 1980).

———. "Kleine Apologie des Erzählens." *Concilium* 9(1973):339ff. (ET *Concilium,* New Series, V, 9, pp. 84–96).

Misner, Paul. "A Note on the Critique of Dogmas." *Theological Studies* 34(1975):690–700.

Moltmann, Jürgen. "Die Zukunft als neues Paradigma der Transzendenz." *Internationale Dialog-Zeitschrift* 1(1969):2–13.

Moore, Sebastian. *The Fire and the Rose Are One.* New York: Seabury Press, 1980.

Needleman, Jacob. *Lost Christianity.* Garden City, NY: Doubleday, 1980.

———. *The New Religions.* Garden City, NY: Doubleday, 1970.

A New Catechism: Catholic Faith for Adults. Translated by Kevin Smyth. New York: Herder and Herder, 1972.

The New Dictionary of Theology. Edited by Joseph A. Komonchak, Mary Collins, Dermot A. Lane. Wilmington, DE: Michael Glazier, 1987.

Newman, John Henry. *Essays Critical and Historical,* 4th ed. vol. 1. London: Basil Montagu Pickering, 1877.

———. *An Essay in Aid of a Grammer of Assent.* Introduced by Nicholas Lash. Notre Dame, IN, and London: University of Notre Dame Press, 1979.

———. *An Essay on the Development of Christian Doctrine.* Garden City, NY: Doubleday, 1960.

———. *Newman's University Sermons: Fifteen Sermons Preached before the University of Oxford 1926–1843,* Reprint from the 3d ed., 1871. Edited by D. M. MacKinnon and J. D. Holmes. London: S. P. C. K., 1970.

Niebuhr, Richard R. *Schleiermacher on Christ and Religion.* London: SCM Press, 1964.

Nock, A. D. *Conversion.* Oxford: Clarendon Press, 1933.

O'Carroll, Michael, *Theotokos: A Theological Encyclopedia of the Blessed Virgin Mary.* Wilmington, DE: Michael Glazier, 1982.

O'Collins, Gerald. *The Case Against Dogma*. New York, Toronto, Paramus, NJ: Paulist Press, 1975.

———. *Jesus Risen: The Resurrection—what actually happened and what does it mean?* London: Darton, Longman and Todd, 1987.

O'Connor, Flannery. *The Habit of Being*. Edited by Sally Fitzgerald. New York: Random House, 1980.

———. *Mystery and Manners*. Edited by Sally and Robert Fitzgerald. New York: Farrar, Straus & Giroux, 1969.

Ong, Walter J. *Fighting for Life: Contest, Sexuality, and Consciousness*. Ithaca, NY, and London: Cornell University Press, 1981.

———. *Interfaces of the Word: Studies in the Evolution of Consciousness and Culture*. Ithaca, NY, and London: Cornell University Press, 1977.

———. *Orality and Literacy: The Technologizing of the Word*. Reprint. London and New York: Methuen, 1985.

———. *The Presence of the Word: Some Prolegomena for Cultural and Religious History*. New York: Simon and Schuster, 1970.

———. *Ramus, Method and the Decay of Dialogue*. Cambridge, MA, and London: Harvard University Press, 1983.

———. *Rhetoric, Romance, and Technology: Studies in the Interaction of Expression and Culture*. Ithaca, NY, and London: Cornell University Press, 1971.

Origen. *Contra Celsum*. Translated by Henry Chadwick. 3d ed. Cambridge: Cambridge University Press, 1980.

———. *Spirit and Fire: A Thematic Anthology of his Writings*. Edited by Hans Urs von Balthasar, translated by Robert J. Daly. Washington, DC: Catholic University of America Press, 1984.

Ott, Heinrich. *Wirklichkeit und Glaube*. Vol. 2, *Der persönliche Gott*. Göttingen and Zürich: Vandenhoeck & Ruprecht, 1969.

Otto, Rudolf. *The Idea of the Holy: An inquiry into the non-rational factor in the idea of the divine and its relation to the rational*. Translated by John W. Harvey. Reprint. London, Oxford, and New York: Oxford University Press, 1970.

Pannenberg, Wolfhart. *Basic Questions in Theology*, vol. 1. Translated by George H. Kehm, Philadelphia: Fortress Press, 1970.

———. *Grundzüge der Christologie*, 2d ed. Gütersloh: Gütersloher Verlagshaus Gerd Mohn, 1966 (ET *Jesus: God and Man*. Philadelphia: The Westminster Press, 1968).

Parain, Brice. *Recherches sur la nature et les fonctions du langage*. Paris: Gallimart, 1942.

Pascal, Blaise. *Pensées*. Edited by Léon Brunschvicg. Paris: Nelson, 1936.

Pascher, Joseph. "Der Friedensgruß der Liturgie." *Münchener Theologische Zeitschrift* 9(1958):34–38.

Peale, Norman Vincent. *The Power of Positive Thinking*, 10th ed. New York: Prentice Hall, 1953.

———. ed. *Faith Made Them Champions*. New York: Prentice Hall, 1954.

Perkins, Pheme. *Love Commands in the New Testament*. New York, Ramsey, NJ: Paulist Press, 1982.

———. *Reading the New Testament: An Introduction*. New York, Ramsey, NJ: Paulist Press, 1977.

_____. *Resurrection: New Testament Witness and Contemporary Reflection.* Garden City, NY: Doubleday, 1984.

Perrin, Norman. *Rediscovering the Teaching of Jesus.* New York and Evanston: Harper & Row, 1967.

[Pliny the Younger]. *C. Plini Caecili Secundi Epistularum Libri Decem.* Edited by R. A. B. Mynors. Oxford: Clarendon Press, 1963.

Pol, W. H. van de. *Het einde van het conventionele christendom.* Roermond and Maaseik: J. J. Romen & Zonen, 1966 (ET *The End of Conventional Christianity.* Translated by Theodore Zuydwijk. New York: Newman Press, 1968).

Poulain, Augustin François. *The Graces of Interior Prayer (Des grâces d'oraison): A Treatise on Mystical Theology.* Translated by Leonora L. Yorke Smith. London: Paul, Trench and Trubner, 1910.

Power, David N. *The Sacrifice We Offer: The Tridentine Dogma and Its Reinterpretation.* Edinburgh: T. & T. Clark, 1987.

Prayers of the Eucharist: Early and Reformed. Translated and edited by R. C. D. Jasper and G. J. Cuming. New York: Oxford University Press, 1980.

Preyer, Robert. "Tennyson as an Oracular Poet." *Modern Philology* 55(1958):239–51.

Punt, Neal. *Unconditional Good News: Toward an Understanding of Biblical Universalism.* Grand Rapids, MI: Wm. B. Eerdmans, 1980.

Rahner, Karl, and Wilhelm Thüsing. *Christologie: systematisch und exegetisch (Quaestiones disputatae, 55).* Freiburg, Basel, and Vienna: Herder, 1972 (ET *A New Christology.* Translated by David Smith and Verdant Green. New York: Seabury, 1980).

_____. See Fries, Heinrich.

_____. *Grundkurs des Glaubens: Einführung in den Begriff des Christentums,* 3d ed. Freiburg, Basel, and Vienna: Herder, 1976 (ET *Foundations of Christian Faith: An Introduction to the Idea of Christianity.* Translated by William V. Dych. New York: Seabury, 1978).

_____. *Hörer des Wortes: Zur Grundlegung einer Religionsphilosophie.* Revised by J. B. Metz. Munich: Kösel, 1963 (ET *Hearers of the Word.* Translated by Michael Richards. New York: Herder and Herder, 1969).

[_____]. *A Rahner Reader.* Edited by Gerald A. McCool. New York: Seabury, 1975.

_____. *Spirit in the World.* Translated by William Dych. New York: Herder and Herder, 1968.

_____. "Towards a Fundamental Theological Interpretation of Vatican II." *Theological Studies* 40(1979):716–27.

_____. "Überlegungen zur Methode der Theologie." Vol. 9 of *Schriften zur Theologie.* Zurich, Einsiedeln, and Cologne: Benziger Verlag, 1970, pp. 79–126 (ET "Reflections on Methodology in Theology." Vol. 11 of *Theological Investigations.* London: DLT; New York: Seabury, 1974, pp. 68–114).

_____. "Was ist eine dogmatische Aussage?" Vol. 5 of *Schriften zur Theologie,* 3d ed. Zurich, Einsiedeln, and Cologne: Benziger Verlag, 1968, pp. 54–81 (ET "What is a Dogmatic Statement?" Vol. 5 of *Theological Investigations.* London: LDT; Baltimore: Helicon, 1966, pp. 42–66).

Ratzinger, Joseph. "Originalität und Überlieferung in Augustins Begriff der *confessio.*" *Revue des études augustiniennes* 3(1957):375–92.

Redwood, John. *Reason, Ridicule and Religion: The Age of Enlightenment in England 1660–1750.* London: Thames and Hudson, 1976.

Riley, Hugh M. *Christian Initiation: A Comparative Study of the Interpretation of the Baptismal Liturgy in the Mystagogical Writings of Cyril of Jerusalem, John Chrysostom, Theodore of Mopsuestia, and Ambrose of Milan.* Catholic University of America Studies in Christian Antiquity, 17. Washington, DC: Catholic University of America Press, Consortium Press, 1974.

Rousseau, J. J. *Émile, ou De l'éducation.* Vol. 4 of *Oeuvres completes,* edited by Bernard Gagnebin and Marcel Raymond (*Bibliotèque de la Pléiade,* 208). 4 vols. [Paris]: Gallimard, 1969, pp. 239–868 (ET *Emile; or, Education.* Translated by Barbara Foxley. Everyman's Library, vol. 518. London and Toronto: Dent & Sons; New York: E. P. Dutton, 1911; Reprint 1930).

Saint-Exupéry, Antoine de. *Un Sens à la Vie: Textes inédits.* Edited by Claude Reynal. Paris: Gallimard, 1956.

Scheeben, Matthias Joseph. *Handbuch der katholischen Dogmatik,* 5/1 (*Gesammelte Schriften,* VI/1). Freiburg: Verlag Herder, 1954.

———. *The Mysteries of Christianity.* Translated by C. Vollert. St. Louis and London: B. Herder, 1946.

Schenk, Erich. *Mozart: Eine Biographie.* [Munich]: Wilhelm Goldmann Verlag, n.d.

Schierse, Franz Joseph. *Verheissung und Heilsvollendung: Zur theologischen Grundfrage des Hebräerbriefes* (*Münchener theologische Studien,* I, Historische Abteilung, Bd. 9). Munich: Karl Zink, 1955.

Schillebeeckx, Edward. *The Church with a Human Face: A New and Expanded Theology of Ministry.* Translated by John Bowden. New York: Crossroad, 1985.

———. *Jezus: Het verhaal van een levende,* 2d ed. Bloemendaal: H. Nelissen, 1974 (ET *Jesus: An Experiment in Christology.* Translated by Hubert Hoskins. New York: Seabury, 1979).

———. *Ministry: Leadership in the Community of Jesus Christ.* Translated by John Bowden. New York: Crossroad, 1981.

Schilson, Arno. *Theologie als Sakramententheologie: Die Mysterientheologie Odo Casels* (*Tübinger theologische Studien,* 18). Mainz: Matthias-Grünewald-Verlag, 1982.

———. "Vergessener und dennoch aktueller Erneuerer: Zum 100. Geburtstag von Odo Casel." *Herder-Korrespondenz* 40(1986):433–36.

Schleiermacher, Friedrich. *Der christliche Glaube,* 7th ed. Edited by Martin Redeker, 2 vols. Berlin: Martin de Gruyter, 1960 (ET *The Christian Faith.* Translated by H. R. Mackintosh and J. S. Stewart. Edinburgh: T. & T. Clark, 1928).

———. *Über die Religion: Reden an die Gebildeten unter ihren Verächtern,* 6th ed. Edited by Rudolf Otto. Göttingen: Vandenhoeck & Ruprecht, 1967 (Also in *Schriften aus der Berliner Zeit, 1796–1799.* Edited by Günter Meckenstock [*Kritische Gesamtausgabe,* I, 2]. Berlin and New York: Walter de Gruyter, 1984, pp. 185–326; also Dritte vermehrte Ausgabe,

Berlin, G. Reimer, 1821; ET *On Religion: Speeches to its Cultured Despisers.* Translated by John Oman. New York: Harper & Row, 1958).

Schoonenberg, Piet. *Hij is een God van mensen.*'s-Hertogenbosch: L. C. G. Malmberg, 1969 (ET *The Christ.* New York: Herder and Herder, 1971).

Schuller, Robert H. *The Be (Happy) Attitudes.* Waco, TX: Word Books, 1985.

———. *Self Esteem: The New Reformation.* Waco, TX: Word Books, 1982.

Segundo, Juan Luis. *A Theology for Artisans of a New Humanity.* Vol. 1, *The Community Called Church;* vol. 2, *Grace and the Human Condition;* vol. 3, *Our Idea of God;* vol. 4, *The Sacraments Today;* vol. 5, *Evolution and Guilt.* Maryknoll, NY: Orbis Books, 1973–74.

Shea, John. *Stories of God: An Unauthorized Biography.* Chicago: Thomas More Press, 1978.

Short, Robert L. *The Gospel According to Peanuts,* Richmond, VA: John Knox Press, 1964.

Smalley, Beryl. *The Study of the Bible in the Middle Ages,* 3d ed. Notre Dame, IN: University of Notre Dame Press, 1978.

Smulders, Pieter. "Dogmengeschichtliche und lehramtliche Entfaltung der Christologie." Vol. 3/I of *Mysterium Salutis,* edited by Johannes Feiner and Magnus Löhrer. Einsiedeln, Zurich, and Cologne: Benziger Verlag, 1970, pp. 389–476.

Sölle, Dorothee. *Stellvertretung: Ein Kapitel Theologie nach dem "Tode Gottes."* Stuttgart and Berlin: Kreuz-Verlag, 1965 (ET *Christ the Representative: An Essay in Theology After the Death of God.* Philadelphia: Fortress Press, 1967).

Solmsen, F. *Isis among the Greeks and Romans.* Martin Classical Lectures, 25. Cambridge, MA: Harvard University Press for Oberlin College, 1979.

Squire, Aelred. *Asking the Fathers: The Art of Meditation and Prayer,* 2d ed. Wilton, CT: Morehouse-Barlow; New York and Ramsey, NJ: Paulist Press, 1976.

———. *Fathers Talking: An Anthology.* Cistercian Studies Series, 93. Kalamazoo, MI: Cistercian Publications, 1986.

———. *Summer in the Seed.* New York, Toronto, Ramsey, NJ: Paulist Press, 1980.

The Study of Liturgy. Edited by Cheslyn Jones, Geoffrey Wainwright, and Edward Yarnold, S.J. New York: Oxford University Press, 1978.

The Study of Spirituality. Edited by Cheslyn Jones, Geoffrey Wainwright, and Edward Yarnold, S.J. New York and Oxford: Oxford University Press, 1986.

Sullivan, Francis A. *Magisterium: Teaching Authority in the Catholic Church.* New York and Ramsey, NJ: Paulist Press, 1983.

Taylor, Vincent. *The Names of Jesus.* New York: St. Martin's Press, 1953.

Teilhard de Chardin, Pierre. *L'Activation de l'Énergie.* Vol. 7 of *Oeuvres.* Paris: Éditions du Seuil, 1963 (ET *Activation of Energy.* New York and London: Harcourt Brace Jovanovich, 1970).

———. *The Phenomenon of Man,* 2d ed. Introduction by Sir Julian Huxley. New York: Harper & Row, Torchbook 1965.

Tertullian. *Apologeticus.* Edited by John E. B. Mayor, translated by Alex. Souter. Cambridge: Cambridge University Press, 1917.

[Theodore of Mopsuestia]. "Theodore on Eucharist and Liturgy." In *Wood-*

brooke Studies: Christian Documents Edited and Translated with a Critical Apparatus, edited by A. Mingana, vol. 6. Cambridge: F. Heffer & Sons, 1933.

Thesaurus spiritualis Societatis Iesu. [Rome]: Typis Polyglottis Vaticanis, 1948.

Thiel, John E. "Theological Responsibility: Beyond the Classical Paradigm." *Theological Studies* 47(1986):573–98.

Thüsing, Wilhelm. See Rahner, Karl.

Tillich, Paul. *The Courage to Be*, 3d ed. London and Glasgow: Collins, 1965.

———. *Systematic Theology* (3 vols. in 1). Chicago: University of Chicago Press, 1967.

Toland, John. *Christianity not Mysterious.* Edited by Günter Gawlick. Stuttgart Bad Cannstatt: Friedrich Fromman Verlag (Günther Holzboog), 1964 (facsimile edition of the original edition of 1696).

———. *Pantheisticon, or, the Form of Celebrating the Socratic-Society.* In *British Philosophers and Theologians of the 17th and 18th Centuries*, edited by René Wellek. New York and London: Garland Publishing, 1976 (facsimile edition of the 1751 translation printed for Sam Paterson and sold by M. Cooper, London).

Torjesen, Karen Jo. *Hermeneutical Procedure and Theological Method in Origen's Exegesis.* Patristische Texte und Studien, 28. Berlin and New York: Walter de Gruyter, 1986.

Unnik, W. C. van. "*Dominus vobiscum*: The Background of a Liturgical Formula." In *New Testament Essays* [Festschrift for Thomas Walter Manson], edited by A. J. B. Higgins. Manchester: Manchester University Press, 1959, pp. 270–305.

Vagaggini, Cypriano. *Theological Dimensions of the Liturgy: A General Treatise on the Theology of the Liturgy.* Translated by Leonard J. Doyle and W. A. Jurgens. Collegeville, MN: Liturgical Press, 1976.

Vatican II, The Documents of. Edited by Walter M. Abbott. New York: America Press and Geoffrey Chapman, 1966.

Vatican II, Documents of. The Conciliar and Postconciliar Documents. Edited by Austin P. Flannery. Rev. ed. Vatican Collection, vol. 1. Grand Rapids, MI: Wm. B. Eerdmans, 1984.

Vatican Council II, More Postconciliar Documents. Edited by Austin P. Flannery. Vatican Collection, vol. 2. Grand Rapids, MI: Wm. B. Eerdmans, 1982.

Verhaar, J. W. M. "Language and Theological Method." *Continuum* 7(1969):3–29.

———. *Some Reflections on Perception, Speech and Thought.* Assen: van Gorcum, 1963.

Wainwright, Geoffrey. *Doxology: The Praise of God in Worship, Doctrine, and Life, A Systematic Theology.* New York: Oxford University Press, 1984.

Weber, Wilhelm. ". . . *nec nostri sæculi est.* Bemerkungen zum Briefwechsel des Plinius und Trajan über die Christen." In *Festgabe für D. Dr. Karl Müller.* Tübingen: J. C. B. Mohr (Paul Siebeck), 1922, pp. 24–45.

Weinrich, H. "Narrative Theologie." *Concilium* 9(1973):329ff.

White, John L. "New Testament Epistolary Literature in the Framework of Ancient Epistolography." Part 2, vol. 25.2 of *Aufstieg und Niedergang der Römischen Welt*, edited by Wolfgang Haase. Berlin and New York: Walter de Gruyter, 1984, pp. 1730–56.

Wilder, Amos. *Early Christian Rhetoric*. New York: Harper & Row, 1964.

Wiles, Maurice. *The Remaking of Christian Doctrine*, 2d ed. London: SCM, 1975.

_____. *What Is Theology?* Oxford: Oxford University Press, 1976.

Wilken, Robert L. *The Christians as the Romans Saw Them*. New Haven and London: Yale University Press, 1984.

Willebrands, Johannes Cardinal. "Address in Cambridge, England." In *Documents on Anglican/Roman Catholic Relations*. Washington: U. S. Catholic Conference, 1972, pp. 32–41.

Wolfson, Harry A. *The Philosophy of the Church Fathers*. Vol. 1, *Faith, Trinity, Incarnation*. Cambridge, MA: Harvard University Press, 1956.

Wordsworth, William. *The Poetical Works of William Wordsworth*. Edited by E. de Selincourt and Helen Darbishire. Vol. 3. Oxford: Clarendon Press, 1946.

Yarnold, Edward. *The Awe-Inspiring Rites of Initiation: Homilies of the Fourth Century*. Slough: St. Paul Publications, 1972.

Subject Index

(Italics refer to footnotes.)

Name Index

Scripture Index